FRESH ROMANCE™

VOLUME 1

ROSY PRESS

ONI PRESS

PUBLISHED BY ROSY PRESS

Janelle Asselin, publisher

PUBLISHED BY ONI PRESS INC.

Joe Nozemack, publisher
James Lucas Jones, editor in chief
Andrew McIntire, v.p. of marketing & sales
Cheyenne Allott, director of sales
Rachel Reed, publicity coordinator
Troy Look, director of design & production
Hilary Thompson, graphic designer
Jared Jones, digital art technician
Ari Yarwood, managing editor
Charlie Chu, senior editor
Robin Herrera, editor
Bess Pallares, editorial assistant
Brad Rooks, director of logistics
Jung Lee, logistics associate

EDITED BY Janelle Asselin
EDITORIAL ASSISTS BY Ari Yarwood
DESIGNED BY Hilary Thompson

onipress.com
facebook.com/onipress
twitter.com/onipress
onipress.tumblr.com
instagram.com/onipress

rosypress.com
facebook.com/rosypress
twitter.com/rosypress
rosypress.tumblr.com

FIRST EDITION: JULY 2016

KICKSTARTER EXCLUSIVE ISBN: 978-1-62010-347-0
DIRECT MARKET ISBN: 978-1-62010-346-3

PRINTED IN CHINA.

LIBRARY OF CONGRESS CONTROL NUMBER: 2016931409

1 2 3 4 5 6 7 8 9 10

TABLE OF CONTENTS

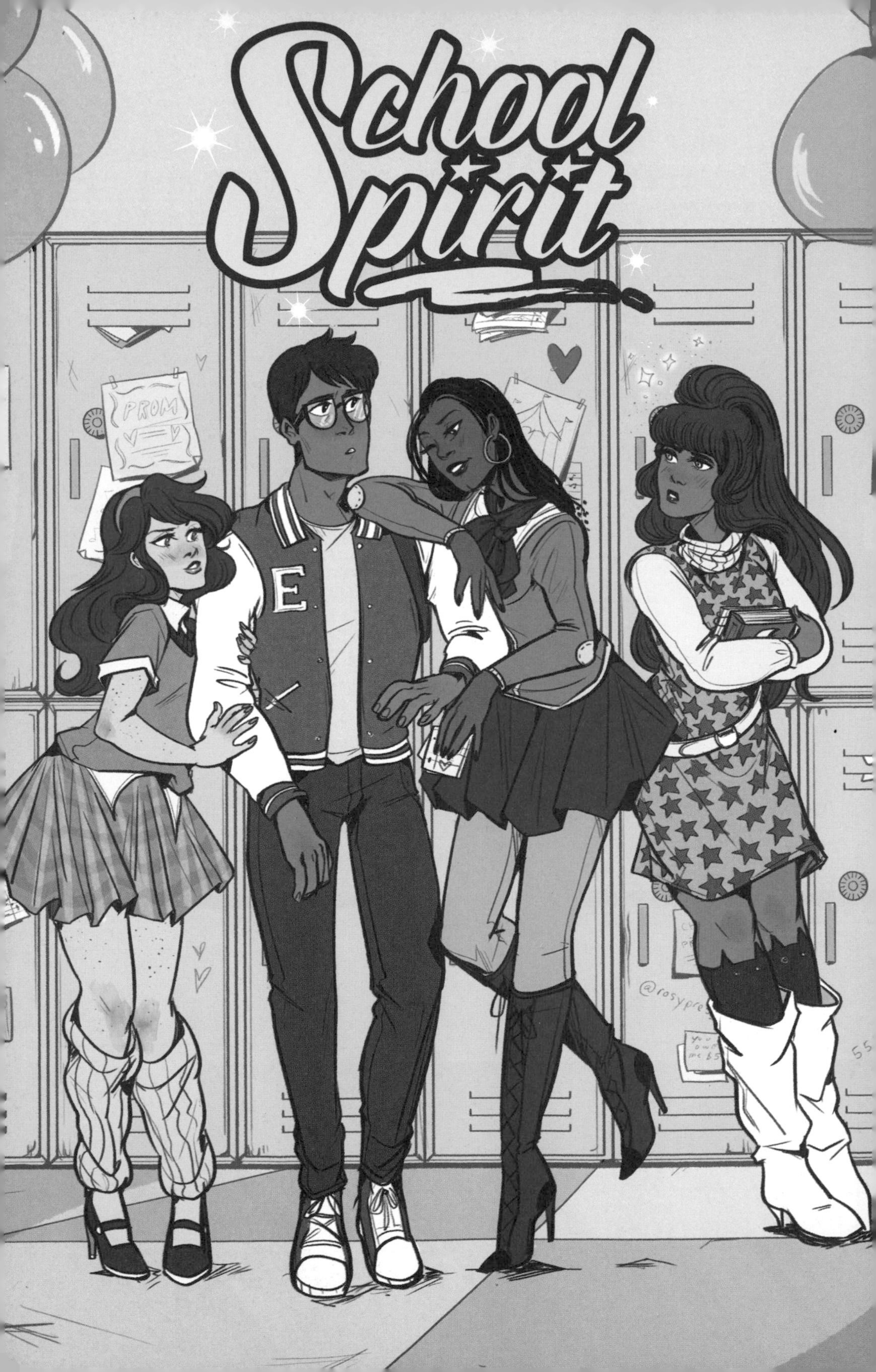
School Spirit
PROM
E
@rosypres

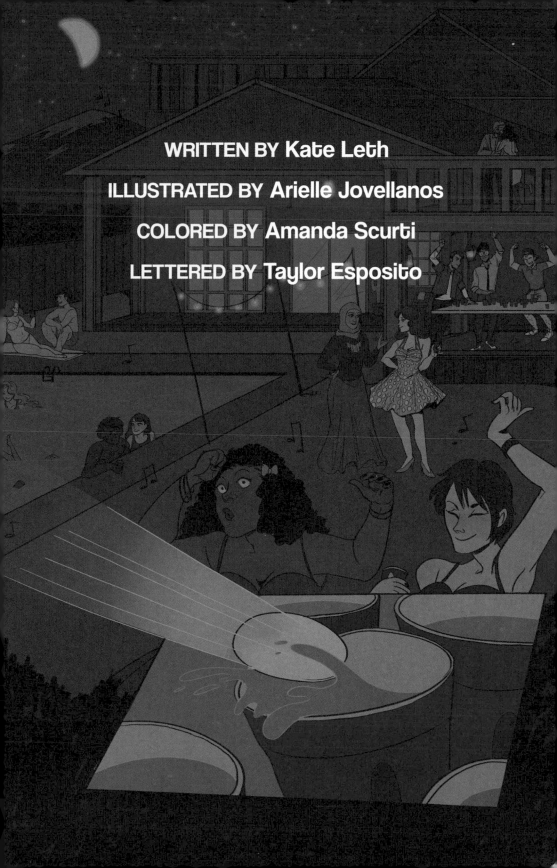

WRITTEN BY **Kate Leth**

ILLUSTRATED BY **Arielle Jovellanos**

COLORED BY **Amanda Scurti**

LETTERED BY **Taylor Esposito**

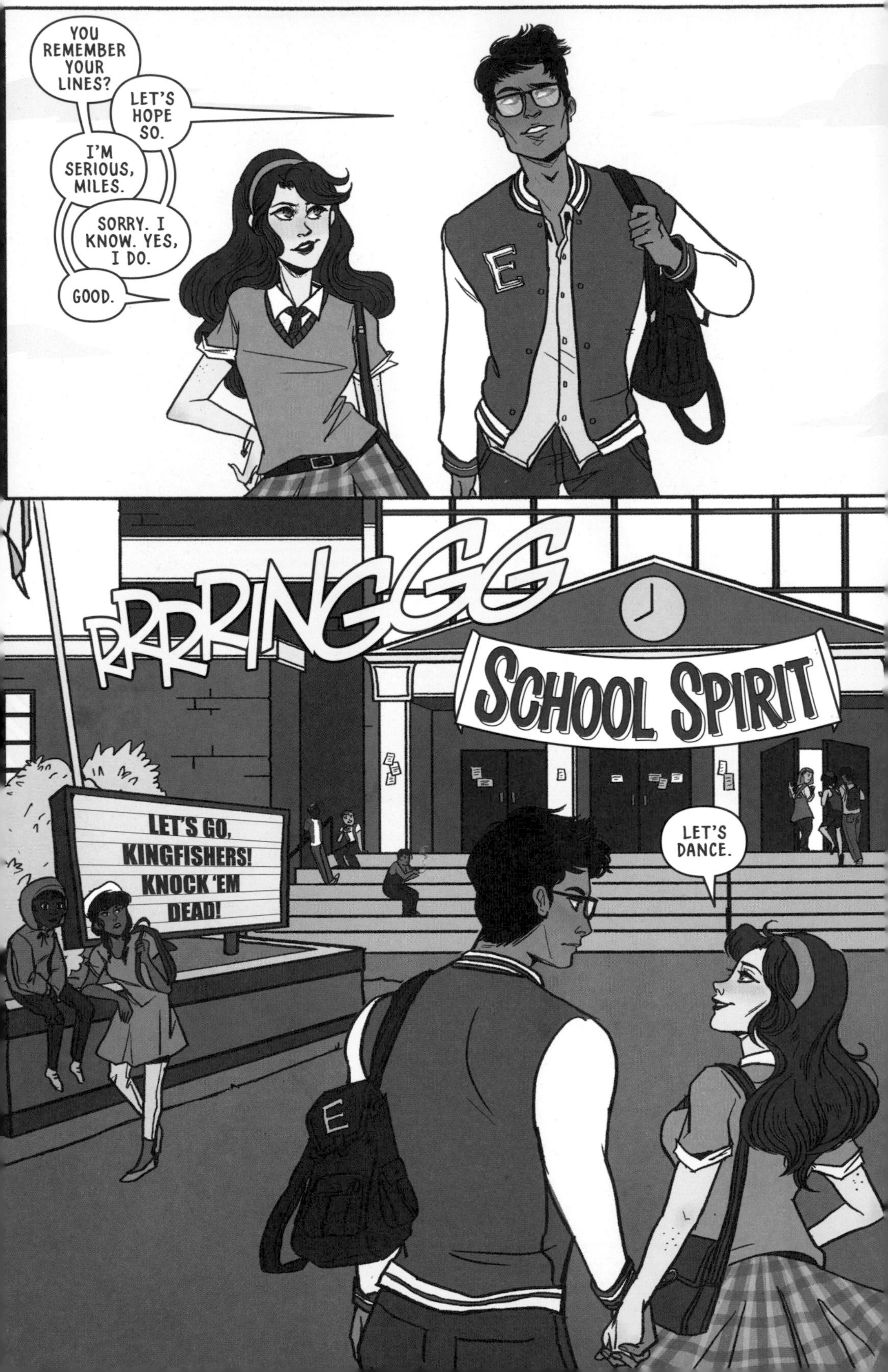
YOU REMEMBER YOUR LINES?
LET'S HOPE SO.
I'M SERIOUS, MILES.
SORRY. I KNOW. YES, I DO.
GOOD.
RRRRINGGG
SCHOOL SPIRIT
LET'S GO, KINGFISHERS! KNOCK 'EM DEAD!
LET'S DANCE.

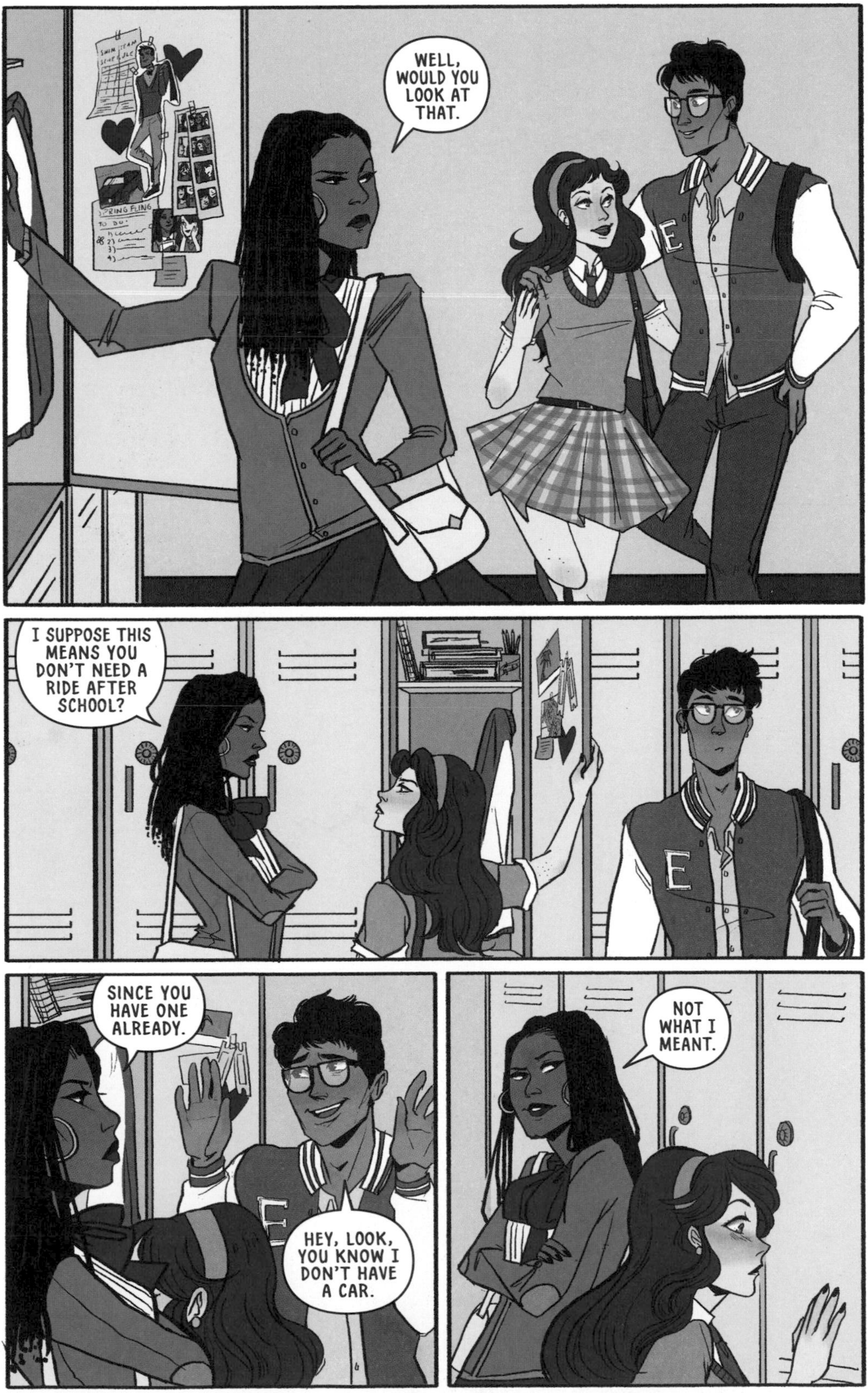
WELL, WOULD YOU LOOK AT THAT.
I SUPPOSE THIS MEANS YOU DON'T NEED A RIDE AFTER SCHOOL?
SINCE YOU HAVE ONE ALREADY.
HEY, LOOK, YOU KNOW I DON'T HAVE A CAR.
NOT WHAT I MEANT.

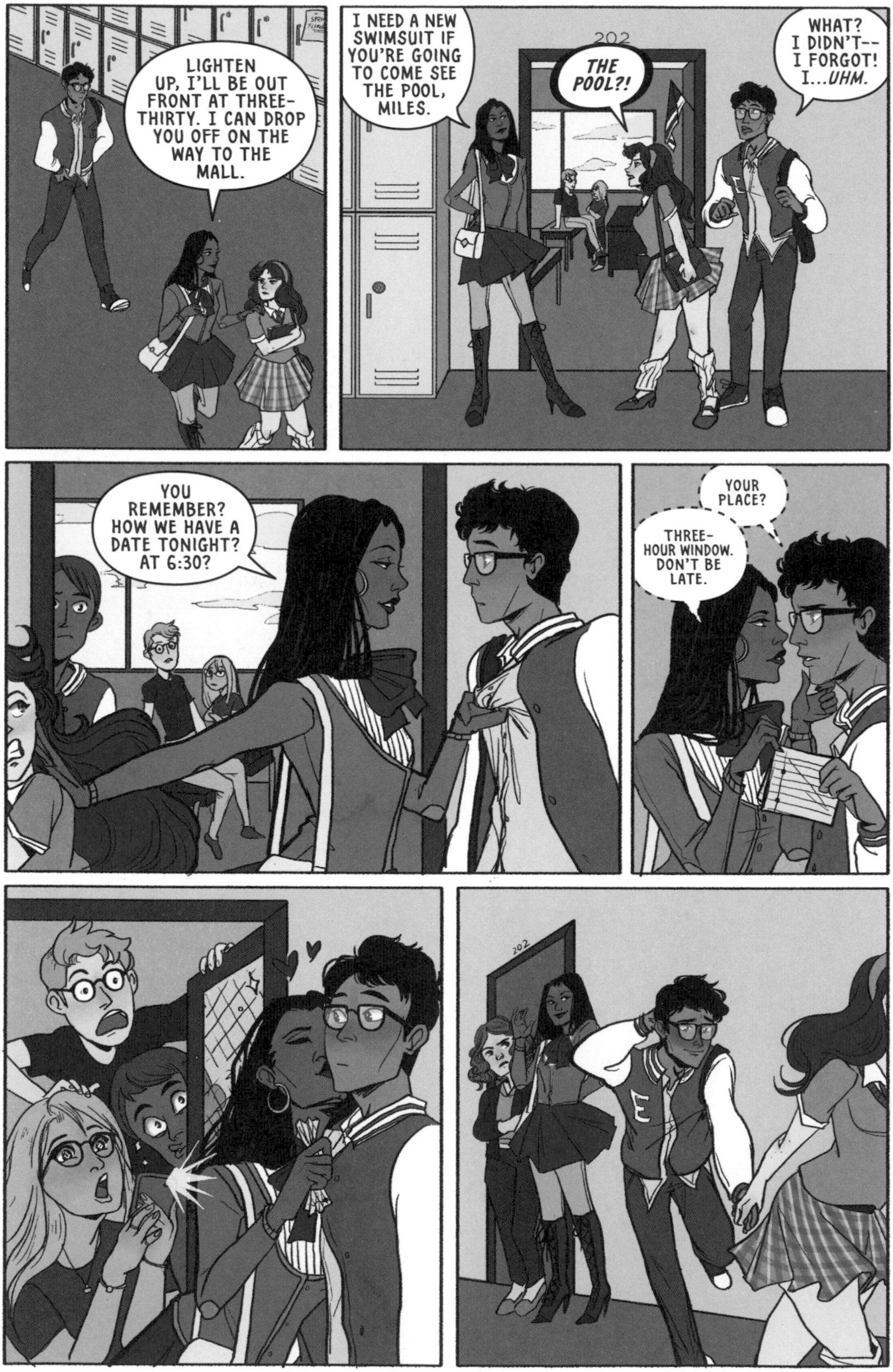
LIGHTEN UP, I'LL BE OUT FRONT AT THREE-THIRTY. I CAN DROP YOU OFF ON THE WAY TO THE MALL.
I NEED A NEW SWIMSUIT IF YOU'RE GOING TO COME SEE THE POOL, MILES.
202
THE POOL?!
WHAT? I DIDN'T-- I FORGOT! I...UHM.
YOU REMEMBER? HOW WE HAVE A DATE TONIGHT? AT 6:30?
YOUR PLACE?
THREE-HOUR WINDOW. DON'T BE LATE.
202
E

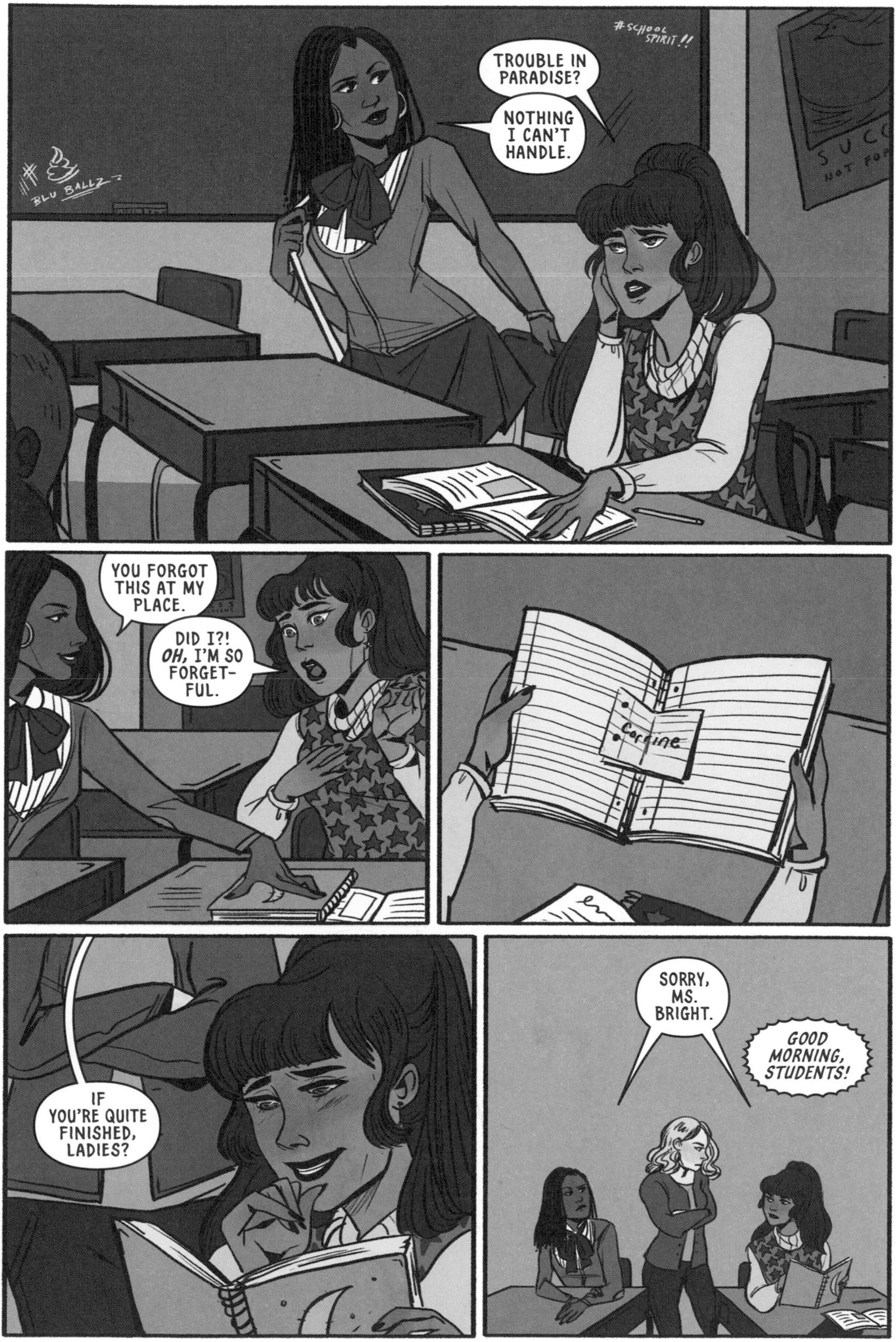

#SCHOOL SPIRIT!!
TROUBLE IN PARADISE?
NOTHING I CAN'T HANDLE.
BLU BALLZ
YOU FORGOT THIS AT MY PLACE.
DID I?! *OH*, I'M SO FORGET-FUL.
IF YOU'RE QUITE FINISHED, LADIES?
SORRY, MS. BRIGHT.
GOOD MORNING, STUDENTS!

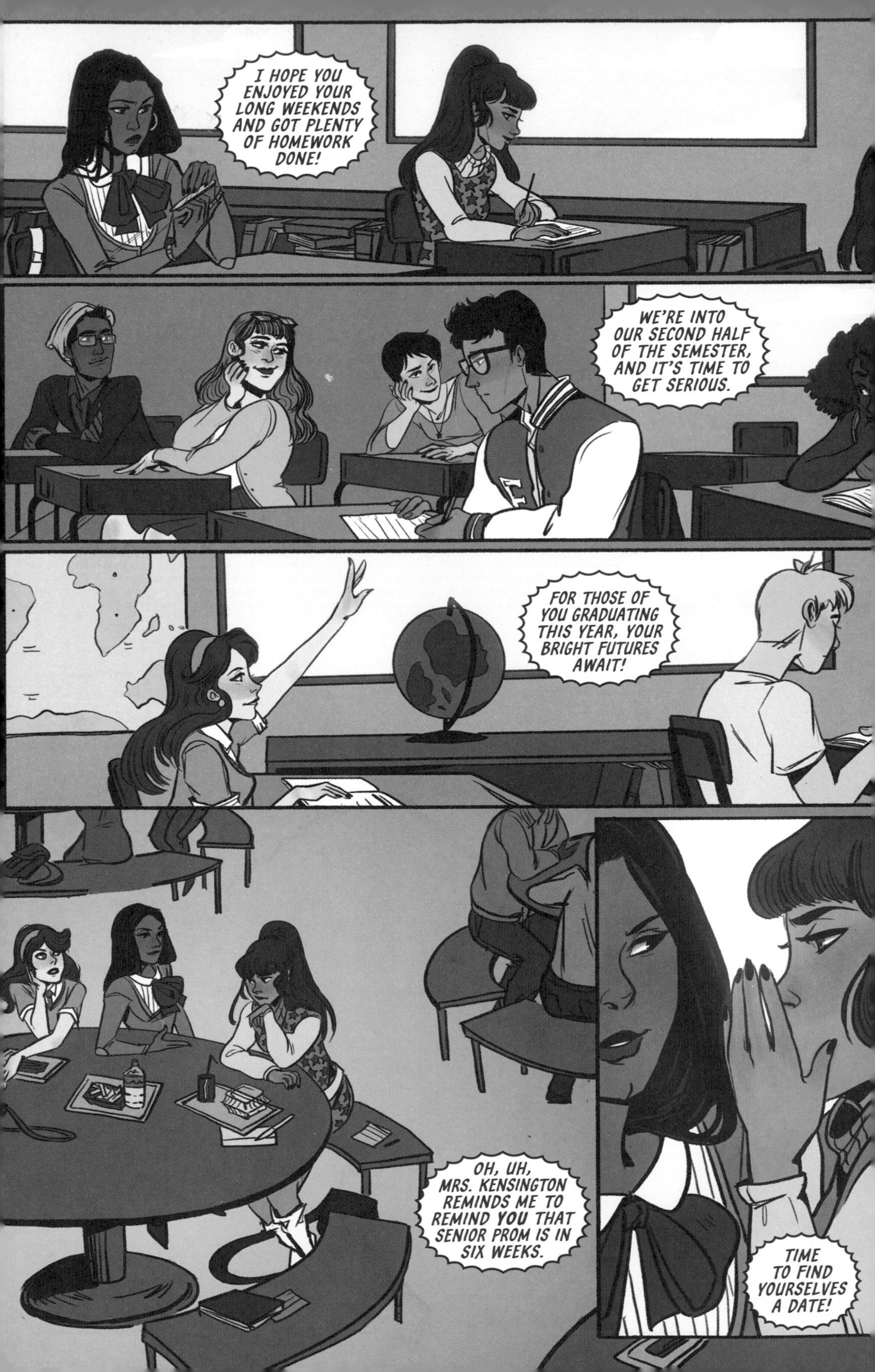
I HOPE YOU ENJOYED YOUR LONG WEEKENDS AND GOT PLENTY OF HOMEWORK DONE!
WE'RE INTO OUR SECOND HALF OF THE SEMESTER, AND IT'S TIME TO GET SERIOUS.
FOR THOSE OF YOU GRADUATING THIS YEAR, YOUR BRIGHT FUTURES AWAIT!
OH, UH, MRS. KENSINGTON REMINDS ME TO REMIND YOU THAT SENIOR PROM IS IN SIX WEEKS.
TIME TO FIND YOURSELVES A DATE!

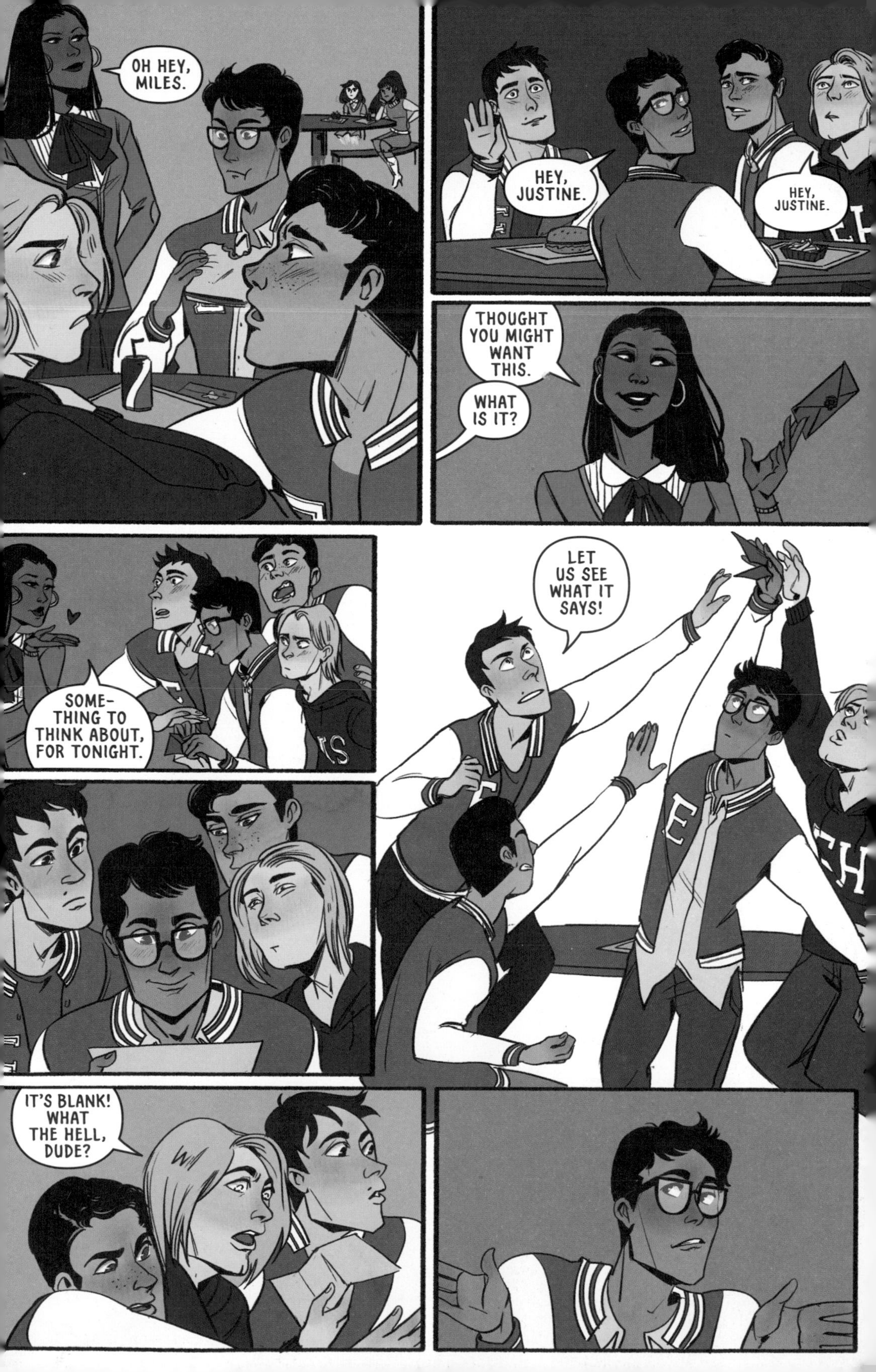
OH HEY, MILES.
HEY, JUSTINE.
HEY, JUSTINE.
THOUGHT YOU MIGHT WANT THIS.
WHAT IS IT?
SOME-THING TO THINK ABOUT, FOR TONIGHT.
LET US SEE WHAT IT SAYS!
IT'S BLANK! WHAT THE HELL, DUDE?

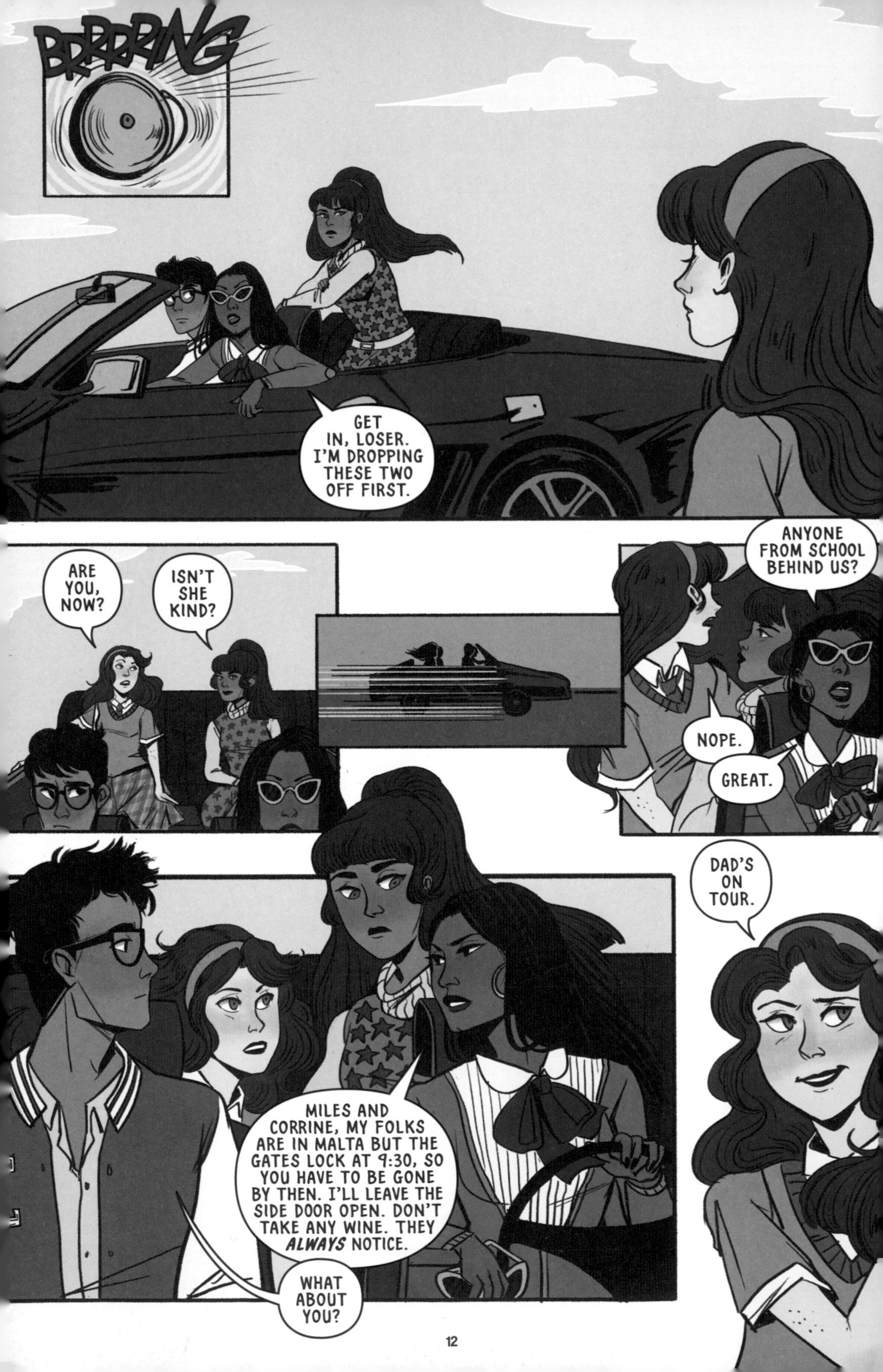
BRRRRING
GET IN, LOSER. I'M DROPPING THESE TWO OFF FIRST.
ARE YOU, NOW?
ISN'T SHE KIND?
ANYONE FROM SCHOOL BEHIND US?
NOPE.
GREAT.
MILES AND CORRINE, MY FOLKS ARE IN MALTA BUT THE GATES LOCK AT 9:30, SO YOU HAVE TO BE GONE BY THEN. I'LL LEAVE THE SIDE DOOR OPEN. DON'T TAKE ANY WINE. THEY *ALWAYS* NOTICE.
WHAT ABOUT YOU?
DAD'S ON TOUR.

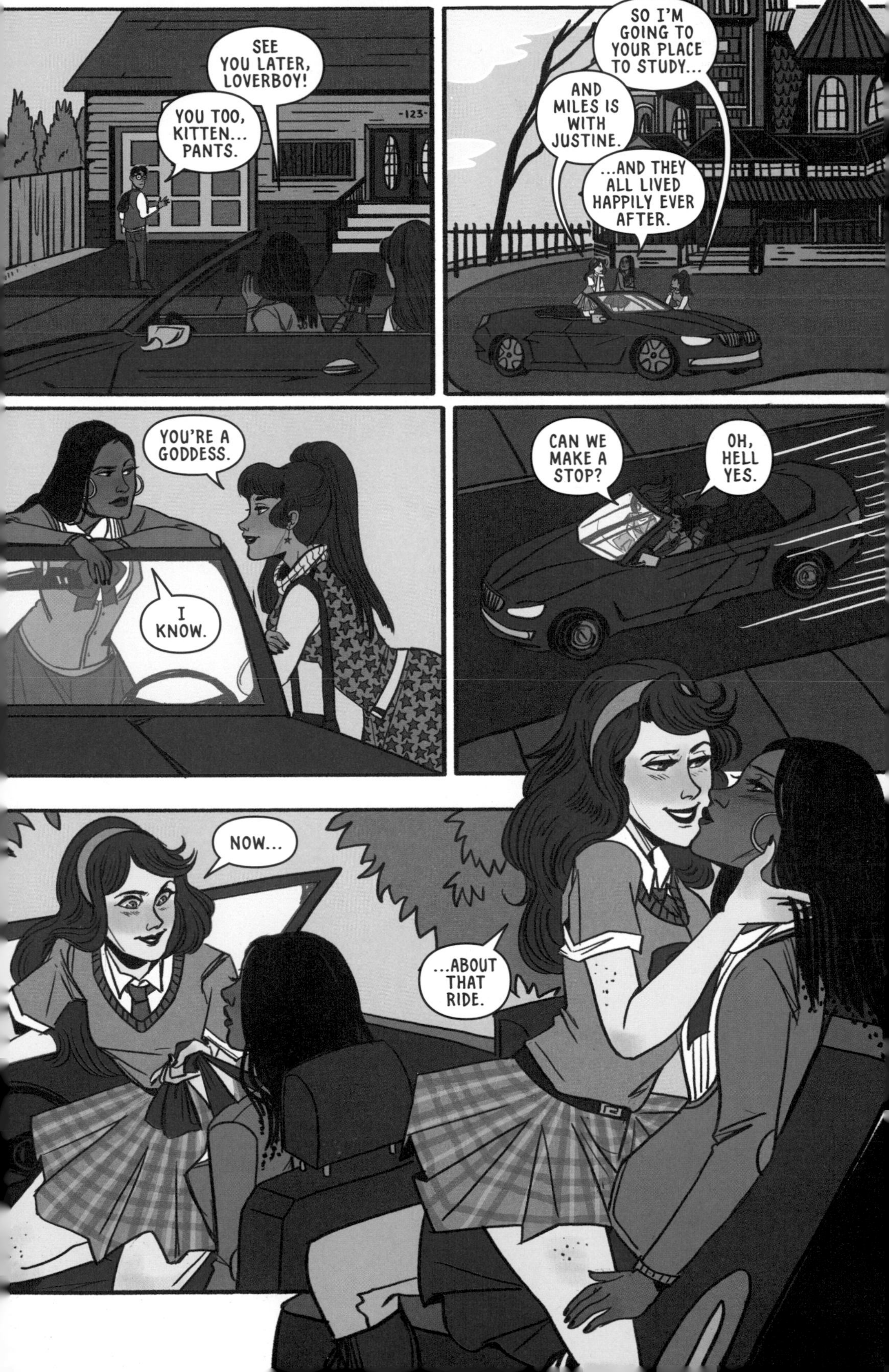
SEE YOU LATER, LOVERBOY!
YOU TOO, KITTEN... PANTS.
-123-
SO I'M GOING TO YOUR PLACE TO STUDY...
AND MILES IS WITH JUSTINE.
...AND THEY ALL LIVED HAPPILY EVER AFTER.
YOU'RE A GODDESS.
I KNOW.
CAN WE MAKE A STOP?
OH, HELL YES.
NOW...
...ABOUT THAT RIDE.

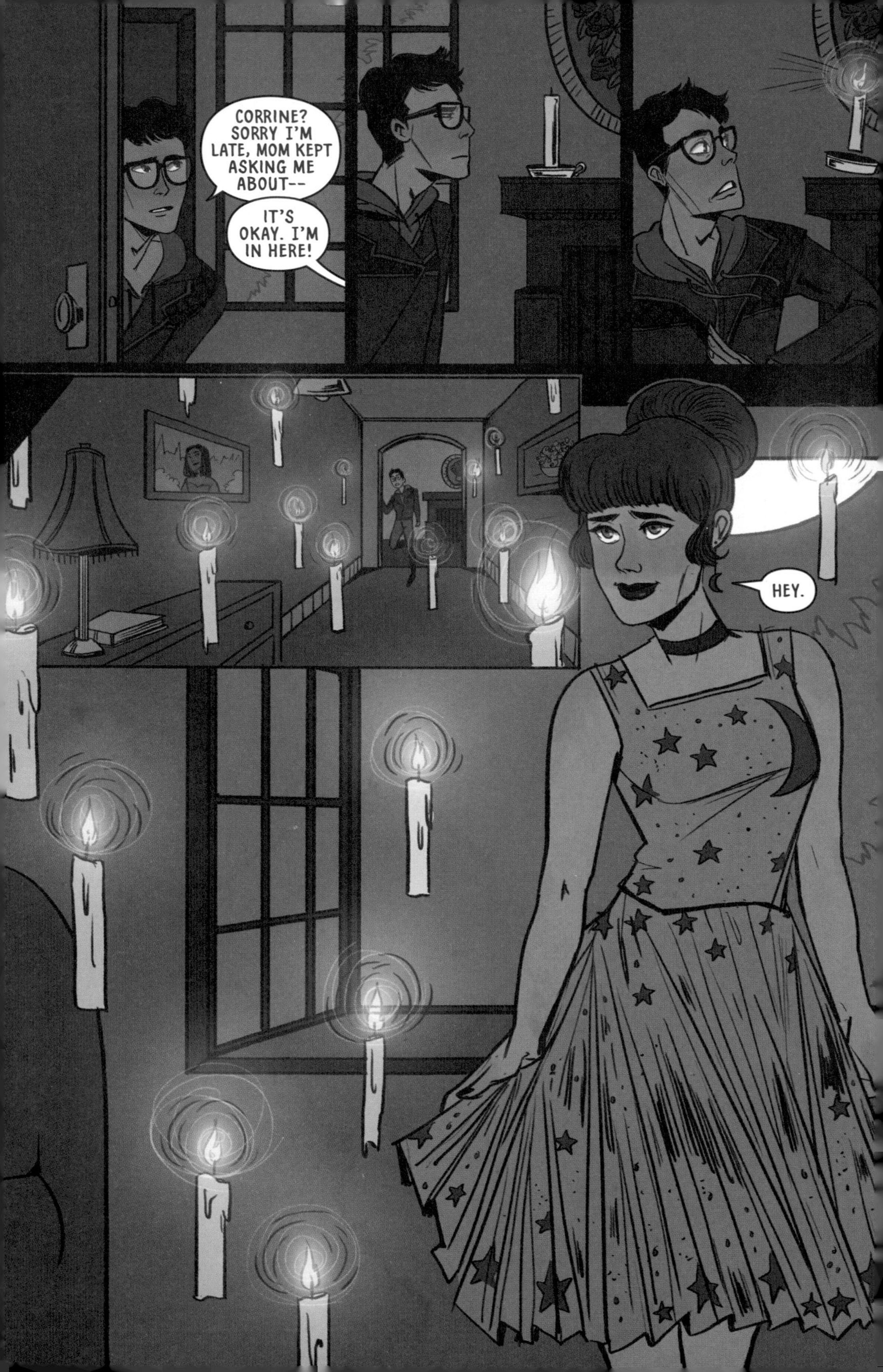
CORRINE? SORRY I'M LATE, MOM KEPT ASKING ME ABOUT--
IT'S OKAY. I'M IN HERE!
HEY.

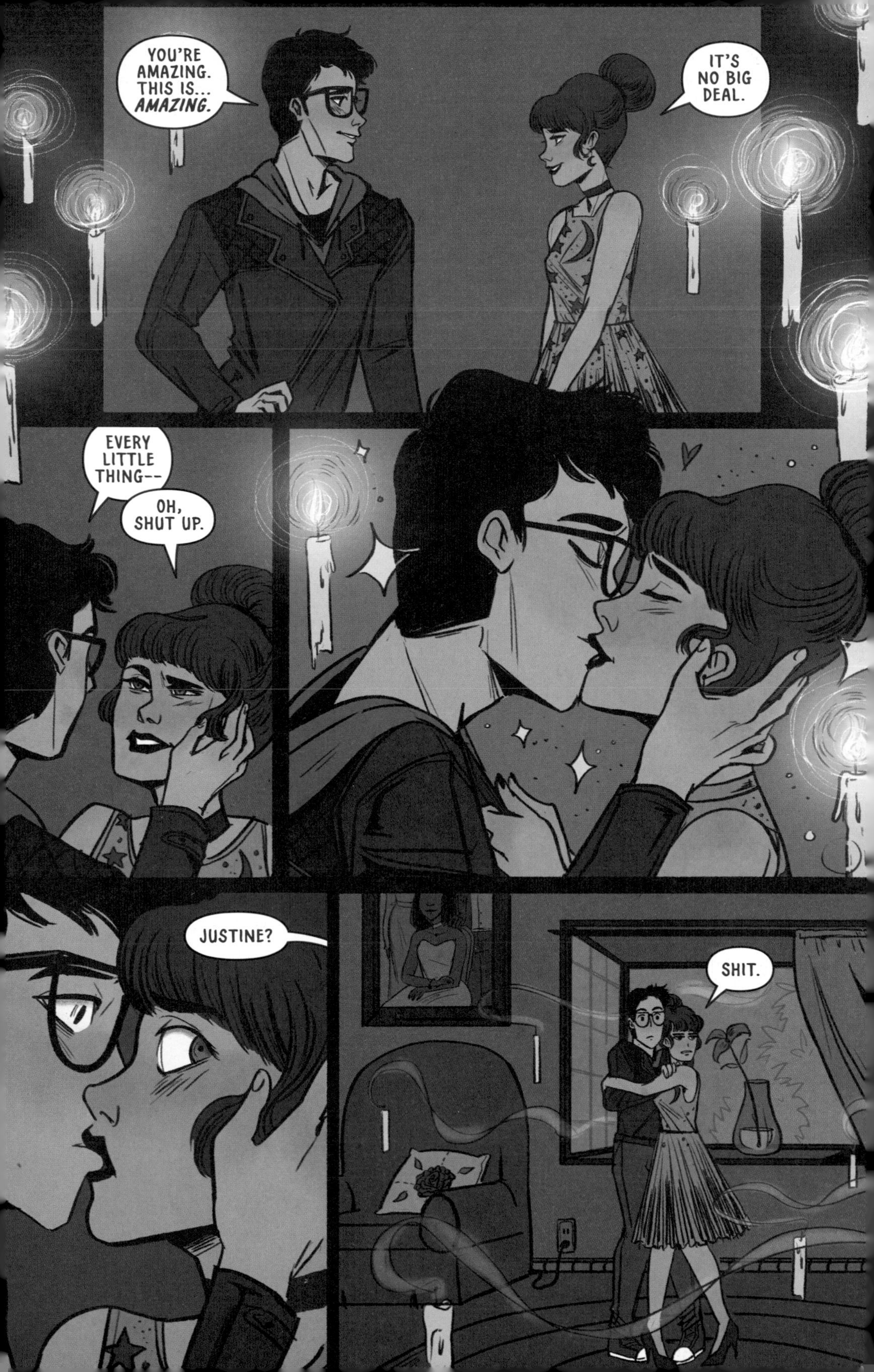
YOU'RE AMAZING. THIS IS... *AMAZING.*
IT'S NO BIG DEAL.
EVERY LITTLE THING--
OH, SHUT UP.
JUSTINE?
SHIT.

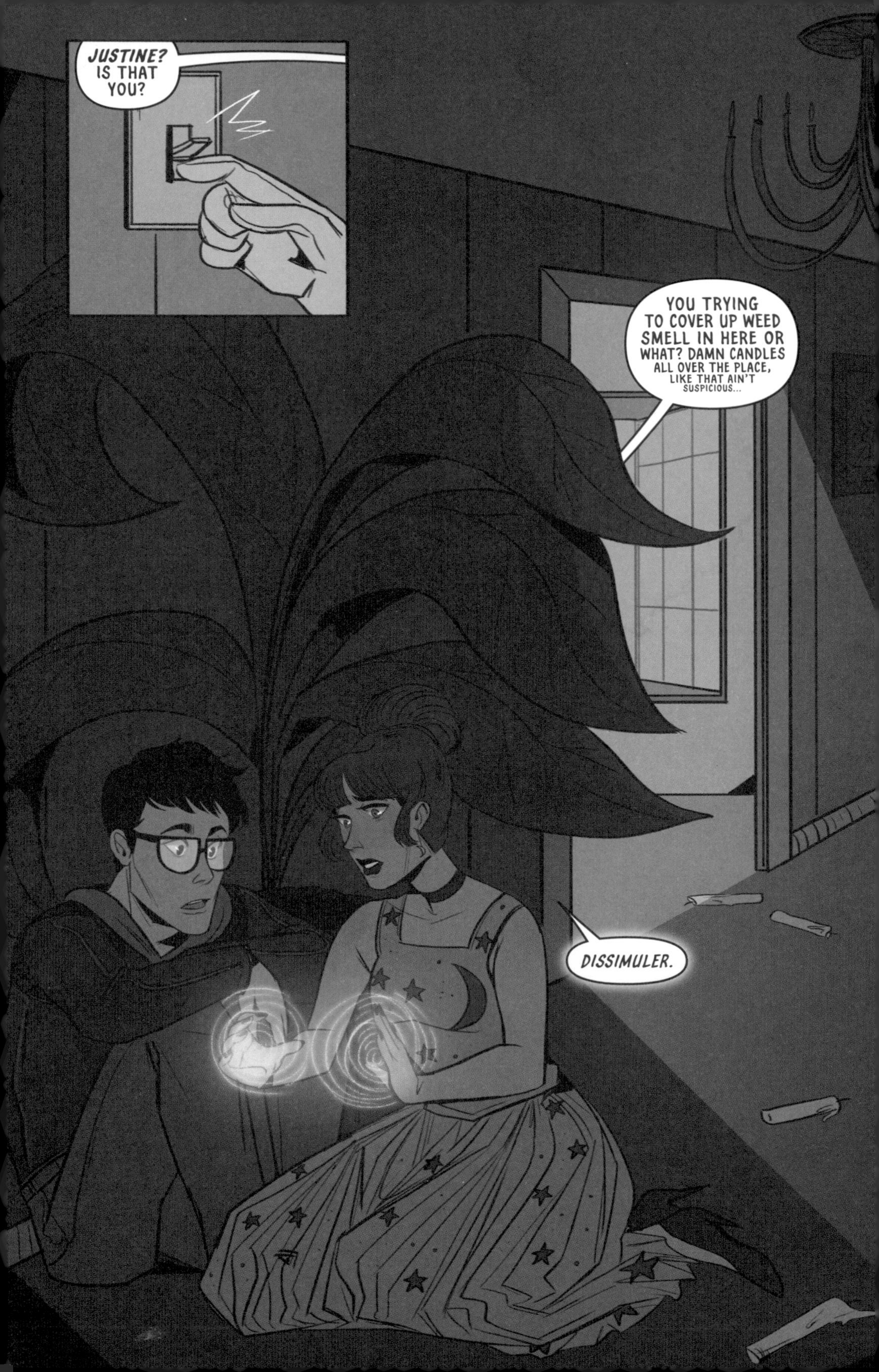
JUSTINE? IS THAT YOU?
YOU TRYING TO COVER UP WEED SMELL IN HERE OR WHAT? DAMN CANDLES ALL OVER THE PLACE, LIKE THAT AIN'T SUSPICIOUS...
DISSIMULER.

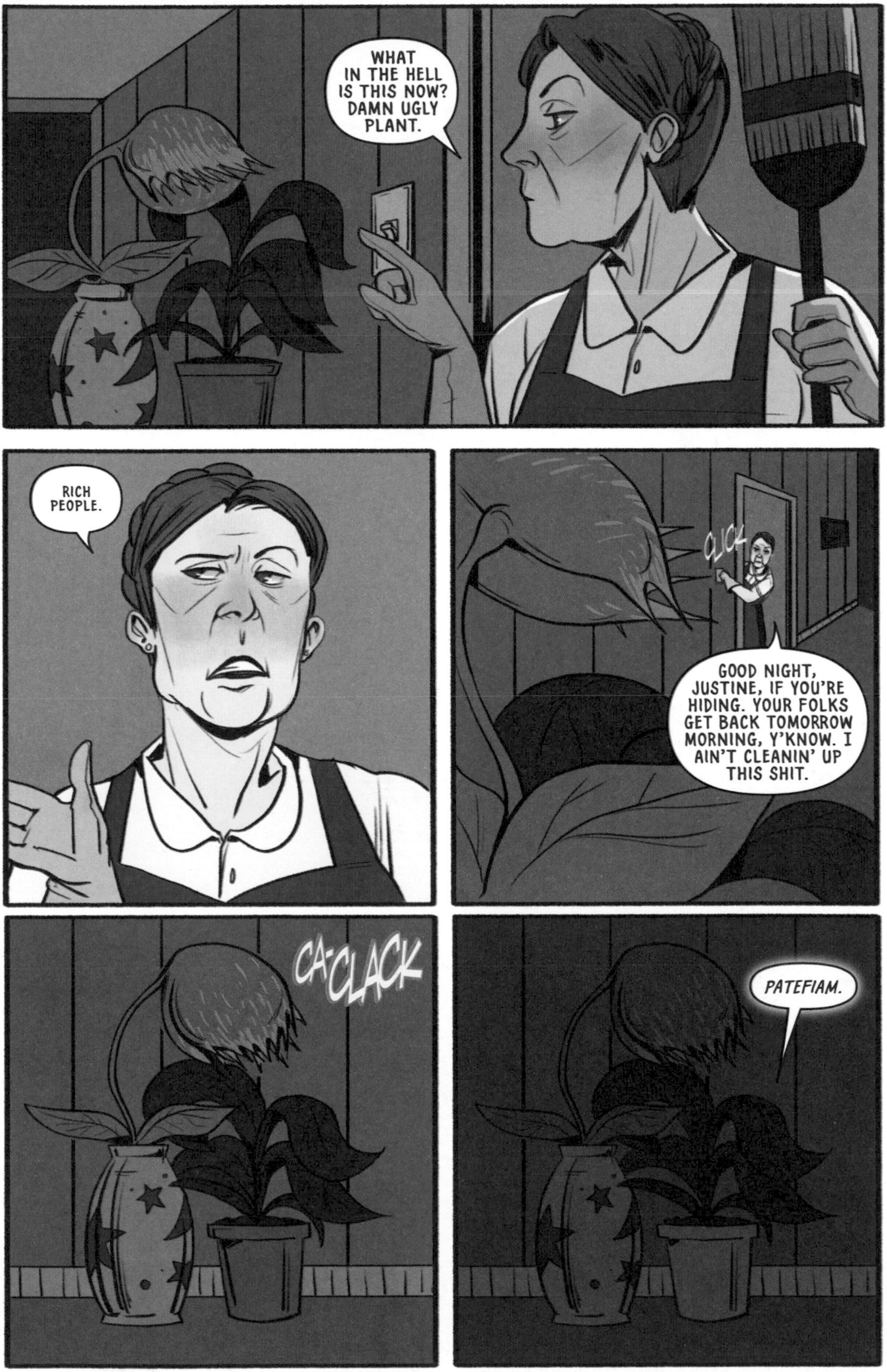
WHAT IN THE HELL IS THIS NOW? DAMN UGLY PLANT.
RICH PEOPLE.
CLICK
GOOD NIGHT, JUSTINE, IF YOU'RE HIDING. YOUR FOLKS GET BACK TOMORROW MORNING, Y'KNOW. I AIN'T CLEANIN' UP THIS SHIT.
CA-CLACK
PATEFIAM.

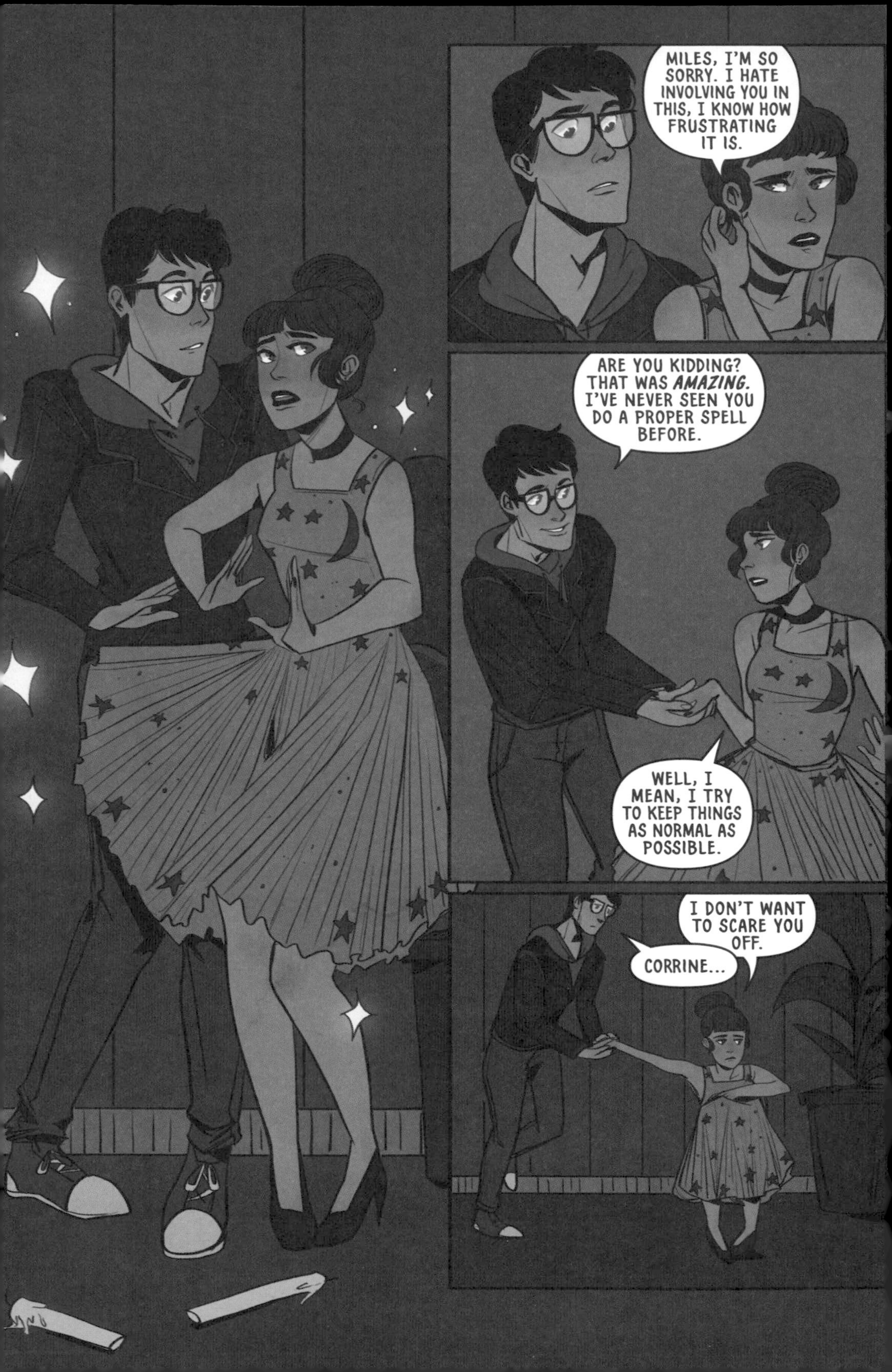
MILES, I'M SO SORRY. I HATE INVOLVING YOU IN THIS, I KNOW HOW FRUSTRATING IT IS.
ARE YOU KIDDING? THAT WAS *AMAZING.* I'VE NEVER SEEN YOU DO A PROPER SPELL BEFORE.
WELL, I MEAN, I TRY TO KEEP THINGS AS NORMAL AS POSSIBLE.
I DON'T WANT TO SCARE YOU OFF.
CORRINE...

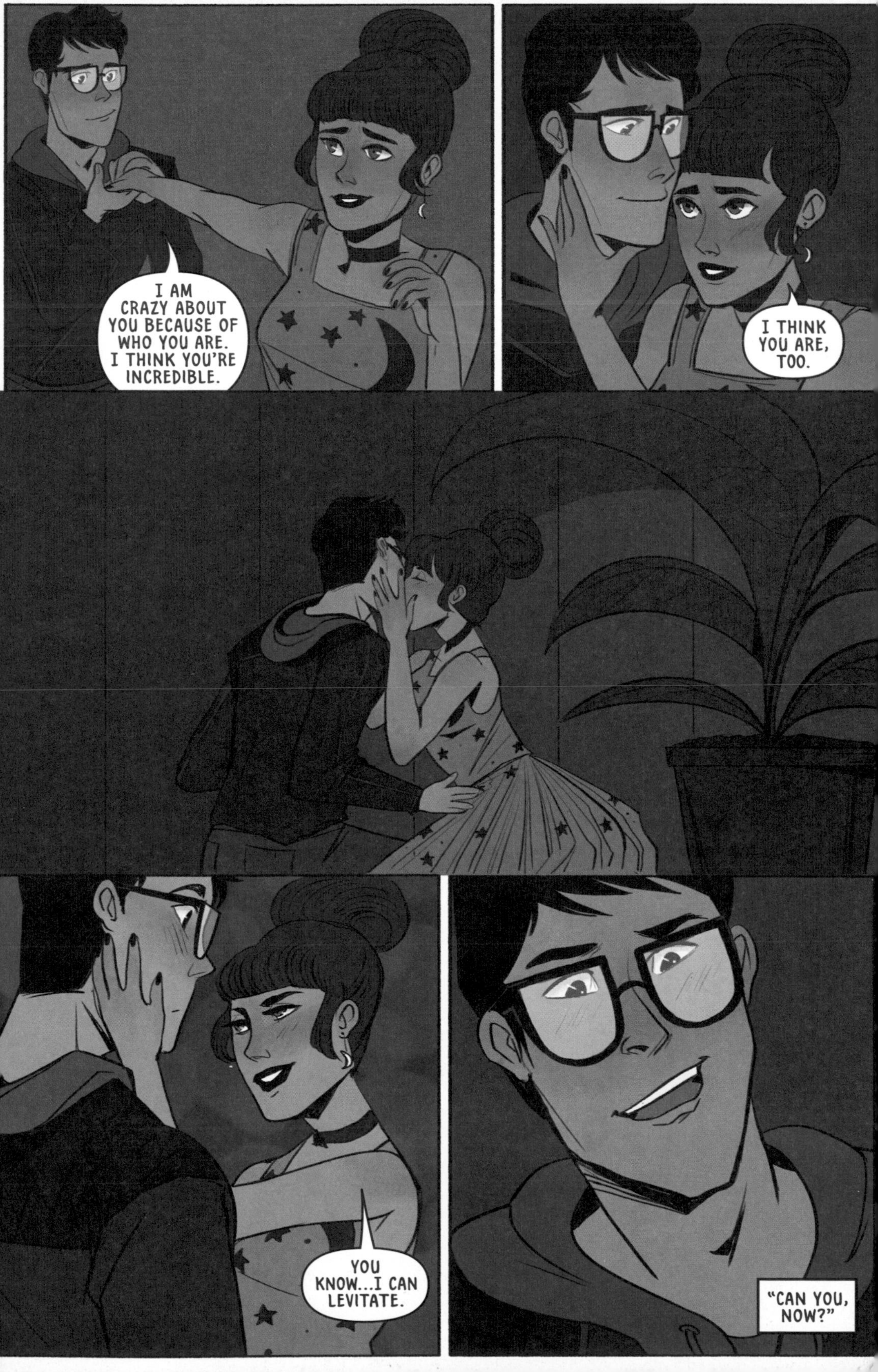
I AM CRAZY ABOUT YOU BECAUSE OF WHO YOU ARE. I THINK YOU'RE INCREDIBLE.
I THINK YOU ARE, TOO.
YOU KNOW...I CAN LEVITATE.
"CAN YOU, NOW?"

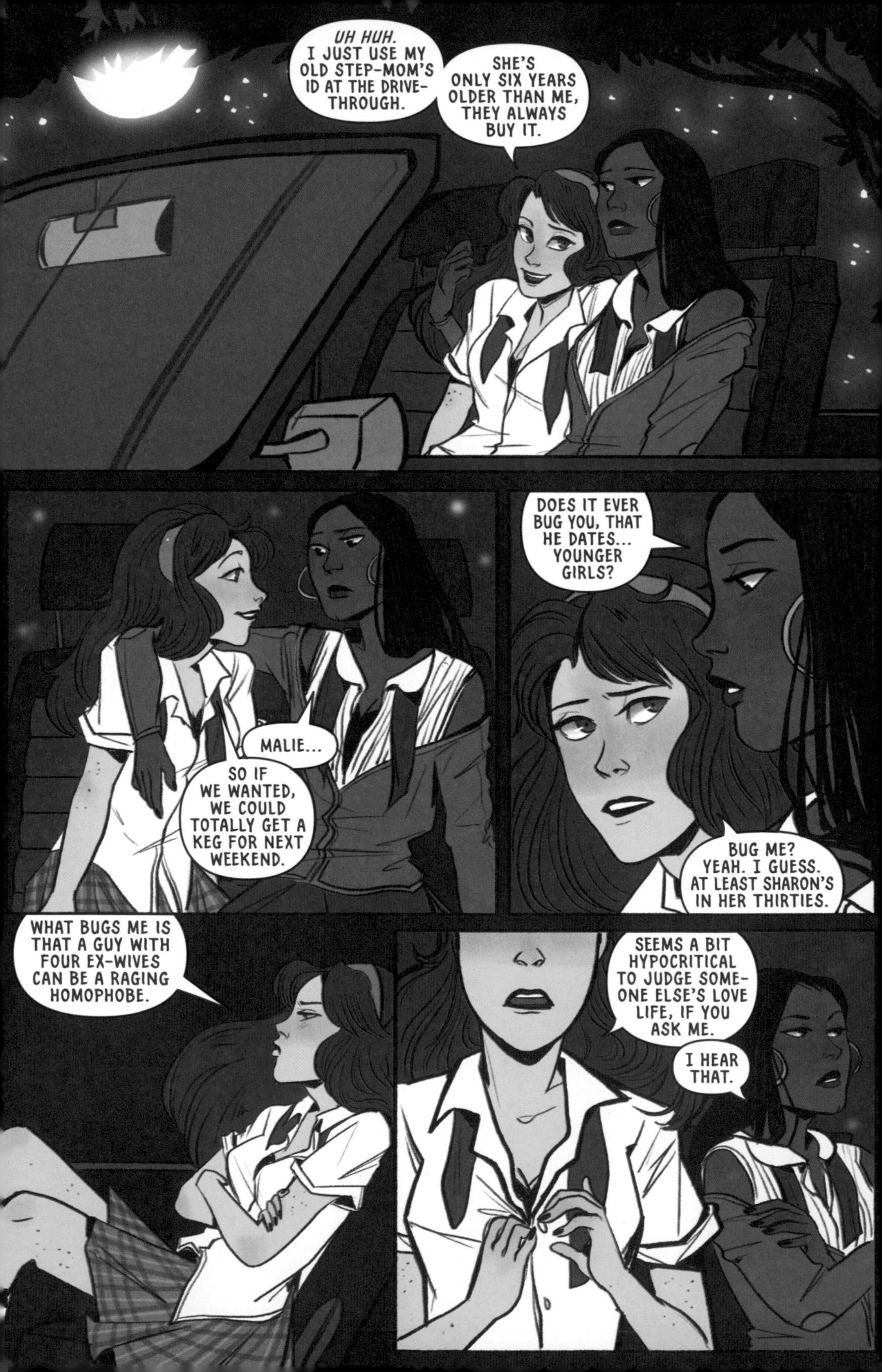
UH HUH. I JUST USE MY OLD STEP-MOM'S ID AT THE DRIVE-THROUGH.
SHE'S ONLY SIX YEARS OLDER THAN ME, THEY ALWAYS BUY IT.
SO IF WE WANTED, WE COULD TOTALLY GET A KEG FOR NEXT WEEKEND.
MALIE...
DOES IT EVER BUG YOU, THAT HE DATES... YOUNGER GIRLS?
BUG ME? YEAH. I GUESS. AT LEAST SHARON'S IN HER THIRTIES.
WHAT BUGS ME IS THAT A GUY WITH FOUR EX-WIVES CAN BE A RAGING HOMOPHOBE.
SEEMS A BIT HYPOCRITICAL TO JUDGE SOME-ONE ELSE'S LOVE LIFE, IF YOU ASK ME.
I HEAR THAT.

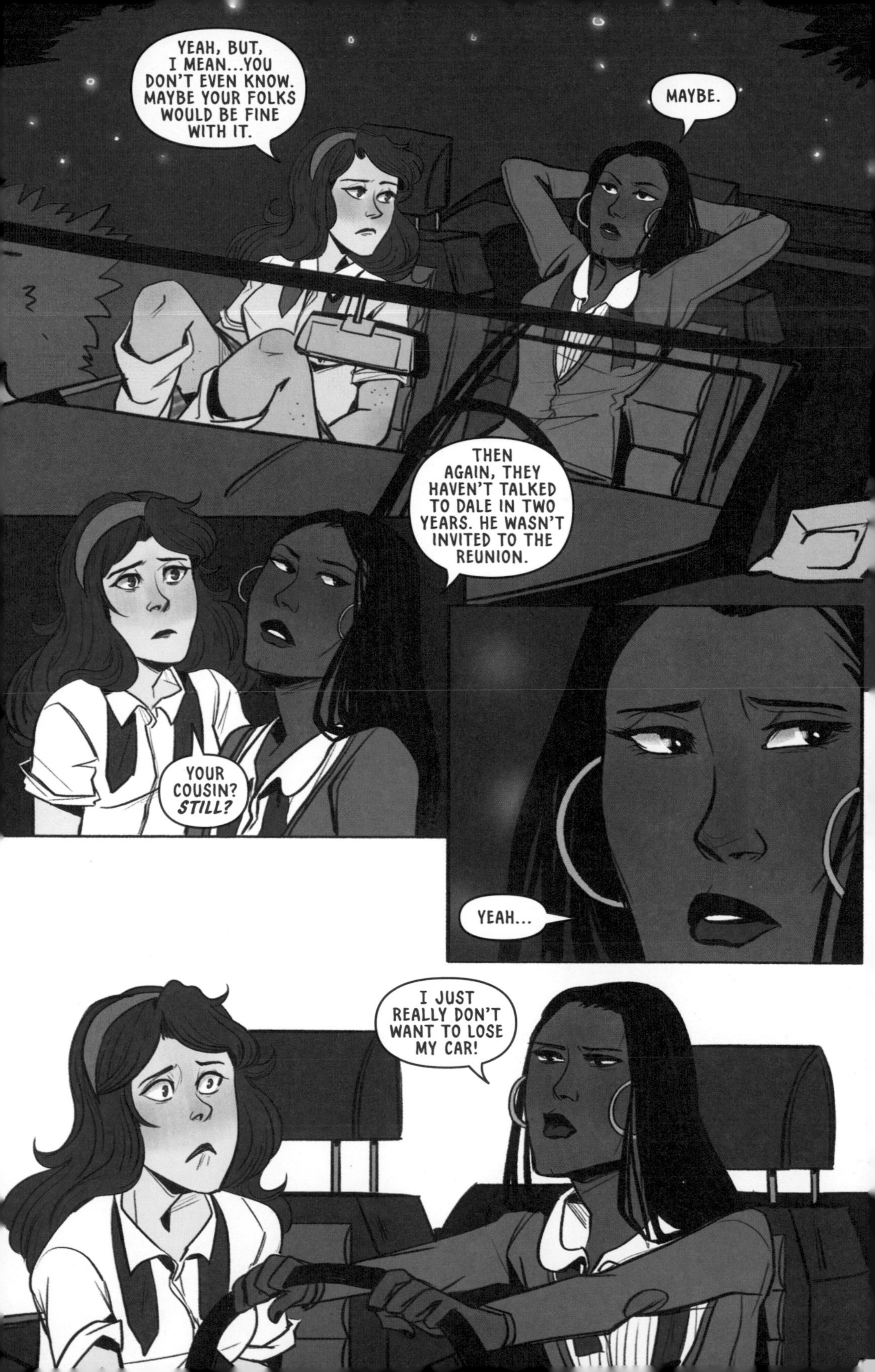
YEAH, BUT, I MEAN...YOU DON'T EVEN KNOW. MAYBE YOUR FOLKS WOULD BE FINE WITH IT.
MAYBE.
THEN AGAIN, THEY HAVEN'T TALKED TO DALE IN TWO YEARS. HE WASN'T INVITED TO THE REUNION.
YOUR COUSIN? *STILL?*
YEAH...
I JUST REALLY DON'T WANT TO LOSE MY CAR!

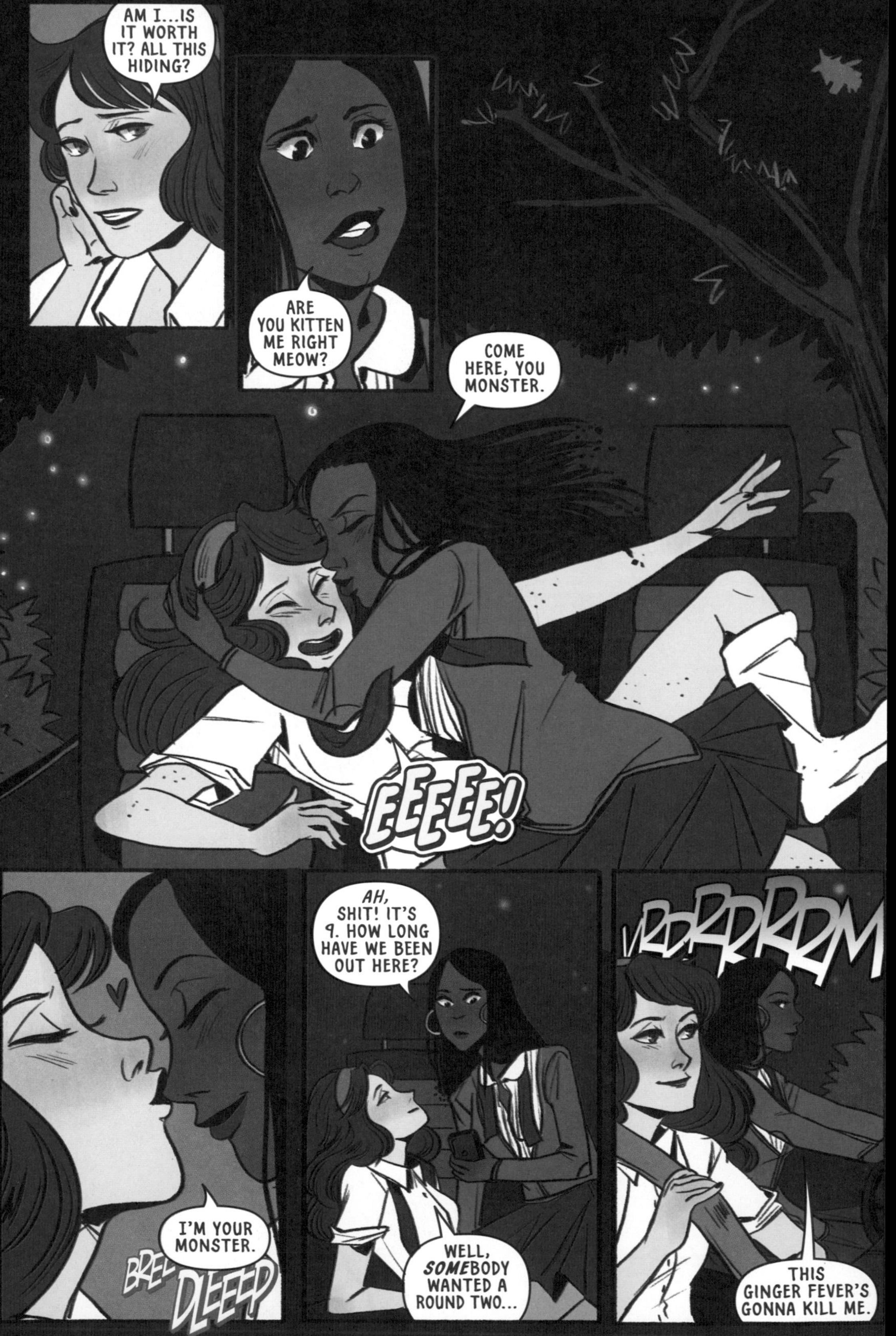

AM I...IS IT WORTH IT? ALL THIS HIDING?
ARE YOU KITTEN ME RIGHT MEOW?
COME HERE, YOU MONSTER.
EEEEE!
I'M YOUR MONSTER.
DLEEEP
AH, SHIT! IT'S 9. HOW LONG HAVE WE BEEN OUT HERE?
WELL, *SOME*BODY WANTED A ROUND TWO...
VRDRDRRRRM
THIS GINGER FEVER'S GONNA KILL ME.

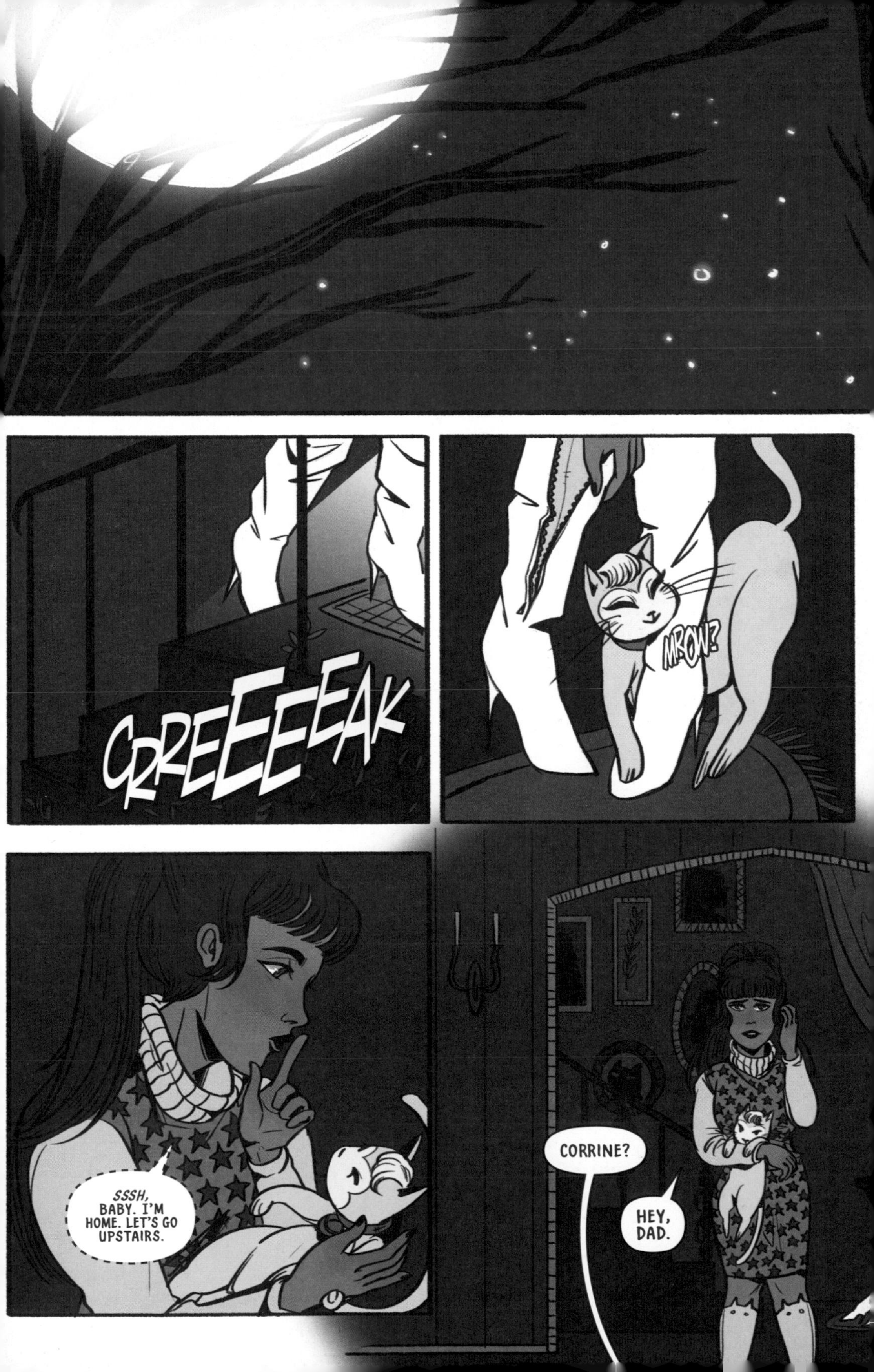
CRREEEEEAK
MROW?
SSSH, BABY. I'M HOME. LET'S GO UPSTAIRS.
CORRINE?
HEY, DAD.

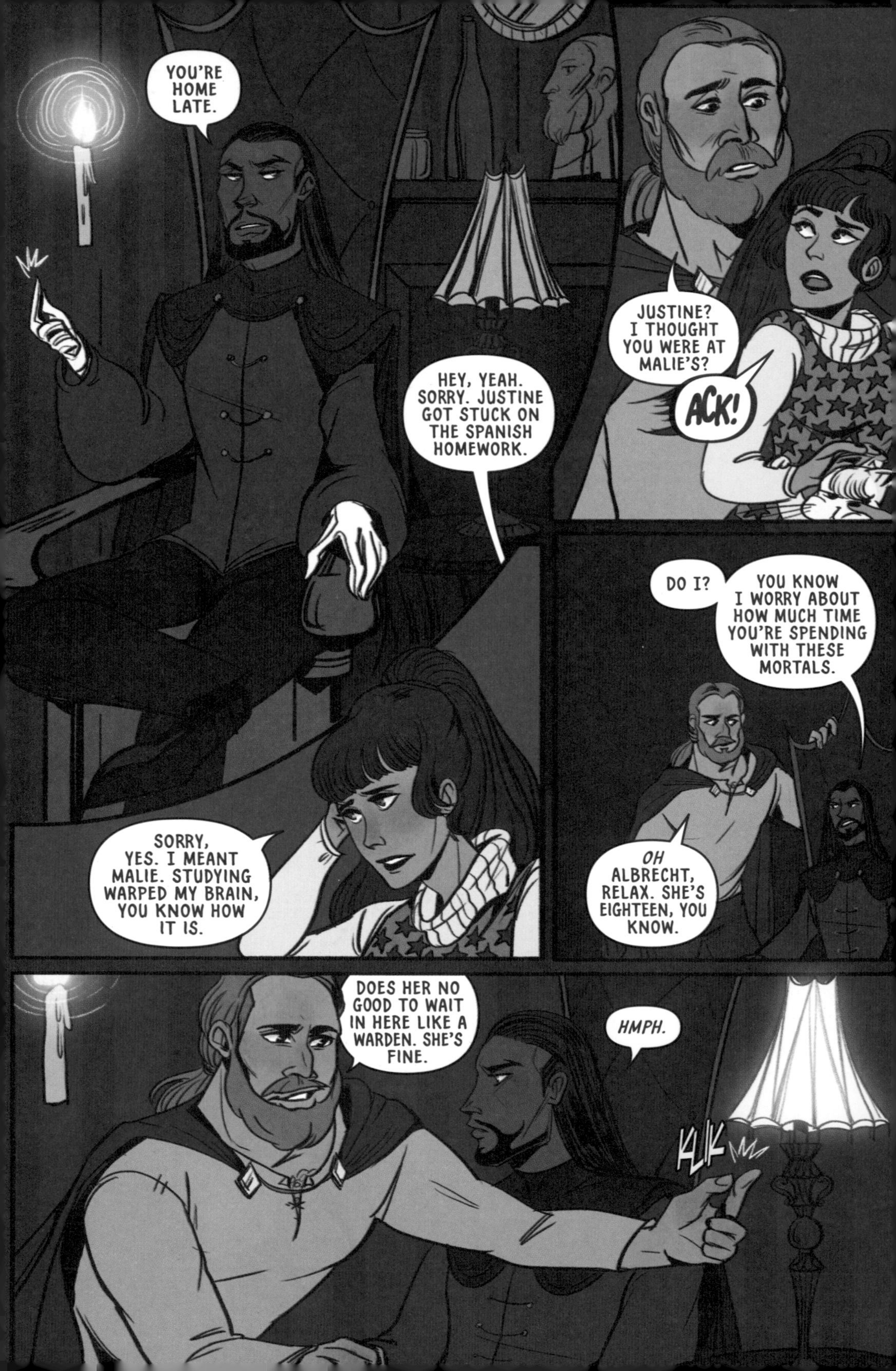
YOU'RE HOME LATE.
HEY, YEAH. SORRY. JUSTINE GOT STUCK ON THE SPANISH HOMEWORK.
JUSTINE? I THOUGHT YOU WERE AT MALIE'S?
ACK!
SORRY, YES. I MEANT MALIE. STUDYING WARPED MY BRAIN, YOU KNOW HOW IT IS.
YOU KNOW I WORRY ABOUT HOW MUCH TIME YOU'RE SPENDING WITH THESE MORTALS.
DO I?
OH ALBRECHT, RELAX. SHE'S EIGHTEEN, YOU KNOW.
DOES HER NO GOOD TO WAIT IN HERE LIKE A WARDEN. SHE'S FINE.
HMPH.
KLIK

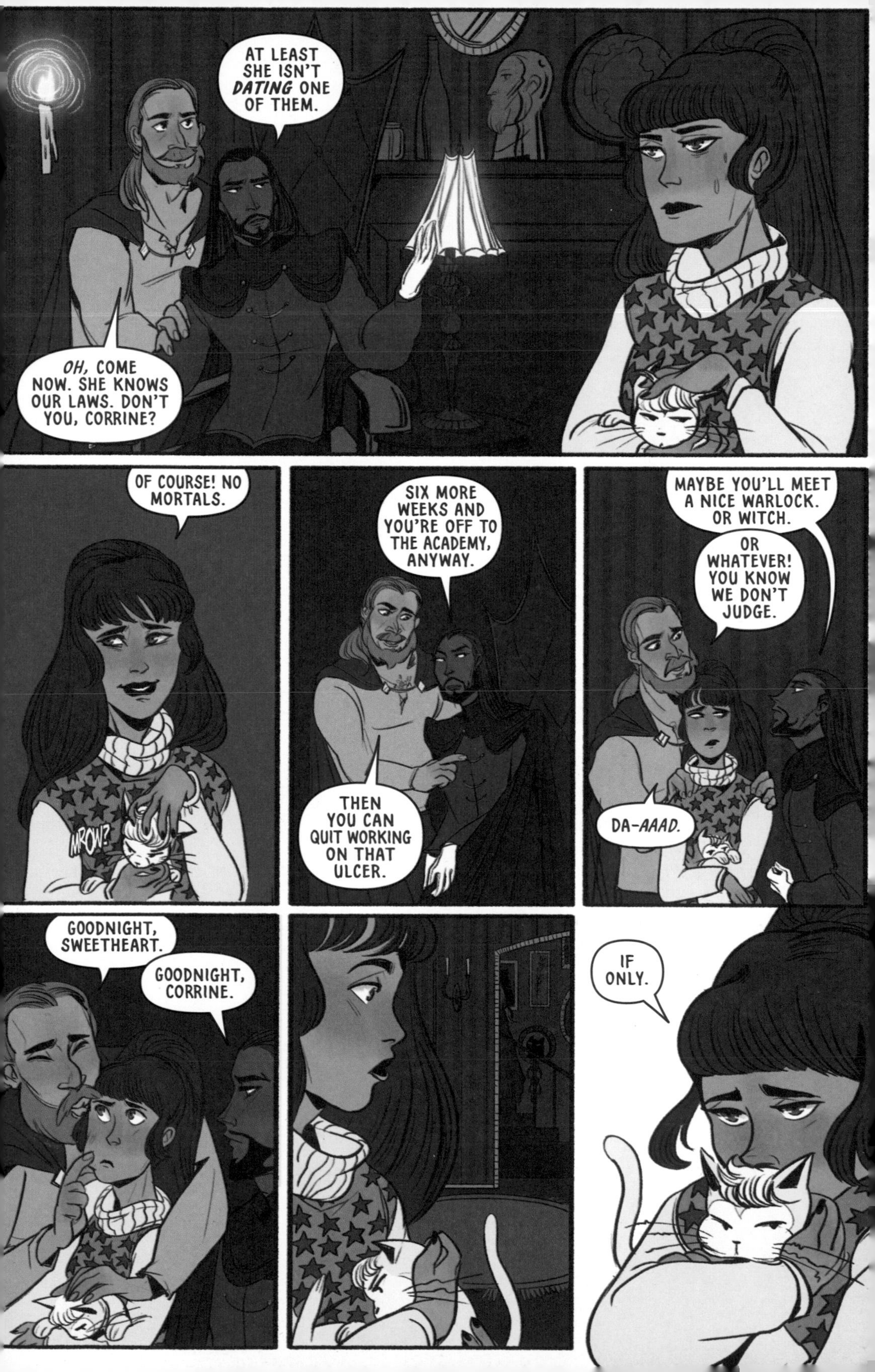
AT LEAST SHE ISN'T *DATING* ONE OF THEM.
OH, COME NOW. SHE KNOWS OUR LAWS. DON'T YOU, CORRINE?
OF COURSE! NO MORTALS.
MROW?
SIX MORE WEEKS AND YOU'RE OFF TO THE ACADEMY, ANYWAY.
THEN YOU CAN QUIT WORKING ON THAT ULCER.
MAYBE YOU'LL MEET A NICE WARLOCK. OR WITCH.
OR WHATEVER! YOU KNOW WE DON'T JUDGE.
DA-*AAAD.*
GOODNIGHT, SWEETHEART.
GOODNIGHT, CORRINE.
IF ONLY.

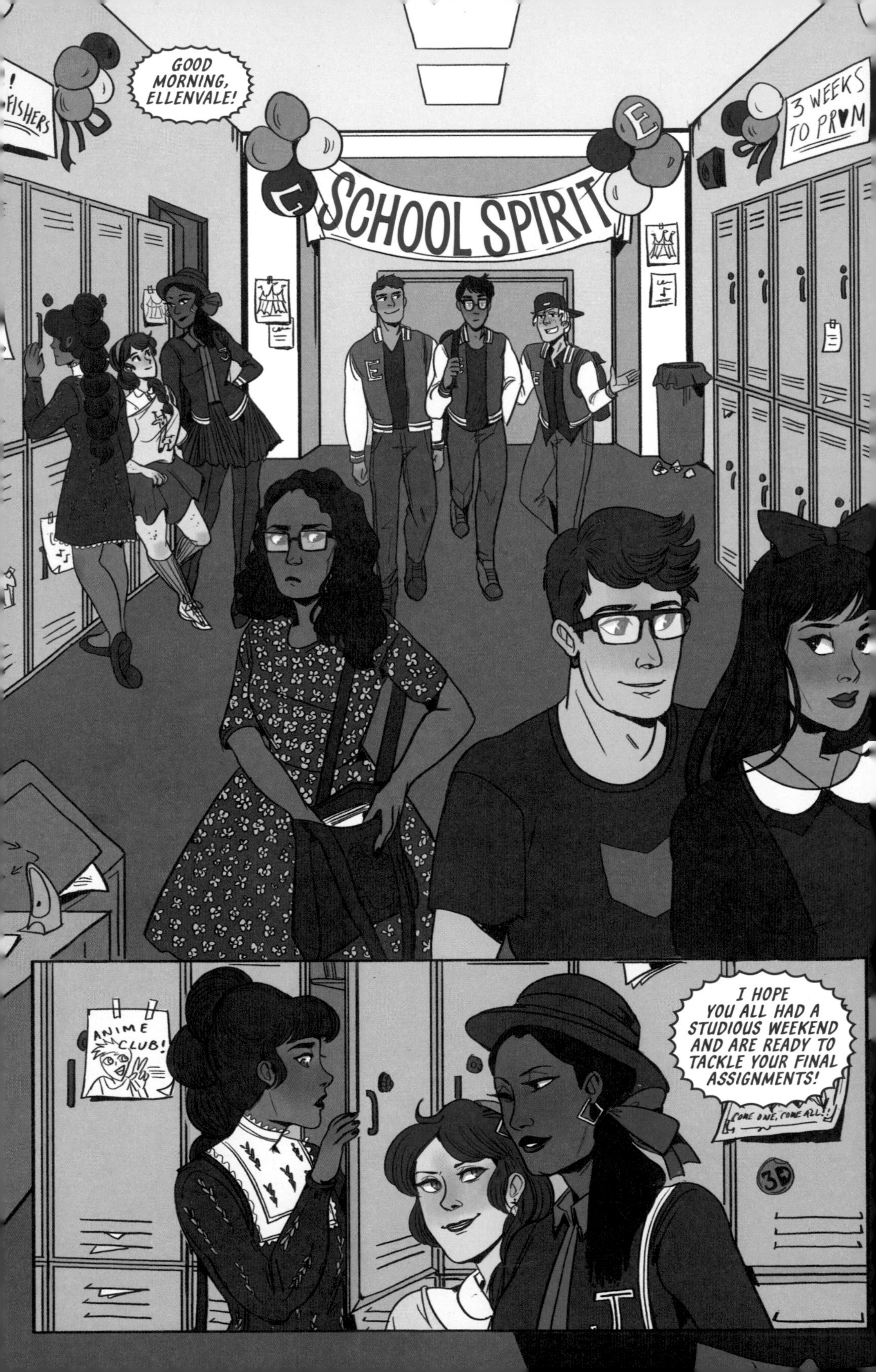
FISHERS
GOOD MORNING, ELLENVALE!
SCHOOL SPIRIT
3 WEEKS TO PR♥M
ANIME CLUB!
I HOPE YOU ALL HAD A STUDIOUS WEEKEND AND ARE READY TO TACKLE YOUR FINAL ASSIGNMENTS!
COME ONE, COME ALL!

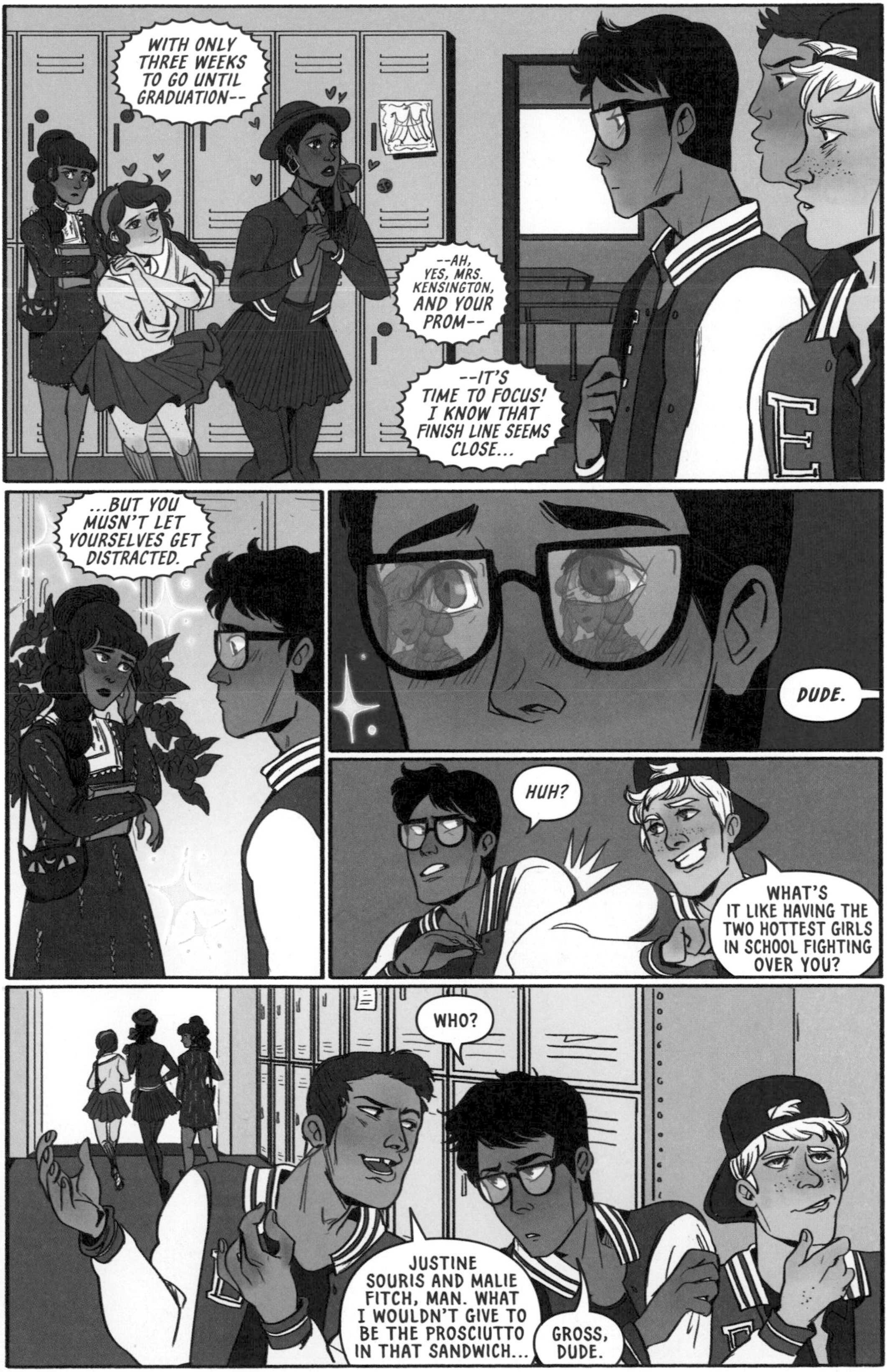

WITH ONLY THREE WEEKS TO GO UNTIL GRADUATION--
--AH, YES, MRS. KENSINGTON, AND YOUR PROM--
--IT'S TIME TO FOCUS! I KNOW THAT FINISH LINE SEEMS CLOSE...
...BUT YOU MUSN'T LET YOURSELVES GET DISTRACTED.
DUDE.
HUH?
WHAT'S IT LIKE HAVING THE TWO HOTTEST GIRLS IN SCHOOL FIGHTING OVER YOU?
WHO?
JUSTINE SOURIS AND MALIE FITCH, MAN. WHAT I WOULDN'T GIVE TO BE THE PROSCIUTTO IN THAT SANDWICH...
GROSS, DUDE.

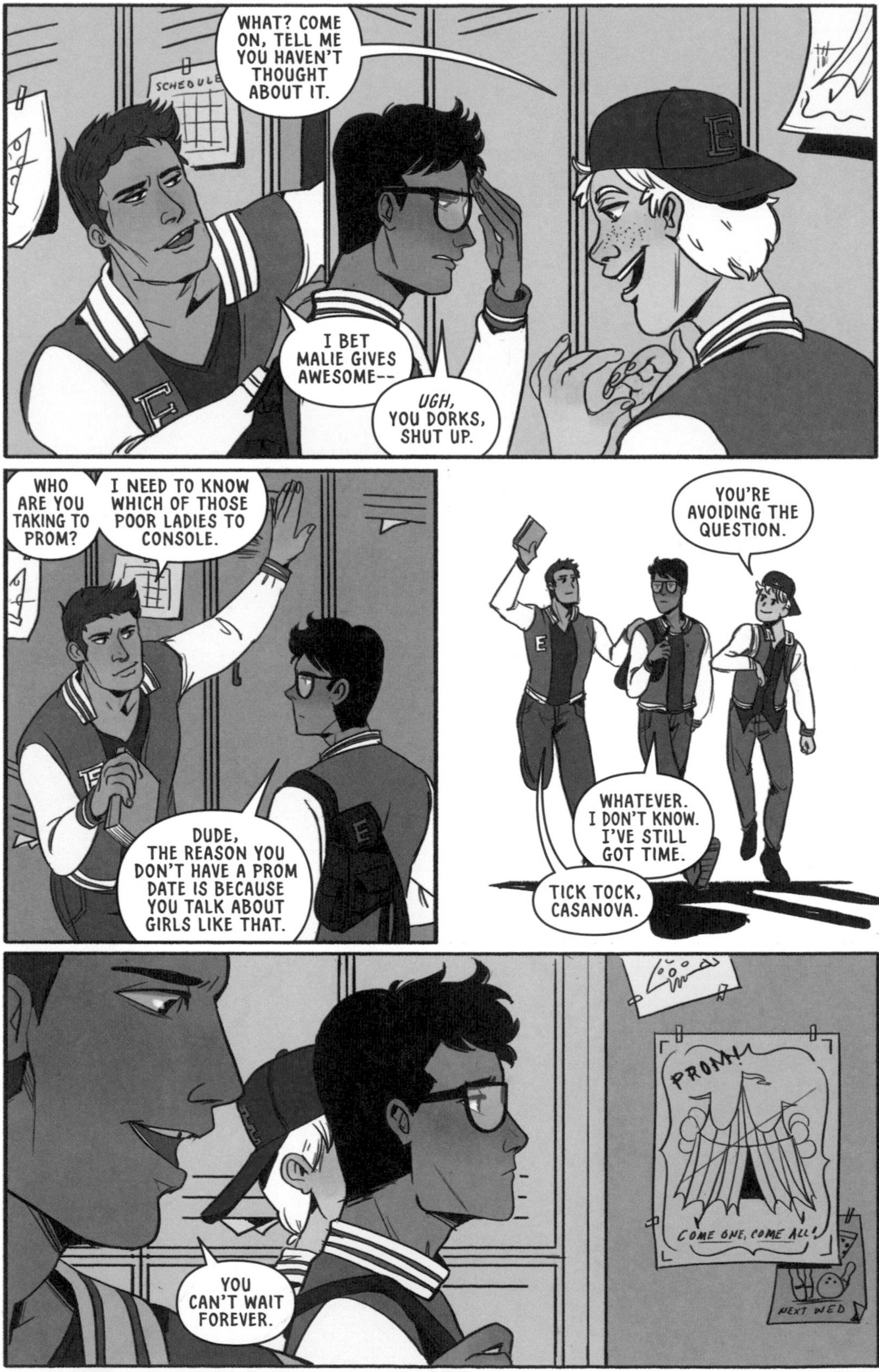
WHAT? COME ON, TELL ME YOU HAVEN'T THOUGHT ABOUT IT.
SCHEDULE
I BET MALIE GIVES AWESOME--
UGH, YOU DORKS, SHUT UP.
WHO ARE YOU TAKING TO PROM?
I NEED TO KNOW WHICH OF THOSE POOR LADIES TO CONSOLE.
DUDE, THE REASON YOU DON'T HAVE A PROM DATE IS BECAUSE YOU TALK ABOUT GIRLS LIKE THAT.
YOU'RE AVOIDING THE QUESTION.
WHATEVER. I DON'T KNOW. I'VE STILL GOT TIME.
TICK TOCK, CASANOVA.
PROM!
COME ONE, COME ALL!
NEXT WED
YOU CAN'T WAIT FOREVER.

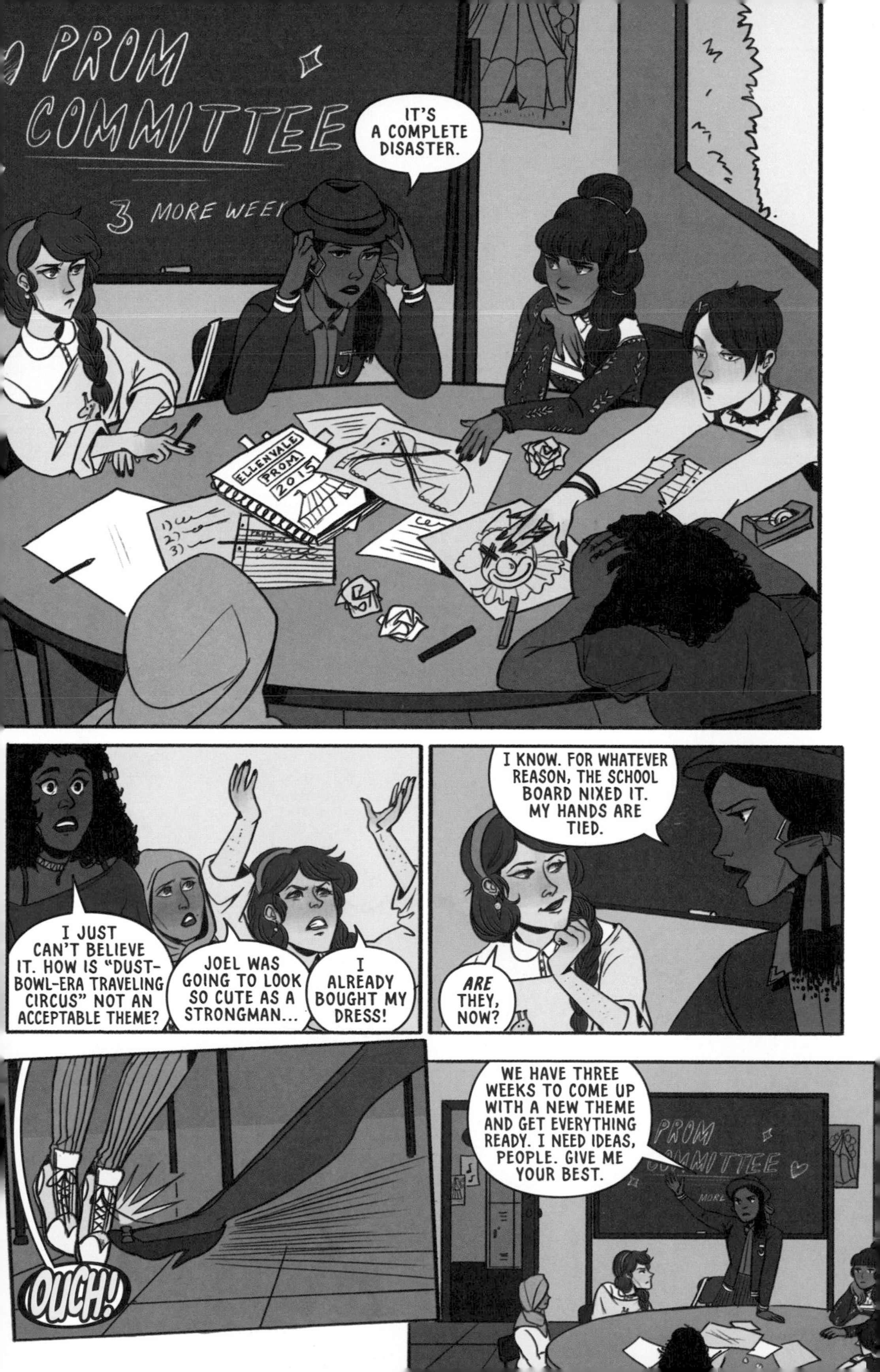
PROM
COMMITTEE
3 MORE WEE
IT'S A COMPLETE DISASTER.
ELLENVALE PROM 2015
I JUST CAN'T BELIEVE IT. HOW IS "DUST-BOWL-ERA TRAVELING CIRCUS" NOT AN ACCEPTABLE THEME?
JOEL WAS GOING TO LOOK SO CUTE AS A STRONGMAN...
I ALREADY BOUGHT MY DRESS!
I KNOW. FOR WHATEVER REASON, THE SCHOOL BOARD NIXED IT. MY HANDS ARE TIED.
ARE THEY, NOW?
OUCH!
WE HAVE THREE WEEKS TO COME UP WITH A NEW THEME AND GET EVERYTHING READY. I NEED IDEAS, PEOPLE. GIVE ME YOUR BEST.
PROM
COMMITTEE
MORE

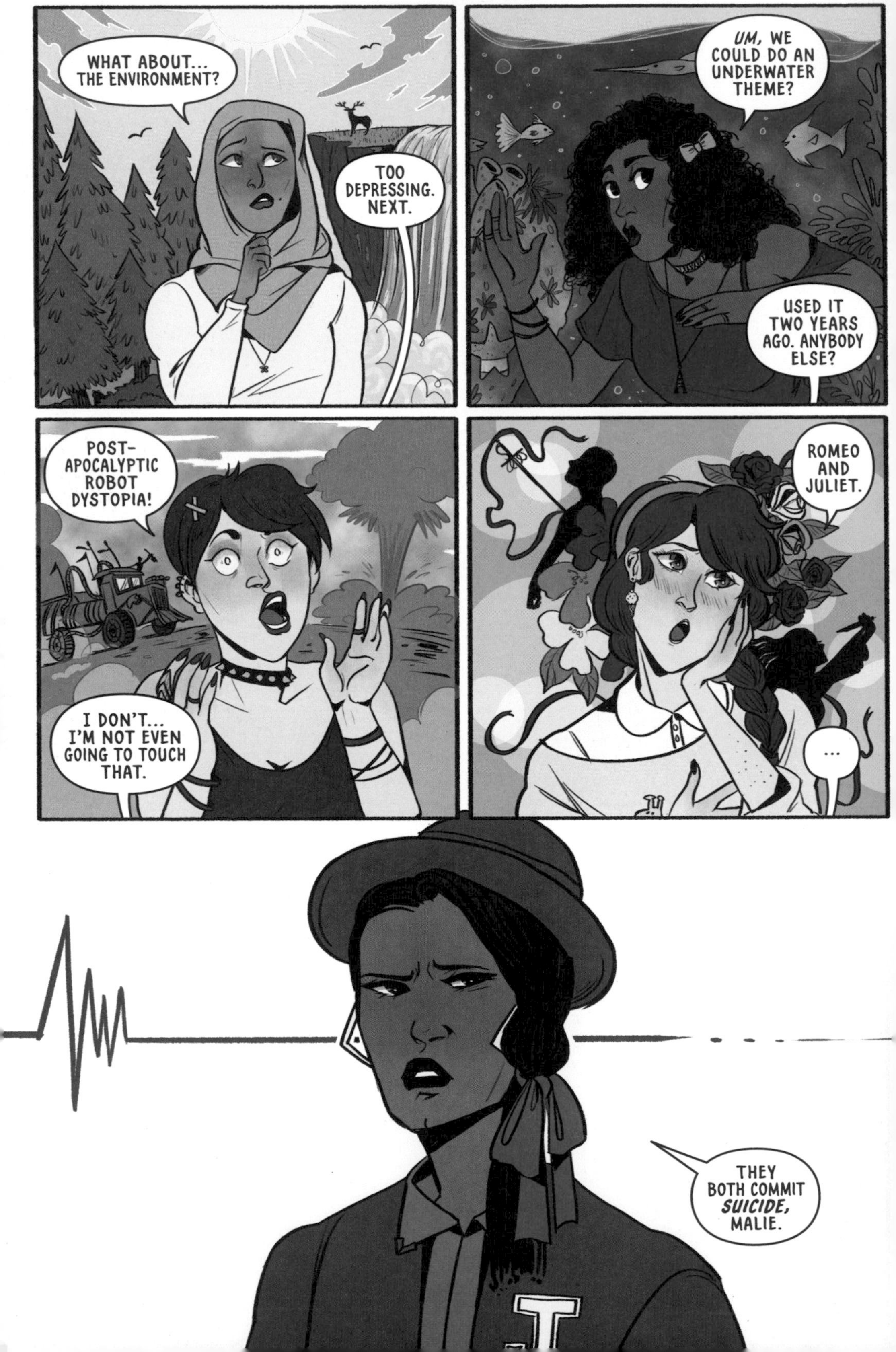
WHAT ABOUT... THE ENVIRONMENT?
TOO DEPRESSING. NEXT.
UM, WE COULD DO AN UNDERWATER THEME?
USED IT TWO YEARS AGO. ANYBODY ELSE?
POST-APOCALYPTIC ROBOT DYSTOPIA!
I DON'T... I'M NOT EVEN GOING TO TOUCH THAT.
ROMEO AND JULIET.
...
THEY BOTH COMMIT SUICIDE, MALIE.

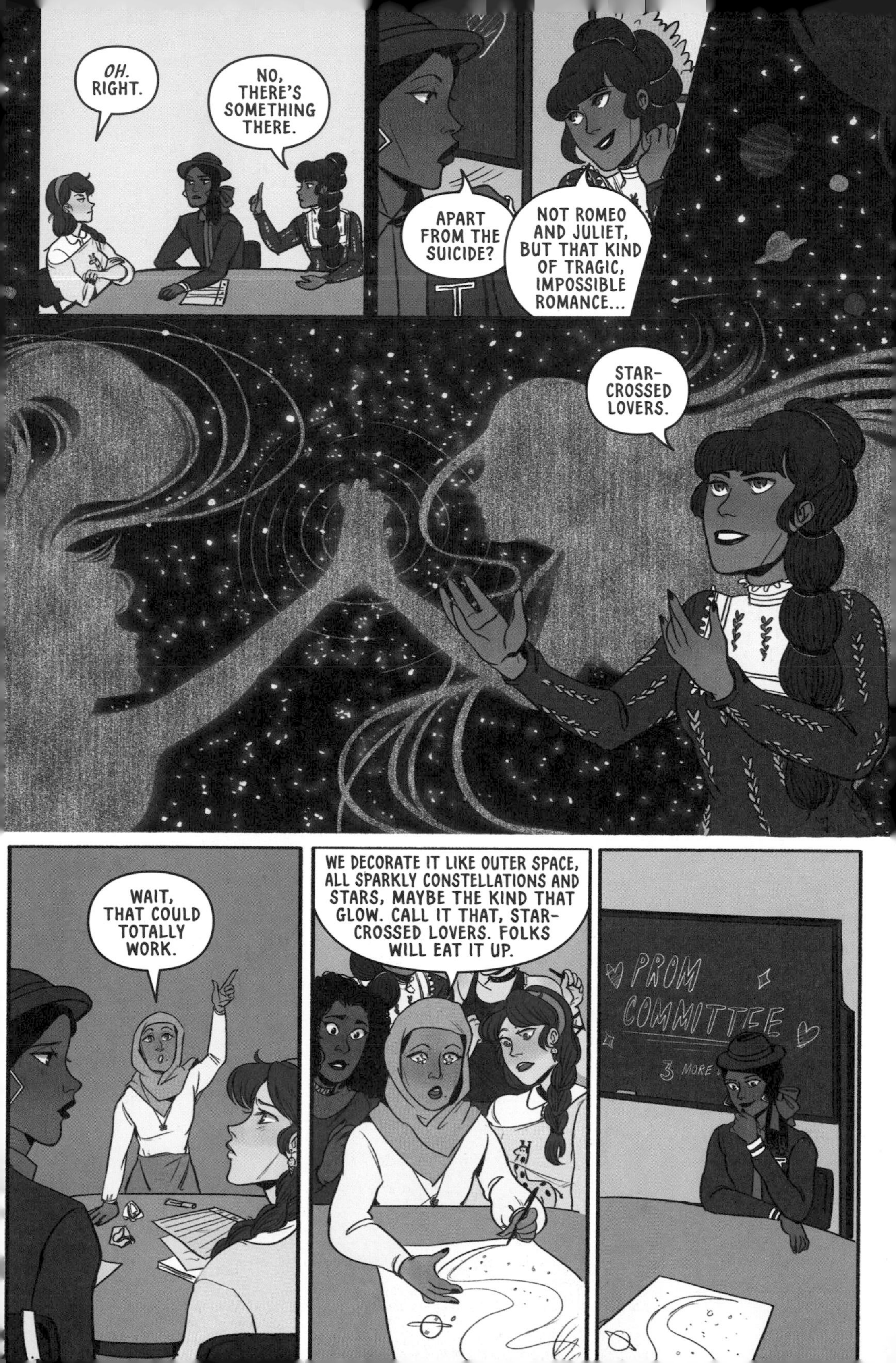
OH. RIGHT.
NO, THERE'S SOMETHING THERE.
APART FROM THE SUICIDE?
NOT ROMEO AND JULIET, BUT THAT KIND OF TRAGIC, IMPOSSIBLE ROMANCE...
STAR-CROSSED LOVERS.
WAIT, THAT COULD TOTALLY WORK.
WE DECORATE IT LIKE OUTER SPACE, ALL SPARKLY CONSTELLATIONS AND STARS, MAYBE THE KIND THAT GLOW. CALL IT THAT, STAR-CROSSED LOVERS. FOLKS WILL EAT IT UP.
PROM COMMITTEE
3 MORE

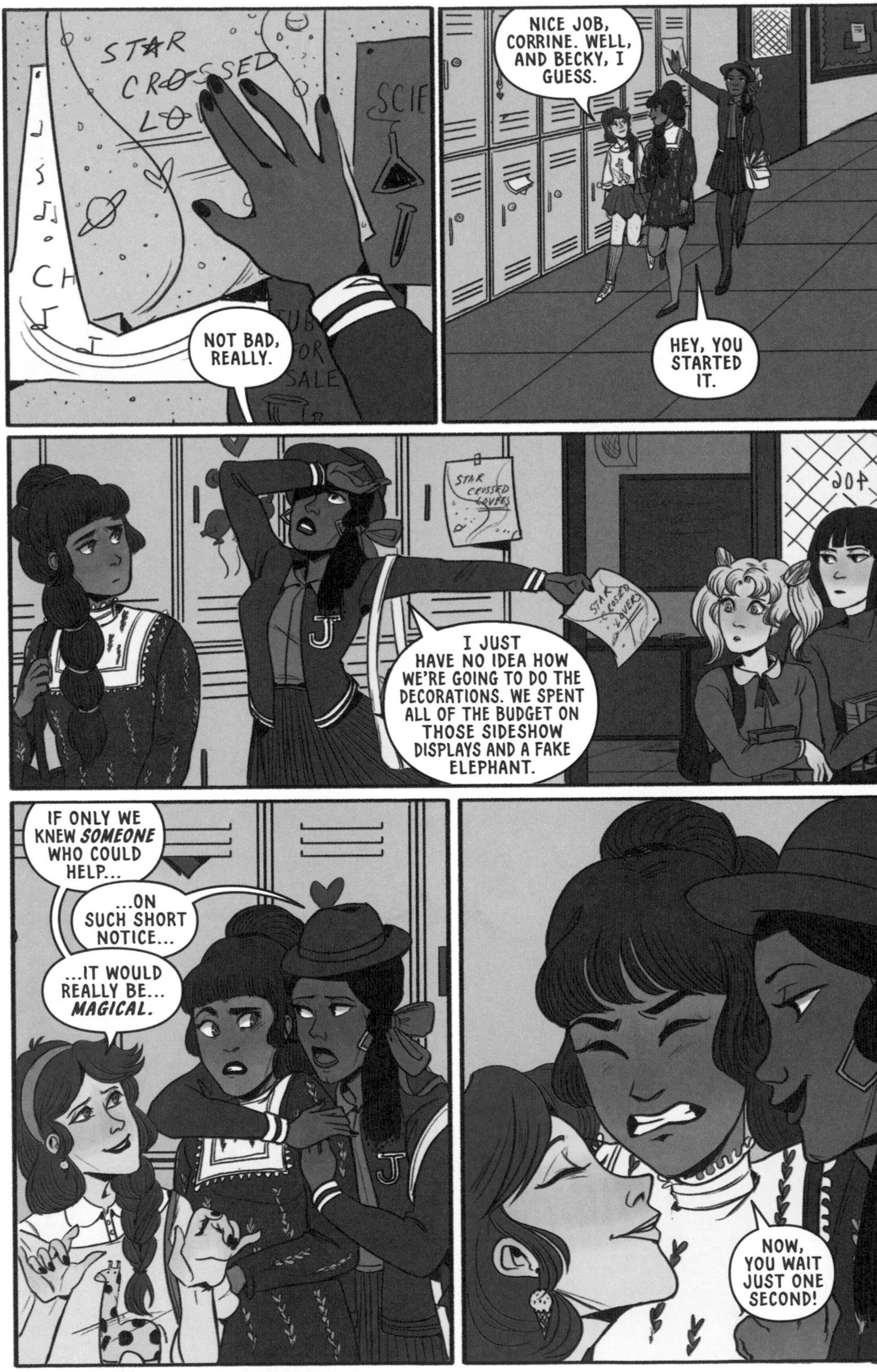
STAR CROSSED LO
SCIF
TUB FOR SALE
NOT BAD, REALLY.
NICE JOB, CORRINE. WELL, AND BECKY, I GUESS.
HEY, YOU STARTED IT.
STAR CROSSED LOVERS
406
I JUST HAVE NO IDEA HOW WE'RE GOING TO DO THE DECORATIONS. WE SPENT ALL OF THE BUDGET ON THOSE SIDESHOW DISPLAYS AND A FAKE ELEPHANT.
IF ONLY WE KNEW *SOMEONE* WHO COULD HELP...
...ON SUCH SHORT NOTICE...
...IT WOULD REALLY BE... ***MAGICAL.***
NOW, YOU WAIT JUST ONE SECOND!

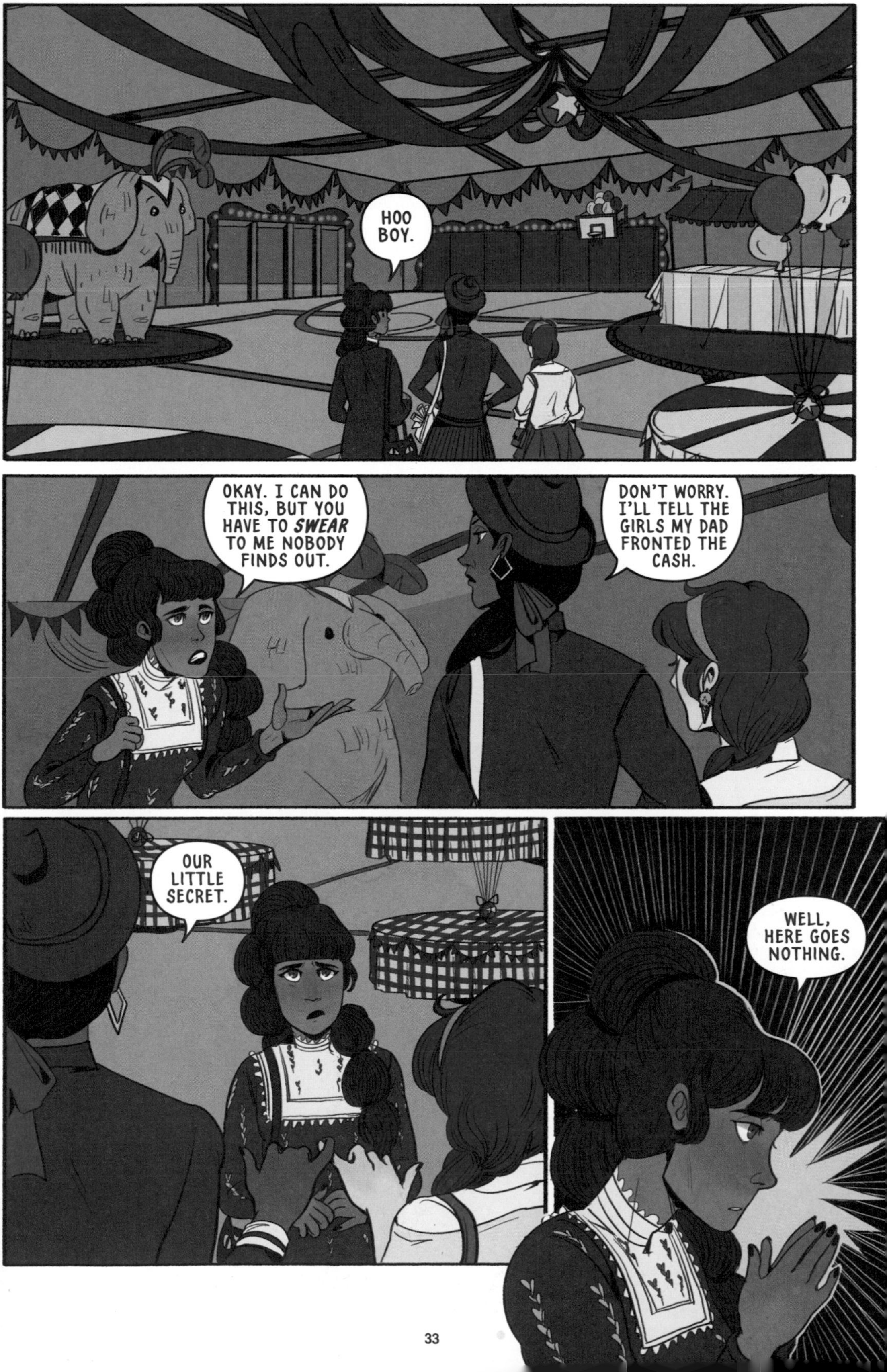
HOO BOY.
OKAY. I CAN DO THIS, BUT YOU HAVE TO *SWEAR* TO ME NOBODY FINDS OUT.
DON'T WORRY. I'LL TELL THE GIRLS MY DAD FRONTED THE CASH.
OUR LITTLE SECRET.
WELL, HERE GOES NOTHING.

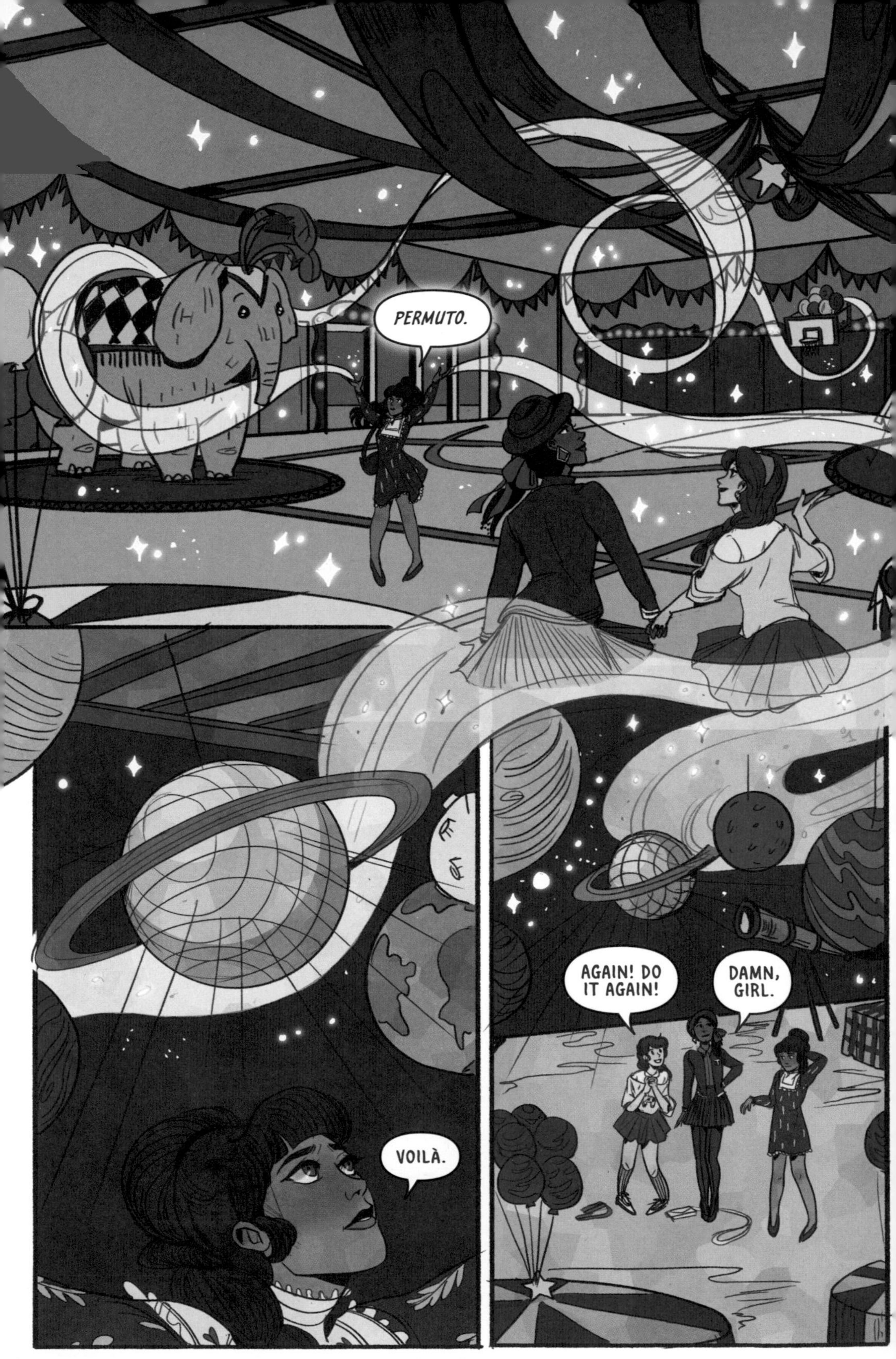
PERMUTO.
VOILÀ.
AGAIN! DO IT AGAIN!
DAMN, GIRL.

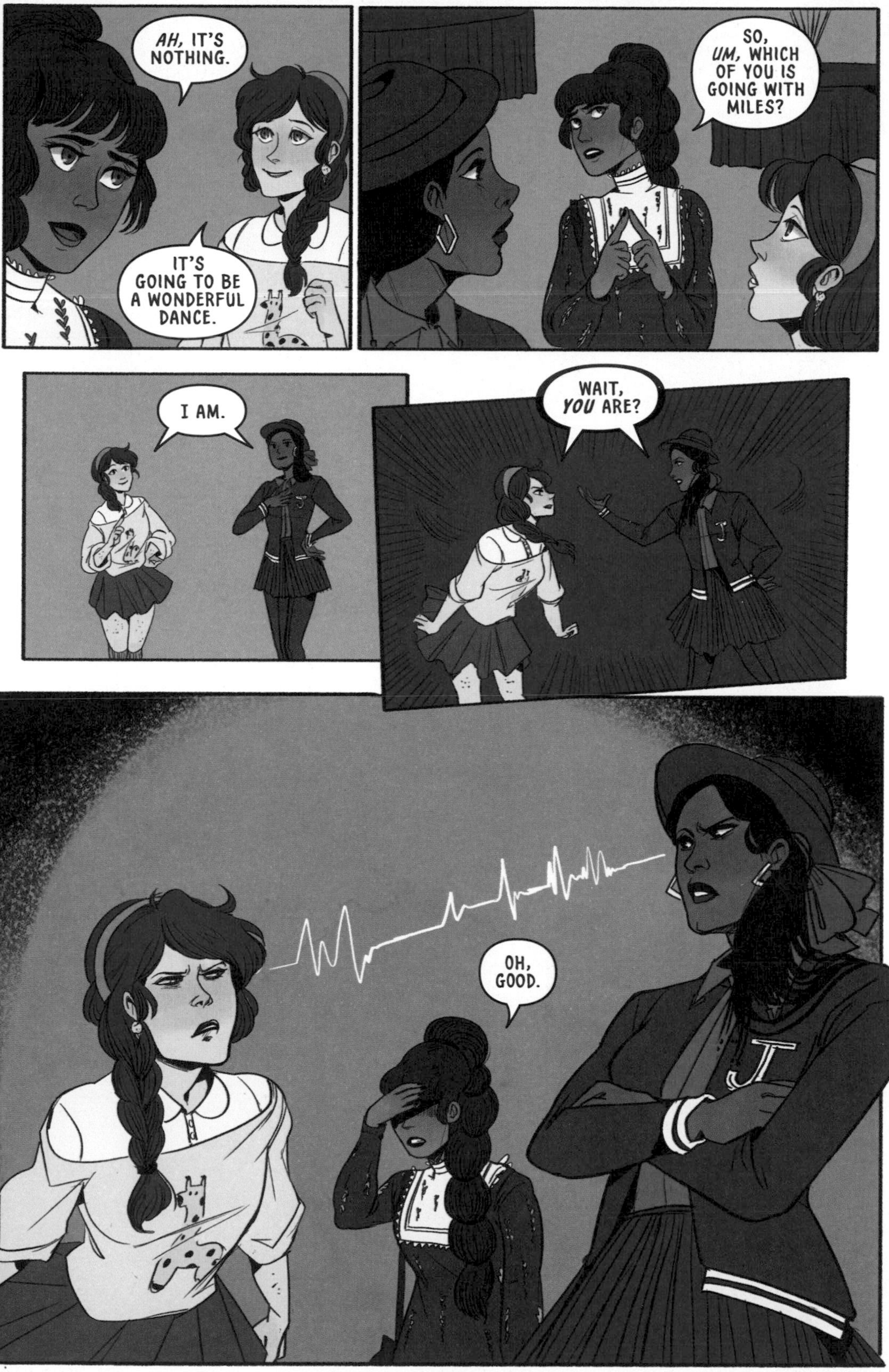
AH, IT'S NOTHING.
IT'S GOING TO BE A WONDERFUL DANCE.
SO, UM, WHICH OF YOU IS GOING WITH MILES?
I AM.
WAIT, YOU ARE?
OH, GOOD.

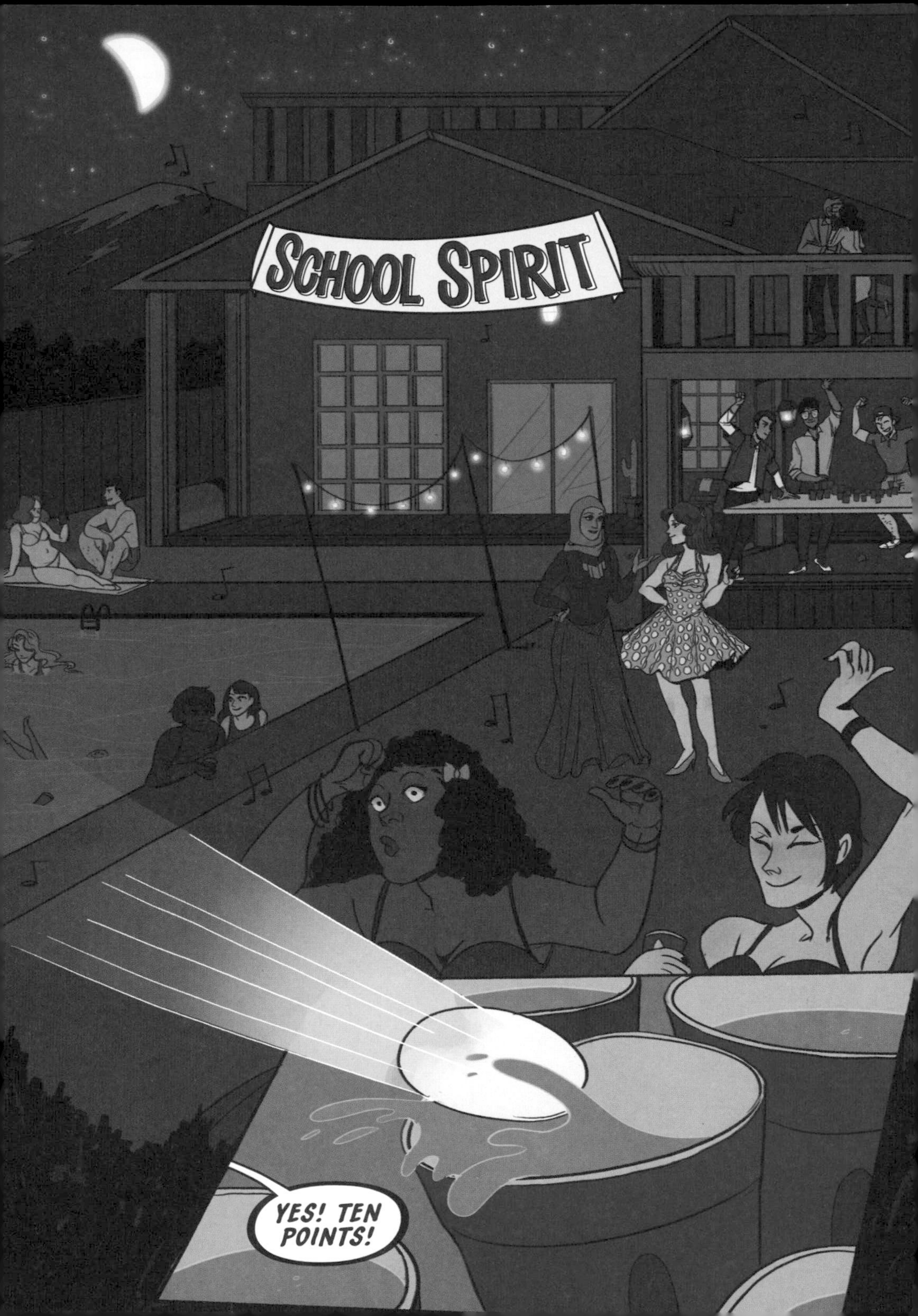
SCHOOL SPIRIT
YES! TEN POINTS!

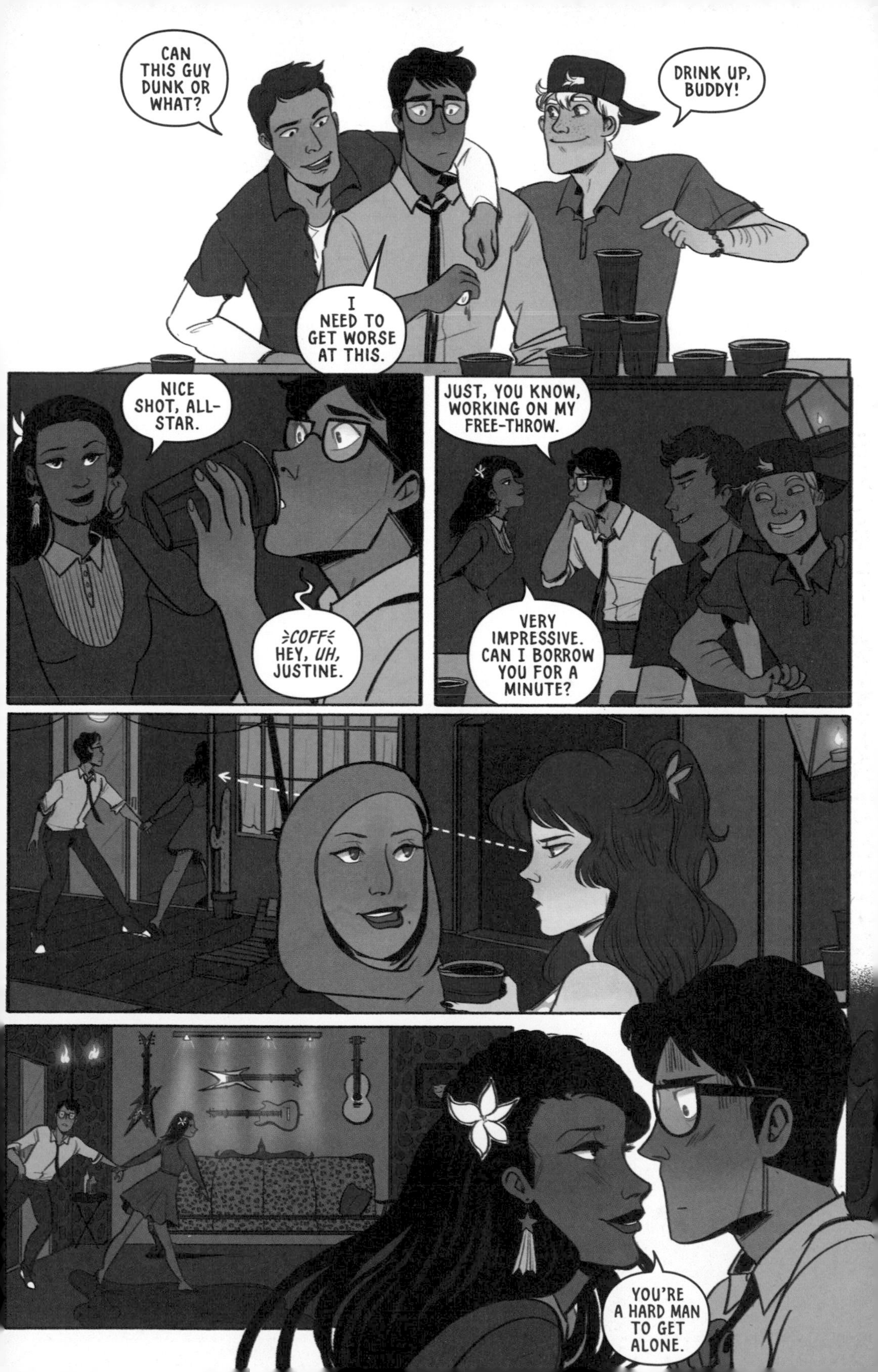
CAN THIS GUY DUNK OR WHAT?
DRINK UP, BUDDY!
I NEED TO GET WORSE AT THIS.
NICE SHOT, ALL-STAR.
≥COFF≤ HEY, UH, JUSTINE.
JUST, YOU KNOW, WORKING ON MY FREE-THROW.
VERY IMPRESSIVE. CAN I BORROW YOU FOR A MINUTE?
YOU'RE A HARD MAN TO GET ALONE.

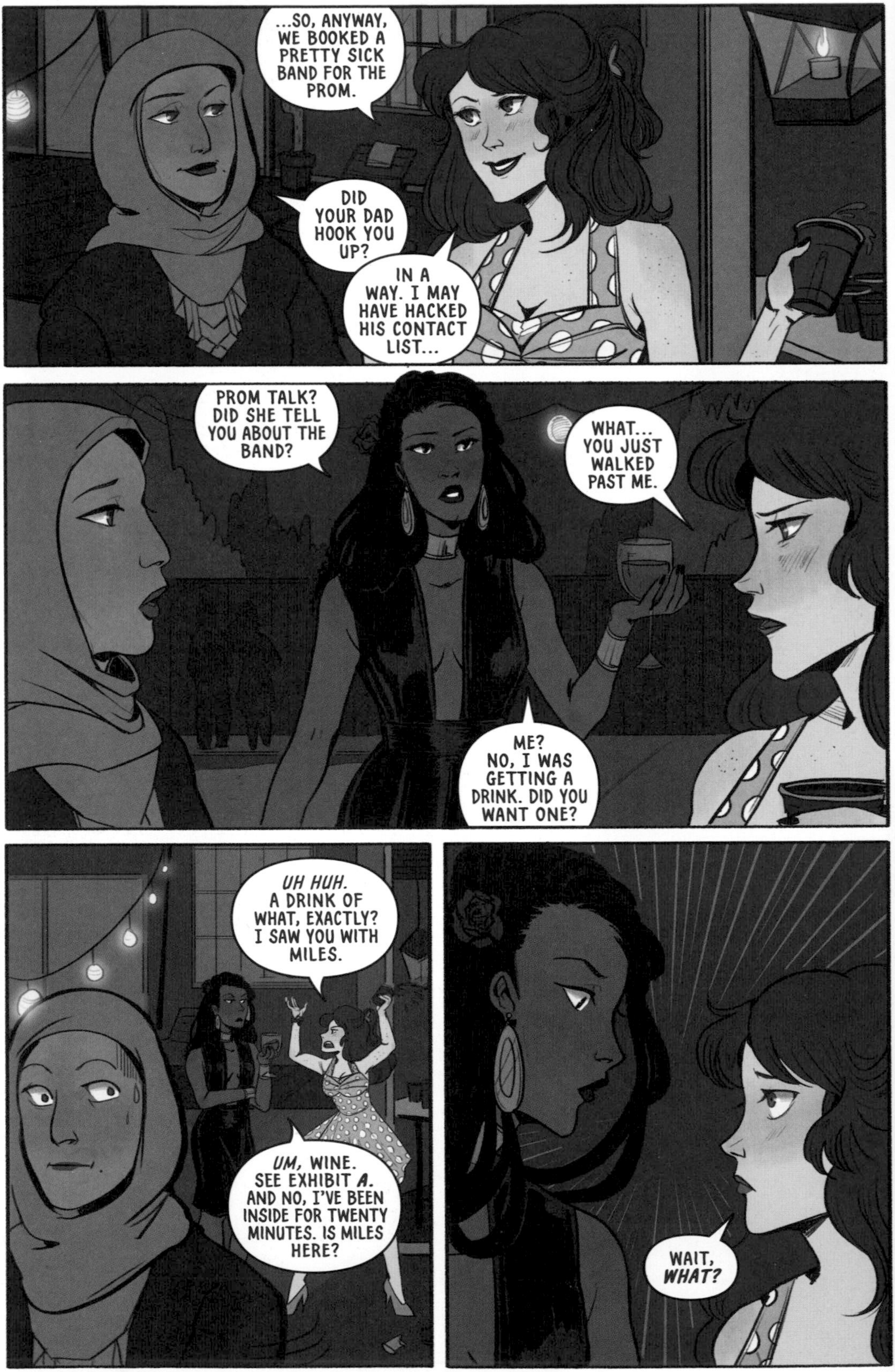
...SO, ANYWAY, WE BOOKED A PRETTY SICK BAND FOR THE PROM.
DID YOUR DAD HOOK YOU UP?
IN A WAY. I MAY HAVE HACKED HIS CONTACT LIST...
PROM TALK? DID SHE TELL YOU ABOUT THE BAND?
WHAT... YOU JUST WALKED PAST ME.
ME? NO, I WAS GETTING A DRINK. DID YOU WANT ONE?
UH HUH. A DRINK OF WHAT, EXACTLY? I SAW YOU WITH MILES.
UM, WINE. SEE EXHIBIT *A.* AND NO, I'VE BEEN INSIDE FOR TWENTY MINUTES. IS MILES HERE?
WAIT, ***WHAT?***

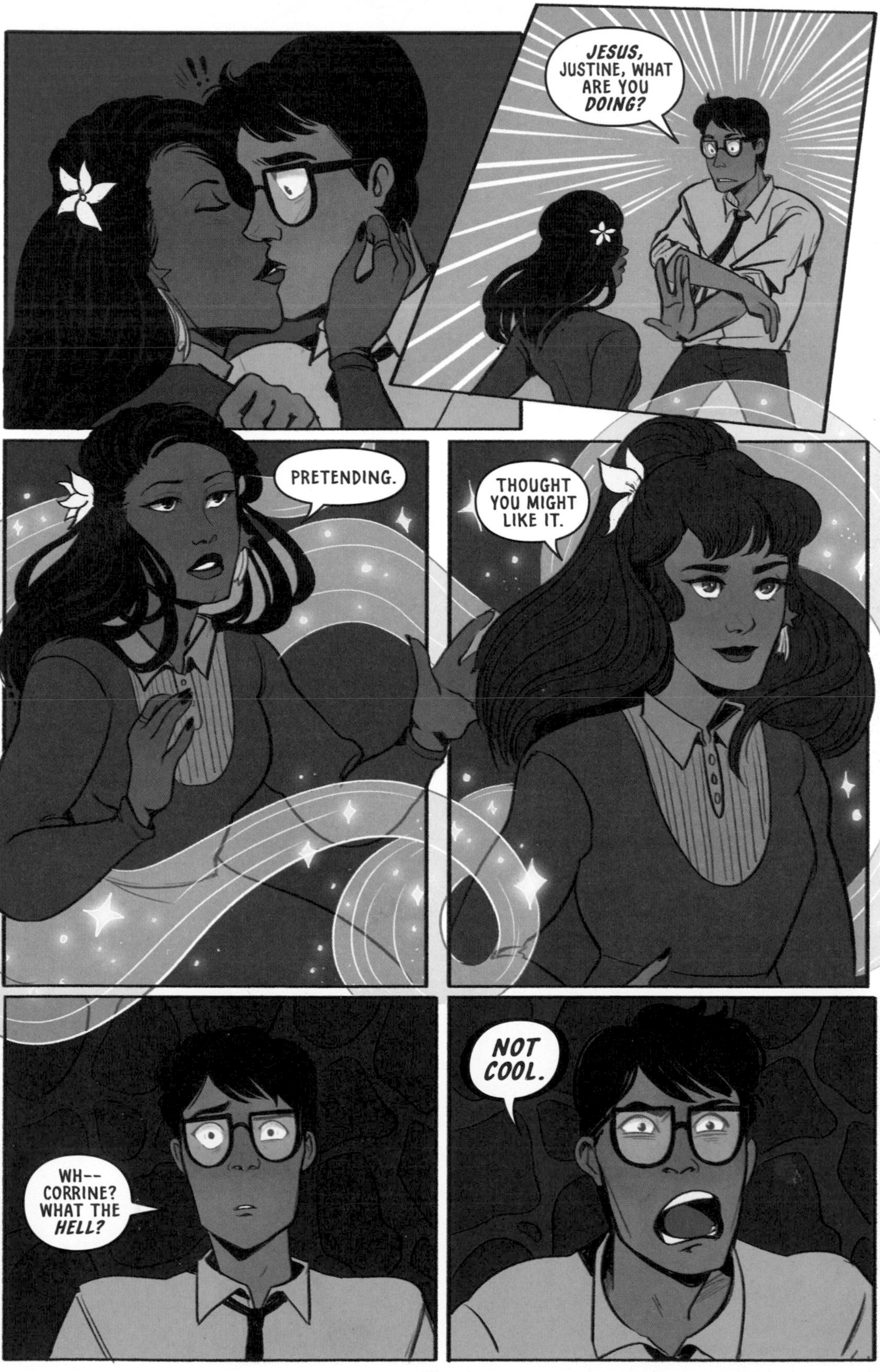
!!
JESUS, JUSTINE, WHAT ARE YOU DOING?
PRETENDING.
THOUGHT YOU MIGHT LIKE IT.
WH-- CORRINE? WHAT THE HELL?
NOT COOL.

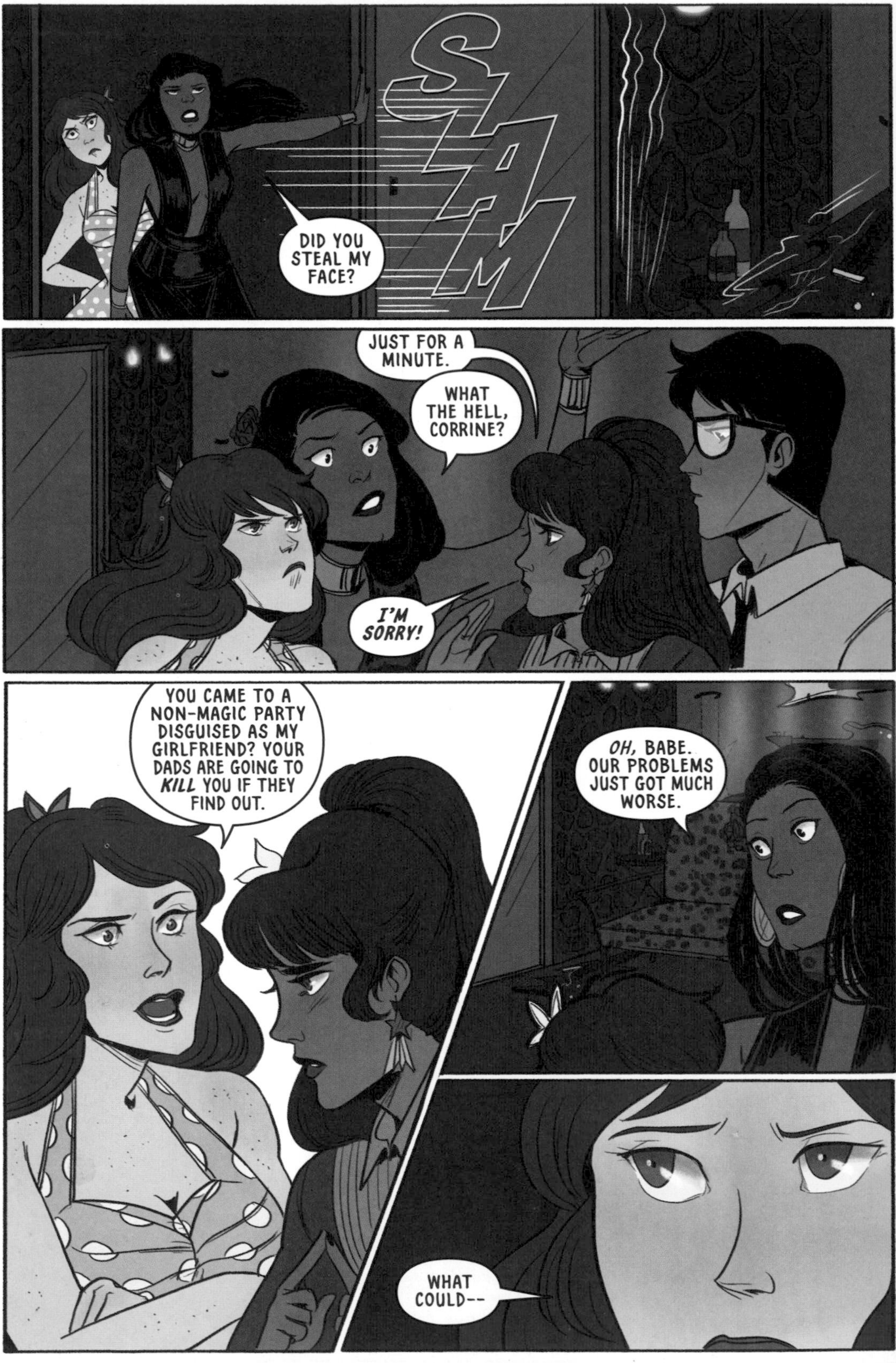
DID YOU STEAL MY FACE?
SLAM
JUST FOR A MINUTE.
WHAT THE HELL, CORRINE?
I'M SORRY!
YOU CAME TO A NON-MAGIC PARTY DISGUISED AS MY GIRLFRIEND? YOUR DADS ARE GOING TO KILL YOU IF THEY FIND OUT.
OH, BABE. OUR PROBLEMS JUST GOT MUCH WORSE.
WHAT COULD--

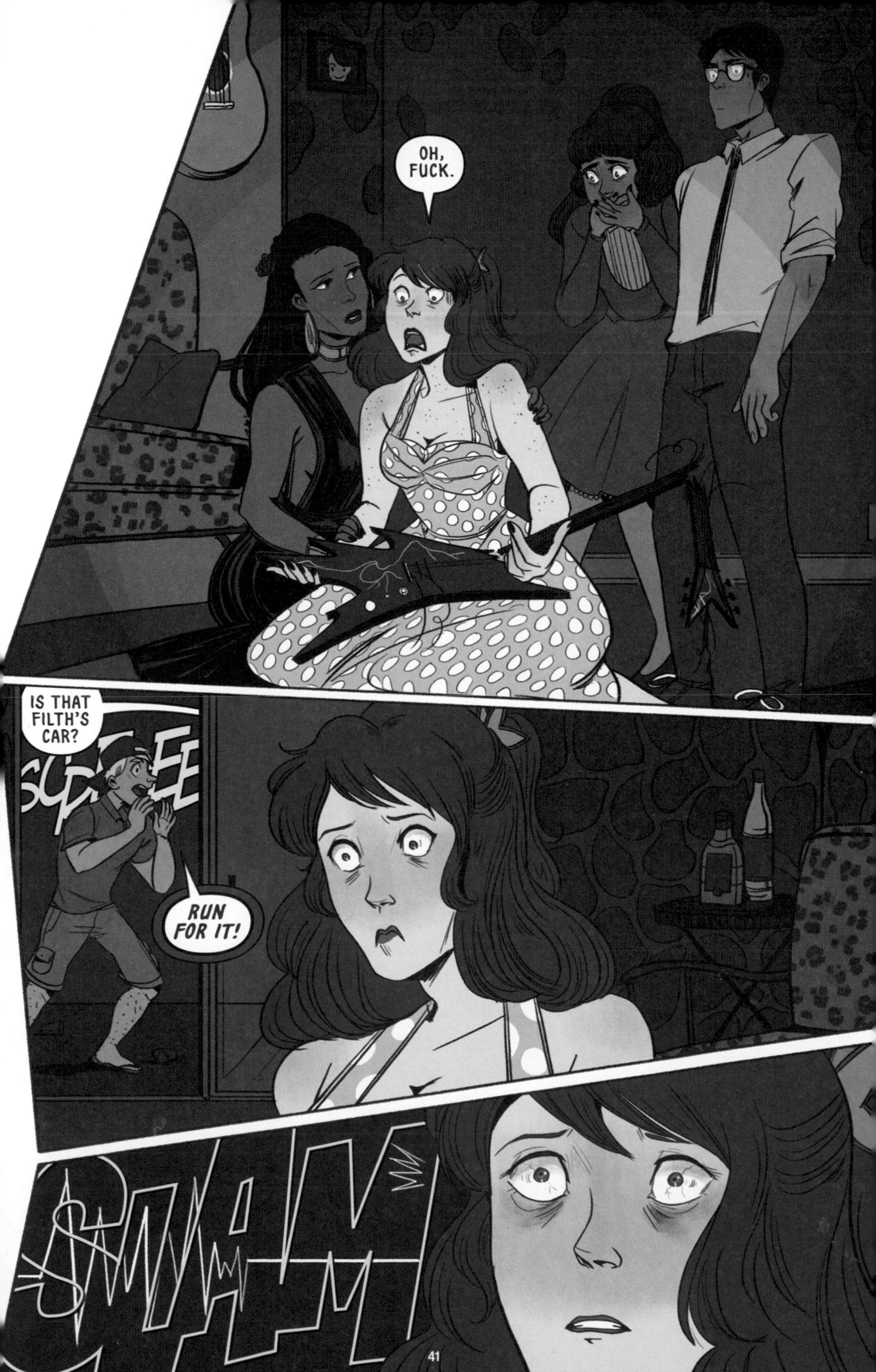
OH, FUCK.
IS THAT FILTH'S CAR?
RUN FOR IT!

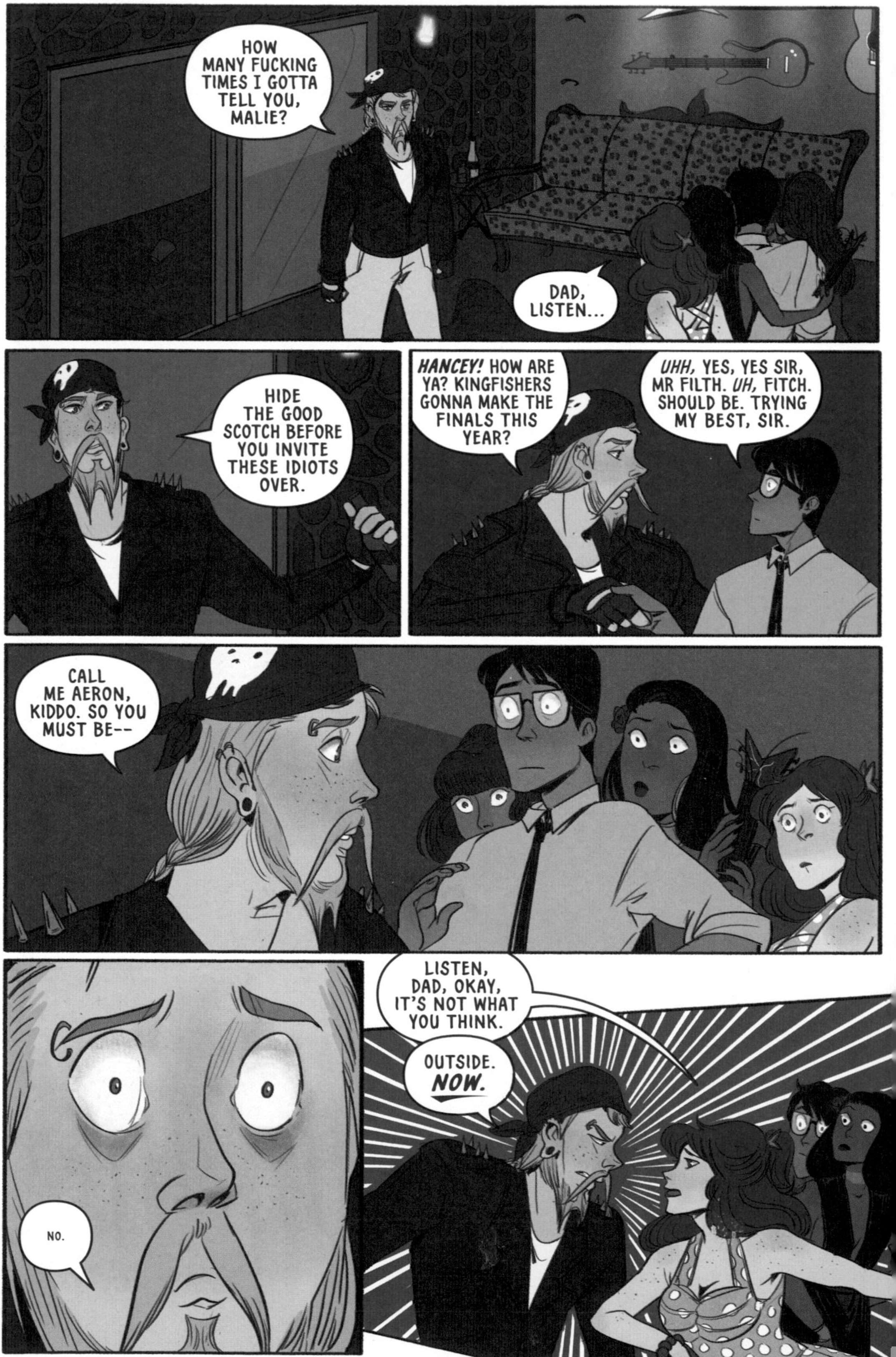
HOW MANY FUCKING TIMES I GOTTA TELL YOU, MALIE?
DAD, LISTEN...
HIDE THE GOOD SCOTCH BEFORE YOU INVITE THESE IDIOTS OVER.
HANCEY! HOW ARE YA? KINGFISHERS GONNA MAKE THE FINALS THIS YEAR?
UHH, YES, YES SIR, MR FILTH. *UH,* FITCH. SHOULD BE. TRYING MY BEST, SIR.
CALL ME AERON, KIDDO. SO YOU MUST BE--
NO.
LISTEN, DAD, OKAY, IT'S NOT WHAT YOU THINK.
OUTSIDE. **NOW.**

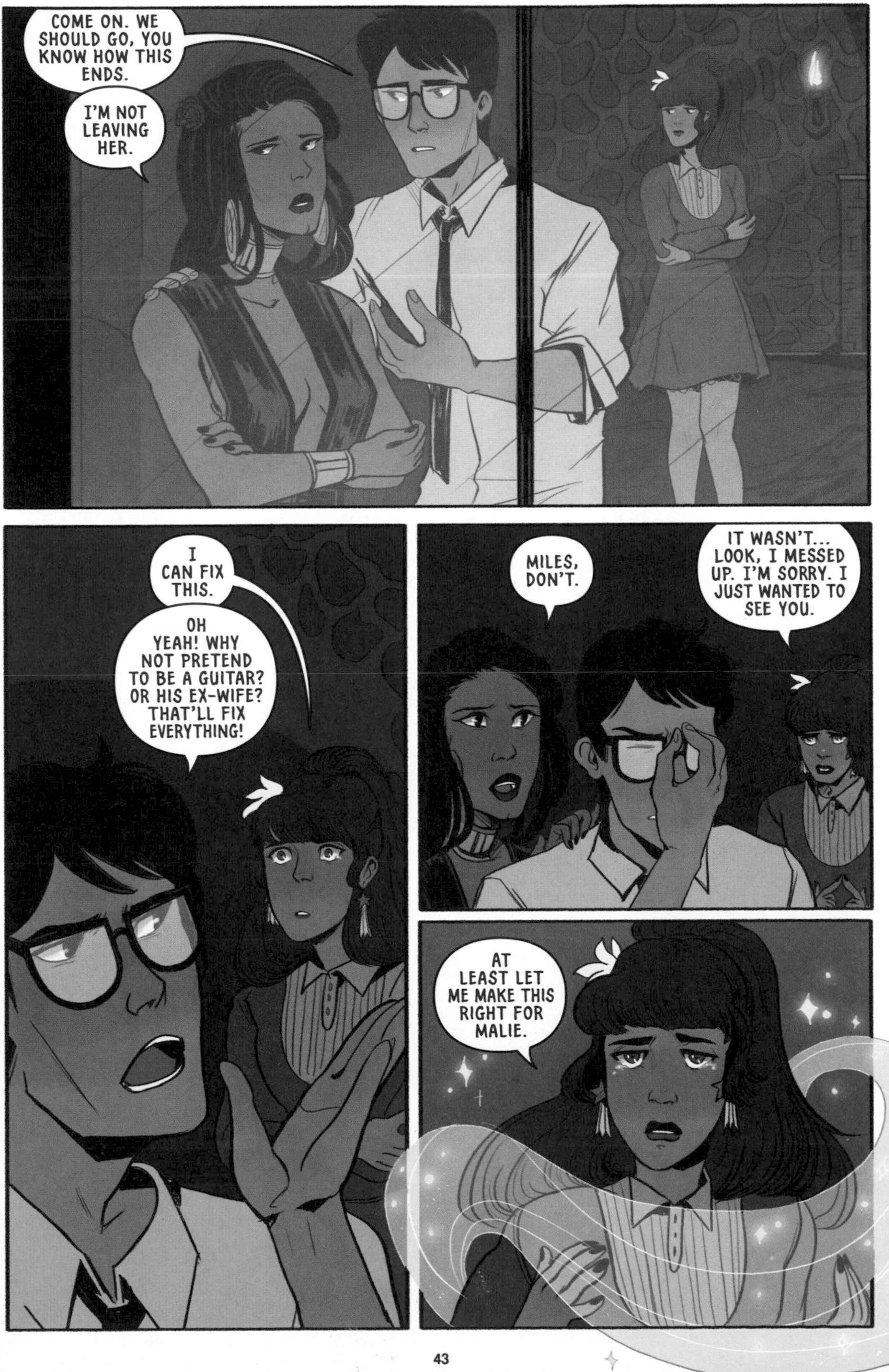

COME ON. WE SHOULD GO, YOU KNOW HOW THIS ENDS.
I'M NOT LEAVING HER.
I CAN FIX THIS.
OH YEAH! WHY NOT PRETEND TO BE A GUITAR? OR HIS EX-WIFE? THAT'LL FIX EVERYTHING!
MILES, DON'T.
IT WASN'T... LOOK, I MESSED UP. I'M SORRY. I JUST WANTED TO SEE YOU.
AT LEAST LET ME MAKE THIS RIGHT FOR MALIE.

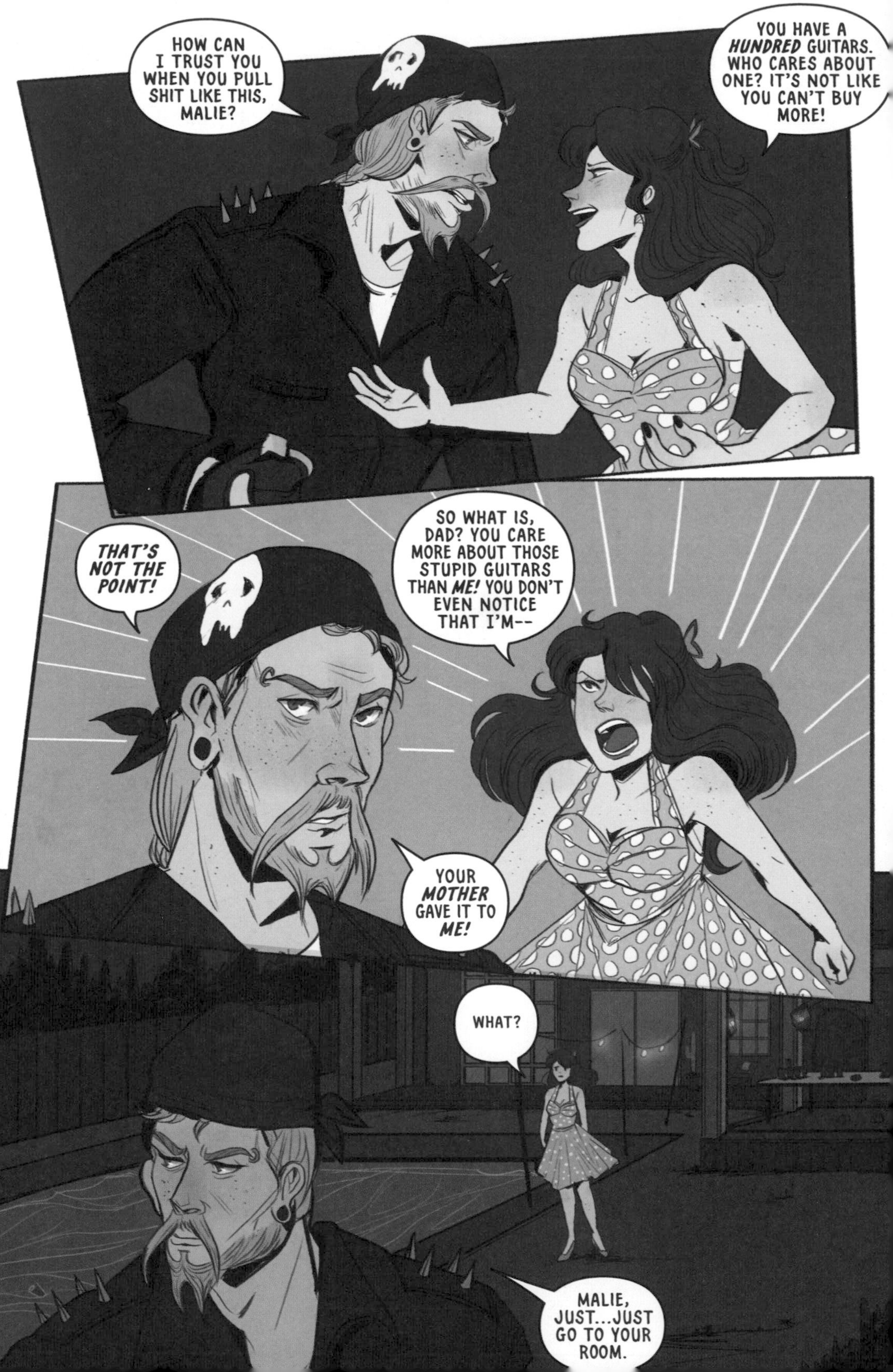

HOW CAN I TRUST YOU WHEN YOU PULL SHIT LIKE THIS, MALIE?
YOU HAVE A *HUNDRED* GUITARS. WHO CARES ABOUT ONE? IT'S NOT LIKE YOU CAN'T BUY MORE!
THAT'S NOT THE POINT!
SO WHAT IS, DAD? YOU CARE MORE ABOUT THOSE STUPID GUITARS THAN *ME!* YOU DON'T EVEN NOTICE THAT I'M--
YOUR *MOTHER* GAVE IT TO *ME!*
WHAT?
MALIE, JUST...JUST GO TO YOUR ROOM.

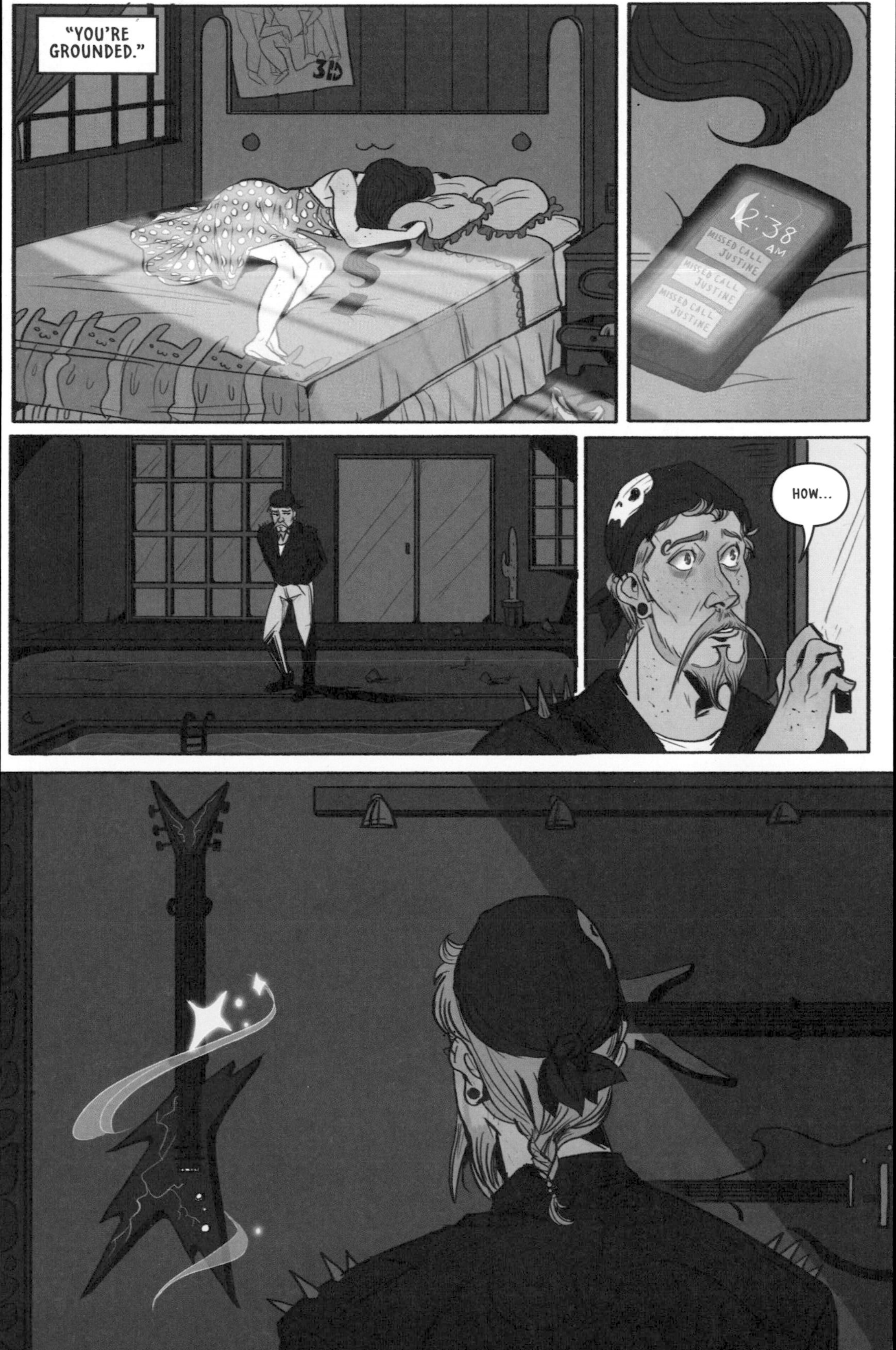
"YOU'RE GROUNDED."
2:38 AM
MISSED CALL JUSTINE
MISSED CALL JUSTINE
MISSED CALL JUSTINE
HOW...

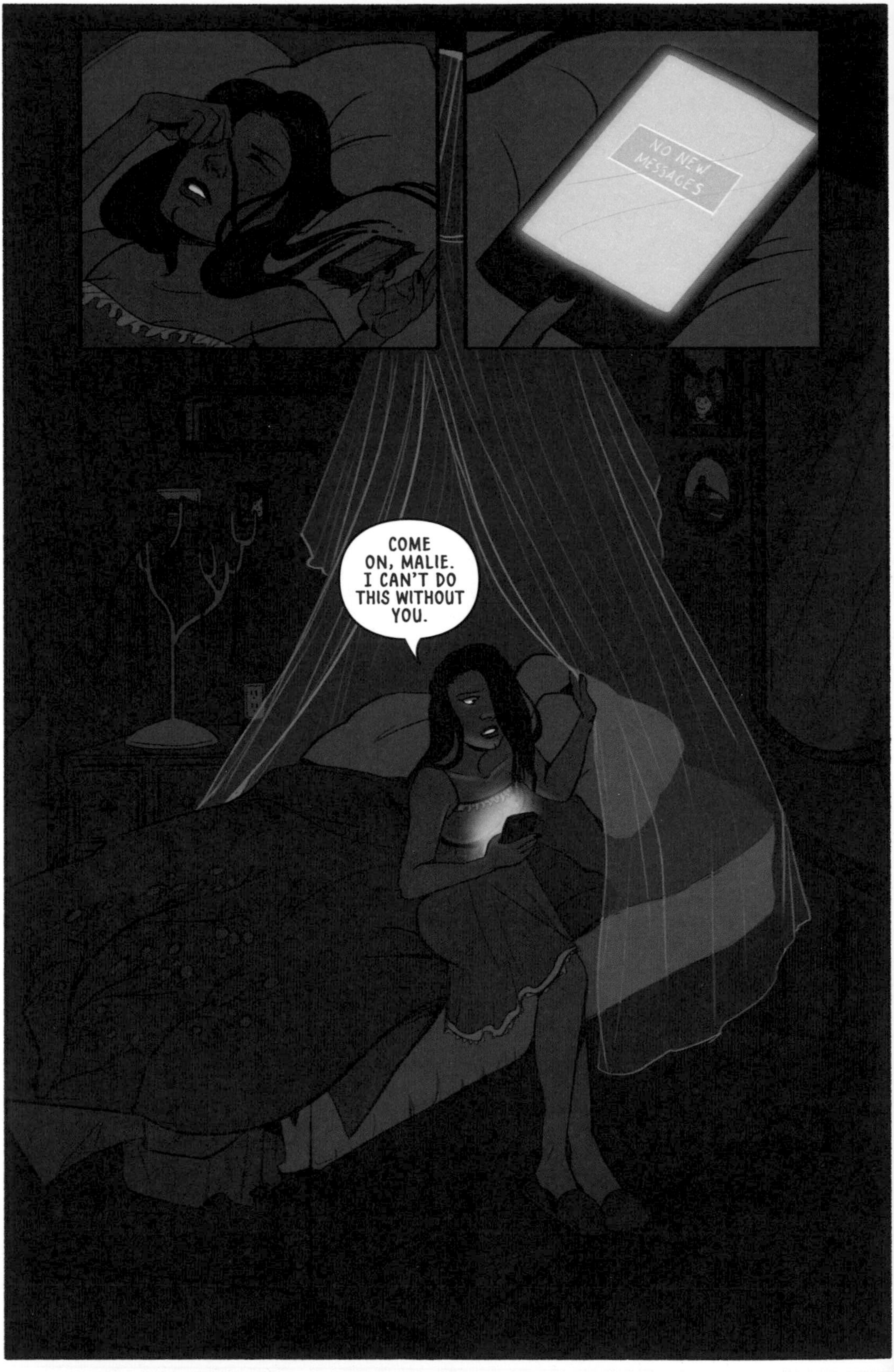
NO NEW MESSAGES.
COME ON, MALIE. I CAN'T DO THIS WITHOUT YOU.

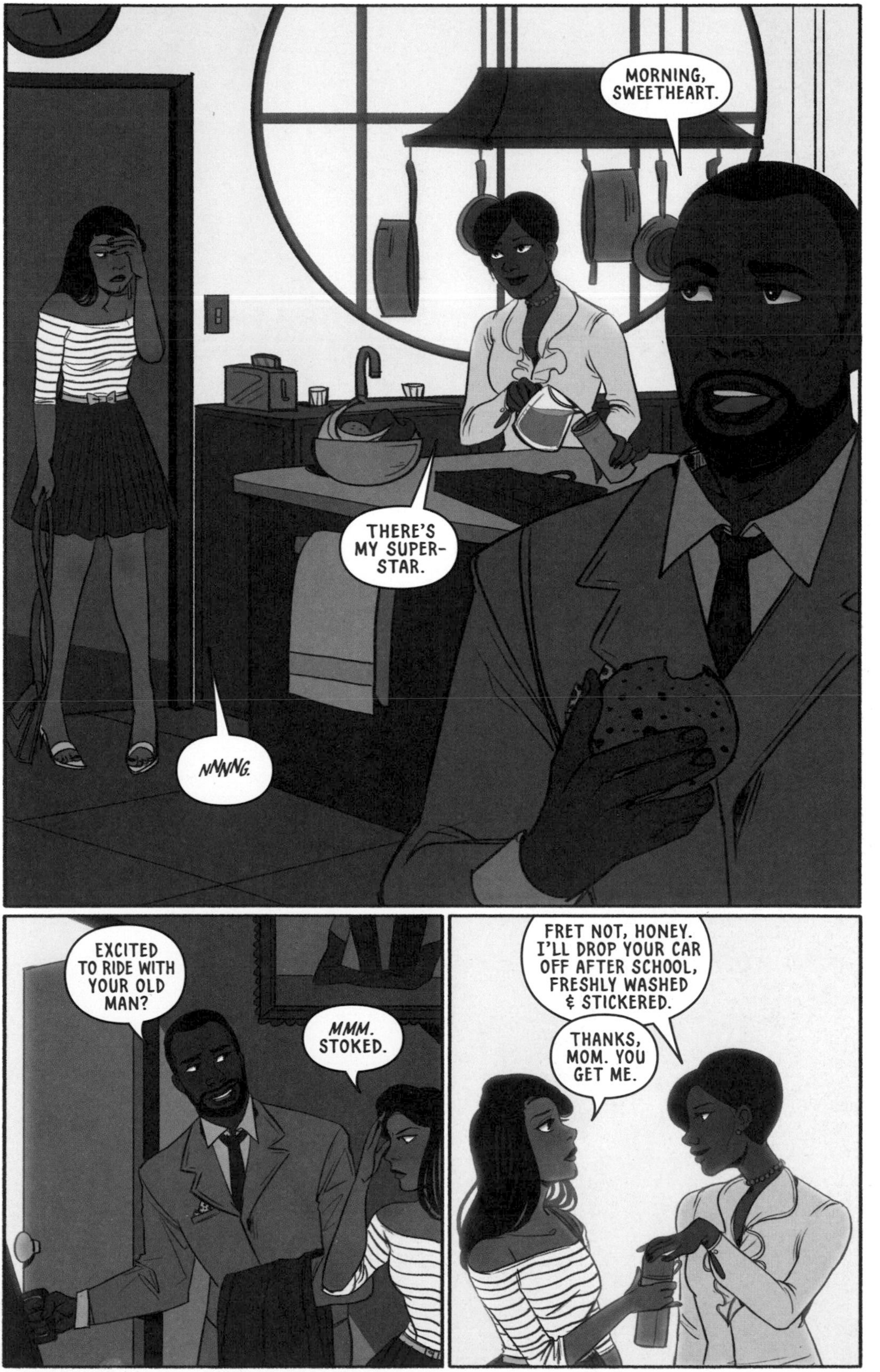
MORNING, SWEETHEART.
THERE'S MY SUPER-STAR.
NNNNG.
EXCITED TO RIDE WITH YOUR OLD MAN?
MMM. STOKED.
FRET NOT, HONEY. I'LL DROP YOUR CAR OFF AFTER SCHOOL, FRESHLY WASHED & STICKERED.
THANKS, MOM. YOU GET ME.

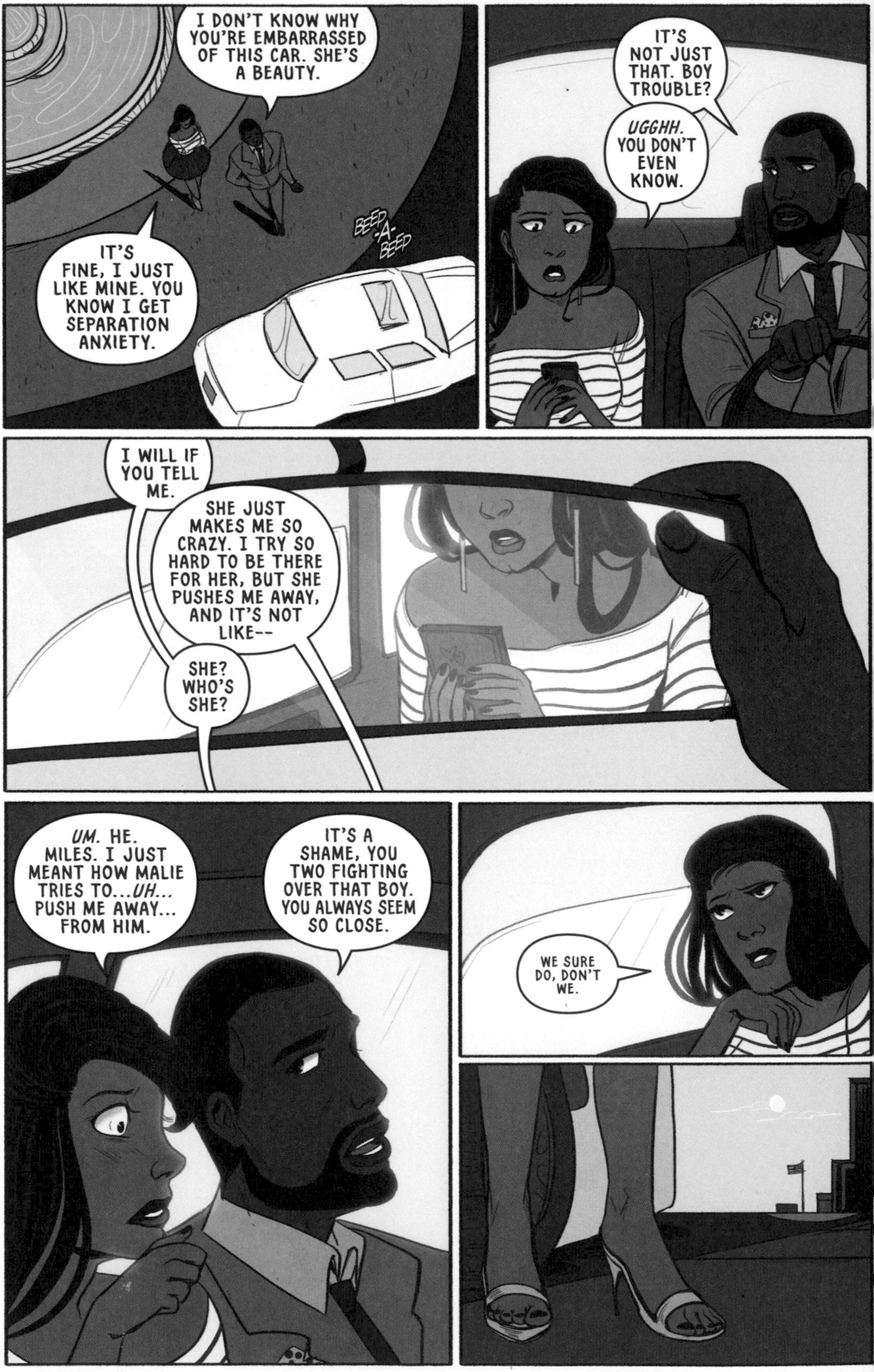
I DON'T KNOW WHY YOU'RE EMBARRASSED OF THIS CAR. SHE'S A BEAUTY.
IT'S FINE, I JUST LIKE MINE. YOU KNOW I GET SEPARATION ANXIETY.
BEEP-A-BEEP
IT'S NOT JUST THAT. BOY TROUBLE?
UGGHH. YOU DON'T EVEN KNOW.
I WILL IF YOU TELL ME.
SHE JUST MAKES ME SO CRAZY. I TRY SO HARD TO BE THERE FOR HER, BUT SHE PUSHES ME AWAY, AND IT'S NOT LIKE--
SHE? WHO'S SHE?
UM. HE. MILES. I JUST MEANT HOW MALIE TRIES TO...*UH...* PUSH ME AWAY... FROM HIM.
IT'S A SHAME, YOU TWO FIGHTING OVER THAT BOY. YOU ALWAYS SEEM SO CLOSE.
WE SURE DO, DON'T WE.

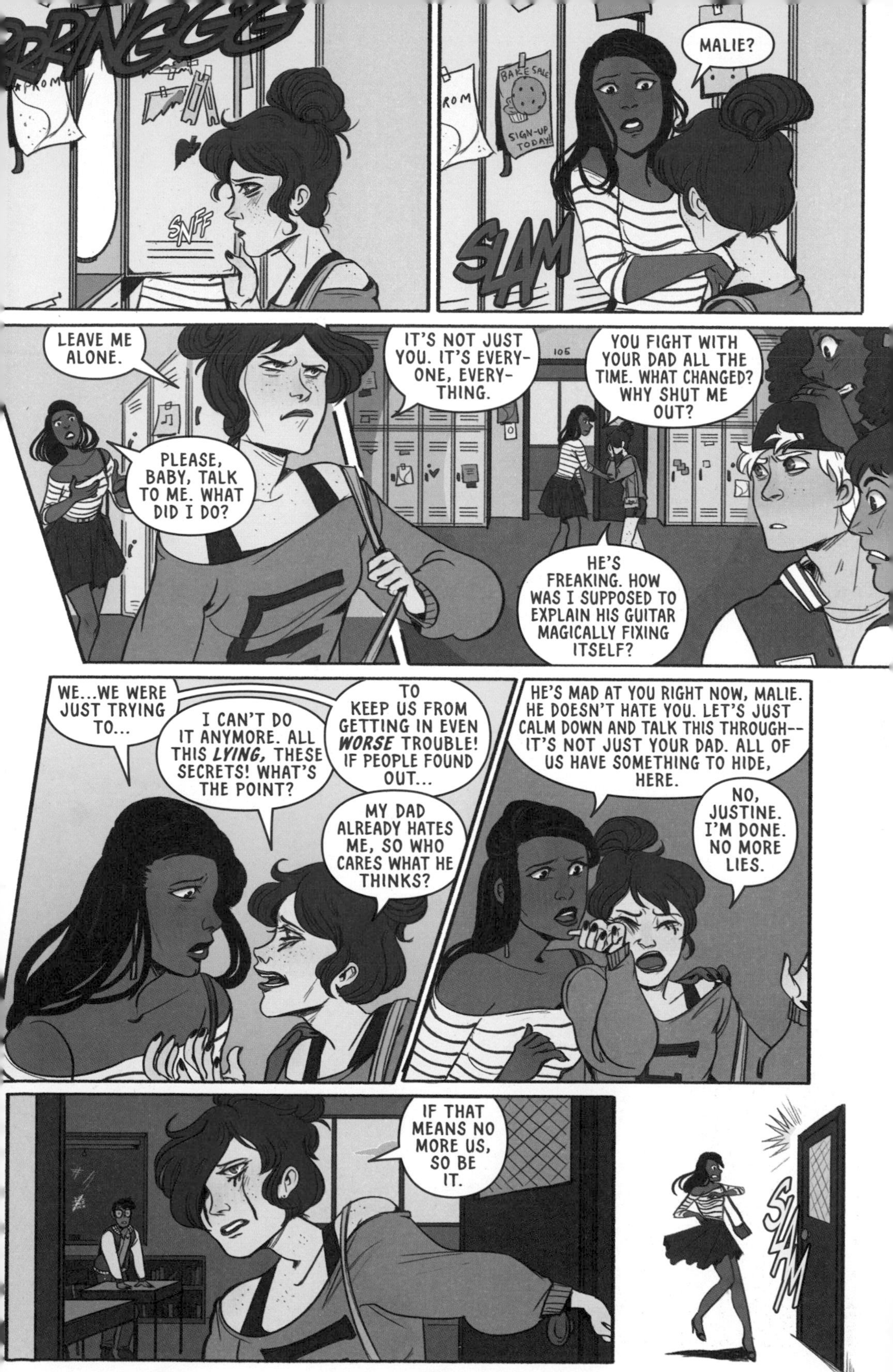
RRINGGG
PROM
SNFF
MALIE?
BAKE SALE SIGN-UP TODAY!!
ROM
SLAM
LEAVE ME ALONE.
PLEASE, BABY, TALK TO ME. WHAT DID I DO?
IT'S NOT JUST YOU. IT'S EVERYONE, EVERYTHING.
105
YOU FIGHT WITH YOUR DAD ALL THE TIME. WHAT CHANGED? WHY SHUT ME OUT?
HE'S FREAKING. HOW WAS I SUPPOSED TO EXPLAIN HIS GUITAR MAGICALLY FIXING ITSELF?
WE...WE WERE JUST TRYING TO...
TO KEEP US FROM GETTING IN EVEN *WORSE* TROUBLE! IF PEOPLE FOUND OUT...
I CAN'T DO IT ANYMORE. ALL THIS *LYING,* THESE SECRETS! WHAT'S THE POINT?
MY DAD ALREADY HATES ME, SO WHO CARES WHAT HE THINKS?
HE'S MAD AT YOU RIGHT NOW, MALIE. HE DOESN'T HATE YOU. LET'S JUST CALM DOWN AND TALK THIS THROUGH-- IT'S NOT JUST YOUR DAD. ALL OF US HAVE SOMETHING TO HIDE, HERE.
NO, JUSTINE. I'M DONE. NO MORE LIES.
IF THAT MEANS NO MORE US, SO BE IT.
SLAM

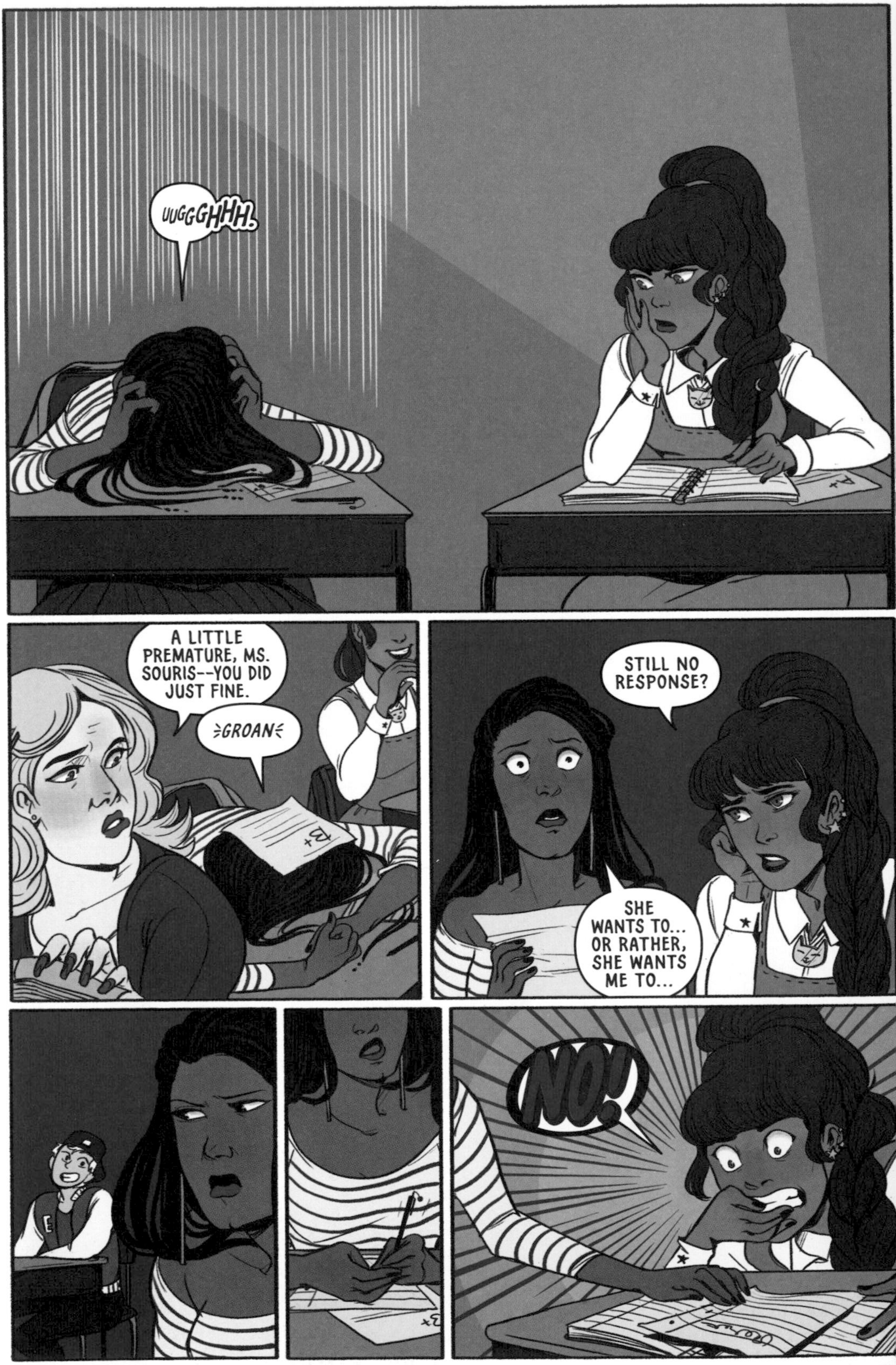

UUGGGHHH.
A LITTLE PREMATURE, MS. SOURIS--YOU DID JUST FINE.
GROAN
STILL NO RESPONSE?
SHE WANTS TO... OR RATHER, SHE WANTS ME TO...
NO!

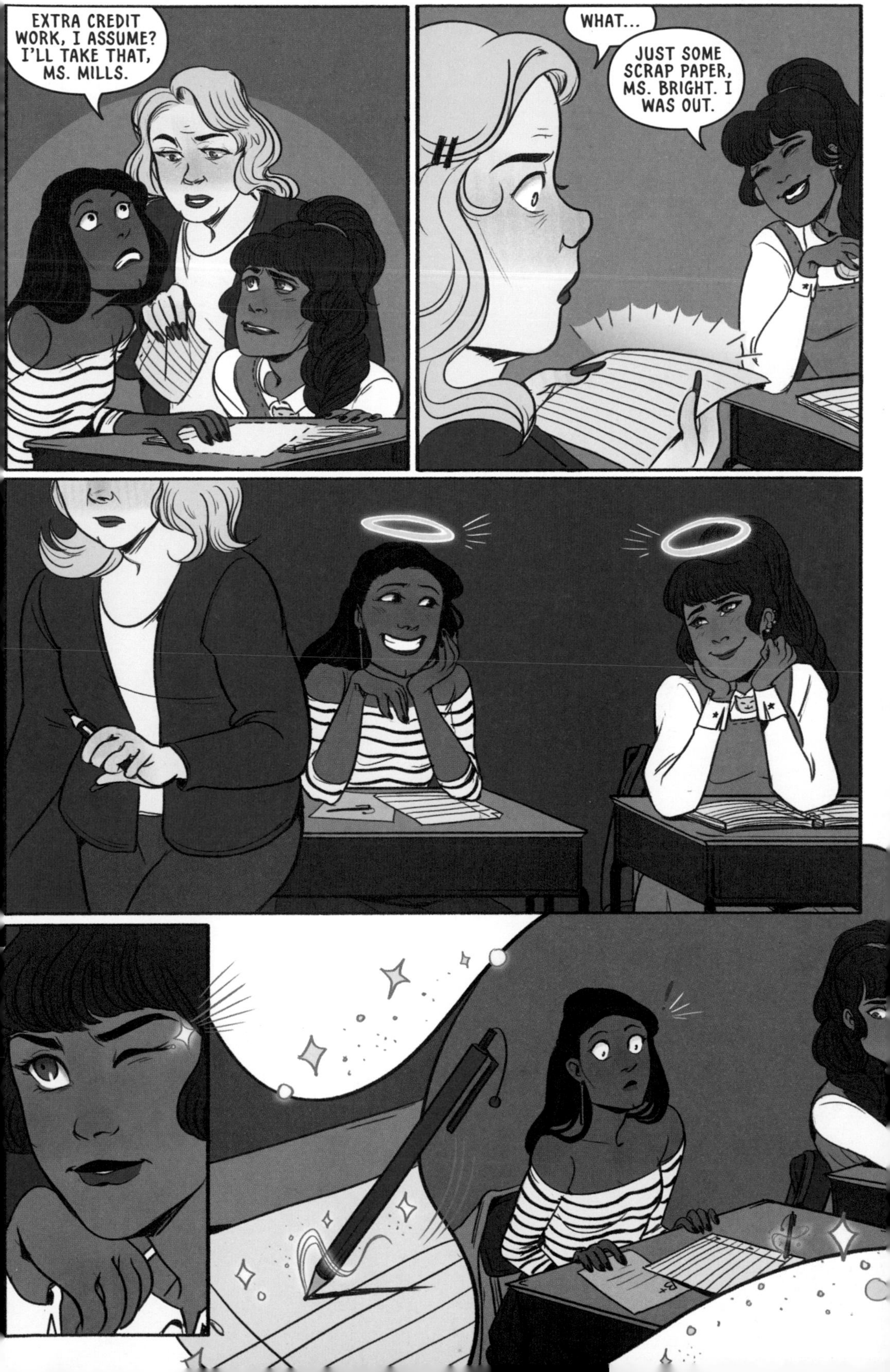
EXTRA CREDIT WORK, I ASSUME? I'LL TAKE THAT, MS. MILLS.
WHAT...
JUST SOME SCRAP PAPER, MS. BRIGHT. I WAS OUT.

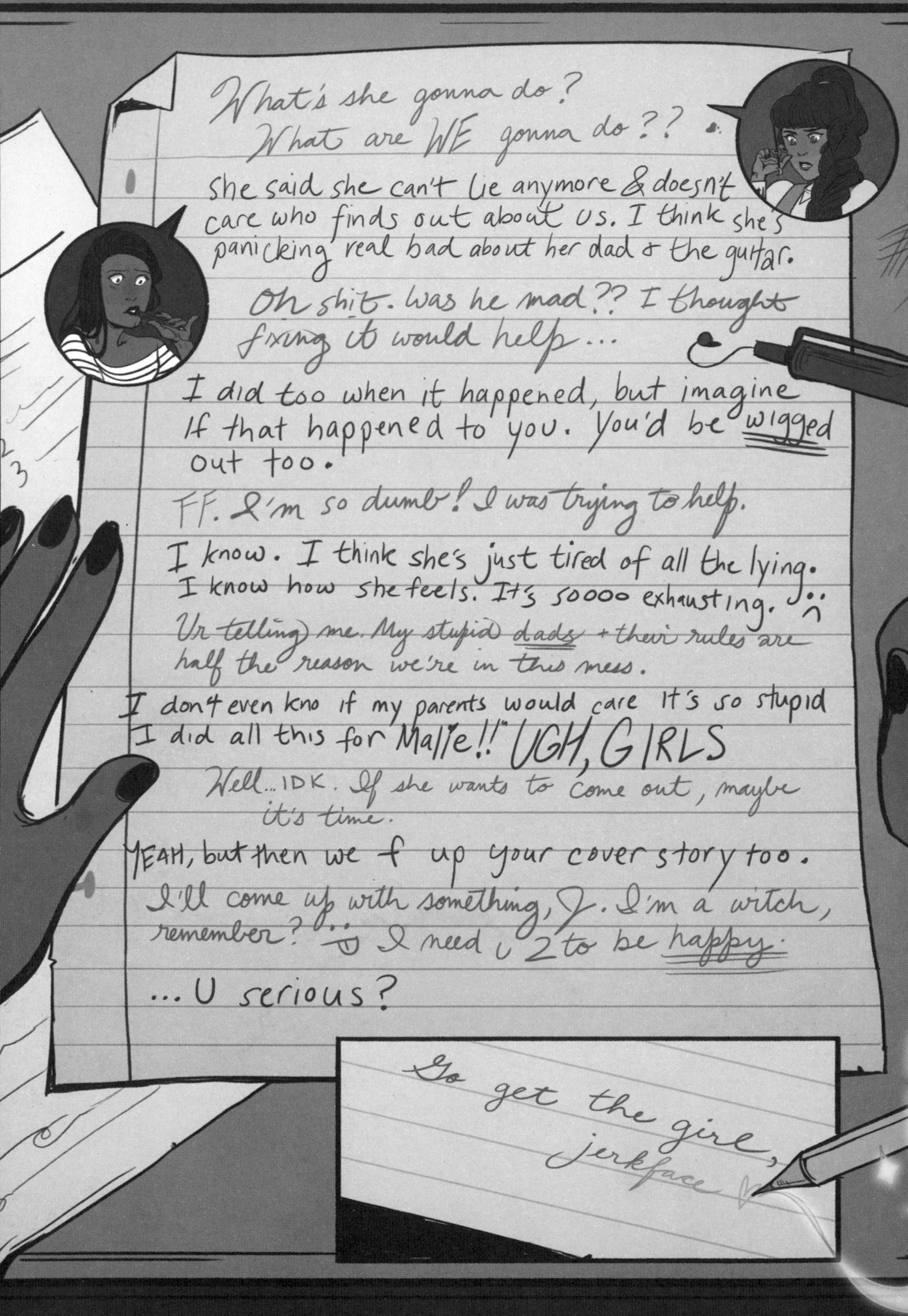
What's she gonna do?
What are WE gonna do??
She said she can't lie anymore & doesn't care who finds out about us. I think she's panicking real bad about her dad & the guitar.
Oh shit. Was he mad?? I thought fixing it would help...
I did too when it happened, but imagine if that happened to you. You'd be wigged out too.
FF. I'm so dumb! I was trying to help.
I know. I think she's just tired of all the lying. I know how she feels. It's soooo exhausting.
Ur telling me. My stupid dads + their rules are half the reason we're in this mess.
I don't even kno if my parents would care It's so stupid I did all this for Malie!! UGH, GIRLS
Well... IDK. If she wants to come out, maybe it's time.
YEAH, but then we f up your cover story too.
I'll come up with something, J. I'm a witch, remember? I need u 2 to be happy.
...U serious?
Go get the girl, jerkface

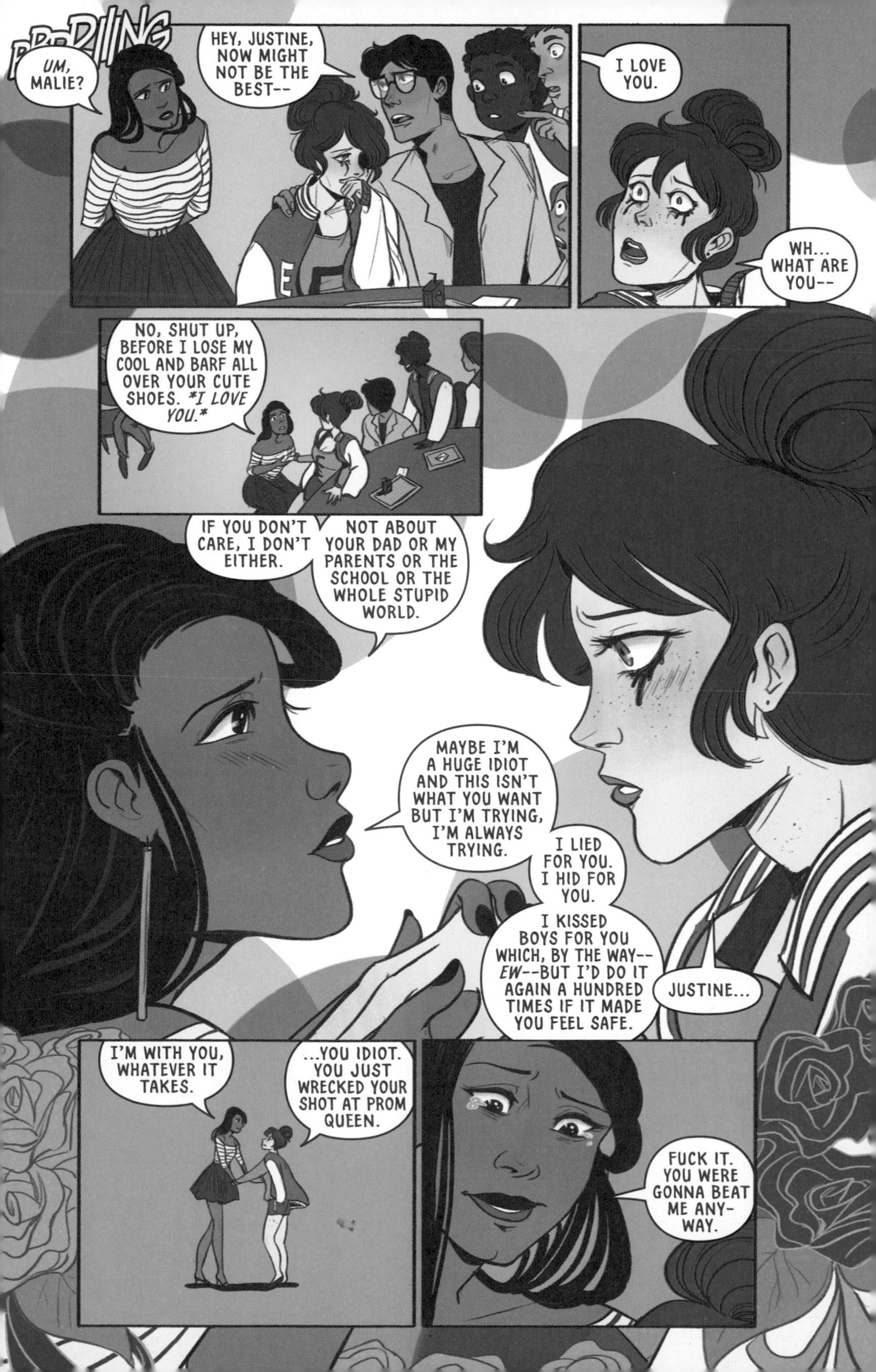
BRRRIIING
UM, MALIE?
HEY, JUSTINE, NOW MIGHT NOT BE THE BEST--
I LOVE YOU.
WH... WHAT ARE YOU--
NO, SHUT UP, BEFORE I LOSE MY COOL AND BARF ALL OVER YOUR CUTE SHOES. *I LOVE YOU.*
IF YOU DON'T CARE, I DON'T EITHER.
NOT ABOUT YOUR DAD OR MY PARENTS OR THE SCHOOL OR THE WHOLE STUPID WORLD.
MAYBE I'M A HUGE IDIOT AND THIS ISN'T WHAT YOU WANT BUT I'M TRYING, I'M ALWAYS TRYING.
I LIED FOR YOU. I HID FOR YOU.
I KISSED BOYS FOR YOU WHICH, BY THE WAY--EW--BUT I'D DO IT AGAIN A HUNDRED TIMES IF IT MADE YOU FEEL SAFE.
JUSTINE...
I'M WITH YOU, WHATEVER IT TAKES.
...YOU IDIOT. YOU JUST WRECKED YOUR SHOT AT PROM QUEEN.
FUCK IT. YOU WERE GONNA BEAT ME ANY-WAY.

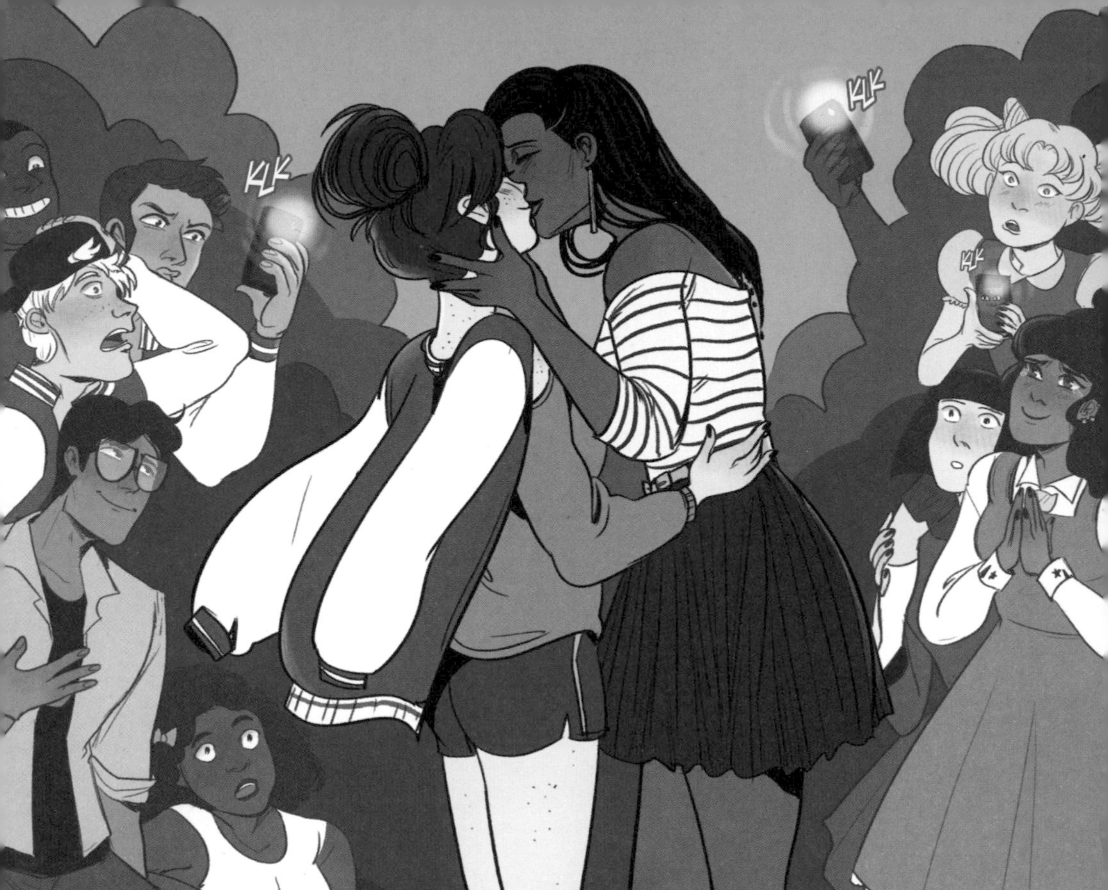
KLK
KLK
KLK

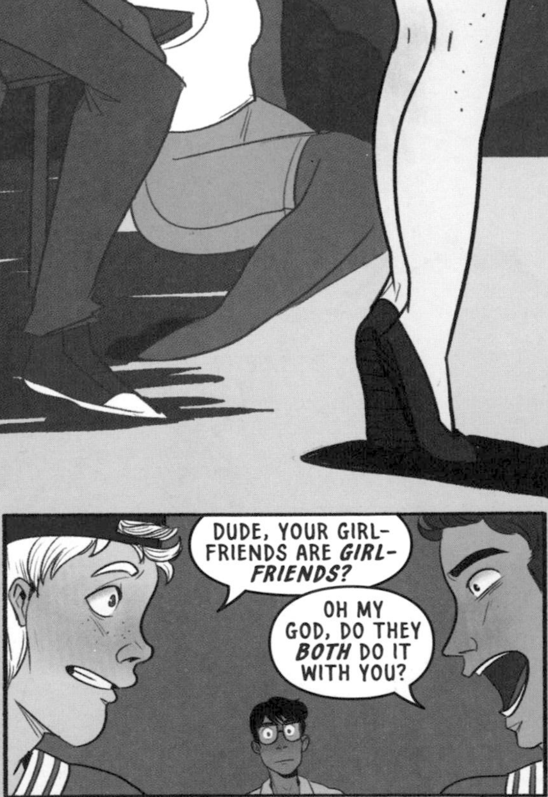
DUDE, YOUR GIRL-FRIENDS ARE *GIRL-FRIENDS?*
OH MY GOD, DO THEY ***BOTH*** DO IT WITH YOU?

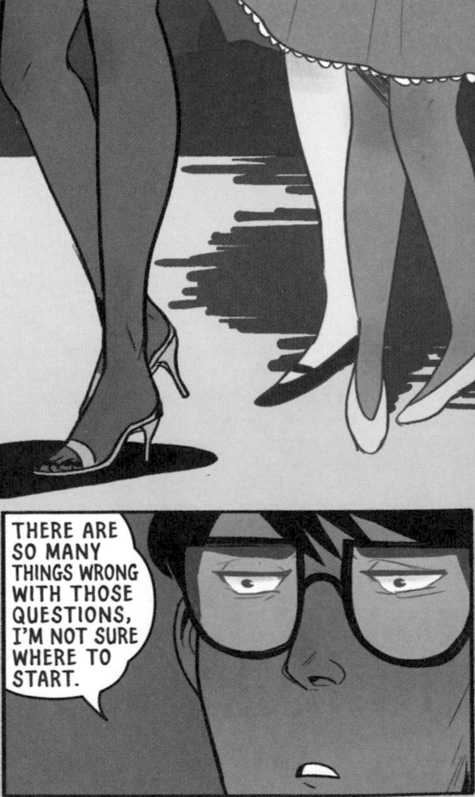
THERE ARE SO MANY THINGS WRONG WITH THOSE QUESTIONS, I'M NOT SURE WHERE TO START.

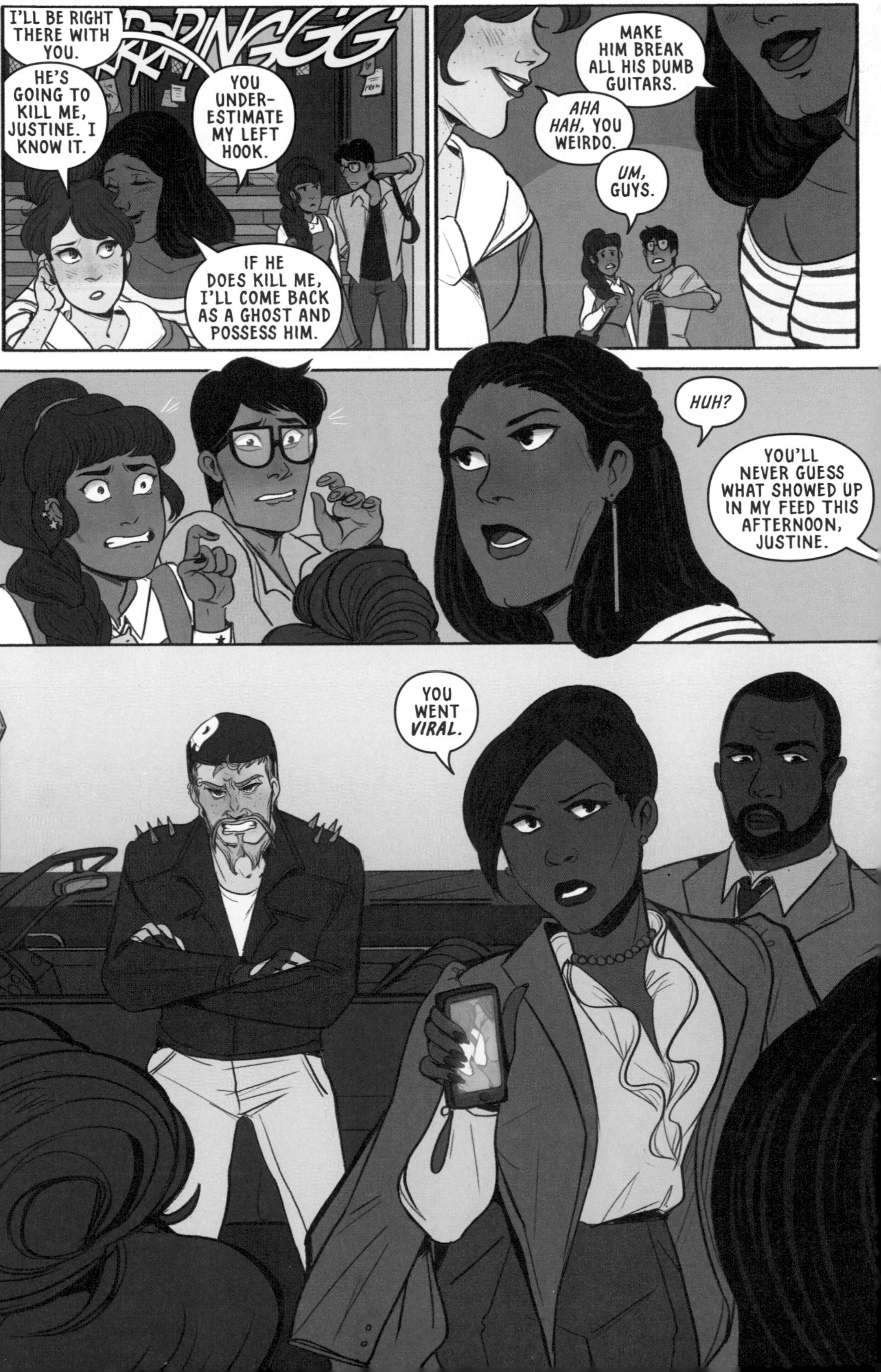
I'LL BE RIGHT THERE WITH YOU.
HE'S GOING TO KILL ME, JUSTINE. I KNOW IT.
YOU UNDER-ESTIMATE MY LEFT HOOK.
IF HE DOES KILL ME, I'LL COME BACK AS A GHOST AND POSSESS HIM.
MAKE HIM BREAK ALL HIS DUMB GUITARS.
AHA HAH, YOU WEIRDO.
UM, GUYS.
HUH?
YOU'LL NEVER GUESS WHAT SHOWED UP IN MY FEED THIS AFTERNOON, JUSTINE.
YOU WENT *VIRAL*.

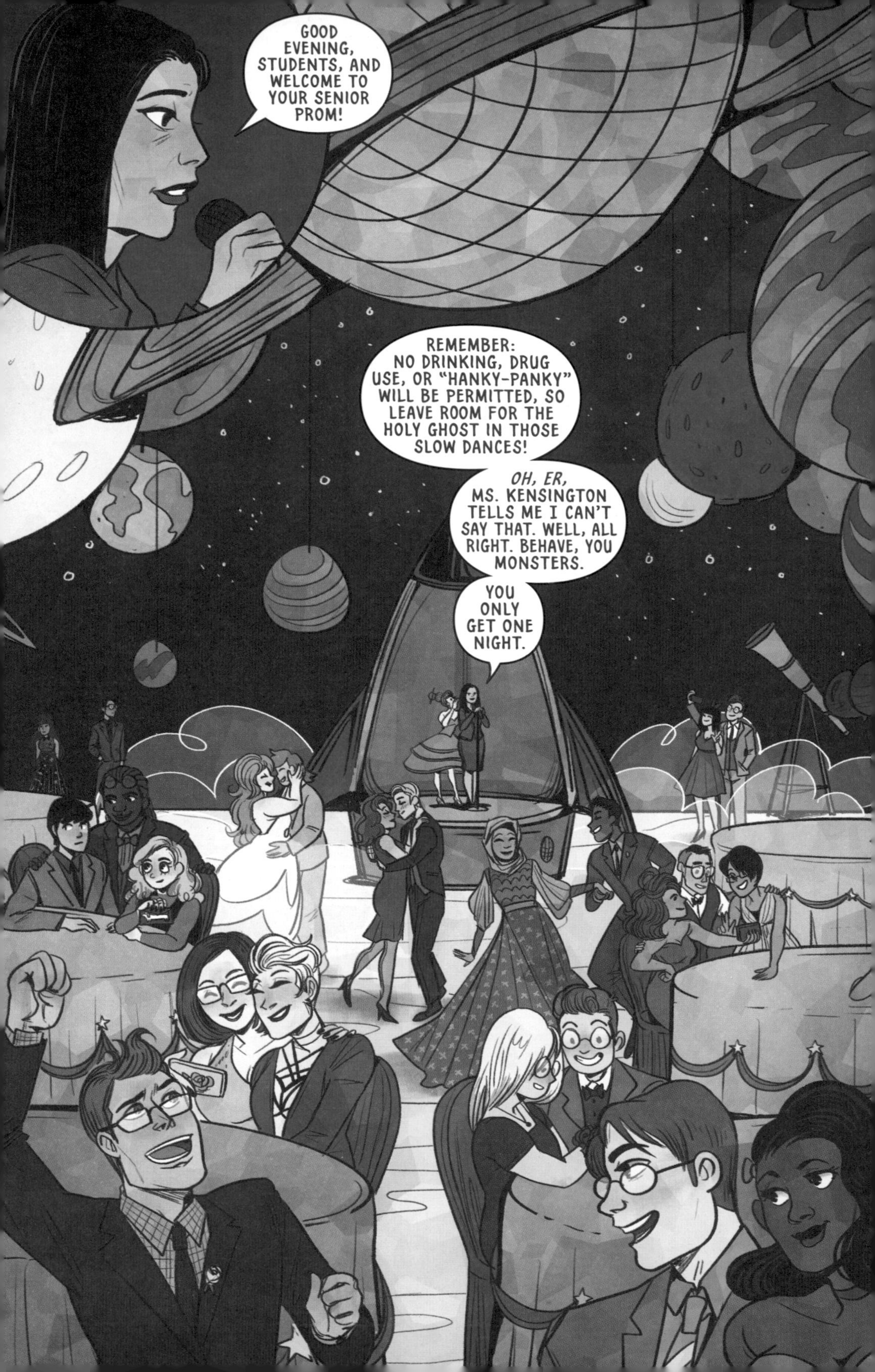
GOOD EVENING, STUDENTS, AND WELCOME TO YOUR SENIOR PROM!
REMEMBER: NO DRINKING, DRUG USE, OR "HANKY-PANKY" WILL BE PERMITTED, SO LEAVE ROOM FOR THE HOLY GHOST IN THOSE SLOW DANCES!
OH, ER, MS. KENSINGTON TELLS ME I CAN'T SAY THAT. WELL, ALL RIGHT. BEHAVE, YOU MONSTERS.
YOU ONLY GET ONE NIGHT.

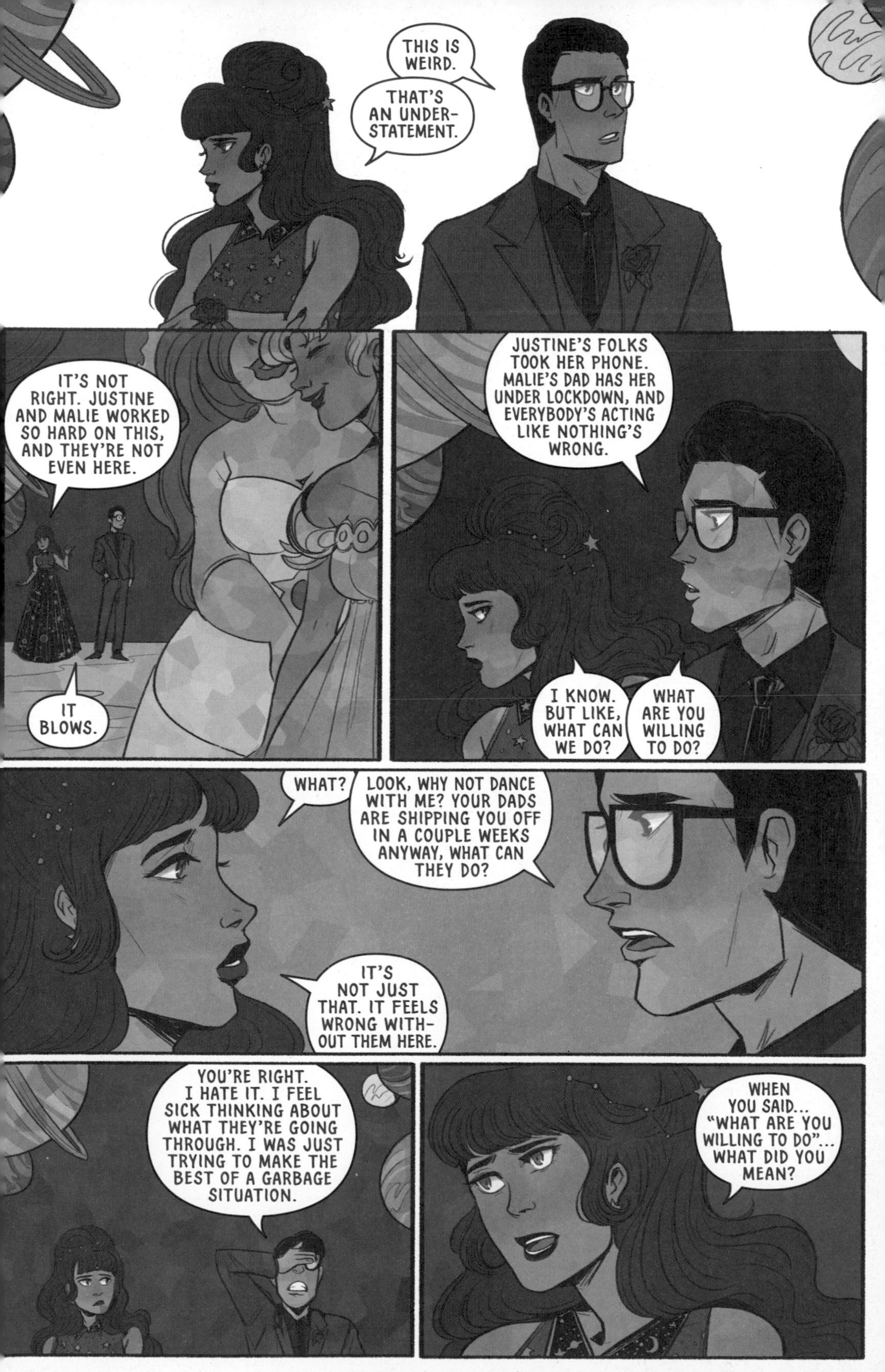

THIS IS WEIRD.
THAT'S AN UNDER-STATEMENT.
IT'S NOT RIGHT. JUSTINE AND MALIE WORKED SO HARD ON THIS, AND THEY'RE NOT EVEN HERE.
IT BLOWS.
JUSTINE'S FOLKS TOOK HER PHONE. MALIE'S DAD HAS HER UNDER LOCKDOWN, AND EVERYBODY'S ACTING LIKE NOTHING'S WRONG.
I KNOW. BUT LIKE, WHAT CAN WE DO?
WHAT ARE YOU WILLING TO DO?
WHAT?
LOOK, WHY NOT DANCE WITH ME? YOUR DADS ARE SHIPPING YOU OFF IN A COUPLE WEEKS ANYWAY, WHAT CAN THEY DO?
IT'S NOT JUST THAT. IT FEELS WRONG WITH-OUT THEM HERE.
YOU'RE RIGHT. I HATE IT. I FEEL SICK THINKING ABOUT WHAT THEY'RE GOING THROUGH. I WAS JUST TRYING TO MAKE THE BEST OF A GARBAGE SITUATION.
WHEN YOU SAID... "WHAT ARE YOU WILLING TO DO"... WHAT DID YOU MEAN?

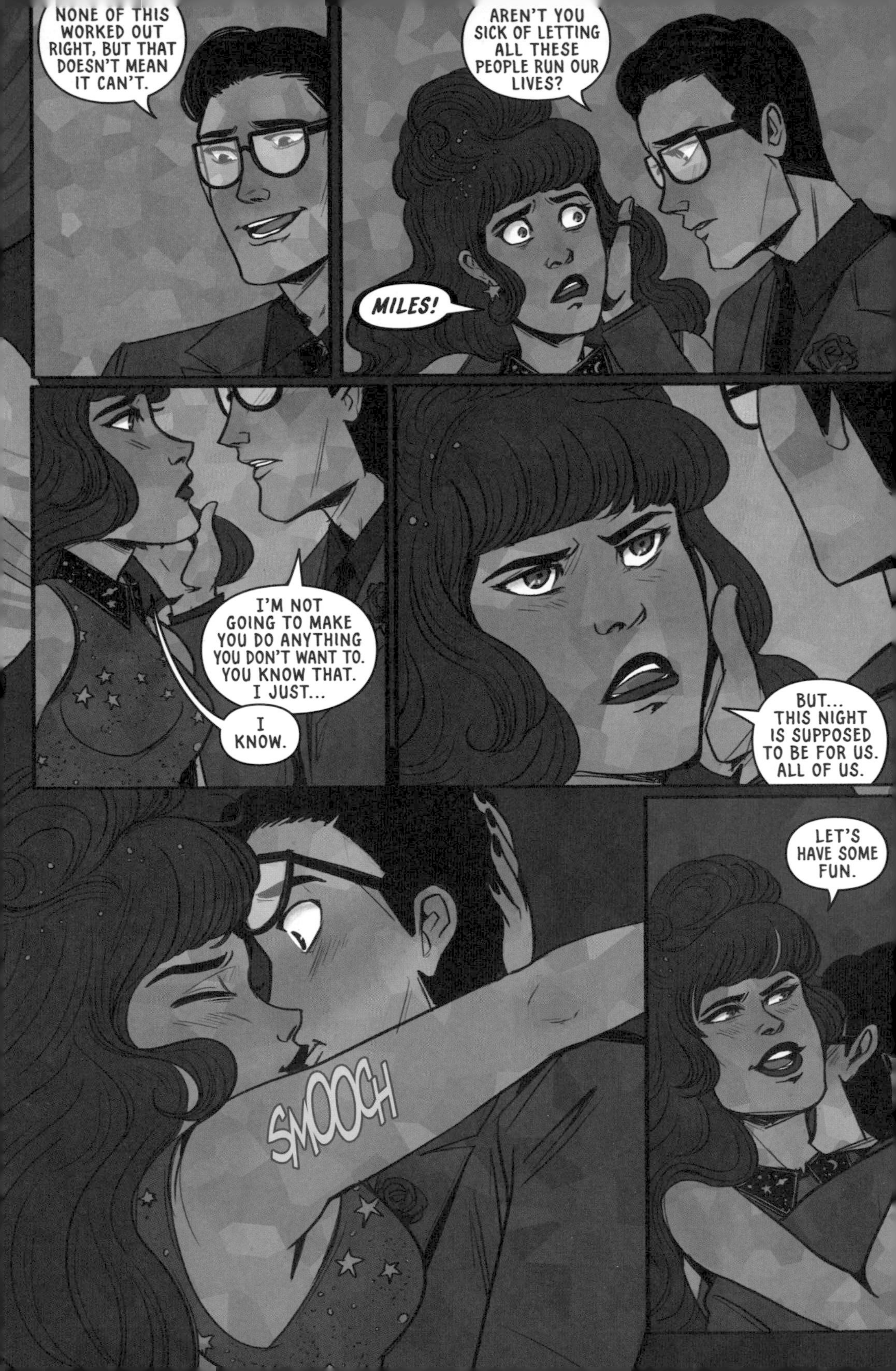
NONE OF THIS WORKED OUT RIGHT, BUT THAT DOESN'T MEAN IT CAN'T.
AREN'T YOU SICK OF LETTING ALL THESE PEOPLE RUN OUR LIVES?
MILES!
I'M NOT GOING TO MAKE YOU DO ANYTHING YOU DON'T WANT TO. YOU KNOW THAT. I JUST...
I KNOW.
BUT... THIS NIGHT IS SUPPOSED TO BE FOR US. ALL OF US.
SMOOCH
LET'S HAVE SOME FUN.

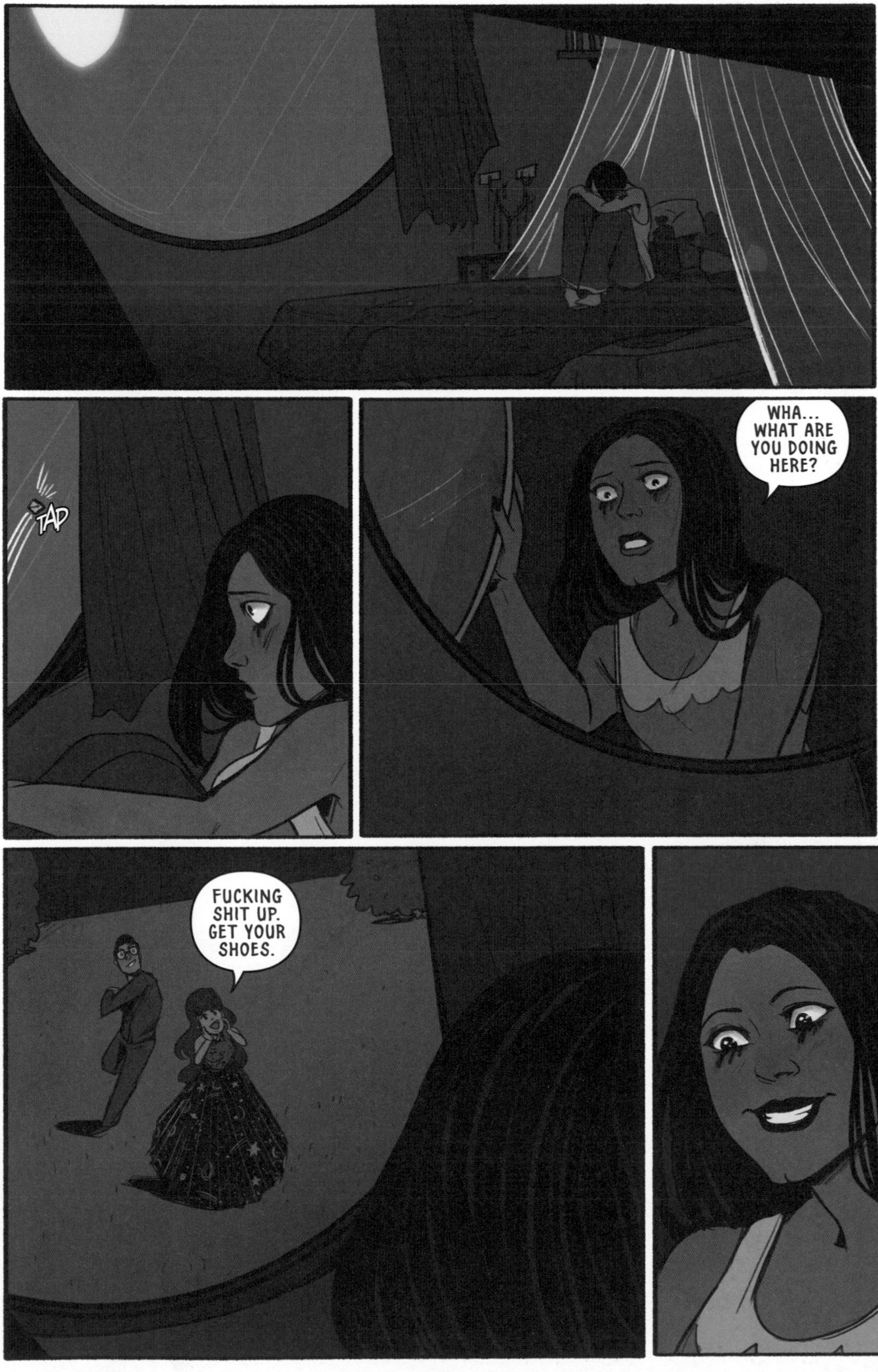
TAP
WHA... WHAT ARE YOU DOING HERE?
FUCKING SHIT UP. GET YOUR SHOES.

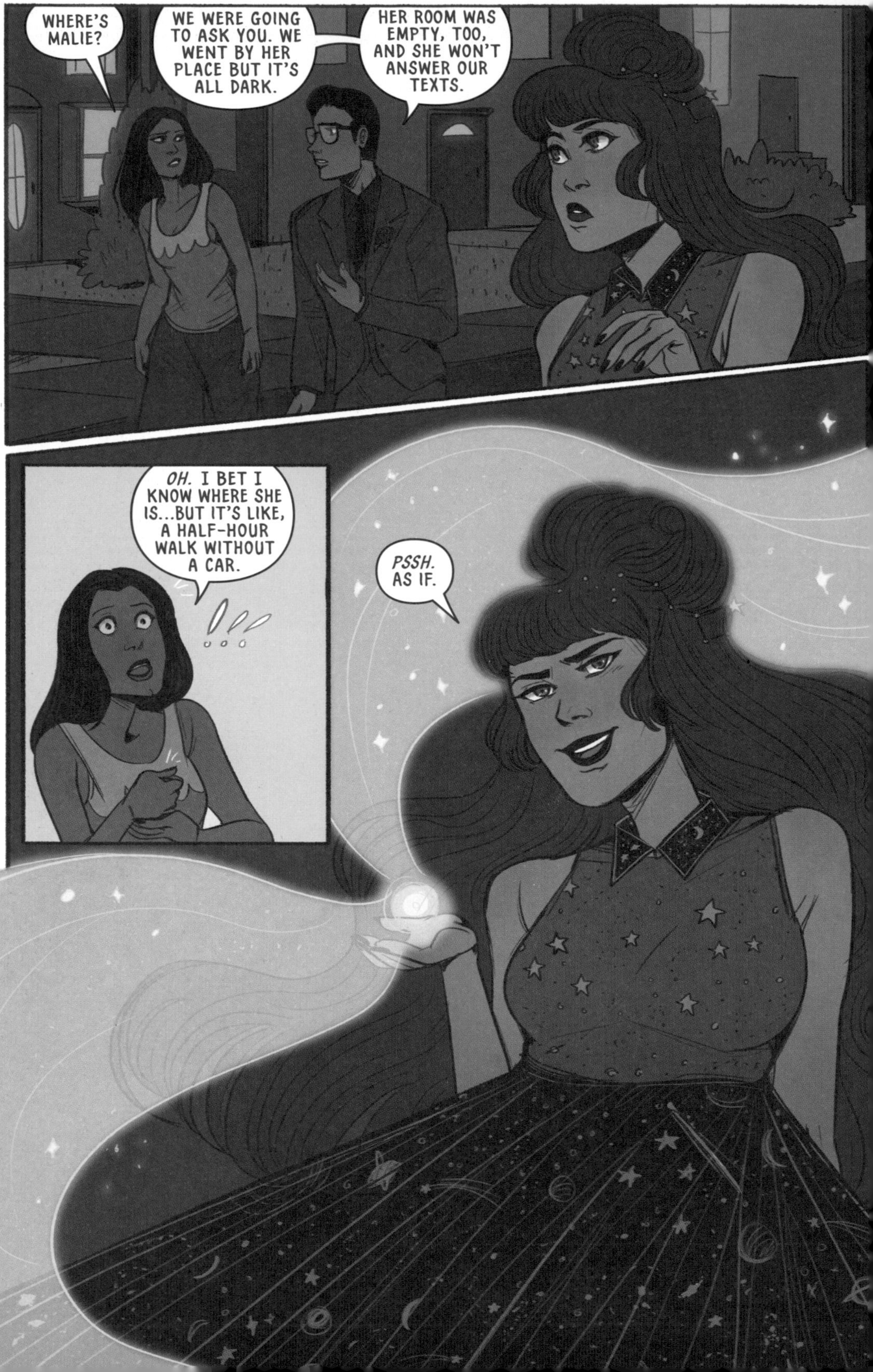
WHERE'S MALIE?
WE WERE GOING TO ASK YOU. WE WENT BY HER PLACE BUT IT'S ALL DARK.
HER ROOM WAS EMPTY, TOO, AND SHE WON'T ANSWER OUR TEXTS.
OH. I BET I KNOW WHERE SHE IS...BUT IT'S LIKE, A HALF-HOUR WALK WITHOUT A CAR.
PSSH. AS IF.

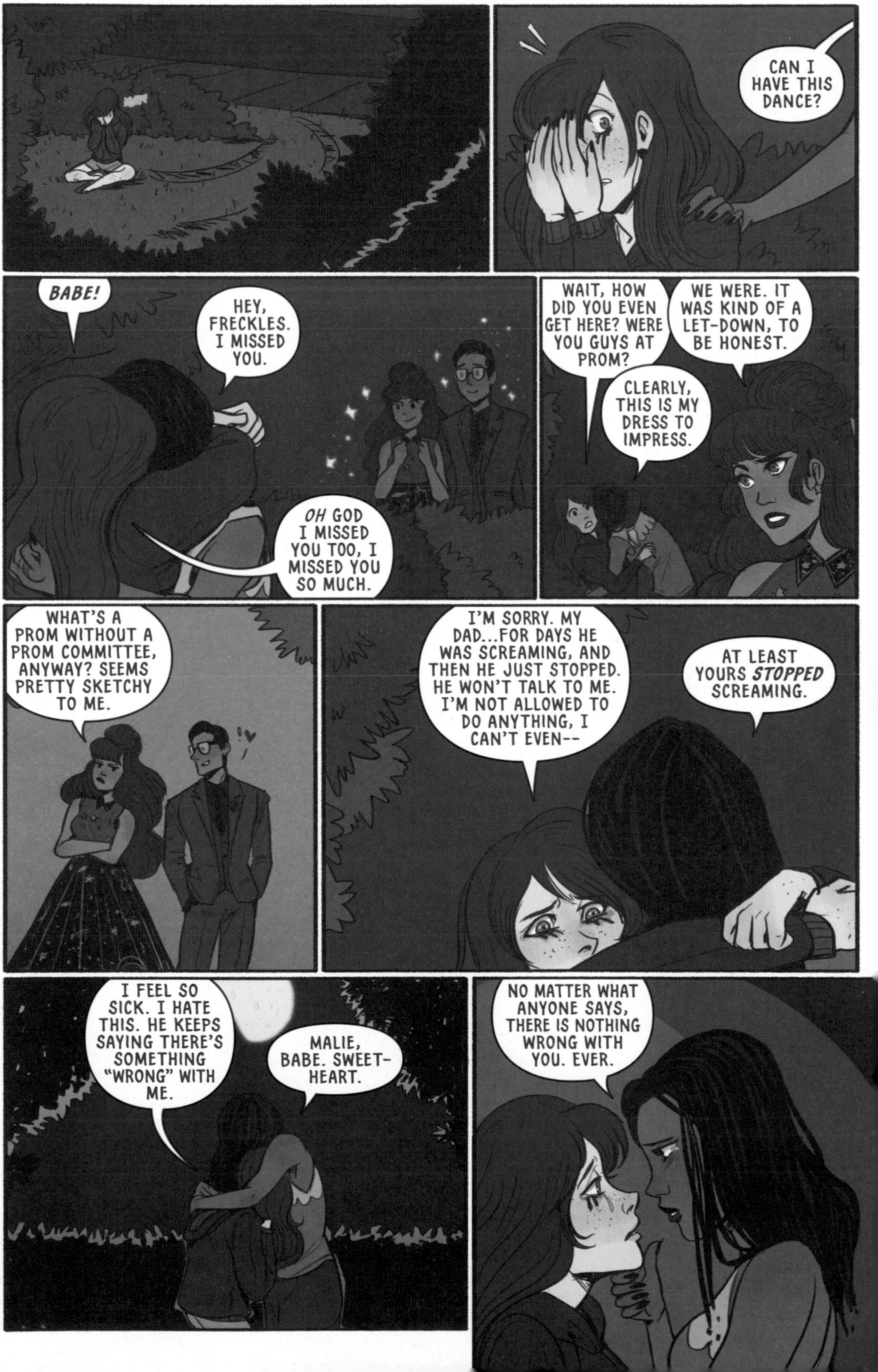
CAN I HAVE THIS DANCE?
BABE!
HEY, FRECKLES. I MISSED YOU.
OH GOD I MISSED YOU TOO, I MISSED YOU SO MUCH.
WAIT, HOW DID YOU EVEN GET HERE? WERE YOU GUYS AT PROM?
WE WERE. IT WAS KIND OF A LET-DOWN, TO BE HONEST.
CLEARLY, THIS IS MY DRESS TO IMPRESS.
WHAT'S A PROM WITHOUT A PROM COMMITTEE, ANYWAY? SEEMS PRETTY SKETCHY TO ME.
I'M SORRY. MY DAD...FOR DAYS HE WAS SCREAMING, AND THEN HE JUST STOPPED. HE WON'T TALK TO ME. I'M NOT ALLOWED TO DO ANYTHING, I CAN'T EVEN--
AT LEAST YOURS STOPPED SCREAMING.
I FEEL SO SICK. I HATE THIS. HE KEEPS SAYING THERE'S SOMETHING "WRONG" WITH ME.
MALIE, BABE. SWEET-HEART.
NO MATTER WHAT ANYONE SAYS, THERE IS NOTHING WRONG WITH YOU. EVER.

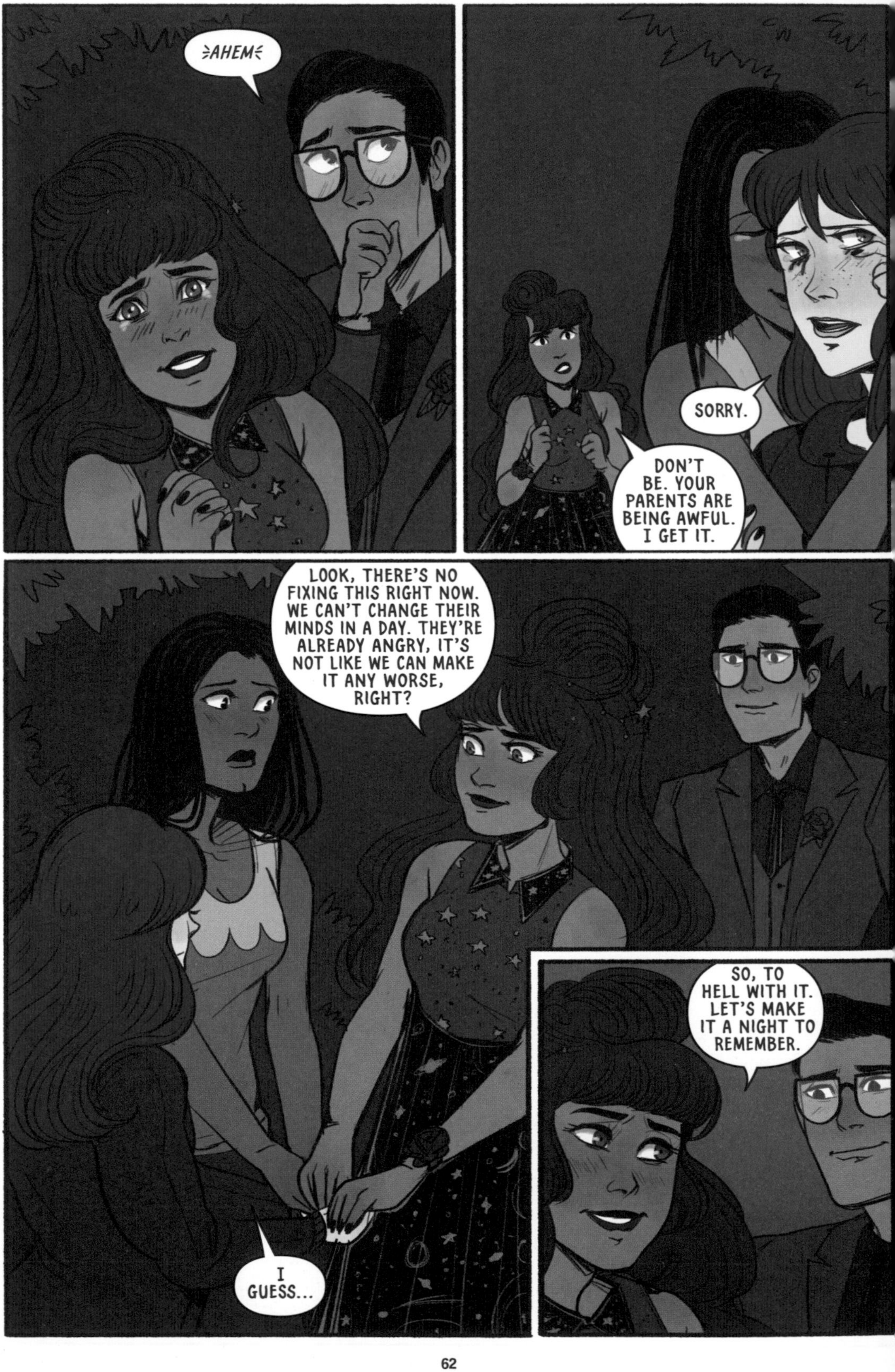
AHEM
SORRY.
DON'T BE. YOUR PARENTS ARE BEING AWFUL. I GET IT.
LOOK, THERE'S NO FIXING THIS RIGHT NOW. WE CAN'T CHANGE THEIR MINDS IN A DAY. THEY'RE ALREADY ANGRY, IT'S NOT LIKE WE CAN MAKE IT ANY WORSE, RIGHT?
I GUESS...
SO, TO HELL WITH IT. LET'S MAKE IT A NIGHT TO REMEMBER.

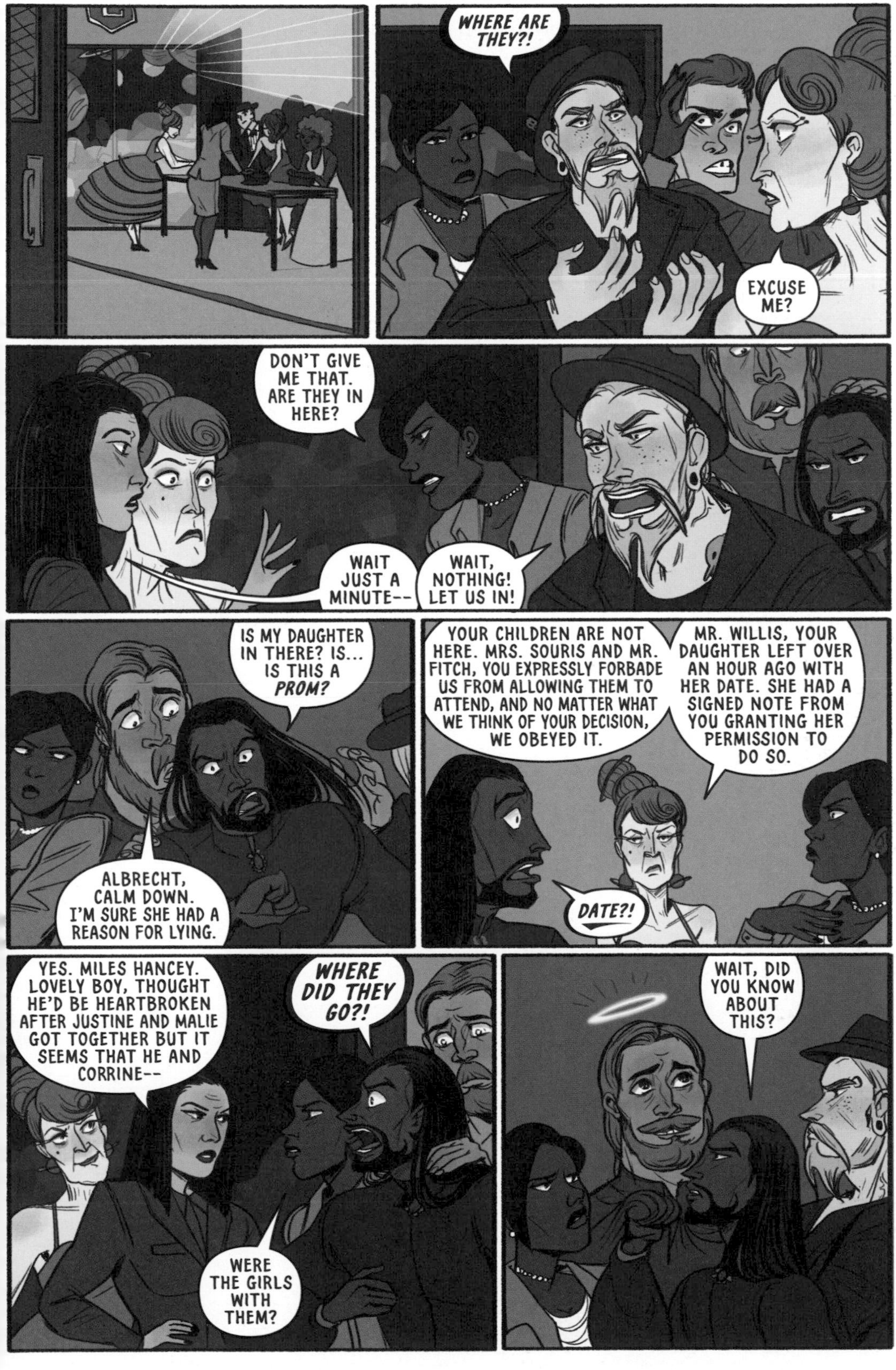
WHERE ARE THEY?!
EXCUSE ME?
DON'T GIVE ME THAT. ARE THEY IN HERE?
WAIT JUST A MINUTE--
WAIT, NOTHING! LET US IN!
IS MY DAUGHTER IN THERE? IS... IS THIS A PROM?
ALBRECHT, CALM DOWN. I'M SURE SHE HAD A REASON FOR LYING.
YOUR CHILDREN ARE NOT HERE. MRS. SOURIS AND MR. FITCH, YOU EXPRESSLY FORBADE US FROM ALLOWING THEM TO ATTEND, AND NO MATTER WHAT WE THINK OF YOUR DECISION, WE OBEYED IT.
MR. WILLIS, YOUR DAUGHTER LEFT OVER AN HOUR AGO WITH HER DATE. SHE HAD A SIGNED NOTE FROM YOU GRANTING HER PERMISSION TO DO SO.
DATE?!
YES. MILES HANCEY. LOVELY BOY, THOUGHT HE'D BE HEARTBROKEN AFTER JUSTINE AND MALIE GOT TOGETHER BUT IT SEEMS THAT HE AND CORRINE--
WHERE DID THEY GO?!
WERE THE GIRLS WITH THEM?
WAIT, DID YOU KNOW ABOUT THIS?

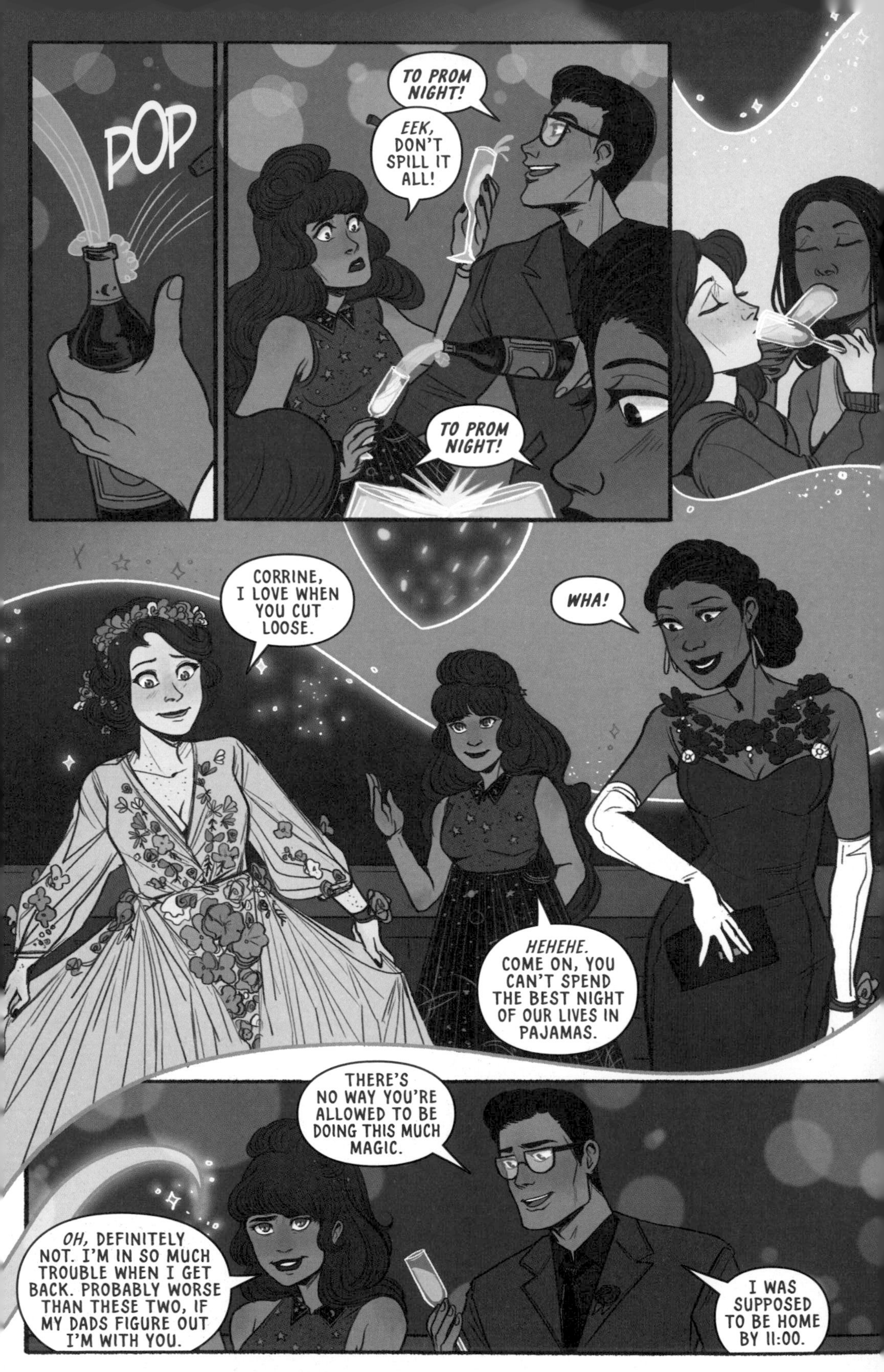
POP
TO PROM NIGHT!
EEK, DON'T SPILL IT ALL!
TO PROM NIGHT!
CORRINE, I LOVE WHEN YOU CUT LOOSE.
WHA!
HEHEHE. COME ON, YOU CAN'T SPEND THE BEST NIGHT OF OUR LIVES IN PAJAMAS.
THERE'S NO WAY YOU'RE ALLOWED TO BE DOING THIS MUCH MAGIC.
OH, DEFINITELY NOT. I'M IN SO MUCH TROUBLE WHEN I GET BACK. PROBABLY WORSE THAN THESE TWO, IF MY DADS FIGURE OUT I'M WITH YOU.
I WAS SUPPOSED TO BE HOME BY 11:00.

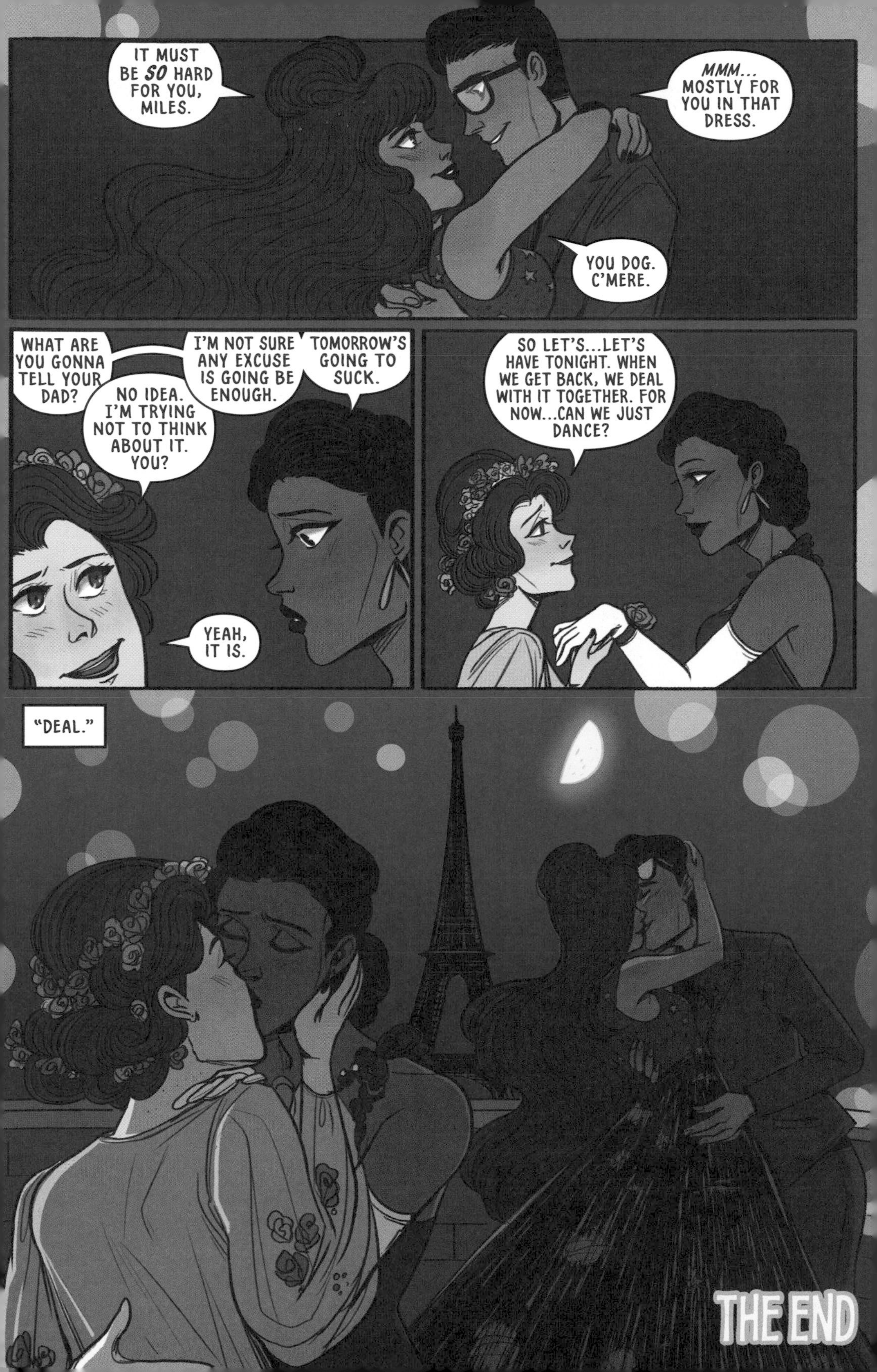

IT MUST BE *SO* HARD FOR YOU, MILES.
MMM... MOSTLY FOR YOU IN THAT DRESS.
YOU DOG. C'MERE.
WHAT ARE YOU GONNA TELL YOUR DAD?
NO IDEA. I'M TRYING NOT TO THINK ABOUT IT. YOU?
I'M NOT SURE ANY EXCUSE IS GOING BE ENOUGH.
TOMORROW'S GOING TO SUCK.
YEAH, IT IS.
SO LET'S...LET'S HAVE TONIGHT. WHEN WE GET BACK, WE DEAL WITH IT TOGETHER. FOR NOW...CAN WE JUST DANCE?
"DEAL."
THE END

School Spirit Roundtable

The entire creative team from *School Spirit* sat down for a roundtable chat about, well… everything. There's some discussion of process in there, too, we promise!

Kate Leth: I'm not really sure what KIND of questions are best so I'll just ask: Arielle, who is your favorite magical girl?

Arielle Jovellanos: AHH!! I want to say either Cardcaptor Sakura because BEST WARDROBE or Sailor Mercury because CUTIE WITH BRAINS but I feel like I need to give a shoutout to this super obscure one I used to love watching on my childhood visits to the Philippines. Akazukin Chacha, in the anime, is both a magical girl AND a witch attending magic academy! Her best friends are a werewolf and an awkward little magician! Her story has the normal "saving the world" beats that come with most magical girl stories, but it also has slice-of-life-y magic school elements that are incredibly charming. I think this is why I love working on *School Spirit*; I have such a soft spot for really close friends who get into silly shenanigans involving magic!

AJ: Amanda, which fictional character would be the best on a date?

Amanda Scurti: I've got so many bizarre attachments to so many weird fictional characters - as I'm sure we all do—but figuring out a realistically dateable one was hard! I think my most vanilla answer would have to be Ned from *Pushing Daisies*—that show was on during the peak of my adolescence so I think my enormous crush on Lee Pace accidentally informed a lot of my non-fictional crushes for a while (oops). Most *interesting* date-o would have to be with Trinity from *The Matrix*, though—I could write an essay on how much I love Trinity and why—but I'll leave it at "she's rad and I'd kick-walk up some walls with her for sure."

AS: Taylor, if you could transform your entire look, whose style would you steal? Assume your choice would be deemed 100% socially acceptable.

Taylor Esposito: That is a loaded question, it depends on my mood. Some days, it's Prof. Jones (*Indiana Jones*), others it's Connery Bond, Bale Bruce Wayne, Cavill *Man from Uncle*. I like the classiness of well-tailored, full suits, regardless of the era. It's completely impractical for a guy hunched over on a Wacom all day, but I love 3 piece suits. I know it's kind of a cop-out because I can't decide, so let's go with just being a scoundrel and the Han Solo look in *Empire*, a dirty, charming space pirate (can you tell I'm on a huge *Empire* kick at the moment?). Definitely a more comfortable look and practical for more everyday stuff.

TE: Kate, what genre would you like to live in, if you could: superheroes, 80s sitcom, 40s noir, D&D, sci fi, etc. and what would you do in that genre if you could have any kind of life/job you wanted?

KL: Can I live in Halloween Town from *The Nightmare Before Christmas*? If not, I just want to live in the movie *Practical Magic*. I have no real historical attachment—the 60s had great style but wasn't great for anyone who wasn't straight and white—but I love fictional versions of the real world. So, I would say, 90s/00s witch movie set in New England. That's my dream. The town from *Hocus Pocus* or *Casper*. Set me up there and I'll die happy on a porch swing covered in bats.

KL: So, Taylor. What's your favorite holiday and how do you celebrate it?

TE: Halloween, easily! Hey, if you moved to Halloween Town, we'd be neighbors! Usually we go to a party or something, but since we got married five years ago on Oct. 30, we try to outdo our "big" Halloween party. It's our Christmas, so we go all out decorating, detailed costumes, and horror movies and drinks with all our local friends.

TE: Amanda, what gives you more enjoyment to color, the personal, intimate scenes/panels, or big crazy splashes with lots going on?

AS: I think personal, intimate scenes are where the role of the colorist can shine through the most, so I always have fun doing those. Big, crazy splashes are very much the draftsperson's thing—they dictate what goes where and the chaos/quiet of a spread by the way they *compose* the spread, but the quiet moments (which often happen in close-ups) tend to lean on the palette a bit more. There's always a different, more contained level of drama that can happen in one page as opposed to two as well, so they're very different playing fields.

AS: Arielle, since you're now well-versed in the area of romance comics, which fictional romantic couples would you say have had the greatest influence on your work?

AJ: Oh man, you know what? I've been shipping characters since elementary school, but somehow I never really thought to draw couple-y art until I saw Heather Campbell's fan art of Lucius and Narcissa Malfoy back in high school. She has such a way of bringing life, history, tragedy, and comedy in her character interaction. I literally did not care about the Malfoy parents until Campbell's supremely adorable depiction

completely humanized them. Her work inspired me to draw a lot of fan art of James Potter and Lily Evans (and other YA book pairings) and that was essentially my training ground for learning to draw people making out and being romantic.

AJ: Kate: one thing that I've really enjoyed about drawing *School Spirit* is all the different characters and finding ways to make them visually distinct! I don't know if this is like asking you to pick a favorite child, but do you have a particular favorite *School Spirit* character voice you love to write?

KL: Oh goodness. That is really hard. I have a lot of fun writing Justine because she's keeping everything together as best she can. I love to write Malie because she's so angsty. I love Corrine because she's quiet. But, really, the characters I wish I could've written a lot more of are Corrine's dads. They have a lot of history.

AJ: AHHH CORRINE'S DADS!!!!

TE: I'd read a whole OGN on just them.

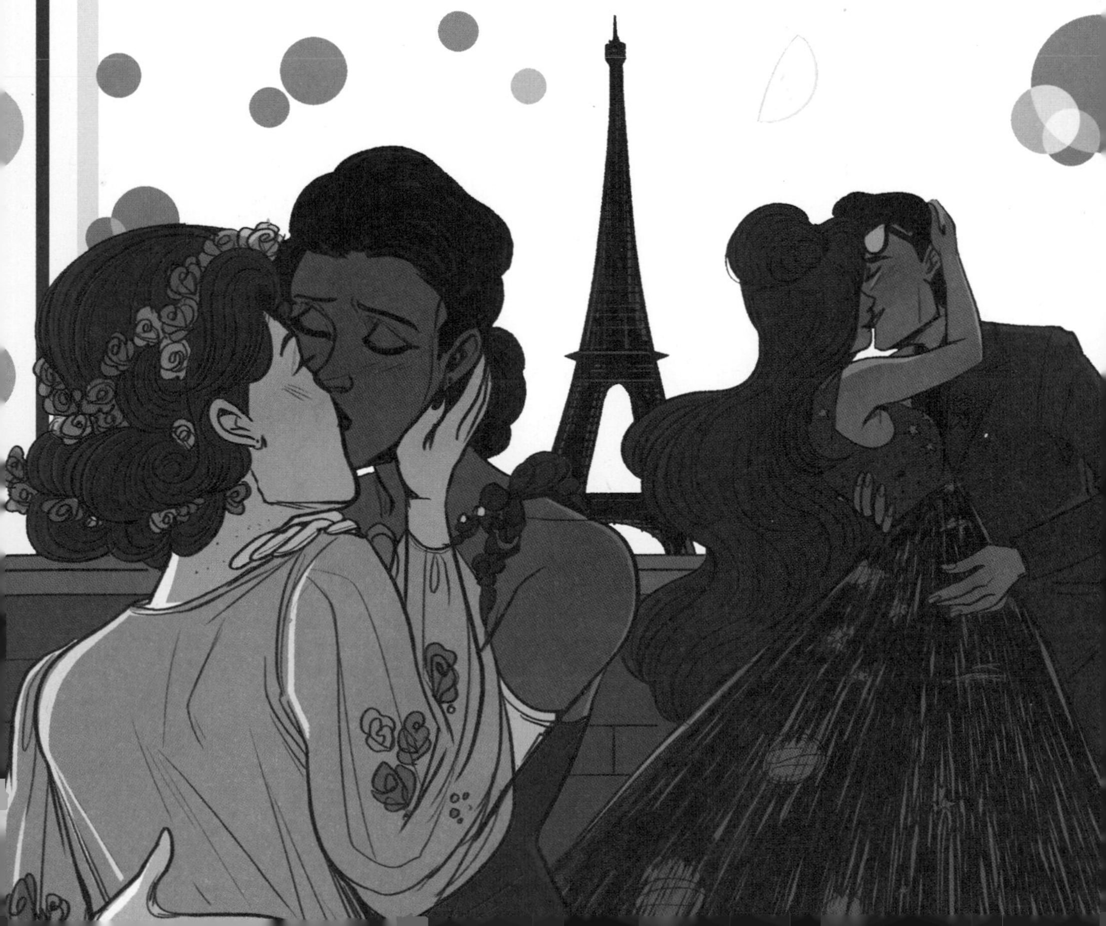

RUINED

VOLUME I.

by SARAH VAUGHN &
SARAH WINIFRED SEARLE

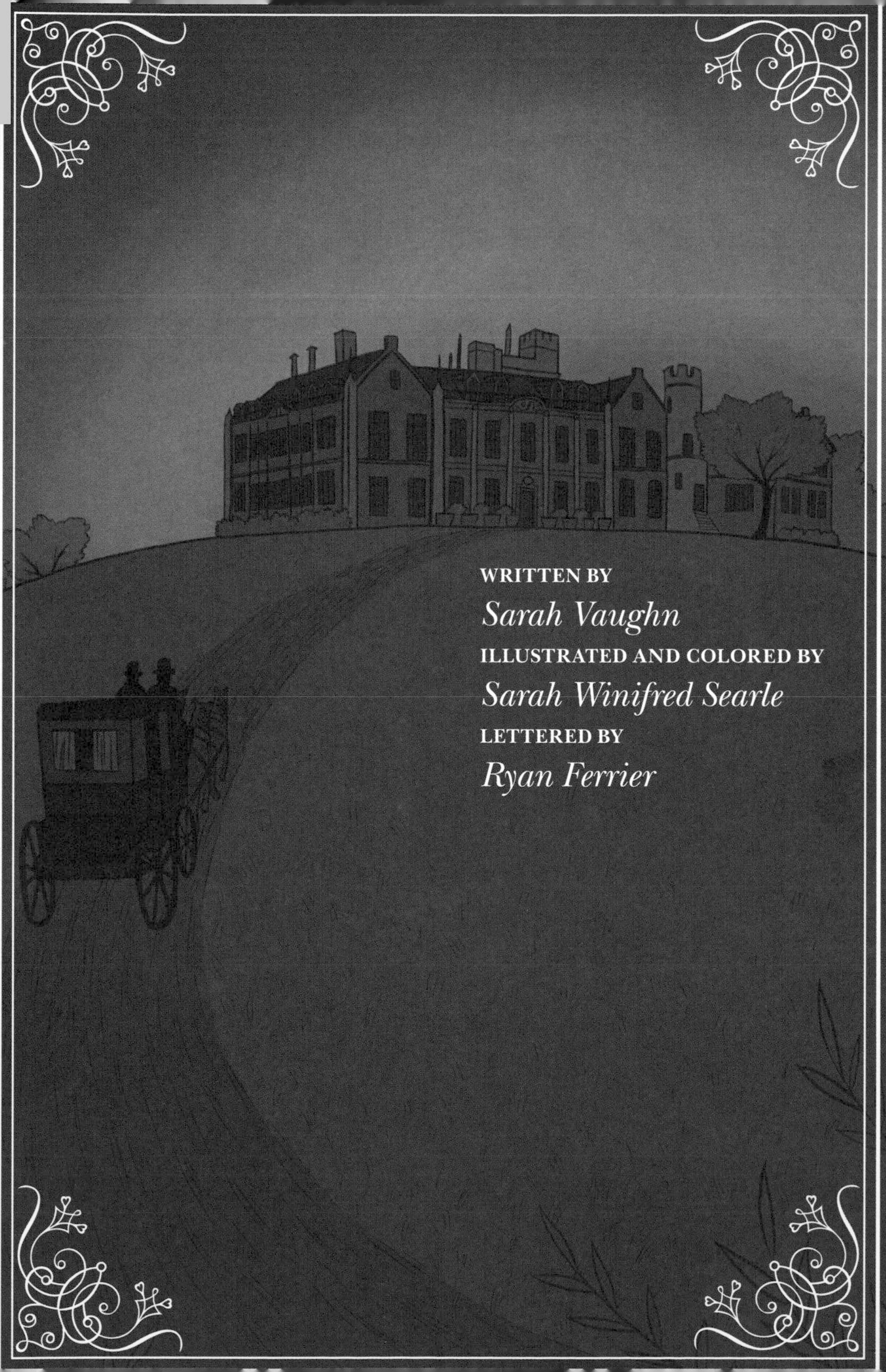

WRITTEN BY

Sarah Vaughn

ILLUSTRATED AND COLORED BY

Sarah Winifred Searle

LETTERED BY

Ryan Ferrier

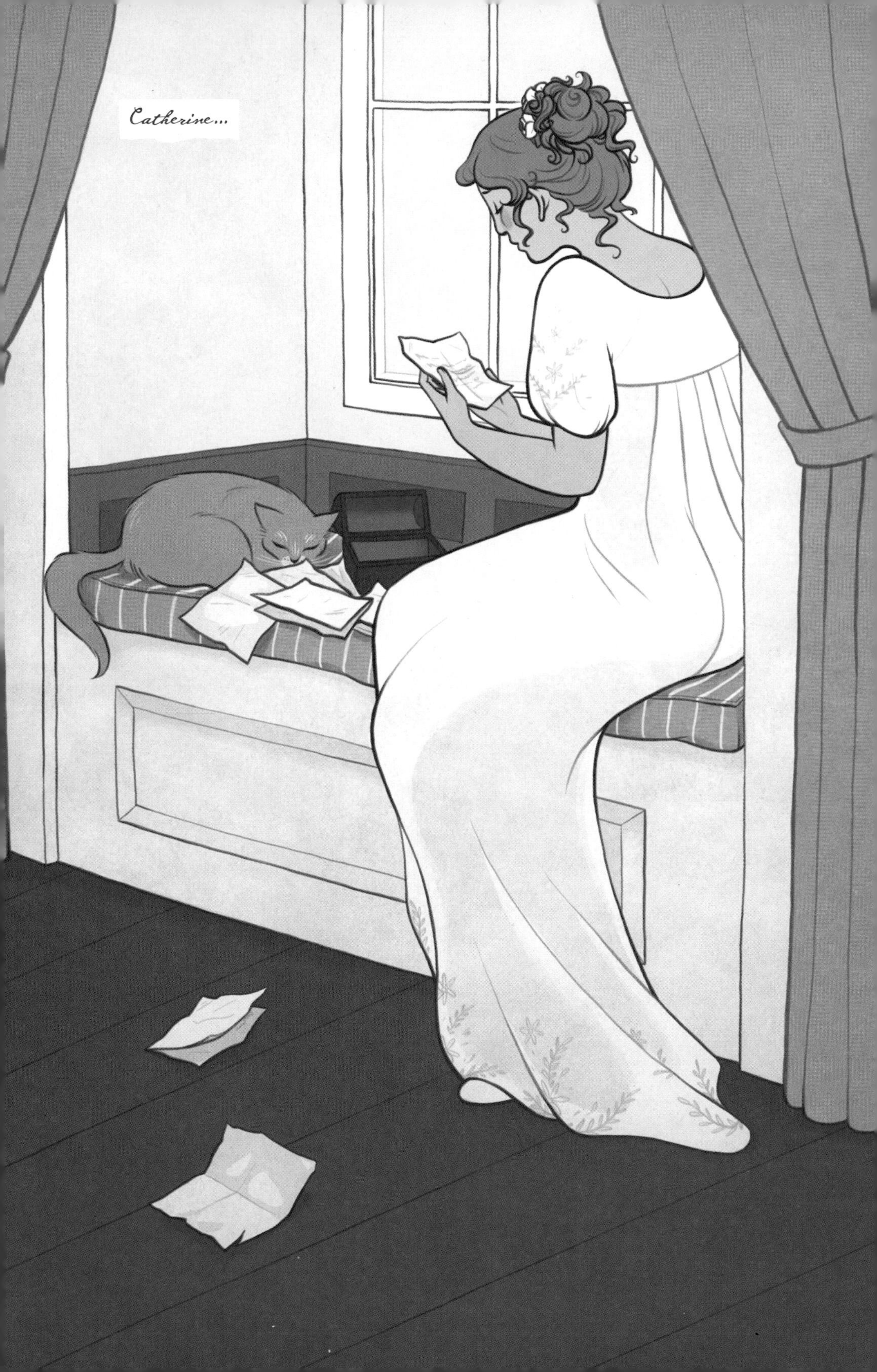
Catherine...

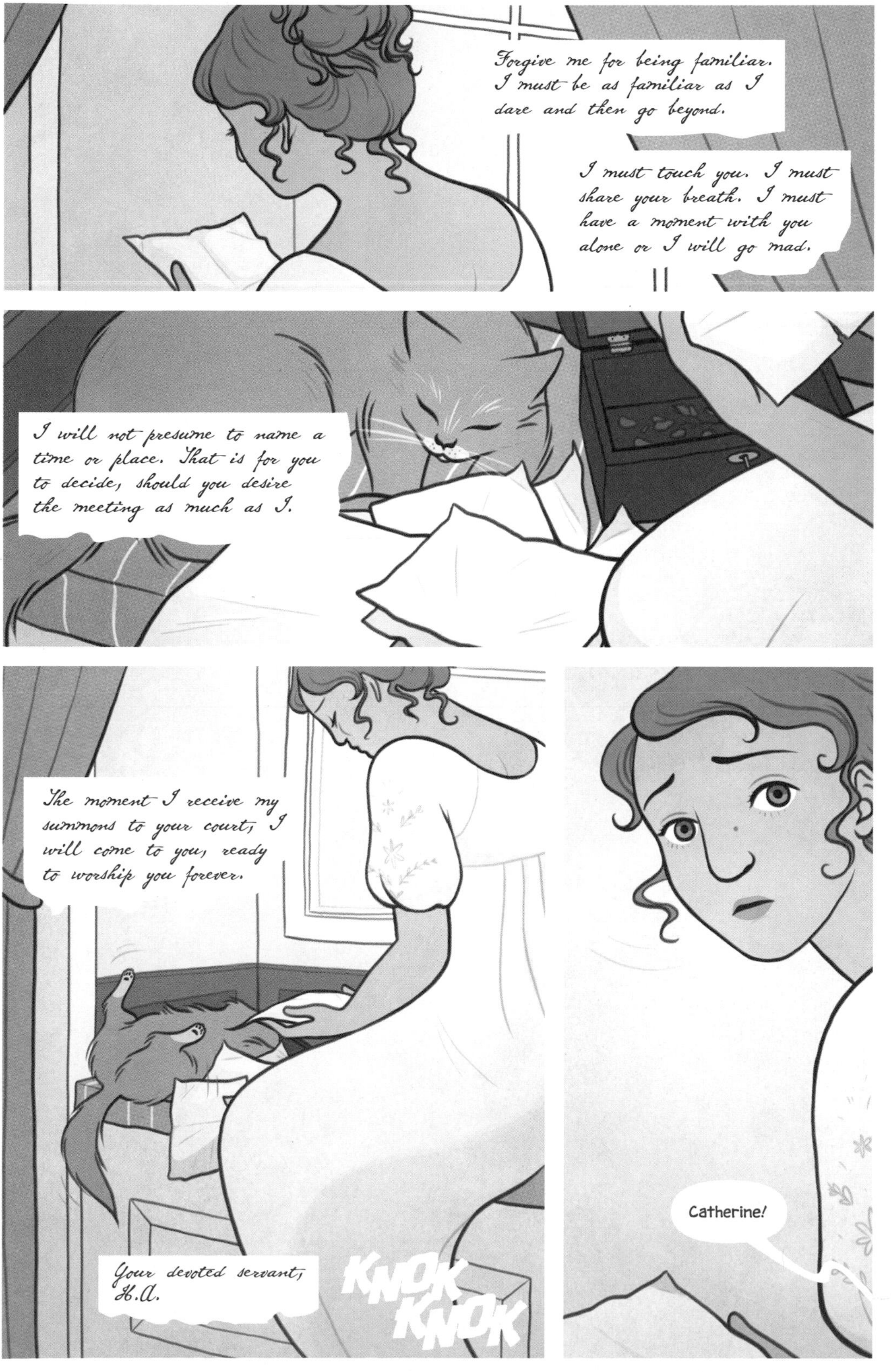
Forgive me for being familiar. I must be as familiar as I dare and then go beyond.
I must touch you. I must share your breath. I must have a moment with you alone or I will go mad.
I will not presume to name a time or place. That is for you to decide, should you desire the meeting as much as I.
The moment I receive my summons to your court, I will come to you, ready to worship you forever.
Your devoted servant, H.A.
KNOK KNOK
Catherine!

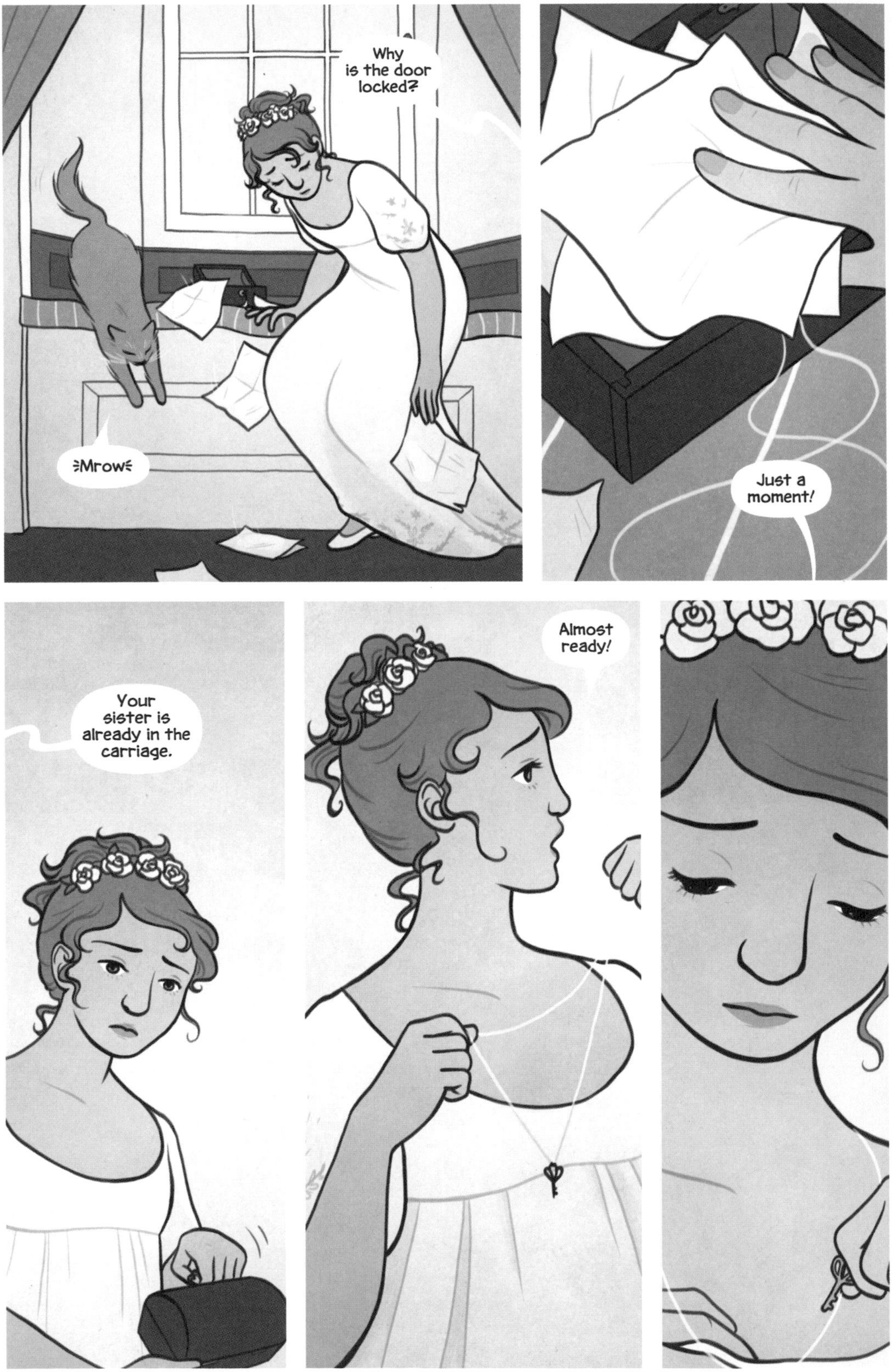
Why is the door locked?
Mrow
Just a moment!
Your sister is already in the carriage.
Almost ready!

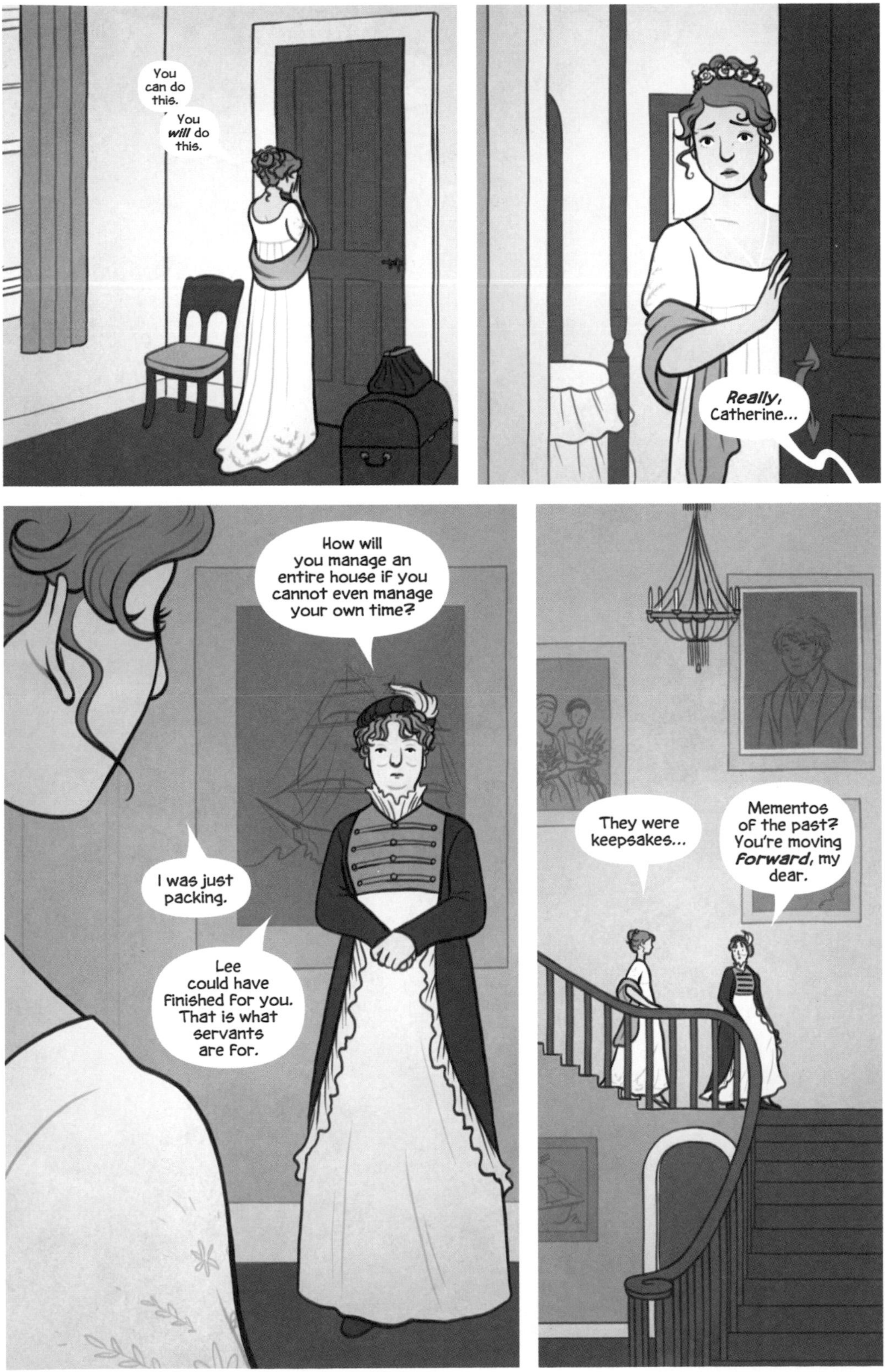
You can do this.
You *will* do this.
Really, Catherine...
How will you manage an entire house if you cannot even manage your own time?
I was just packing.
Lee could have finished for you. That is what servants are for.
They were keepsakes...
Mementos of the past? You're moving *forward*, my dear.

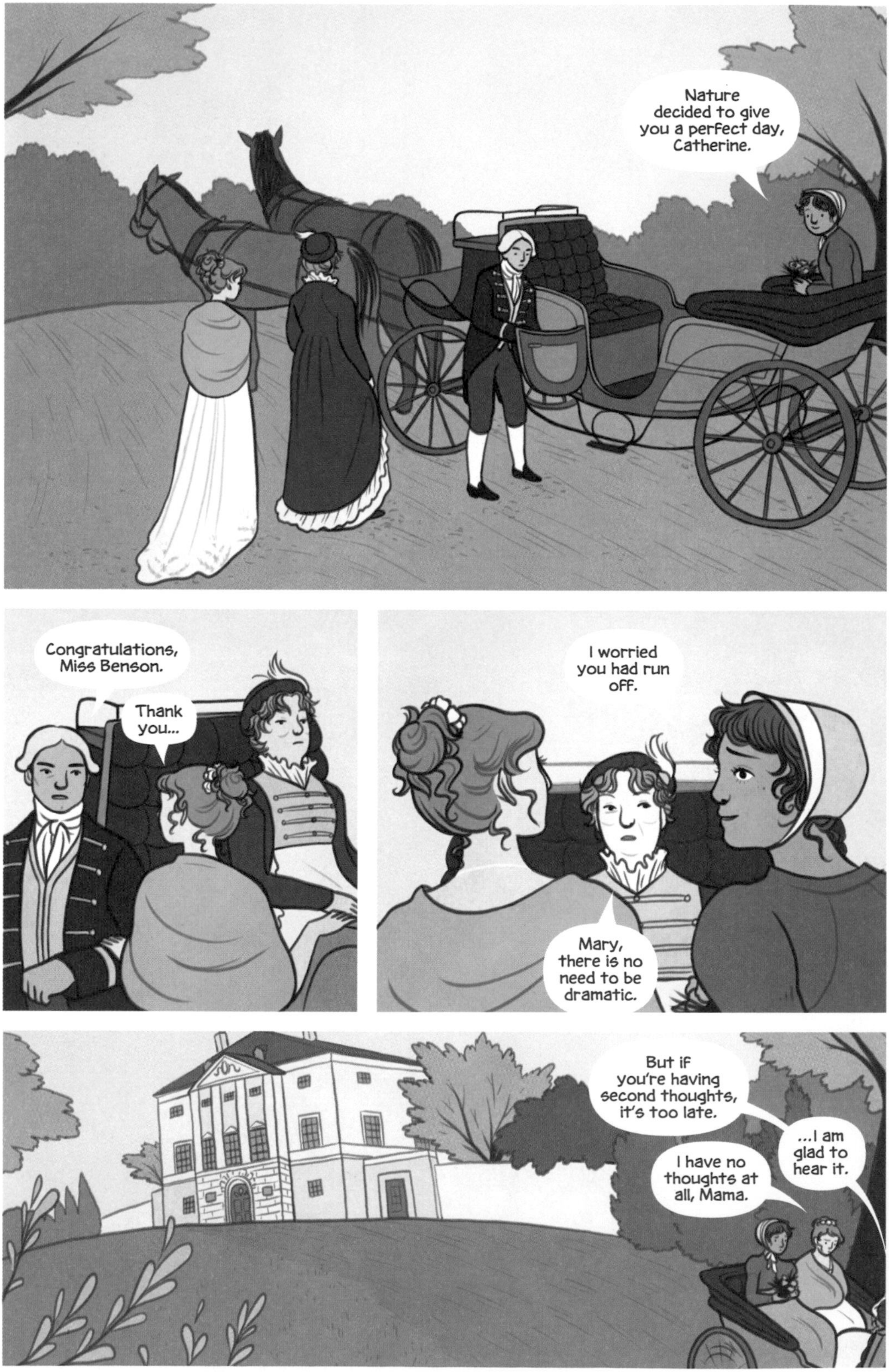
Nature decided to give you a perfect day, Catherine.
Congratulations, Miss Benson.
Thank you...
I worried you had run off.
Mary, there is no need to be dramatic.
But if you're having second thoughts, it's too late.
I have no thoughts at all, Mama.
...I am glad to hear it.

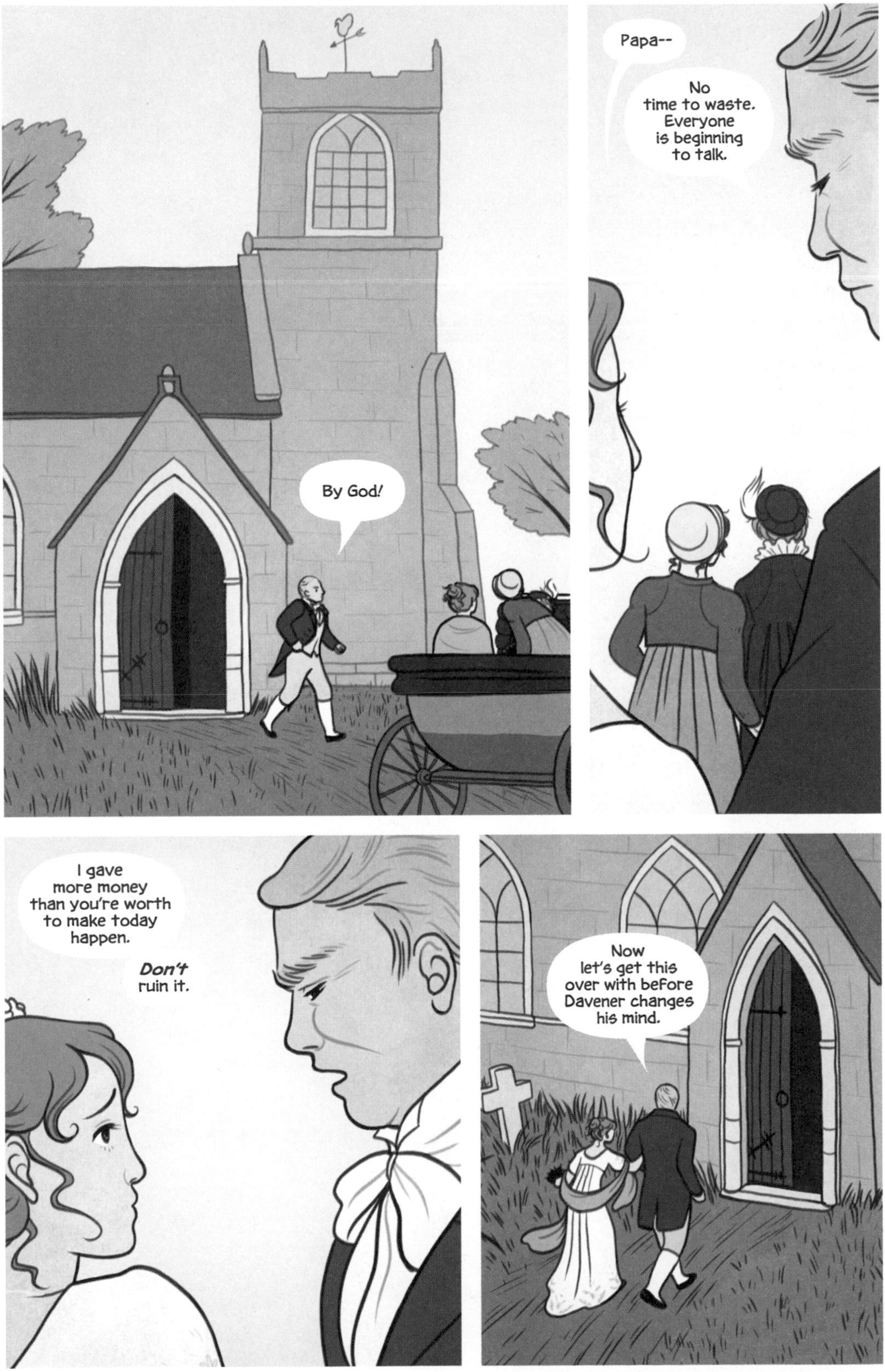
By God!
Papa--
No time to waste. Everyone is beginning to talk.
I gave more money than you're worth to make today happen.
Don't ruin it.
Now let's get this over with before Davener changes his mind.

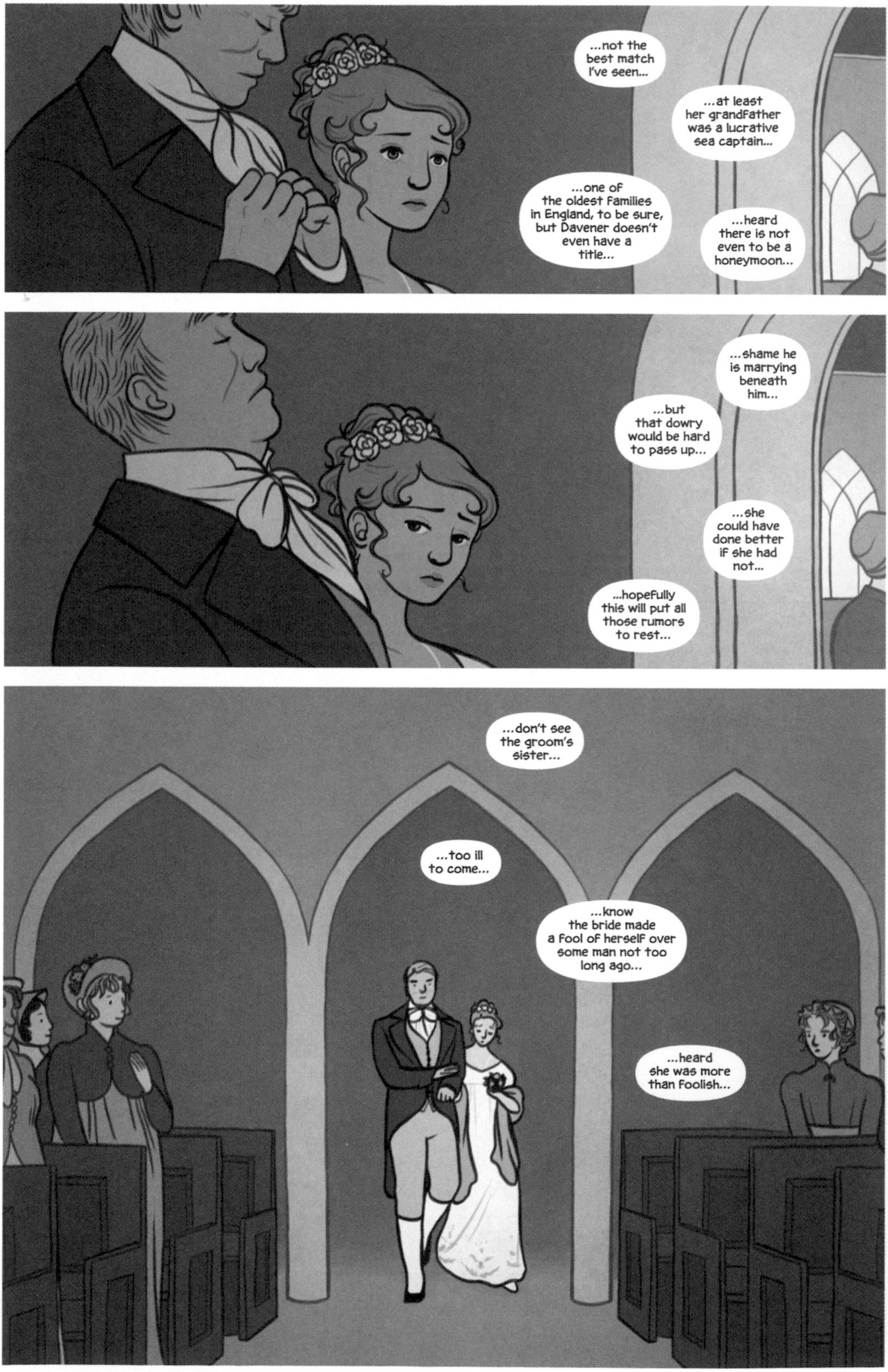
...not the best match I've seen...
...at least her grandfather was a lucrative sea captain...
...one of the oldest families in England, to be sure, but Davener doesn't even have a title...
...heard there is not even to be a honeymoon...
...shame he is marrying beneath him...
...but that dowry would be hard to pass up...
...she could have done better if she had not...
...hopefully this will put all those rumors to rest...
...don't see the groom's sister...
...too ill to come...
...know the bride made a fool of herself over some man not too long ago...
...heard she was more than foolish...

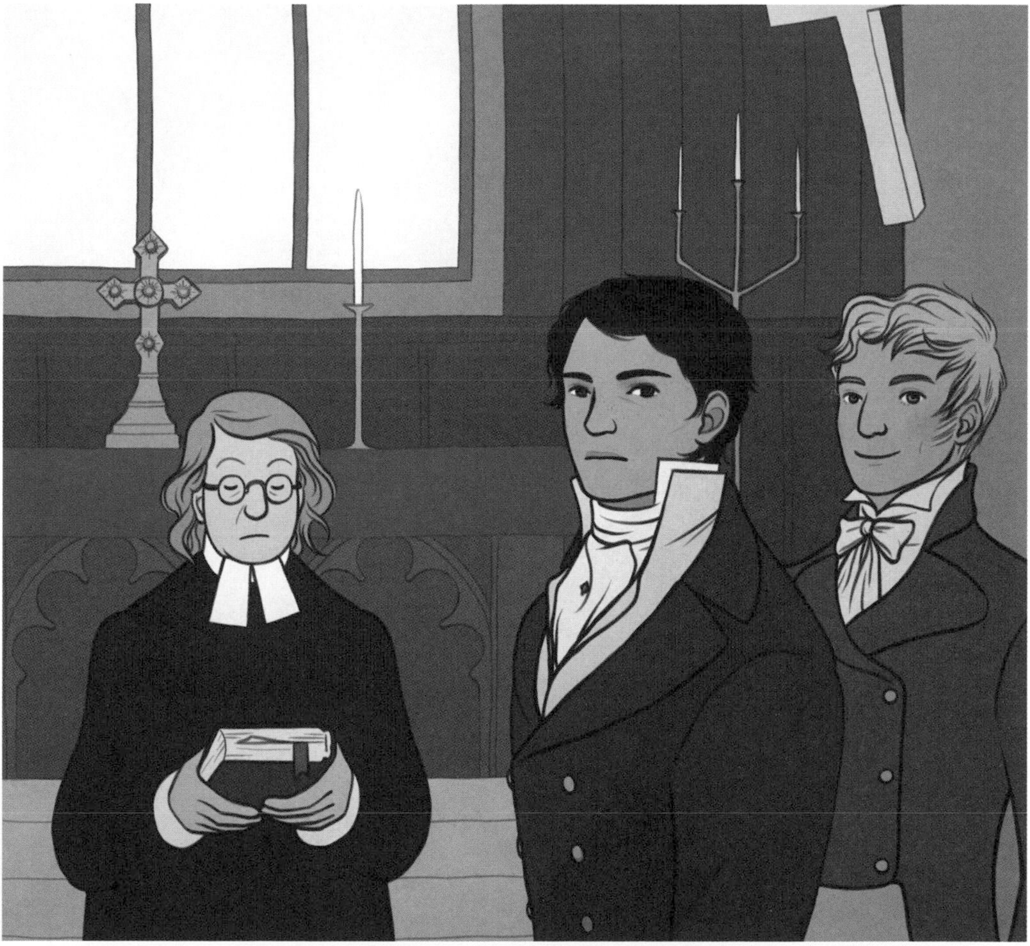

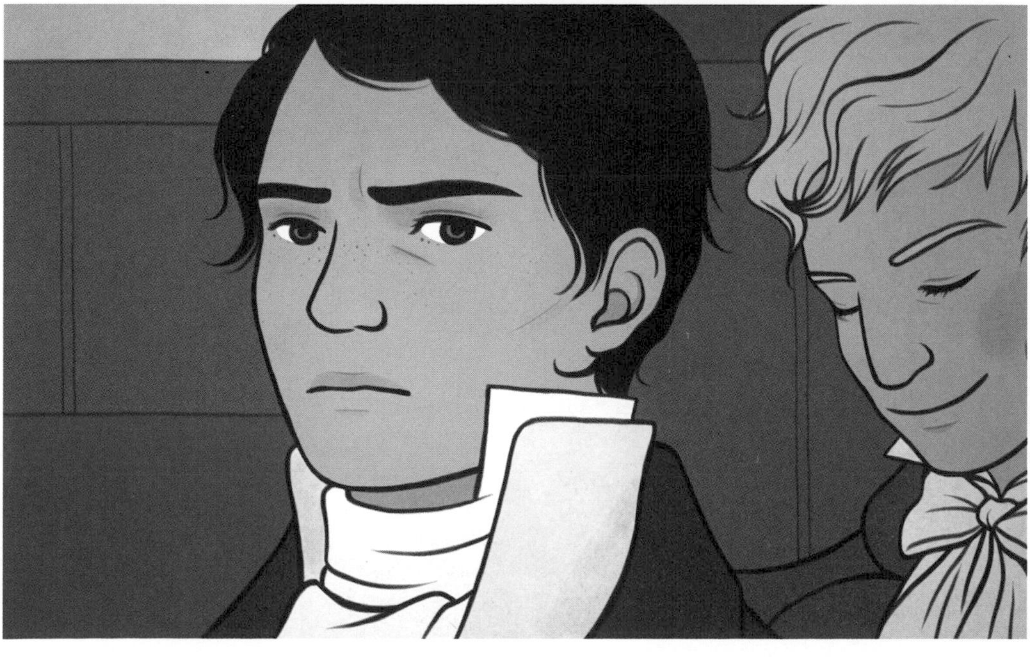

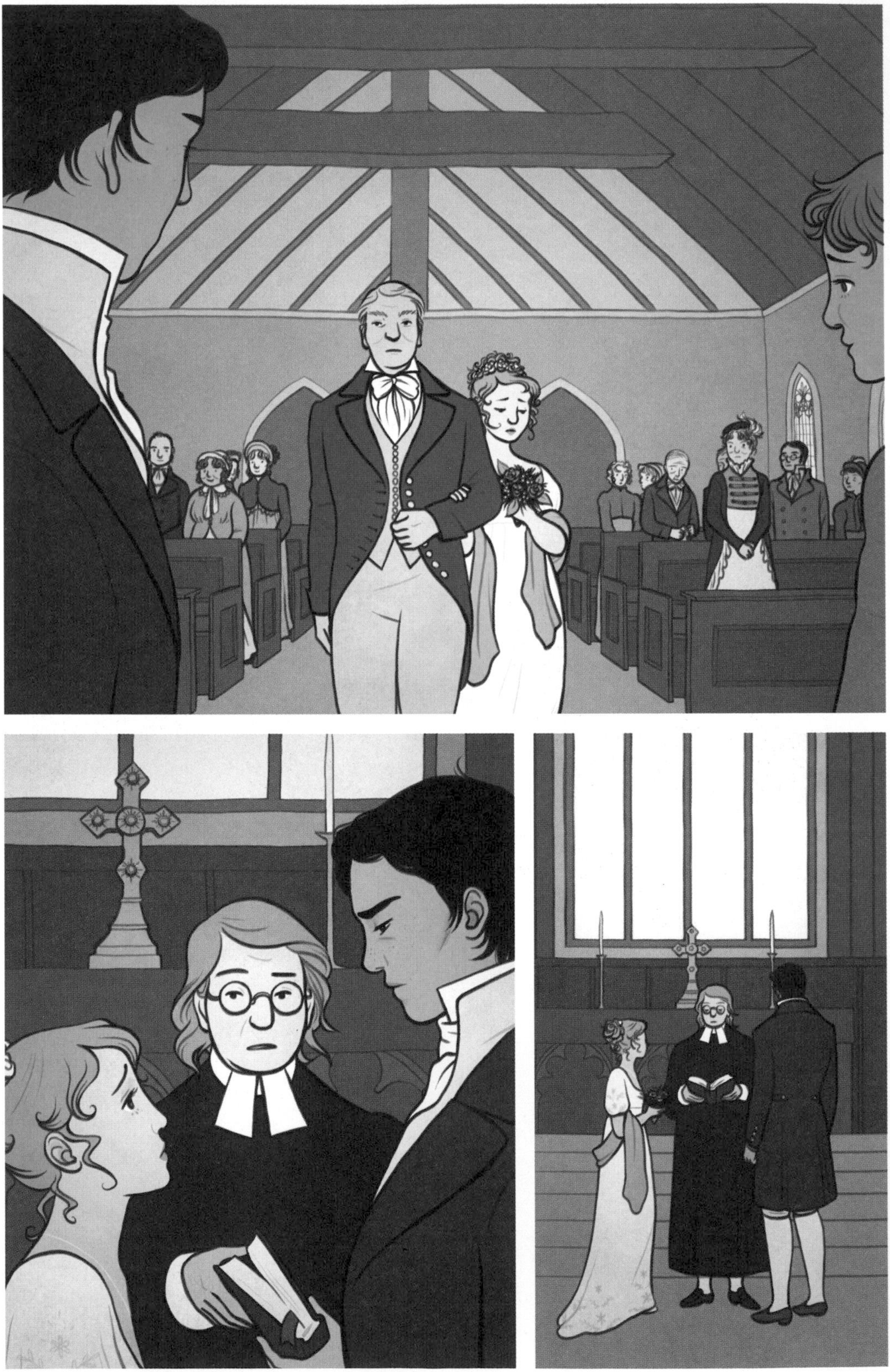

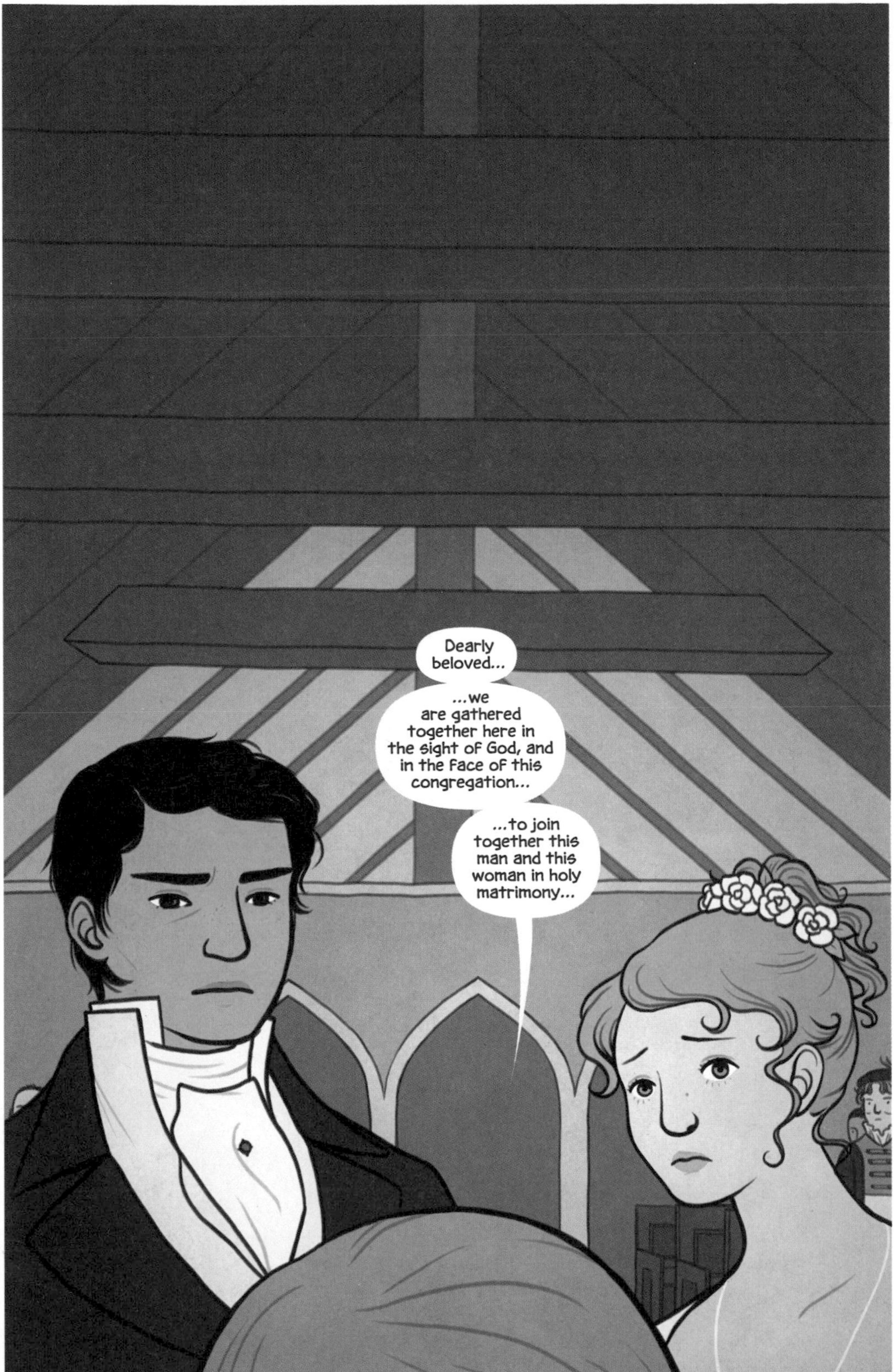
Dearly beloved...
...we are gathered together here in the sight of God, and in the face of this congregation...
...to join together this man and this woman in holy matrimony...

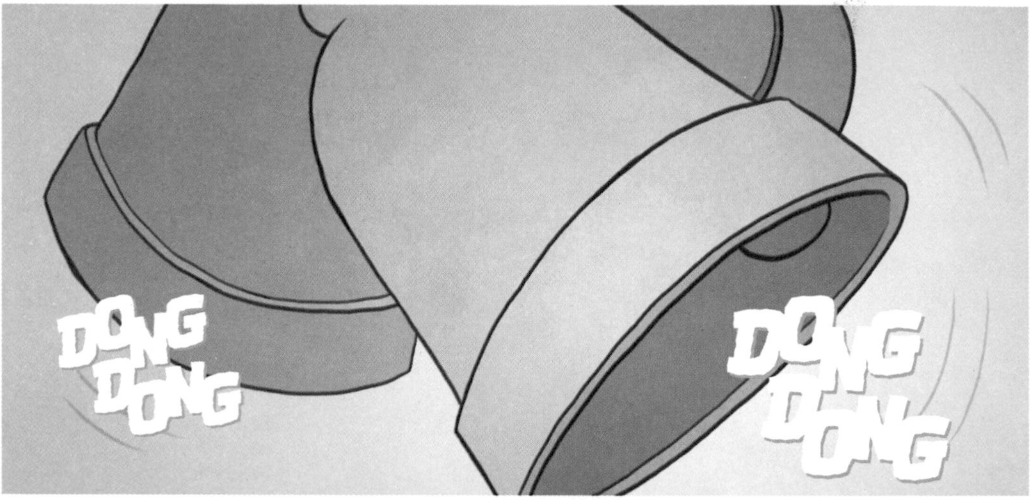
DONG DONG
DONG DONG

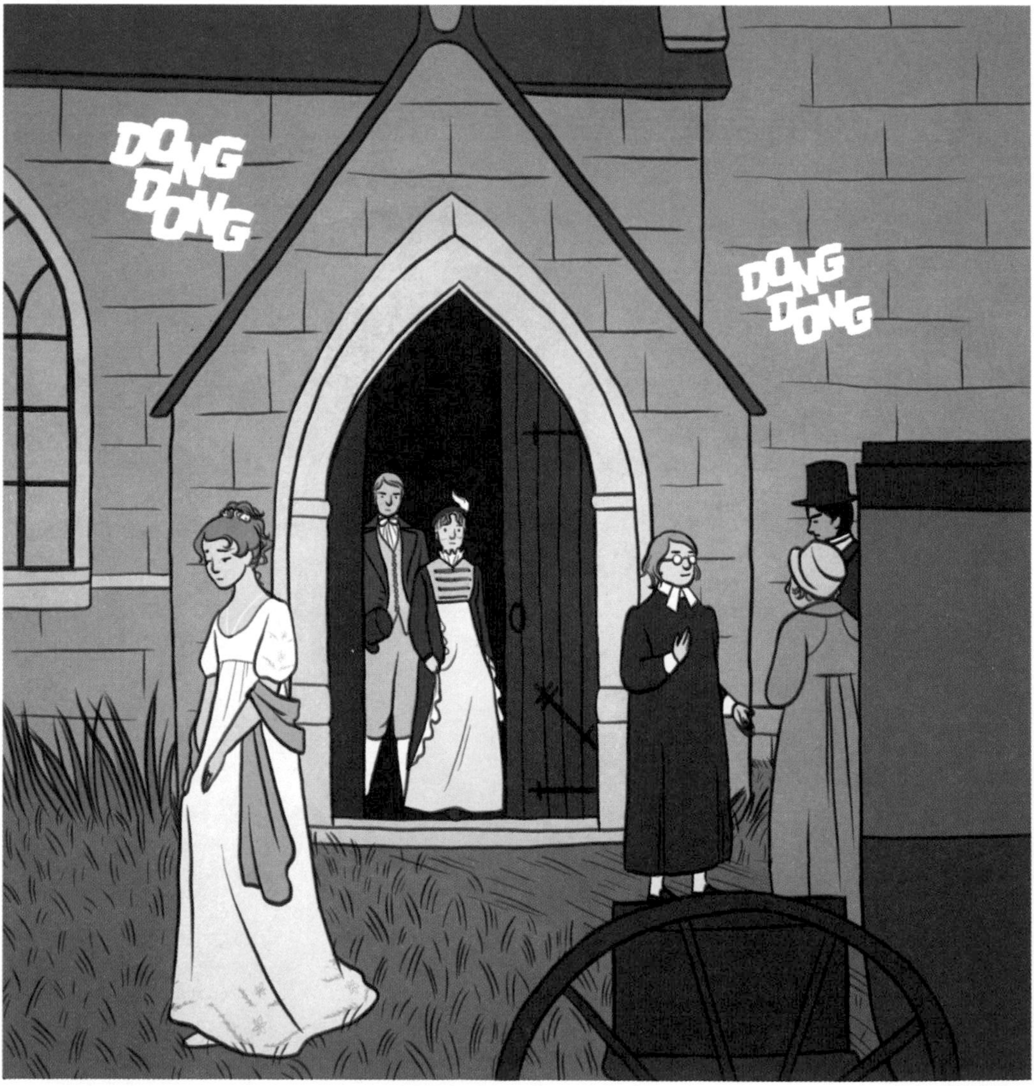
DONG DONG
DONG DONG

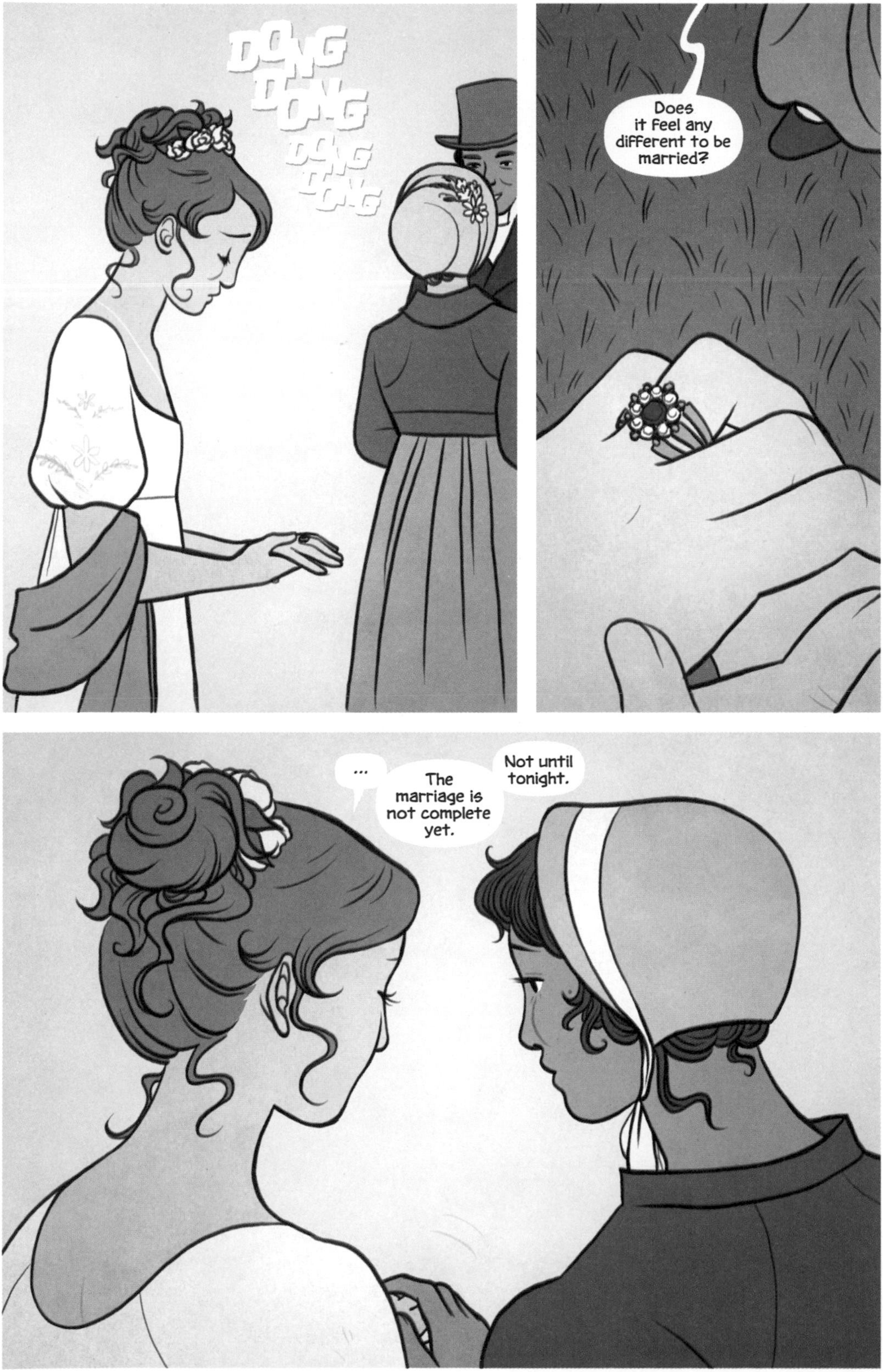
DONG
DONG
DONG
DONG
Does it feel any different to be married?
...
The marriage is not complete yet.
Not until tonight.

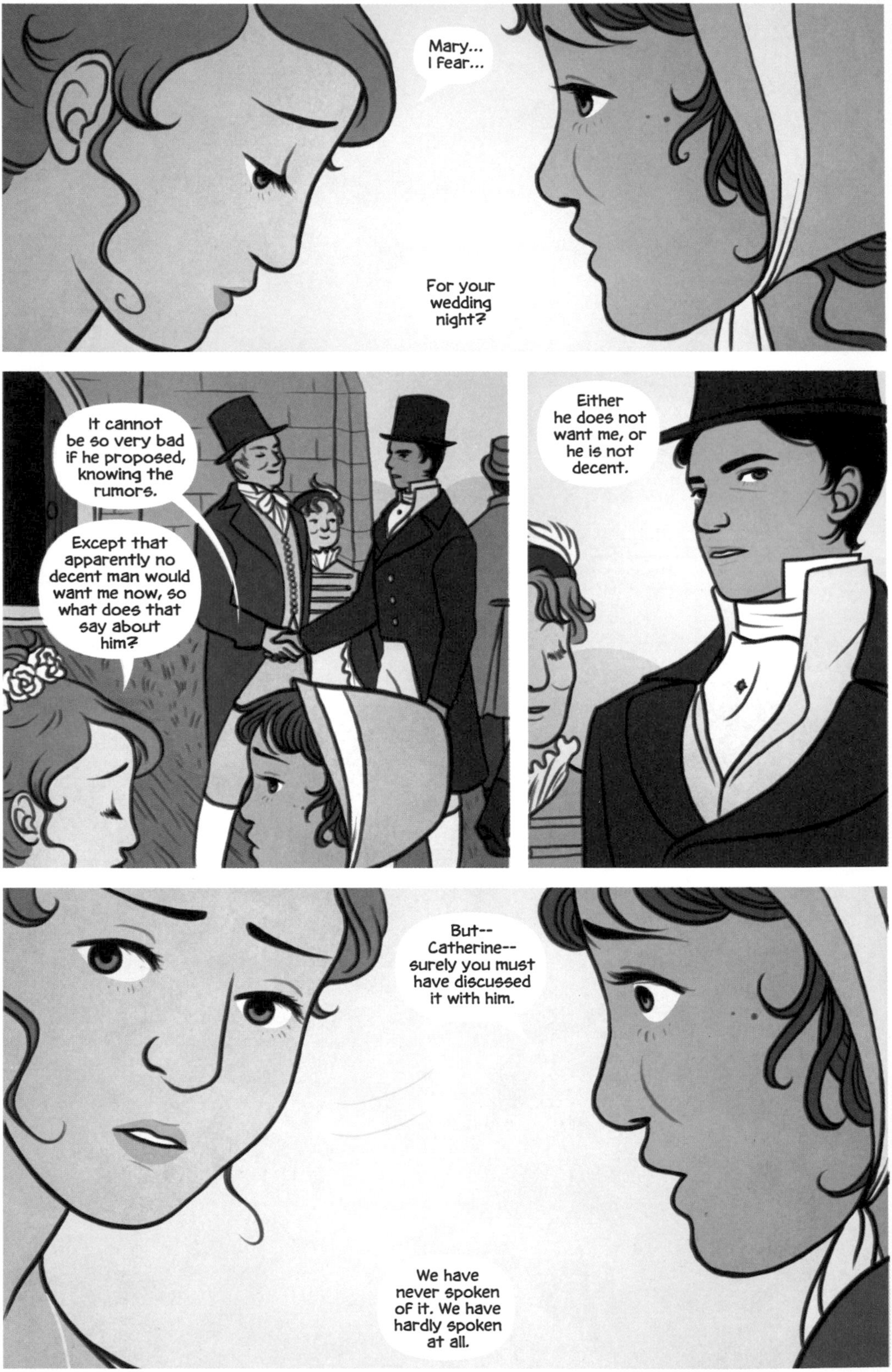
Mary... I fear...
For your wedding night?
It cannot be so very bad if he proposed, knowing the rumors.
Except that apparently no decent man would want me now, so what does that say about him?
Either he does not want me, or he is not decent.
But-- Catherine-- surely you must have discussed it with him.
We have never spoken of it. We have hardly spoken at all.

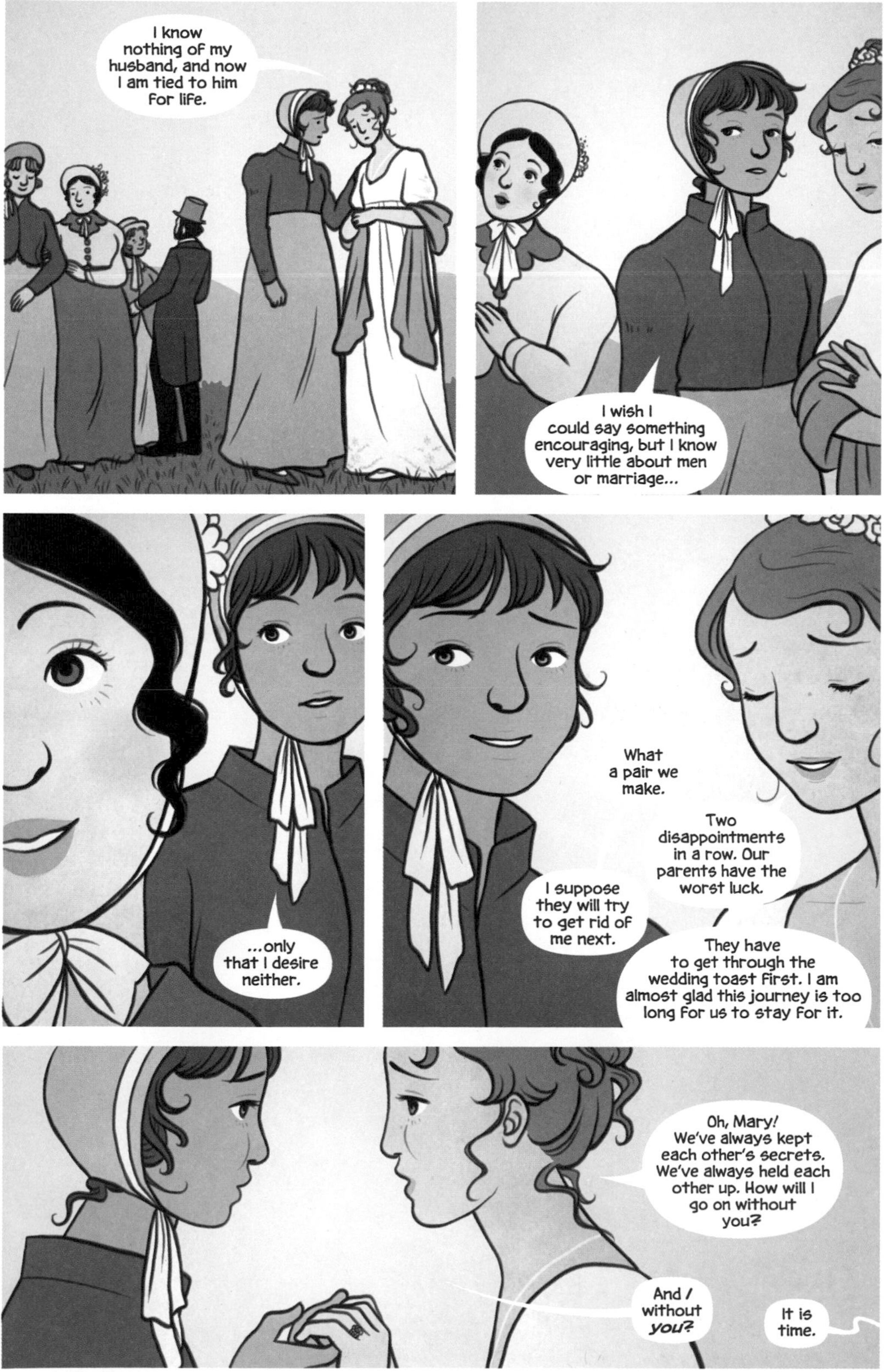
I know nothing of my husband, and now I am tied to him for life.
I wish I could say something encouraging, but I know very little about men or marriage...
...only that I desire neither.
What a pair we make.
Two disappointments in a row. Our parents have the worst luck.
I suppose they will try to get rid of me next.
They have to get through the wedding toast first. I am almost glad this journey is too long for us to stay for it.
Oh, Mary! We've always kept each other's secrets. We've always held each other up. How will I go on without you?
And *I* without *you?*
It is time.

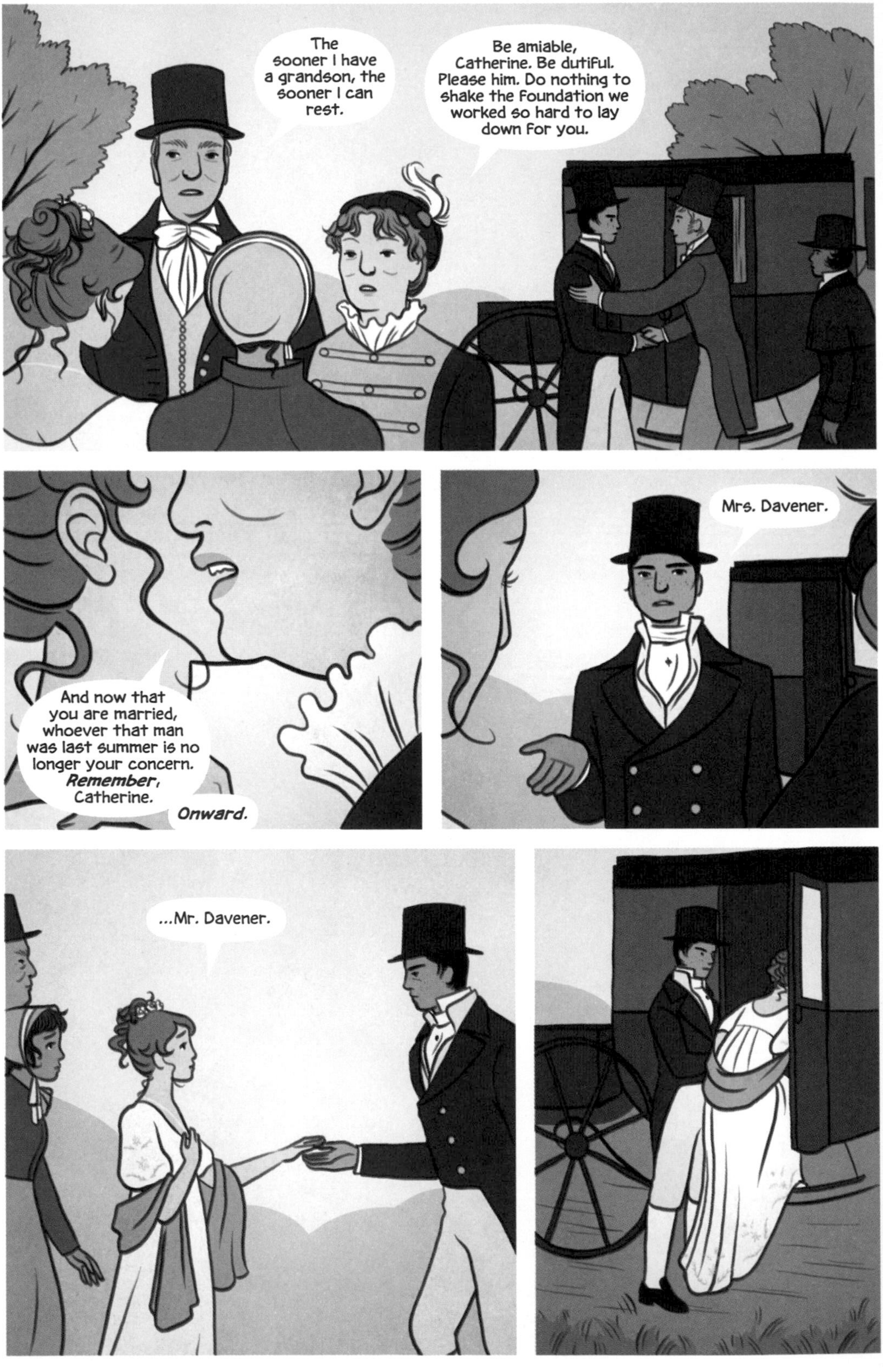
The sooner I have a grandson, the sooner I can rest.
Be amiable, Catherine. Be dutiful. Please him. Do nothing to shake the foundation we worked so hard to lay down for you.
And now that you are married, whoever that man was last summer is no longer your concern. *Remember*, Catherine.
Onward.
Mrs. Davener.
...Mr. Davener.

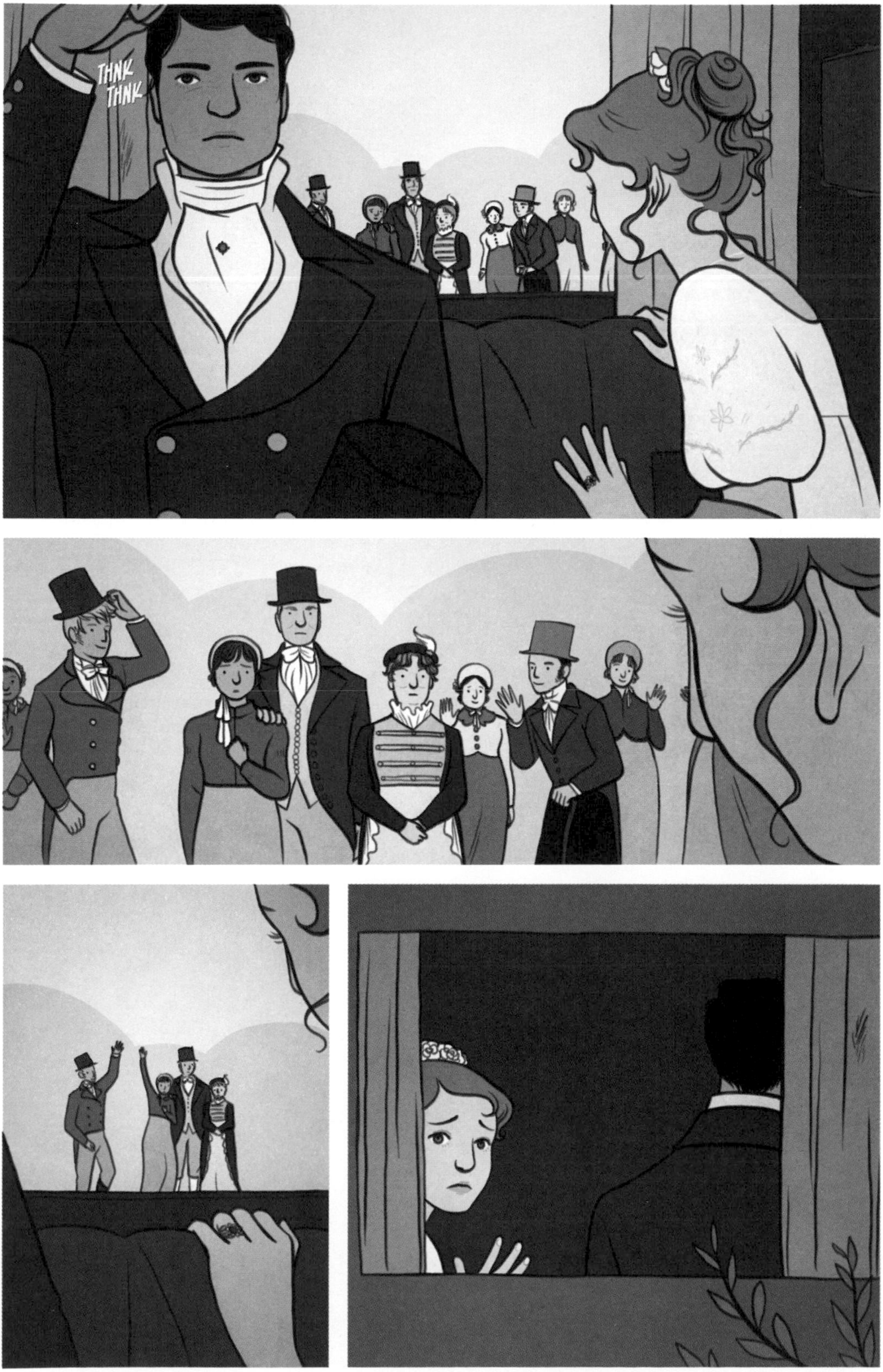
THNK
THNK

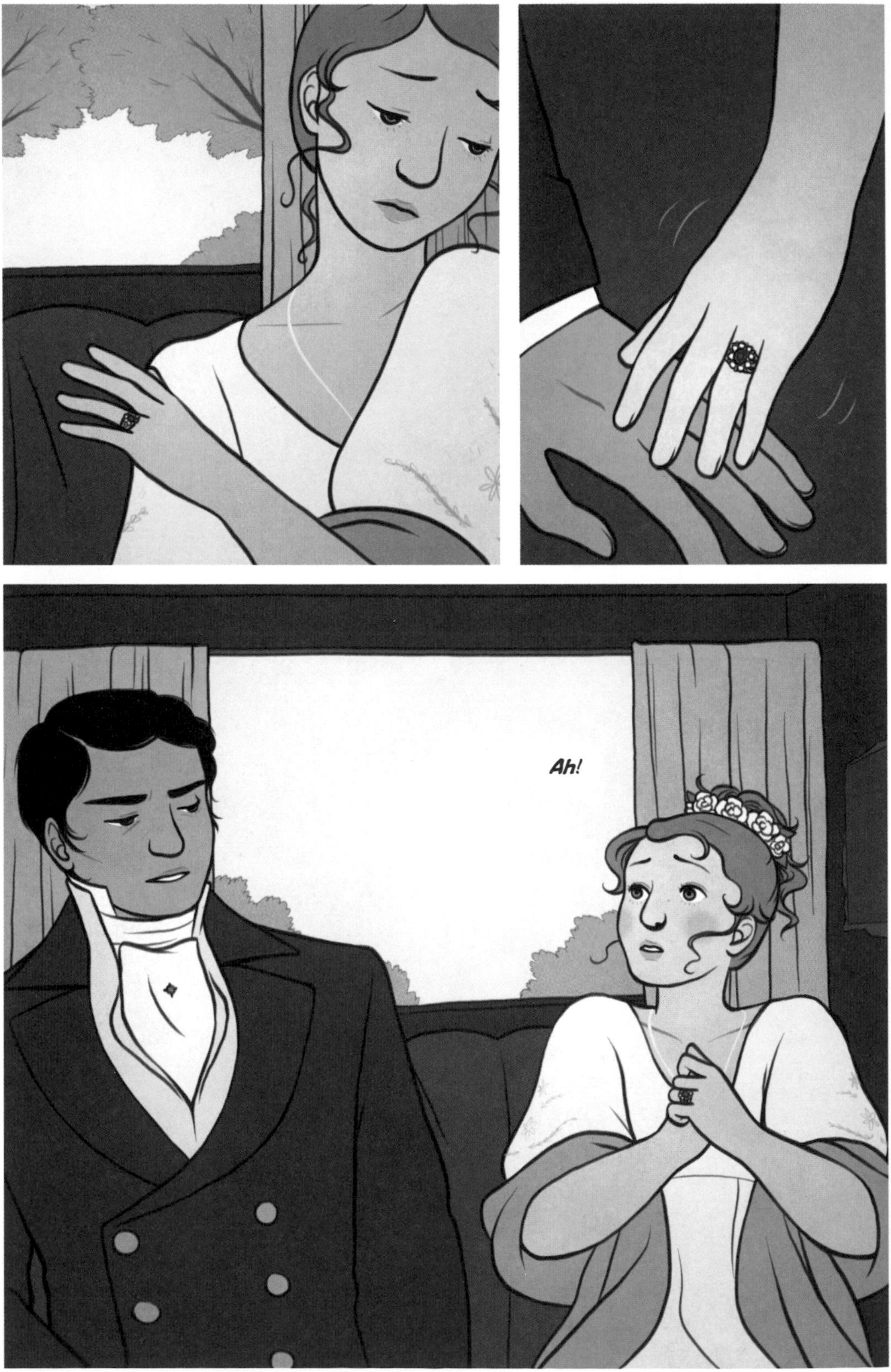
Ah!

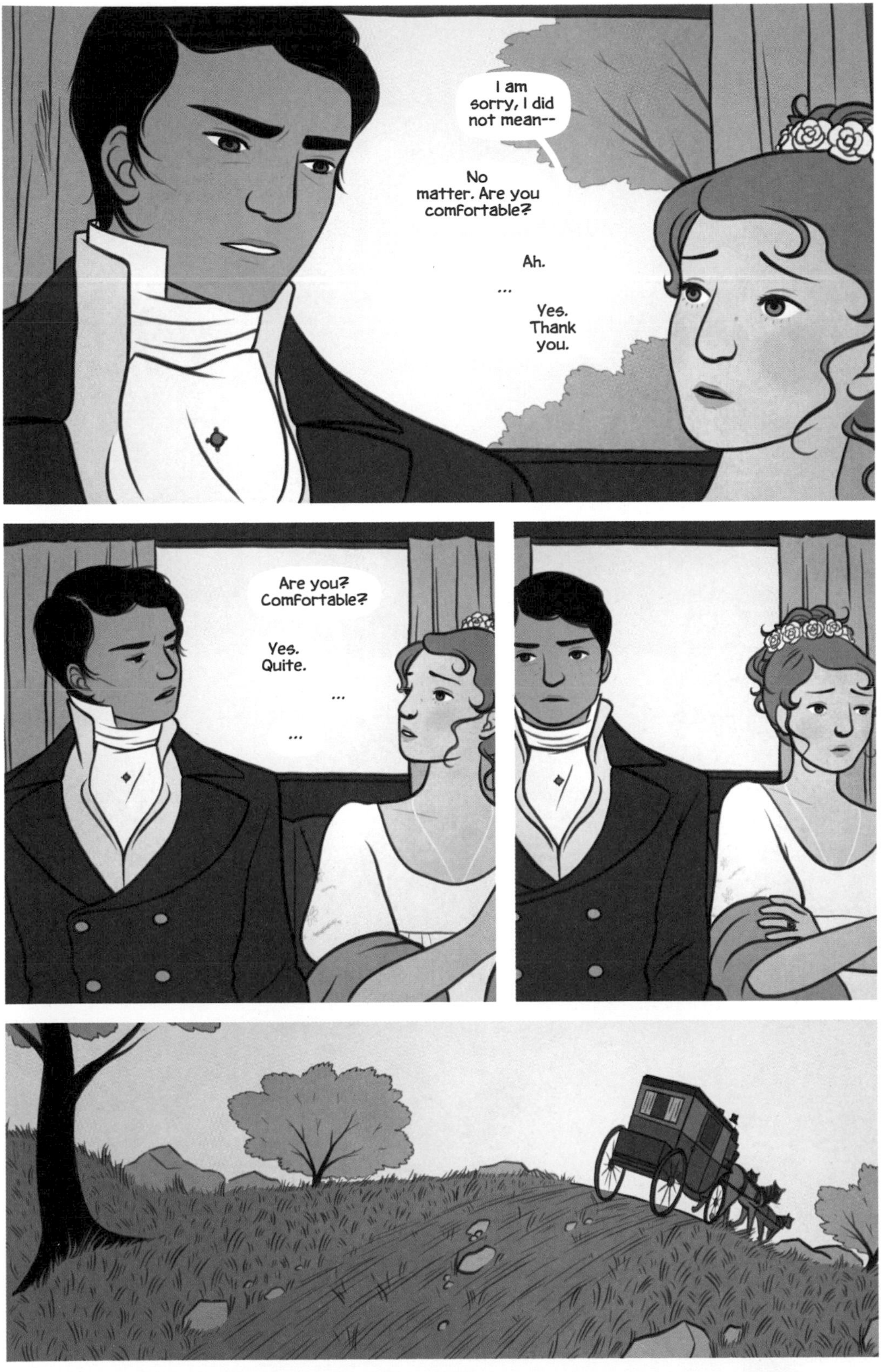
I am sorry, I did not mean--
No matter. Are you comfortable?
Ah.
...
Yes. Thank you.
Are you? Comfortable?
Yes. Quite.
...
...

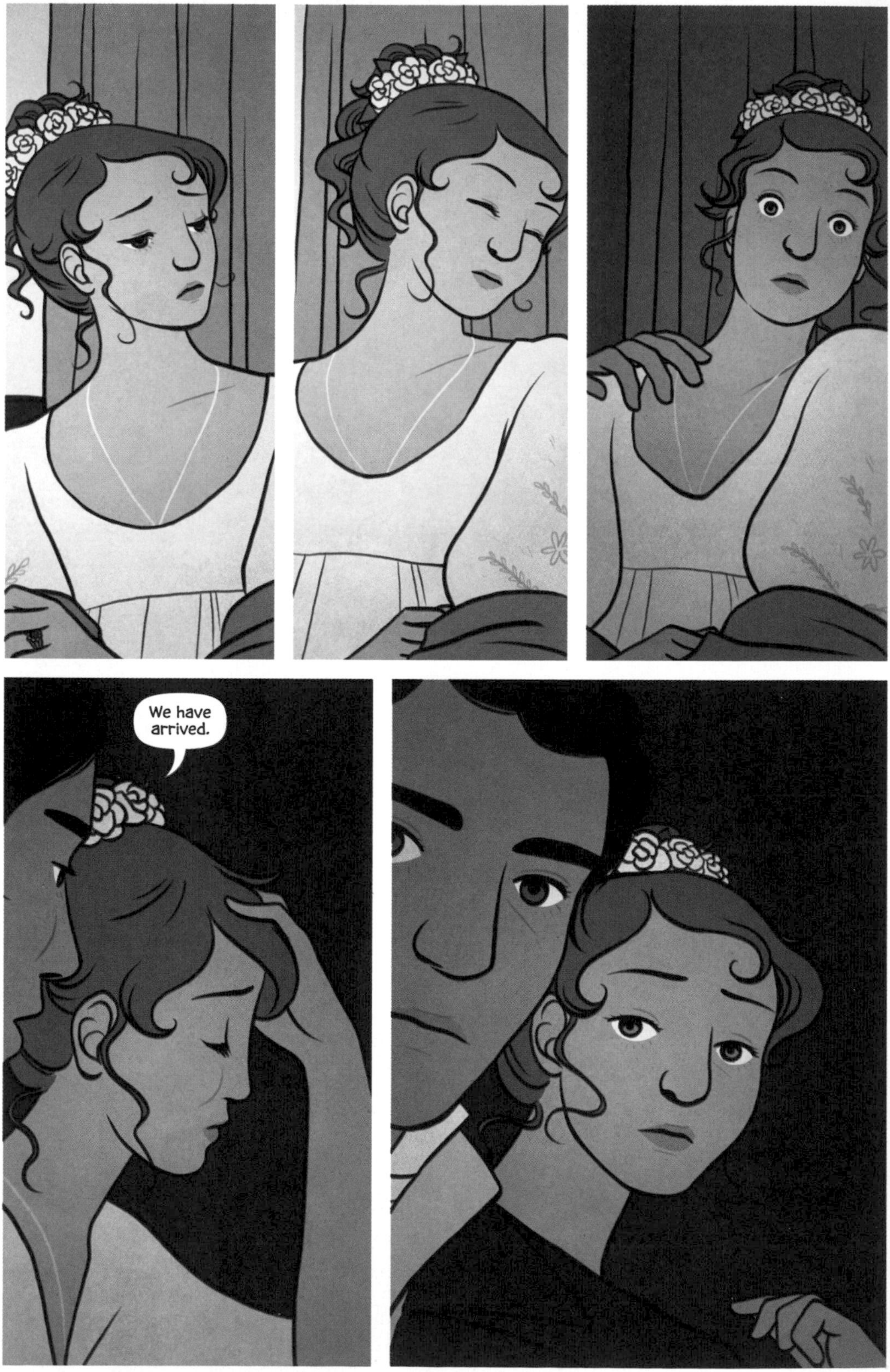
We have arrived.

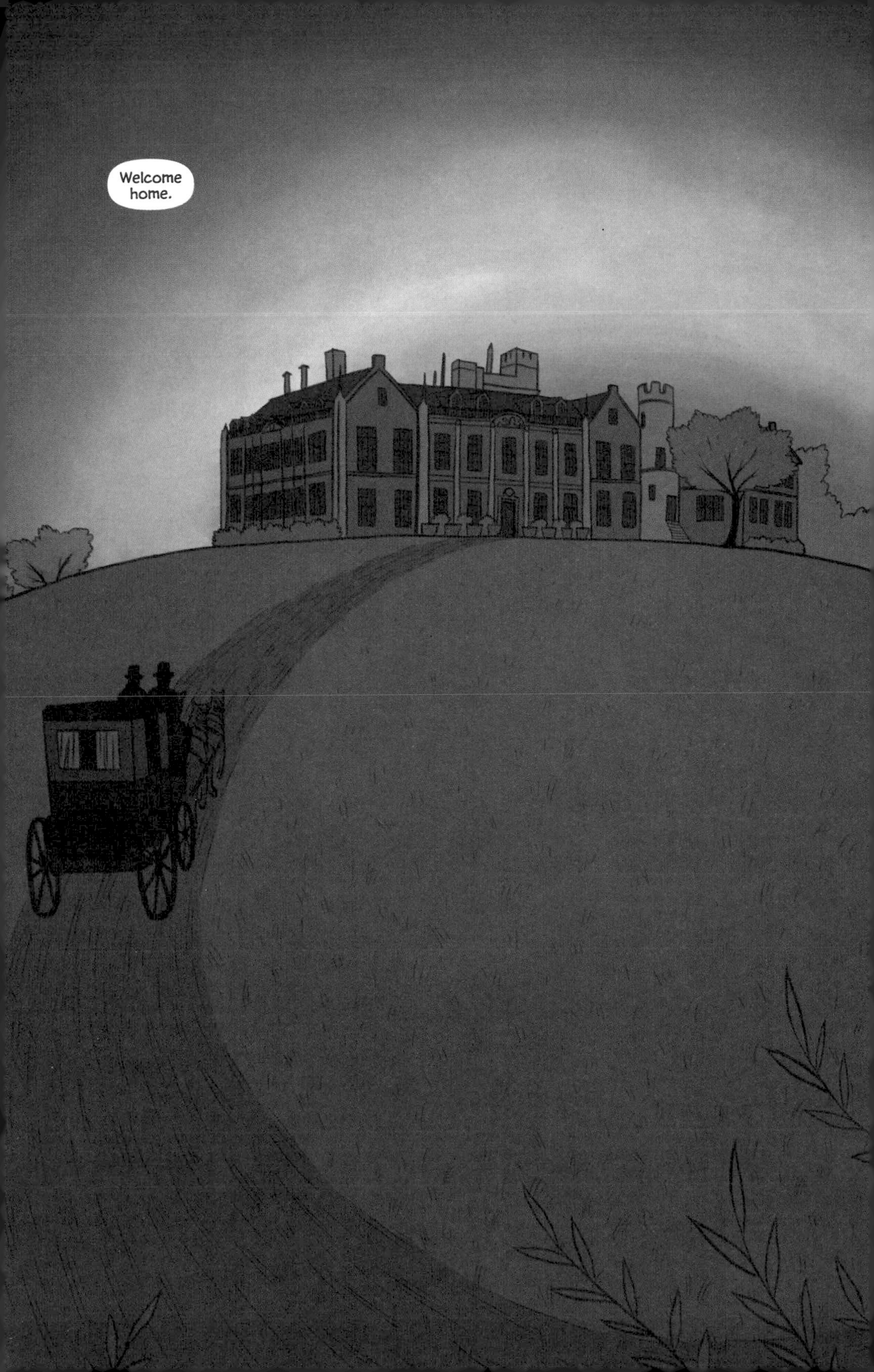
Welcome home.

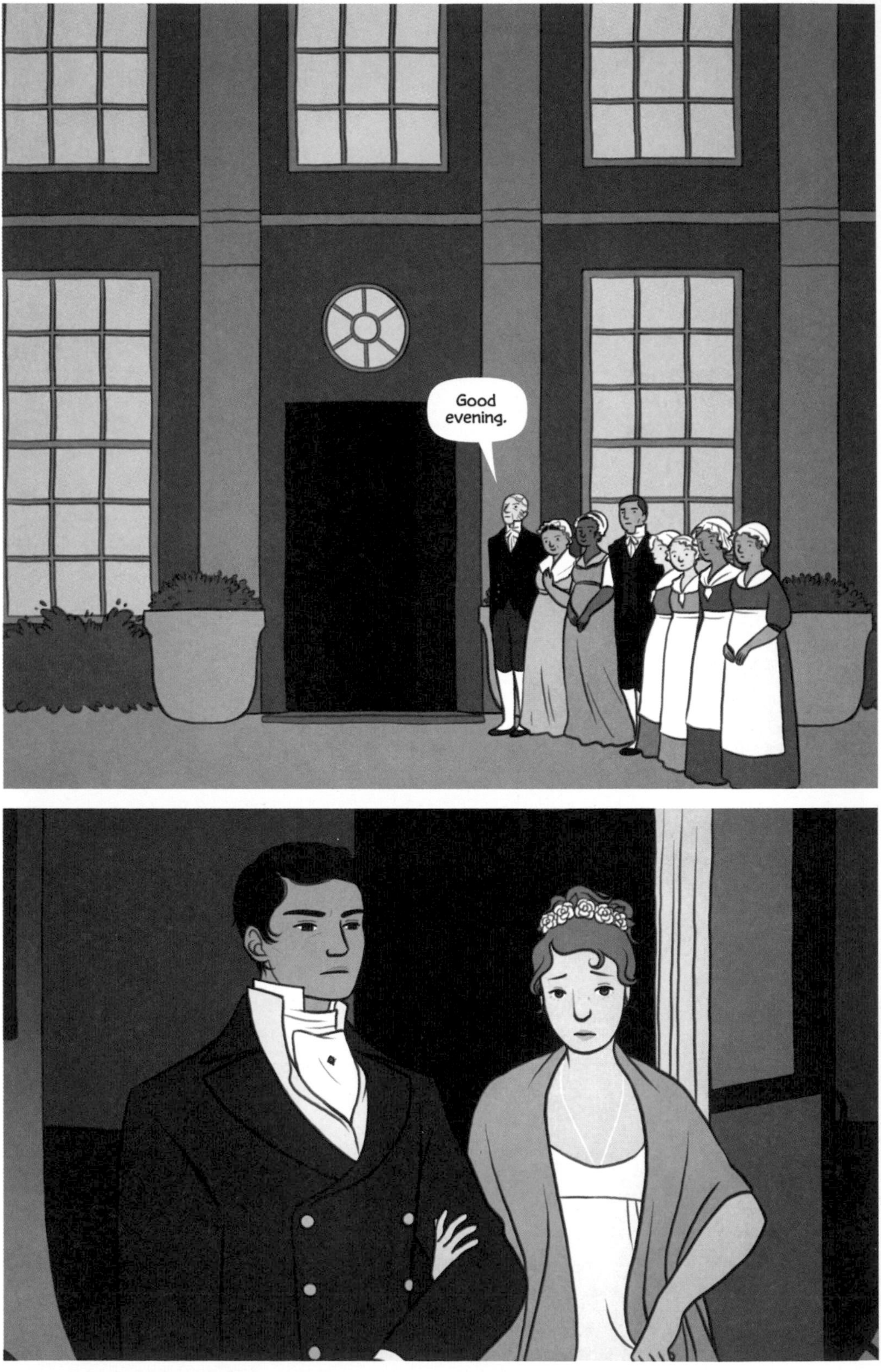
Good evening.

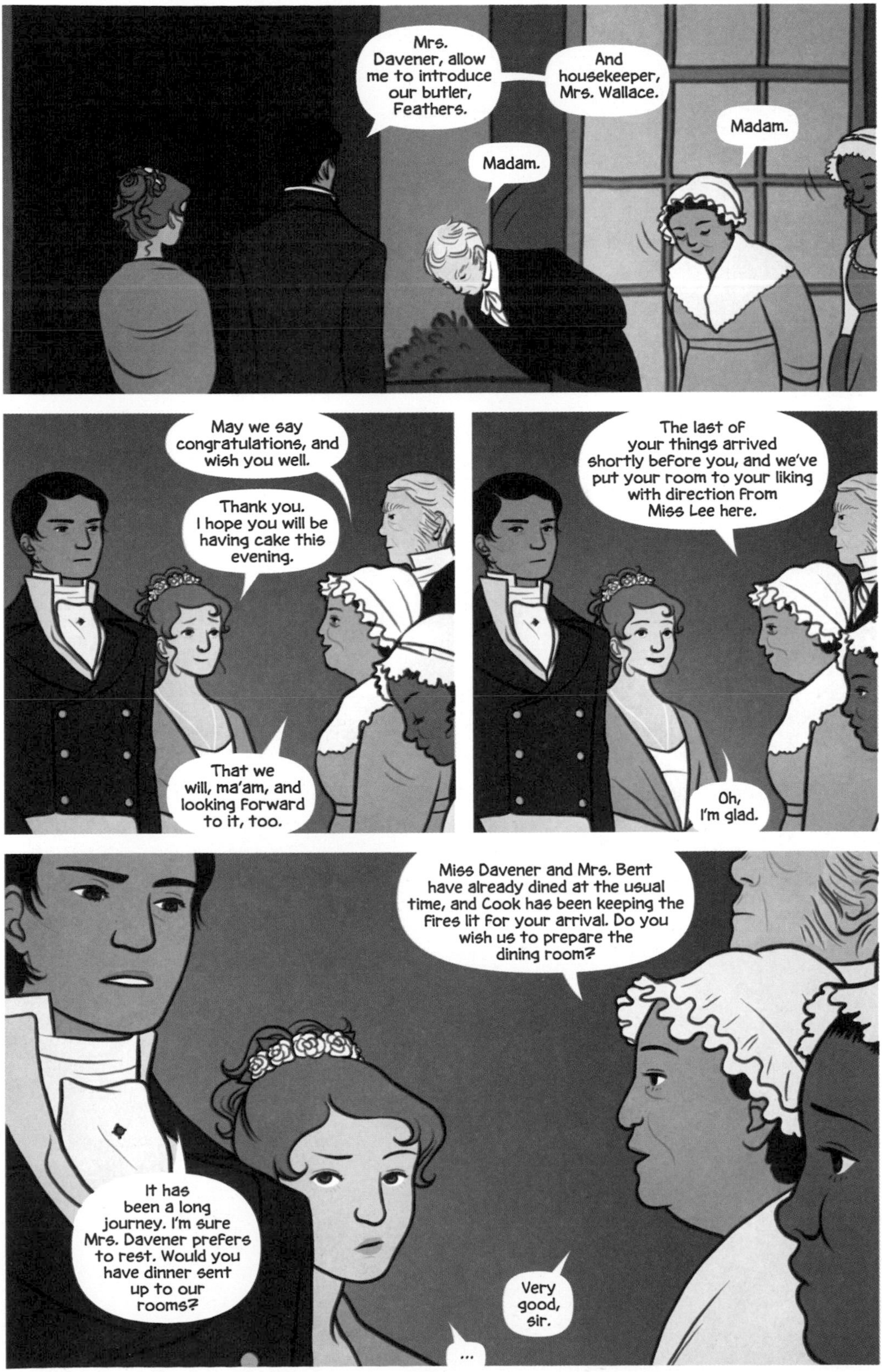

Mrs. Davener, allow me to introduce our butler, Feathers.
And housekeeper, Mrs. Wallace.
Madam.
Madam.
May we say congratulations, and wish you well.
Thank you. I hope you will be having cake this evening.
That we will, ma'am, and looking forward to it, too.
The last of your things arrived shortly before you, and we've put your room to your liking with direction from Miss Lee here.
Oh, I'm glad.
Miss Davener and Mrs. Bent have already dined at the usual time, and Cook has been keeping the fires lit for your arrival. Do you wish us to prepare the dining room?
It has been a long journey. I'm sure Mrs. Davener prefers to rest. Would you have dinner sent up to our rooms?
Very good, sir.
...

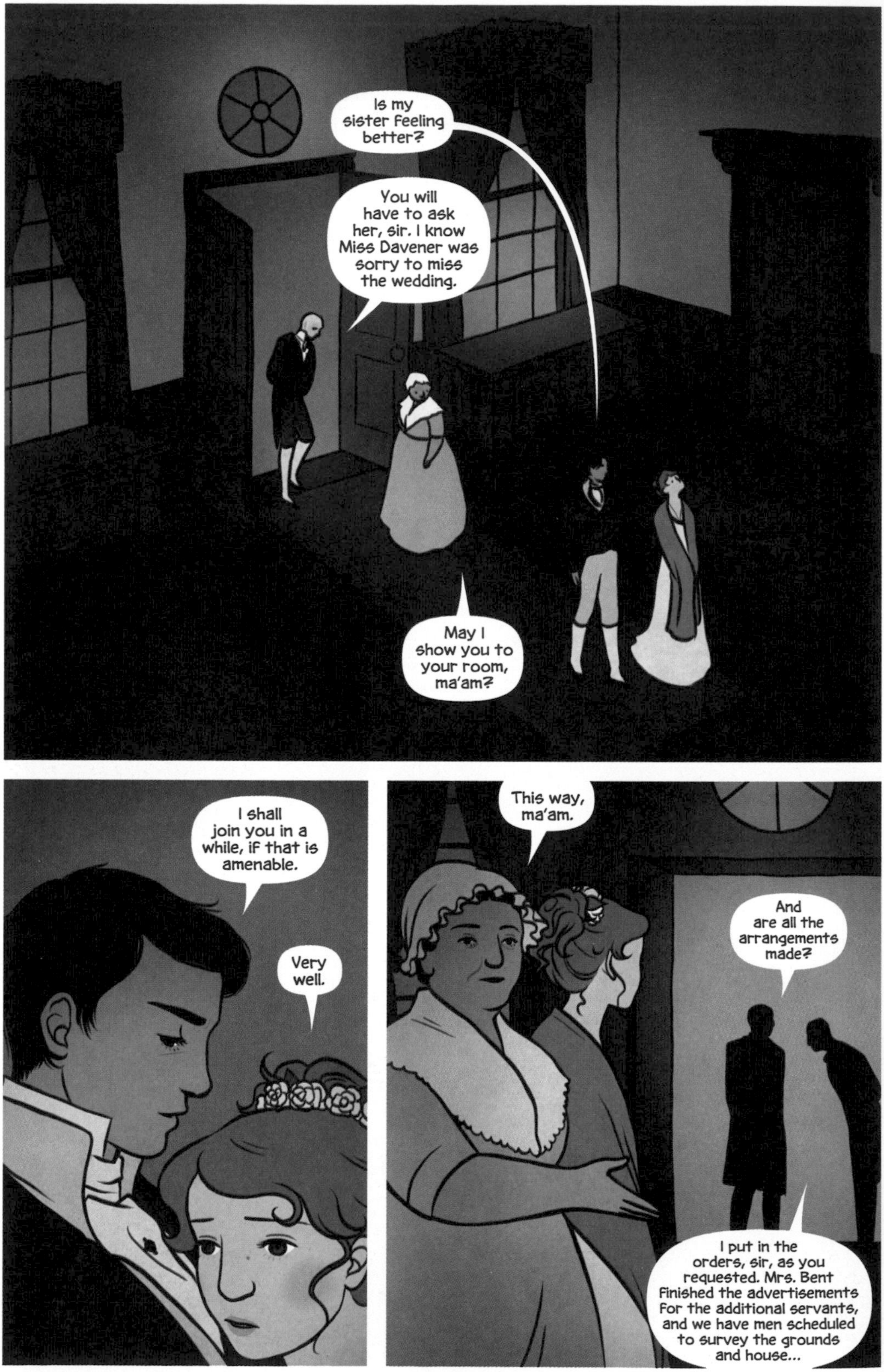
Is my sister feeling better?
You will have to ask her, sir. I know Miss Davener was sorry to miss the wedding.
May I show you to your room, ma'am?
I shall join you in a while, if that is amenable.
Very well.
This way, ma'am.
And are all the arrangements made?
I put in the orders, sir, as you requested. Mrs. Bent finished the advertisements for the additional servants, and we have men scheduled to survey the grounds and house...

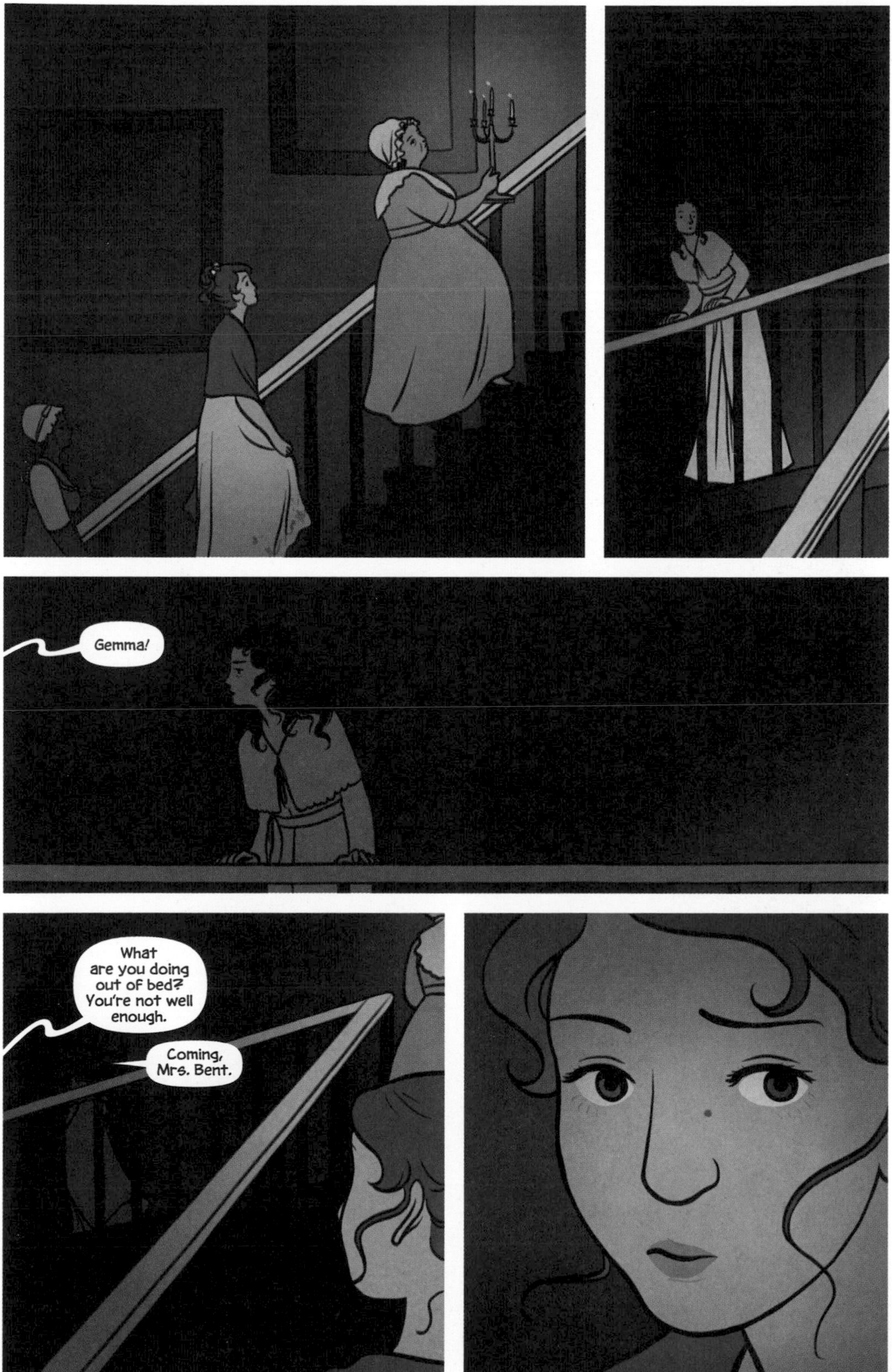
Gemma!
What are you doing out of bed? You're not well enough.
Coming, Mrs. Bent.

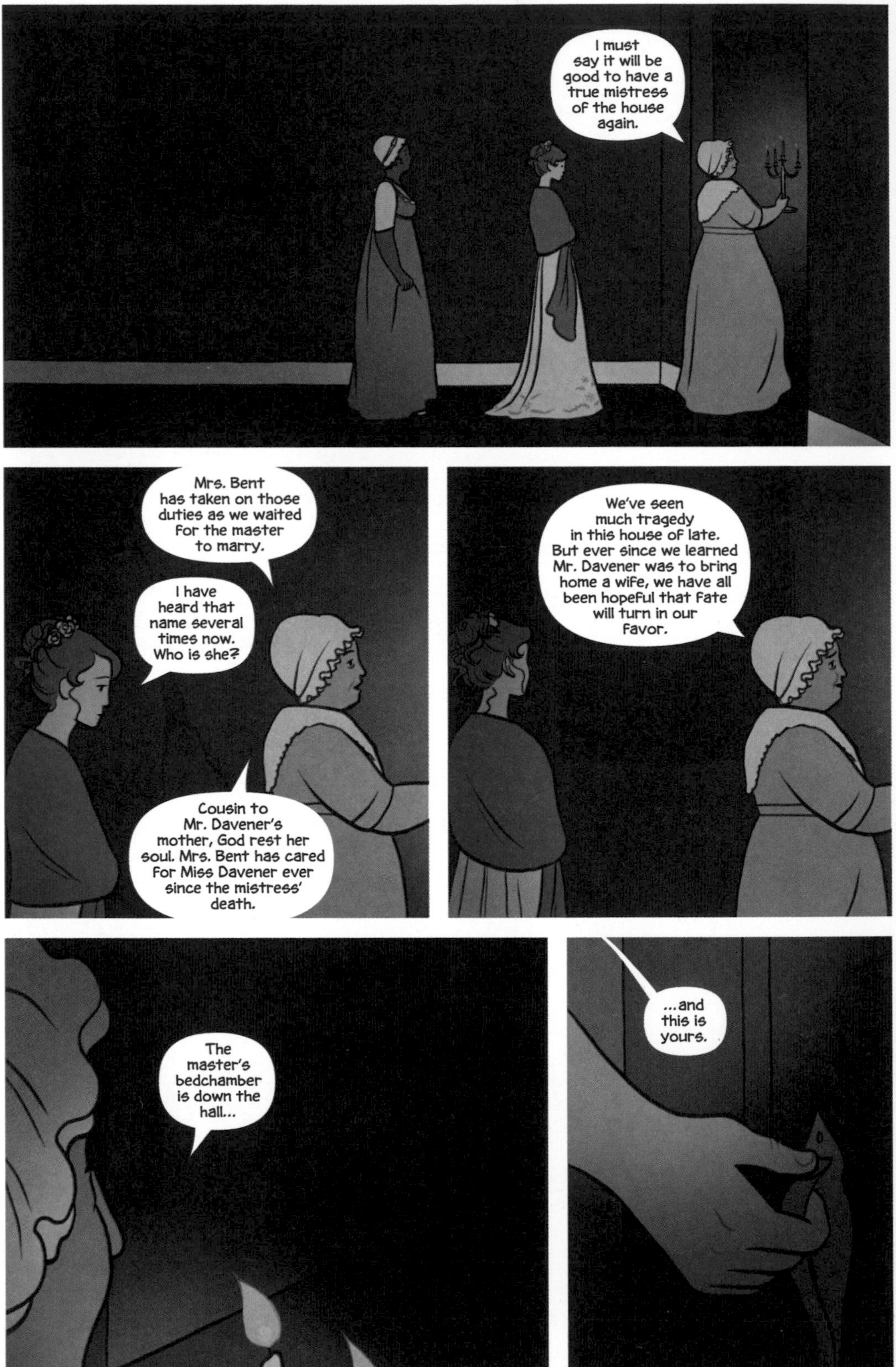
I must say it will be good to have a true mistress of the house again.
Mrs. Bent has taken on those duties as we waited for the master to marry.
I have heard that name several times now. Who is she?
Cousin to Mr. Davener's mother, God rest her soul. Mrs. Bent has cared for Miss Davener ever since the mistress' death.
We've seen much tragedy in this house of late. But ever since we learned Mr. Davener was to bring home a wife, we have all been hopeful that Fate will turn in our favor.
The master's bedchamber is down the hall...
...and this is yours.

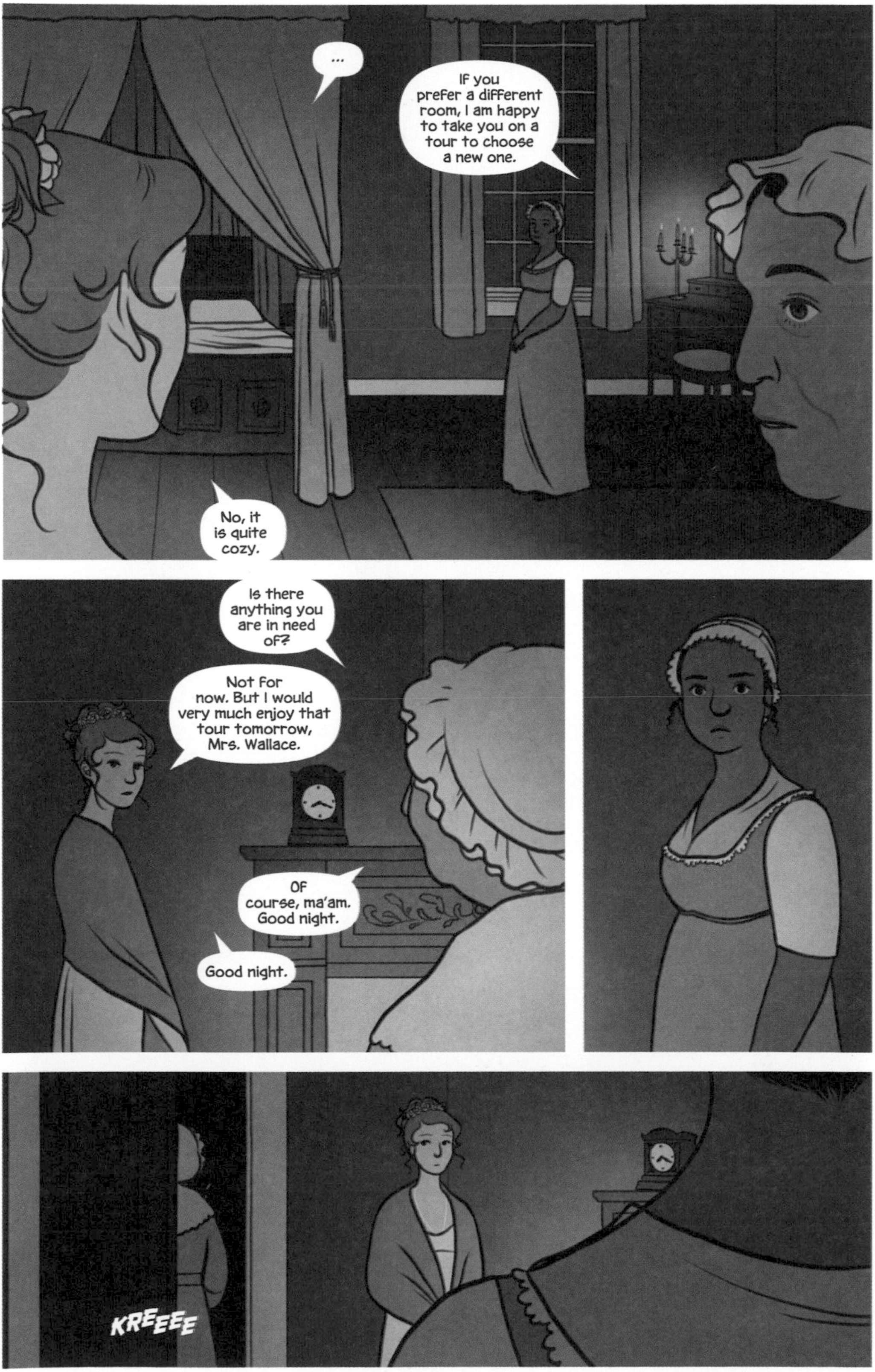
...
If you prefer a different room, I am happy to take you on a tour to choose a new one.
No, it is quite cozy.
Is there anything you are in need of?
Not for now. But I would very much enjoy that tour tomorrow, Mrs. Wallace.
Of course, ma'am. Good night.
Good night.
KREEEE

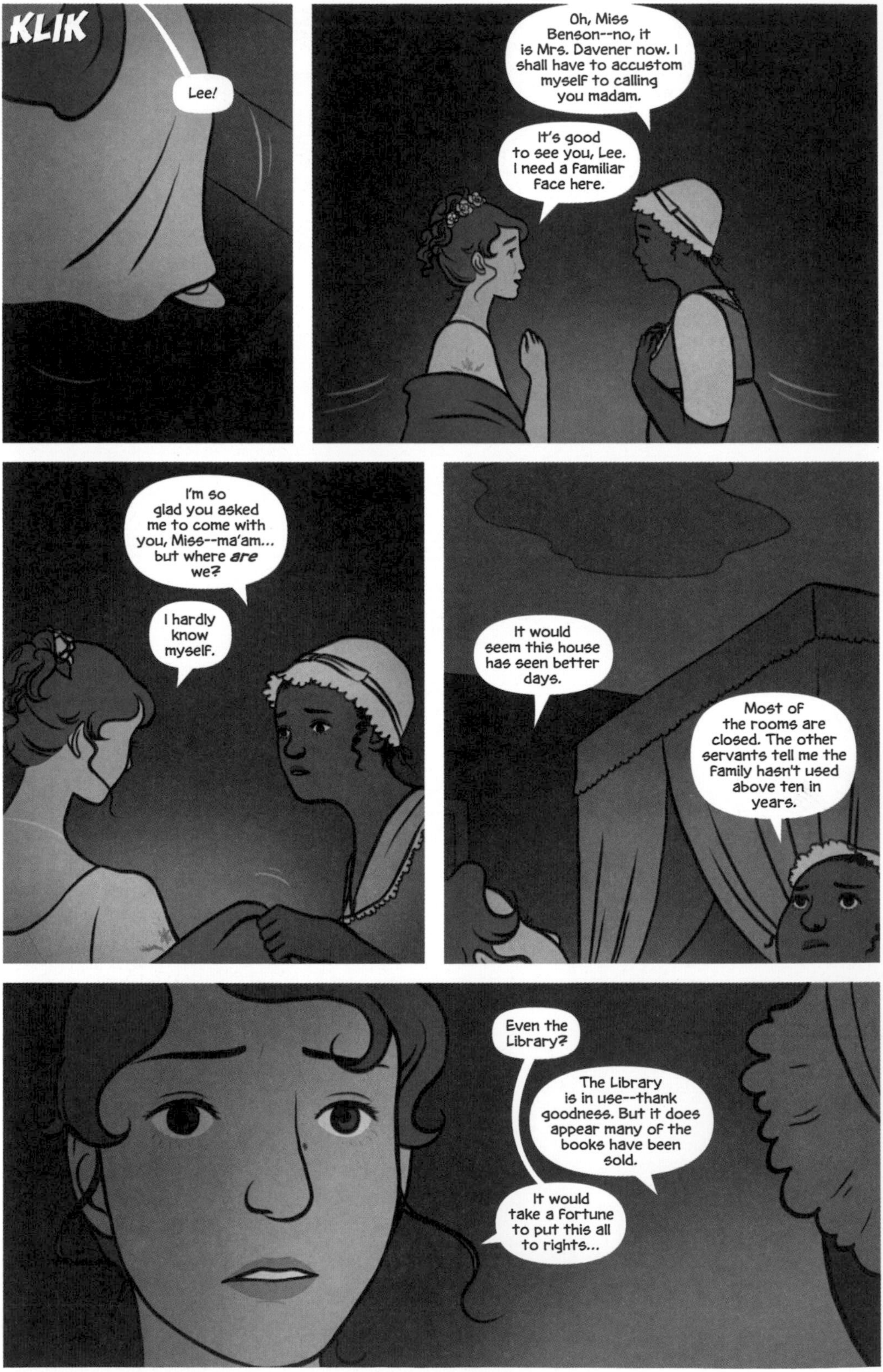
KLIK
Lee!
Oh, Miss Benson--no, it is Mrs. Davener now. I shall have to accustom myself to calling you madam.
It's good to see you, Lee. I need a familiar face here.
I'm so glad you asked me to come with you, Miss--ma'am... but where *are* we?
I hardly know myself.
It would seem this house has seen better days.
Most of the rooms are closed. The other servants tell me the family hasn't used above ten in years.
Even the Library?
The Library is in use--thank goodness. But it does appear many of the books have been sold.
It would take a fortune to put this all to rights...

Shall we get you more comfortable?

Yes, please. I am ready to be out of this gown, as beautiful as it is. There is no embroidery like yours.

You flatter me.

Your mother packed lace caps for you. I could not stop her.

...You know how I feel about caps.

I'll just leave them in the drawer then, should you ever wish to wear one.

They will be in that drawer a very long time.

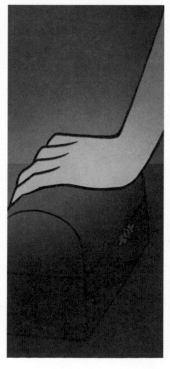

Lee?

Yes?

Would you ever marry, given the chance?

It depends on the chance, I suppose.

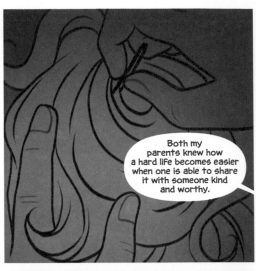

Both my parents knew how a hard life becomes easier when one is able to share it with someone kind and worthy.

But a woman loses her legal existence once she marries. I have seen too many marry cruel men for me to make that decision lightly.

Yet...I do want to be mistress of a house, one day, with servants of my own, and a good man to enjoy the days with.

You mean you *don't* wish to stay with me the rest of your life?

Terribly unprofessional for me to admit, I know.

There.

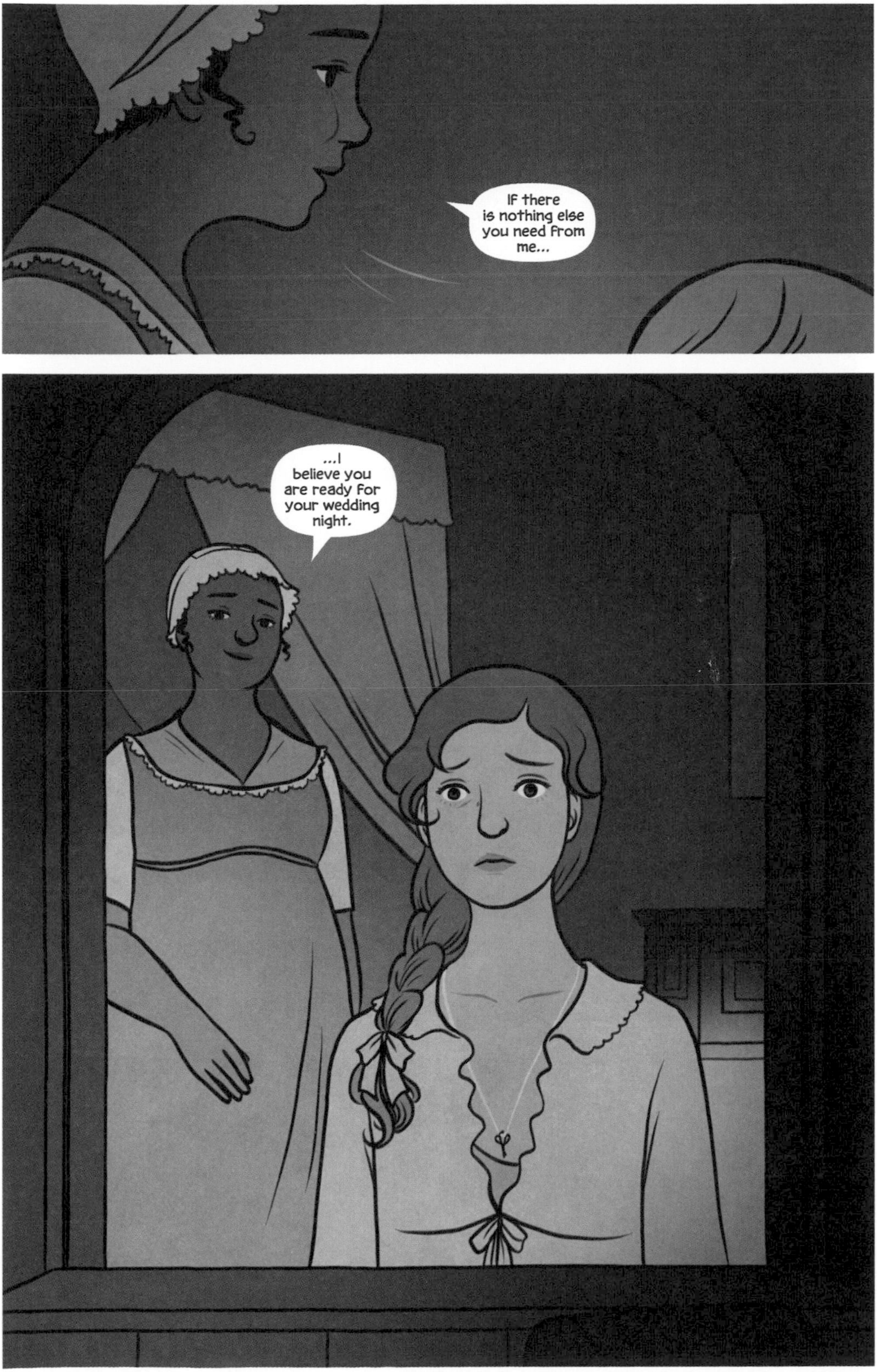
If there is nothing else you need from me...
...I believe you are ready for your wedding night.

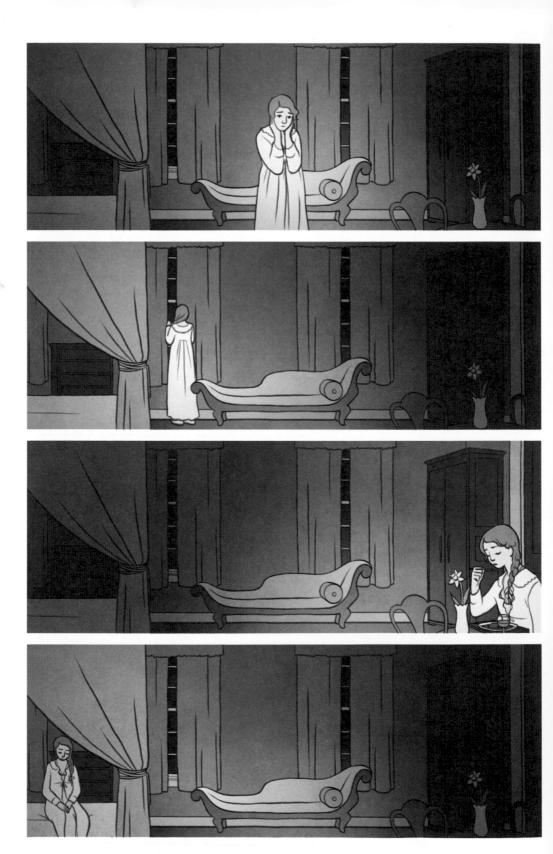

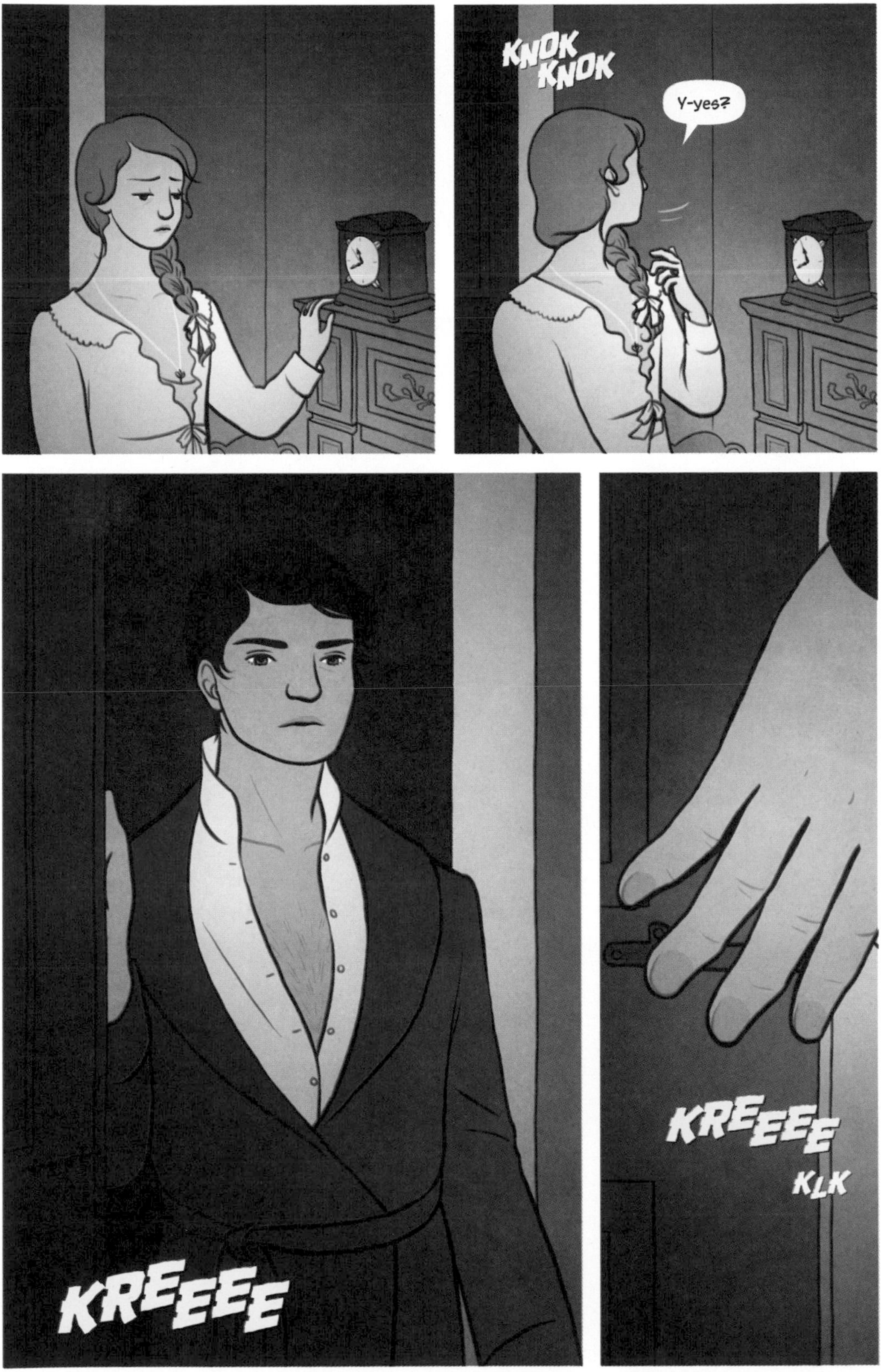
KNOK KNOK
Y-yes?
KREEEE
KREEEE
KLK

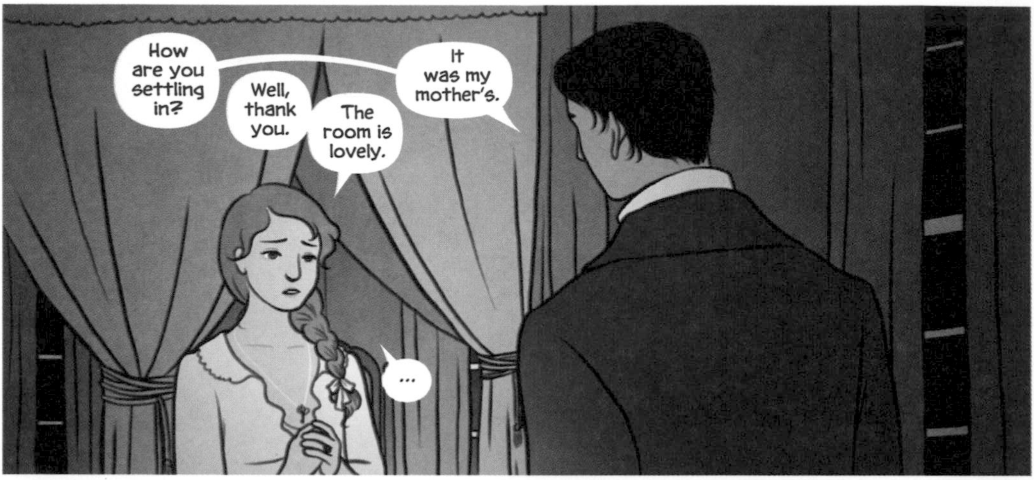
How are you settling in?
Well, thank you.
The room is lovely.
It was my mother's.
...

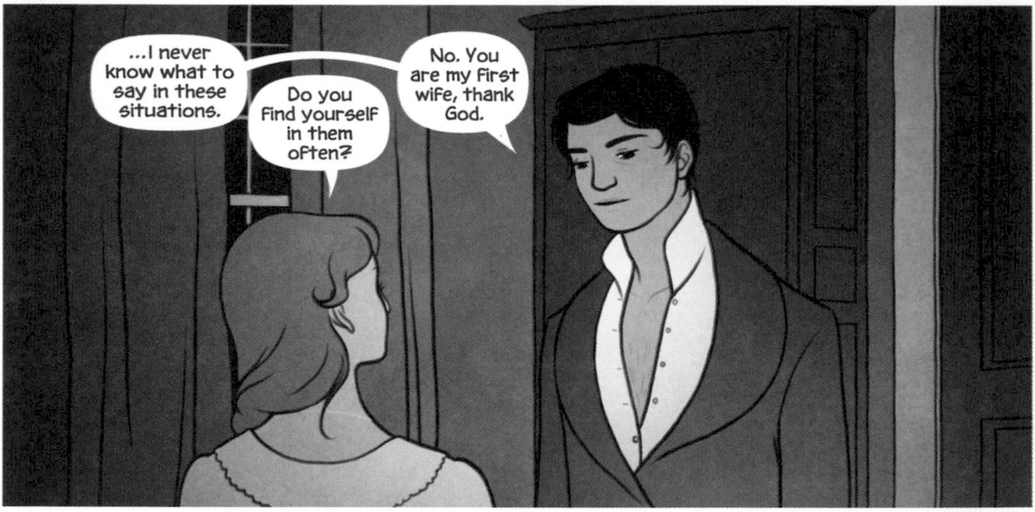
...I never know what to say in these situations.
Do you find yourself in them often?
No. You are my first wife, thank God.

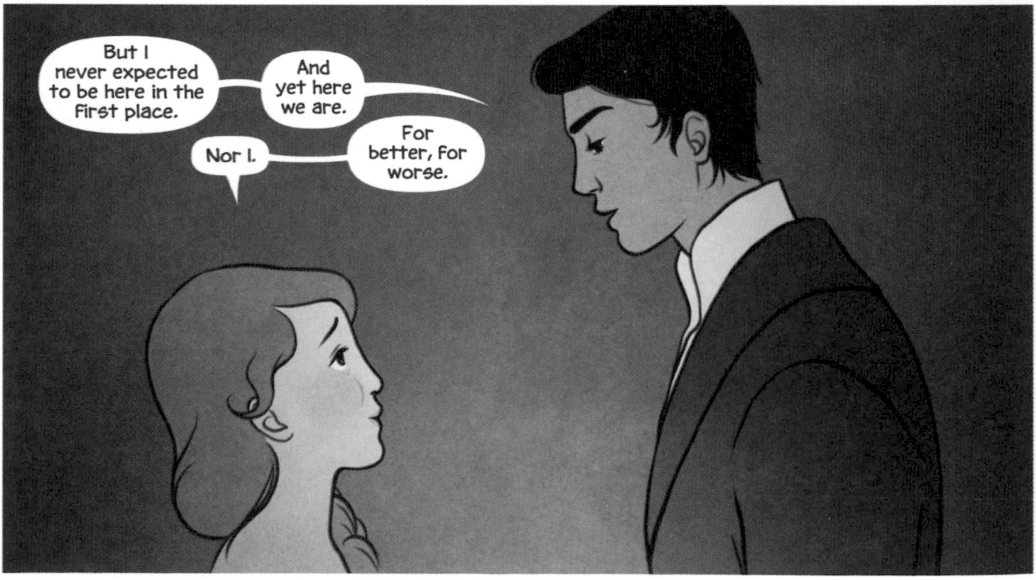
But I never expected to be here in the first place.
And yet here we are.
Nor I.
For better, for worse.

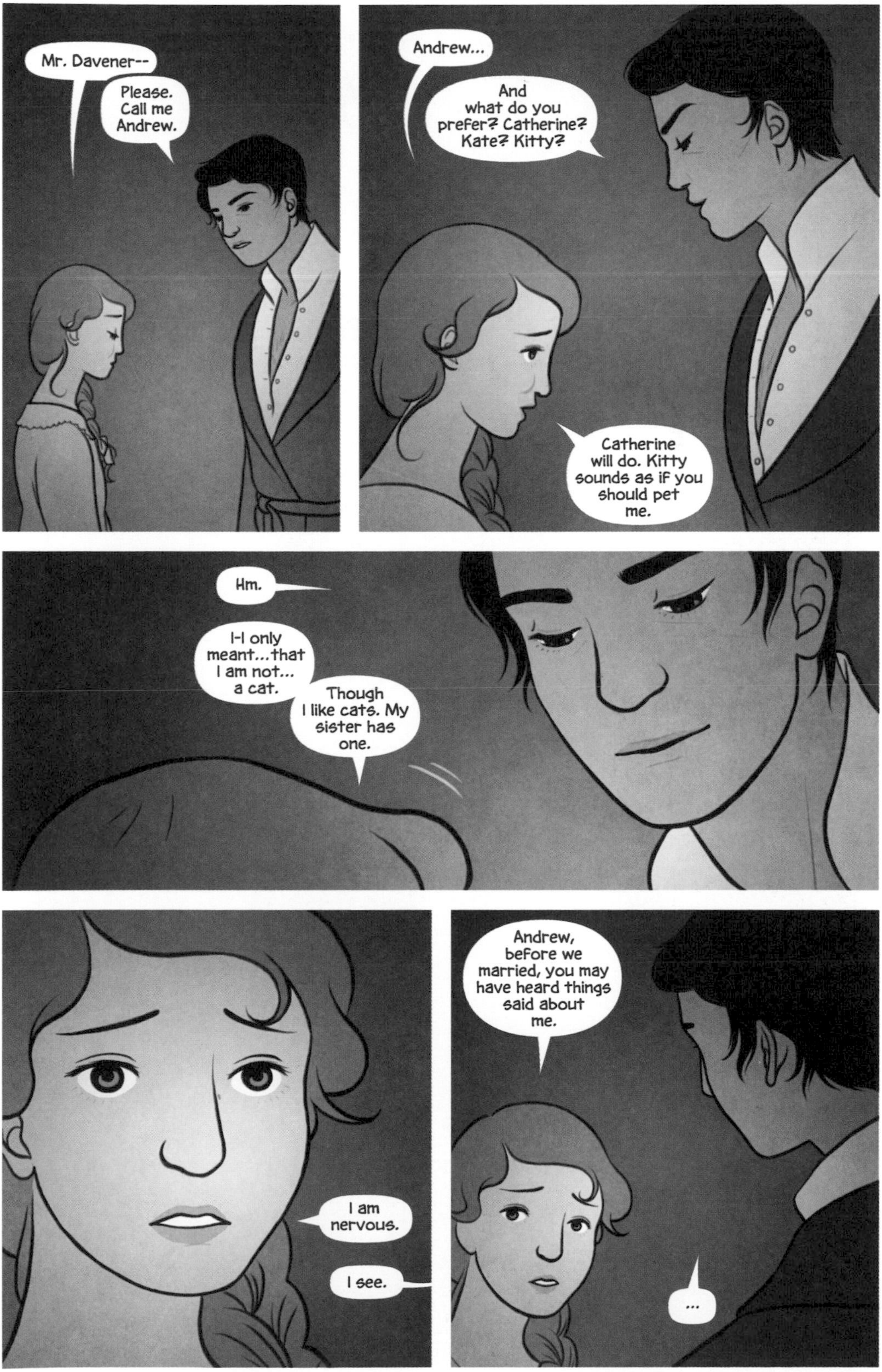
Mr. Davener--
Please. Call me Andrew.
Andrew...
And what do you prefer? Catherine? Kate? Kitty?
Catherine will do. Kitty sounds as if you should pet me.
Hm.
I-I only meant...that I am not... a cat.
Though I like cats. My sister has one.
I am nervous.
I see.
Andrew, before we married, you may have heard things said about me.
...

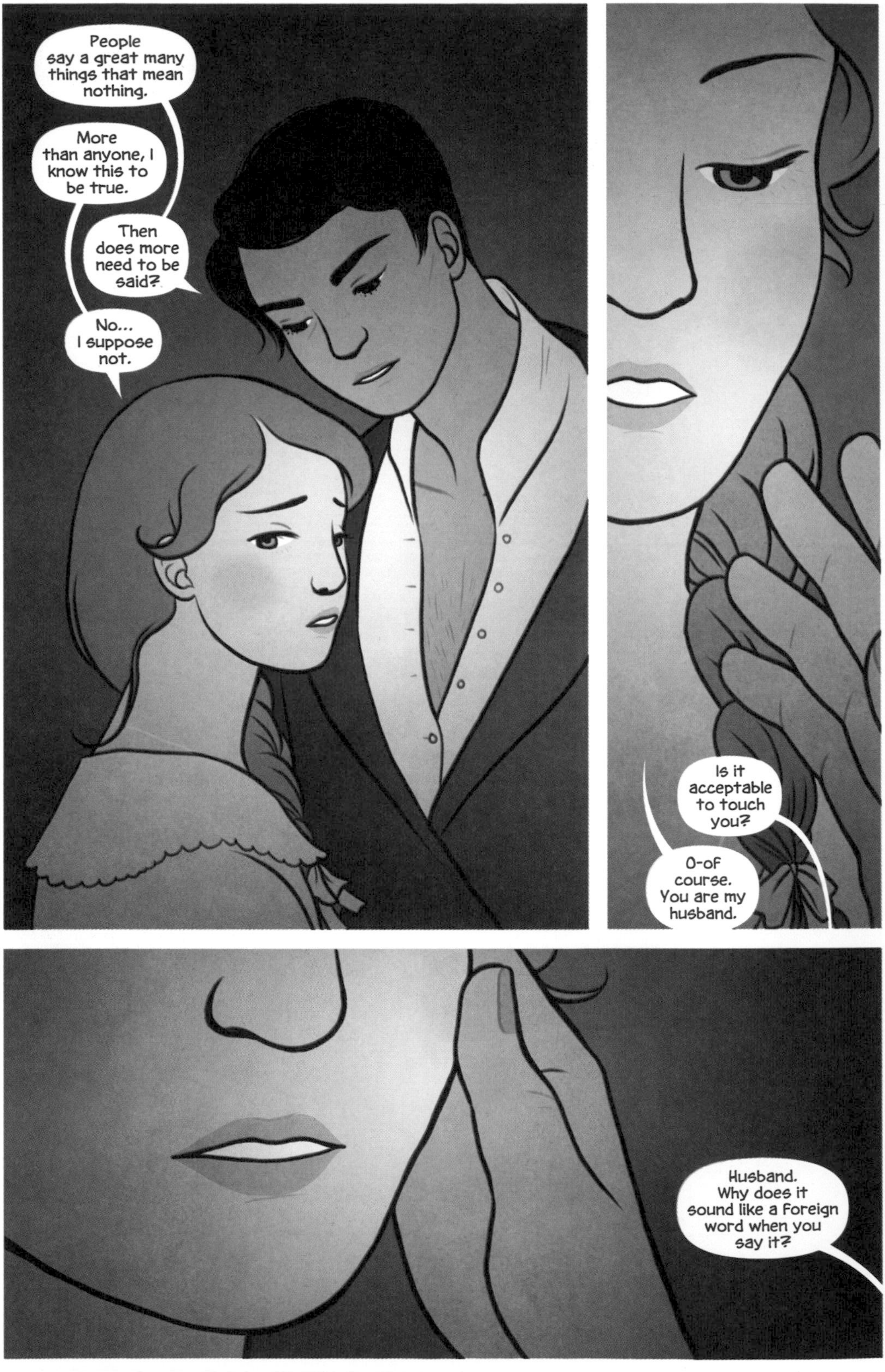

People say a great many things that mean nothing.
More than anyone, I know this to be true.
Then does more need to be said?
No... I suppose not.
Is it acceptable to touch you?
O-of course. You are my husband.
Husband. Why does it sound like a foreign word when you say it?

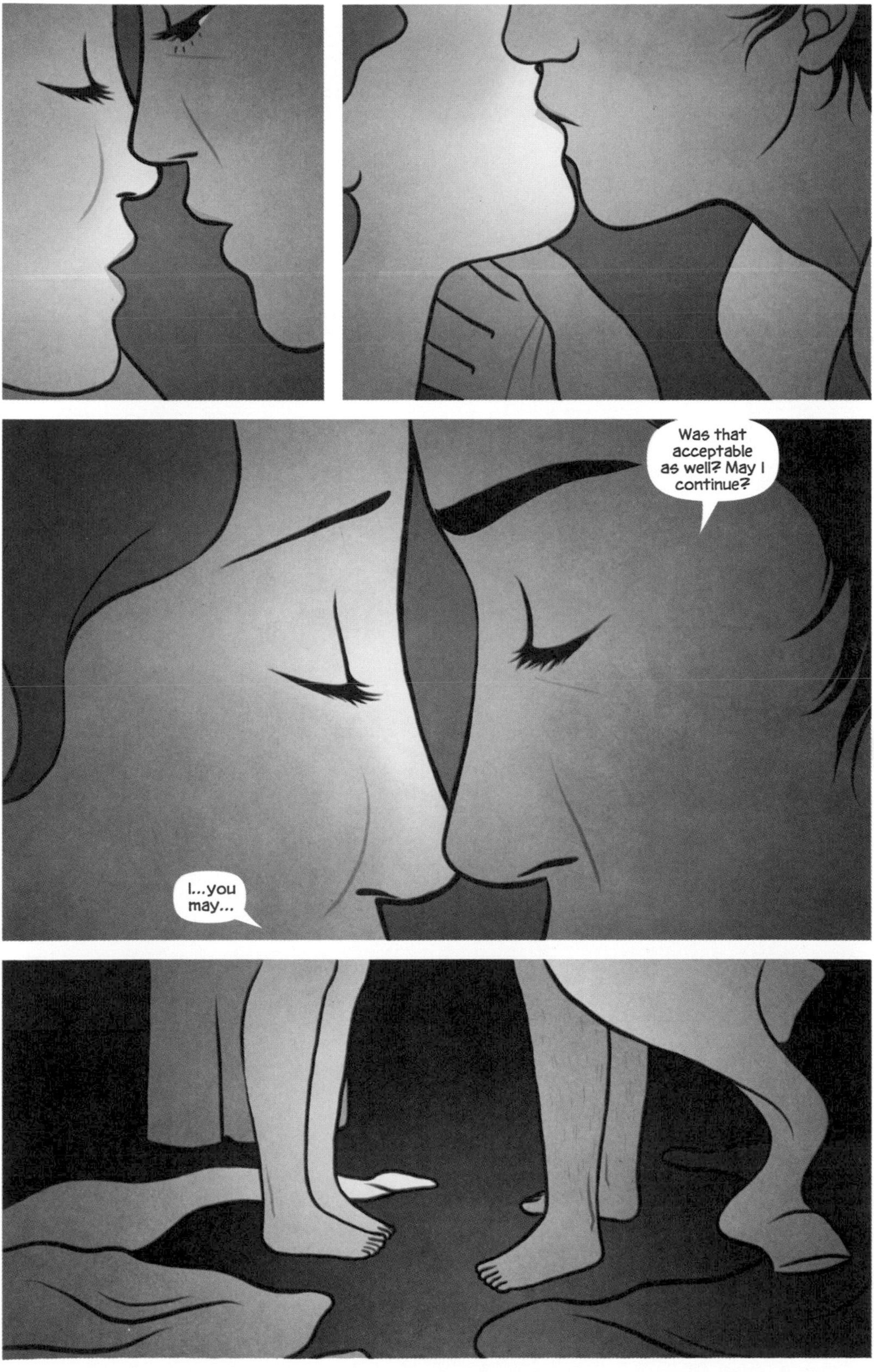
Was that acceptable as well? May I continue?
I...you may...

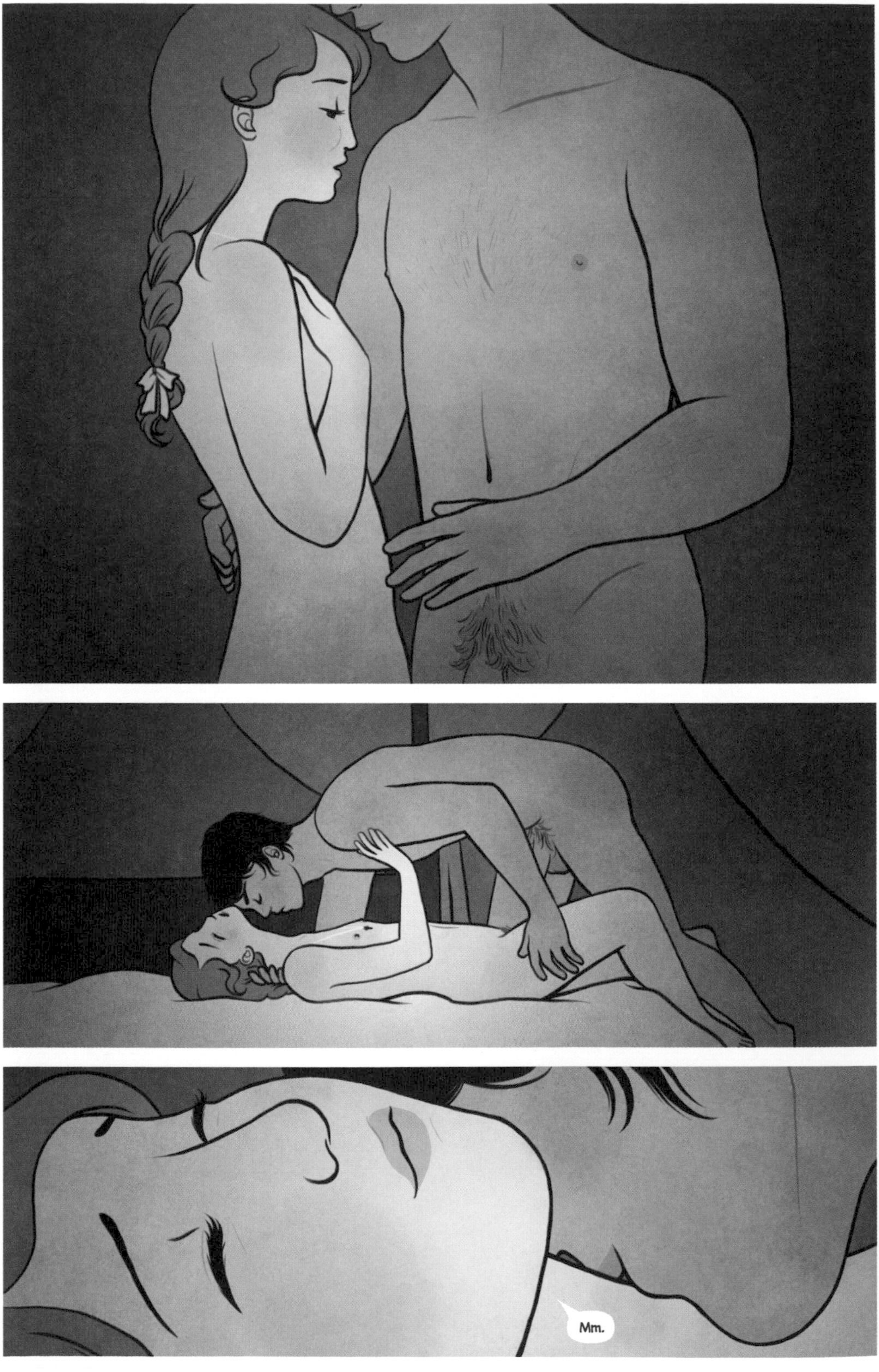
Mm.

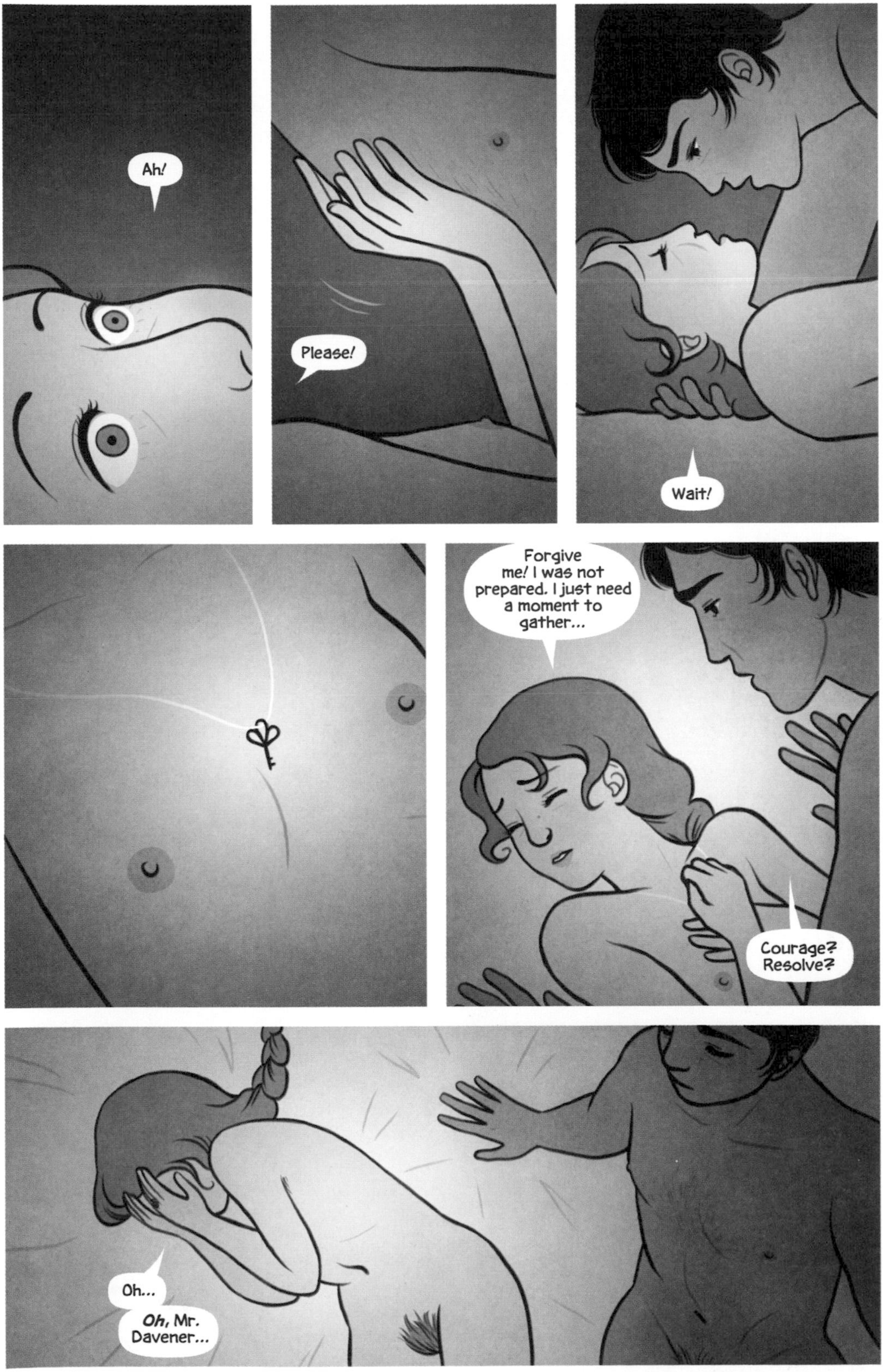
Ah!
Please!
Wait!
Forgive me! I was not prepared. I just need a moment to gather...
Courage? Resolve?
Oh...
Oh, Mr. Davener...

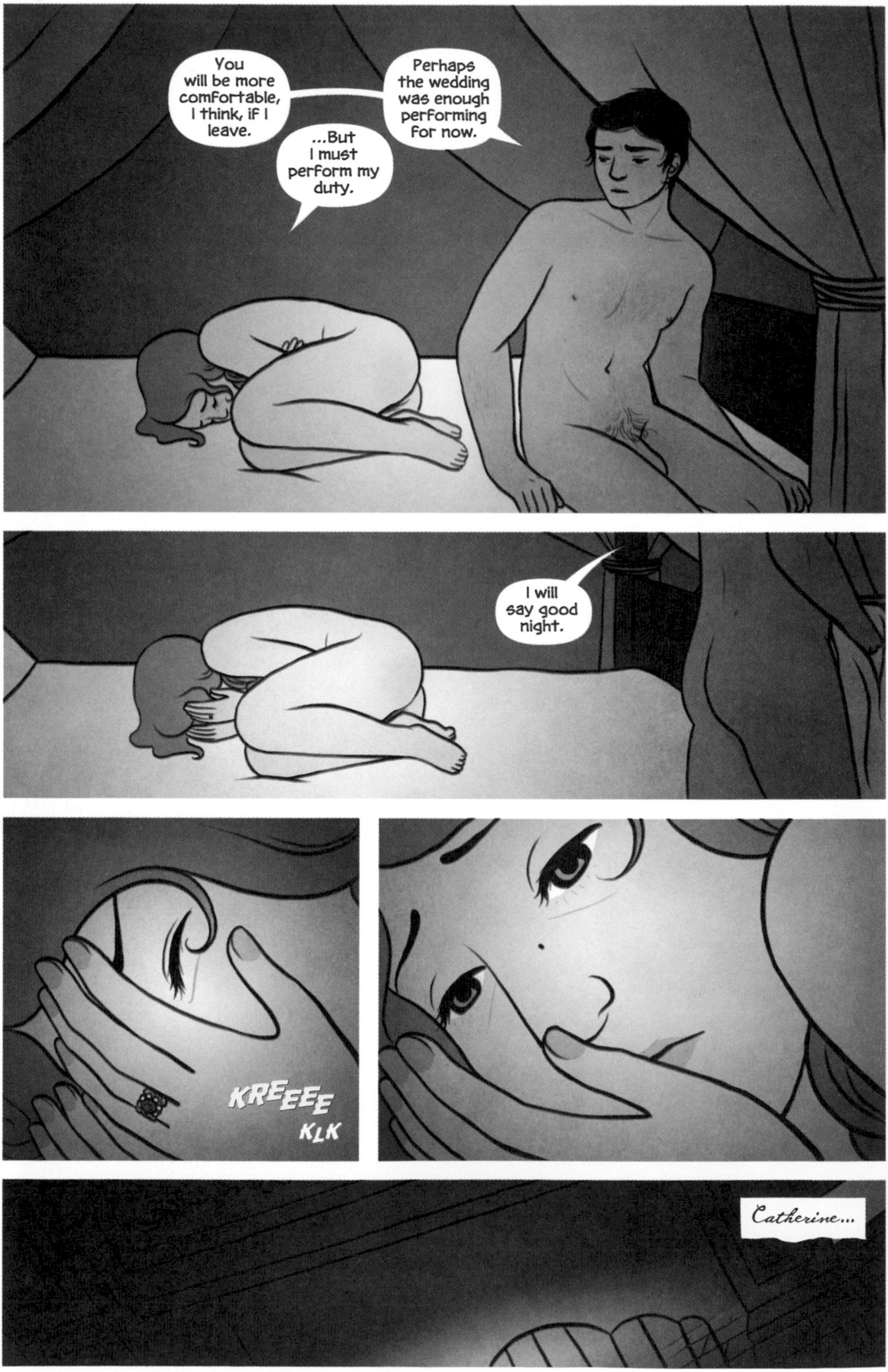
You will be more comfortable, I think, if I leave.
Perhaps the wedding was enough performing for now.
...But I must perform my duty.
I will say good night.
KREEEE
KLK
Catherine...

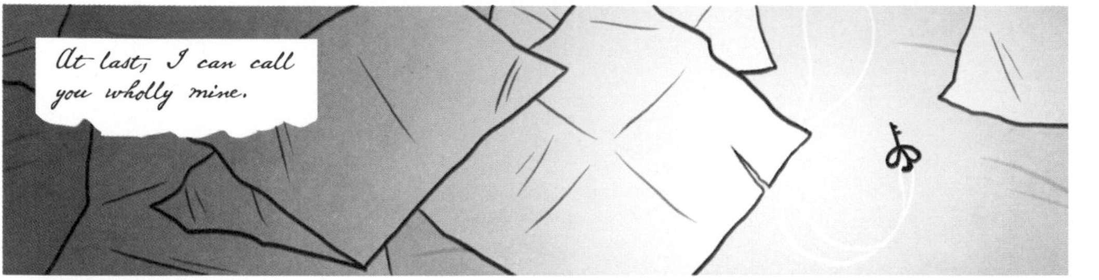
At last, I can call you wholly mine.

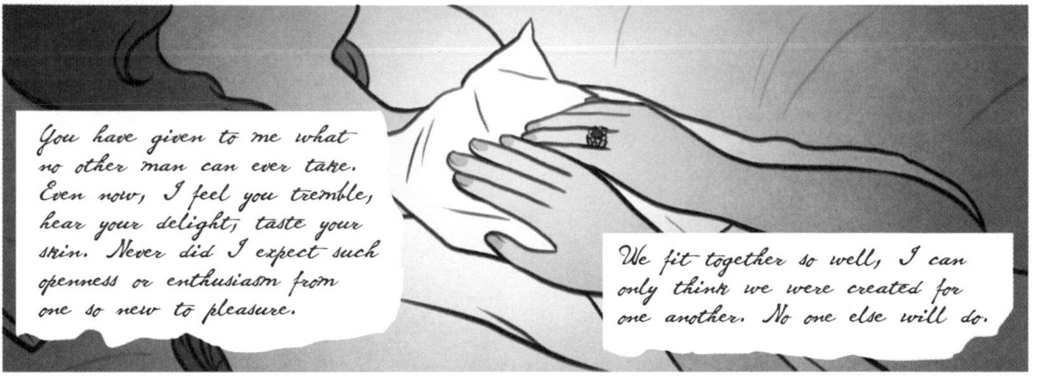
You have given to me what no other man can ever take. Even now, I feel you tremble, hear your delight, taste your skin. Never did I expect such openness or enthusiasm from one so new to pleasure.
We fit together so well, I can only think we were created for one another. No one else will do.

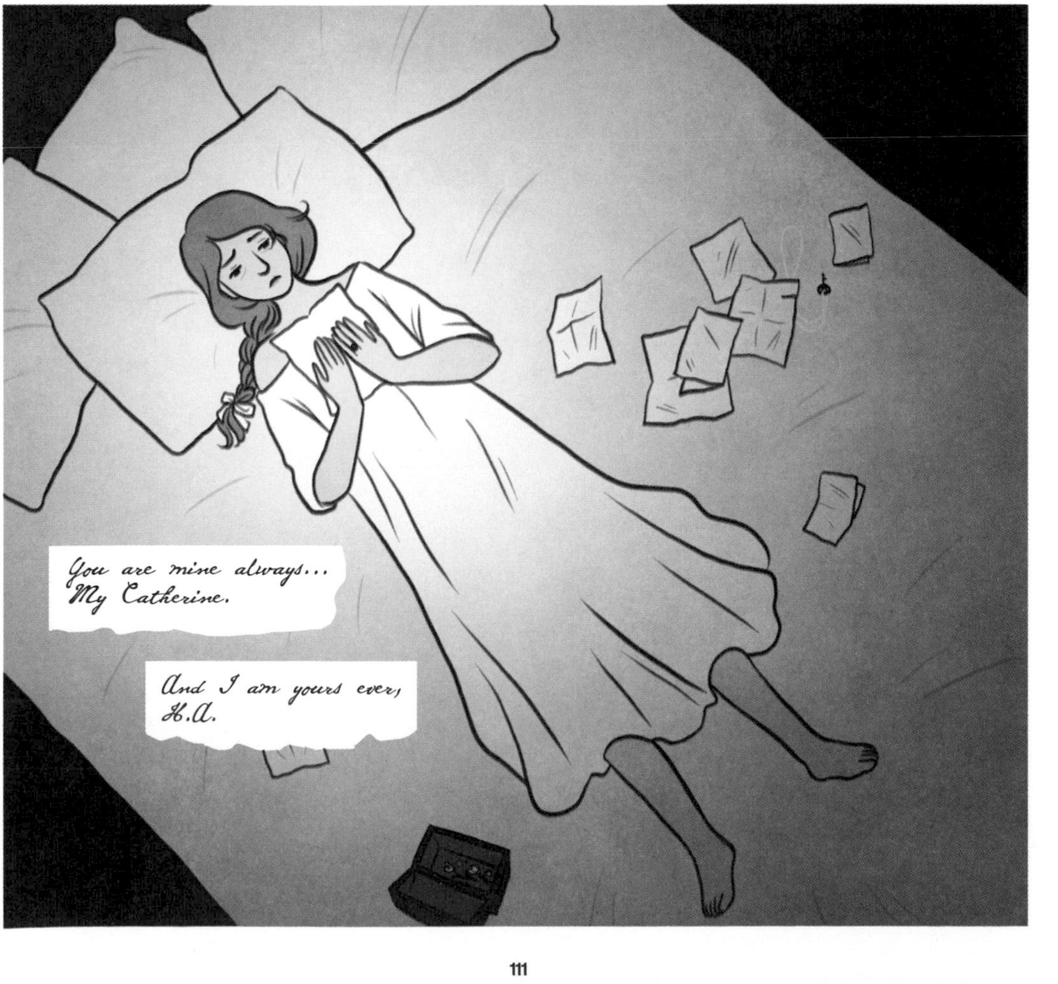
You are mine always... My Catherine.
And I am yours ever, H.A.

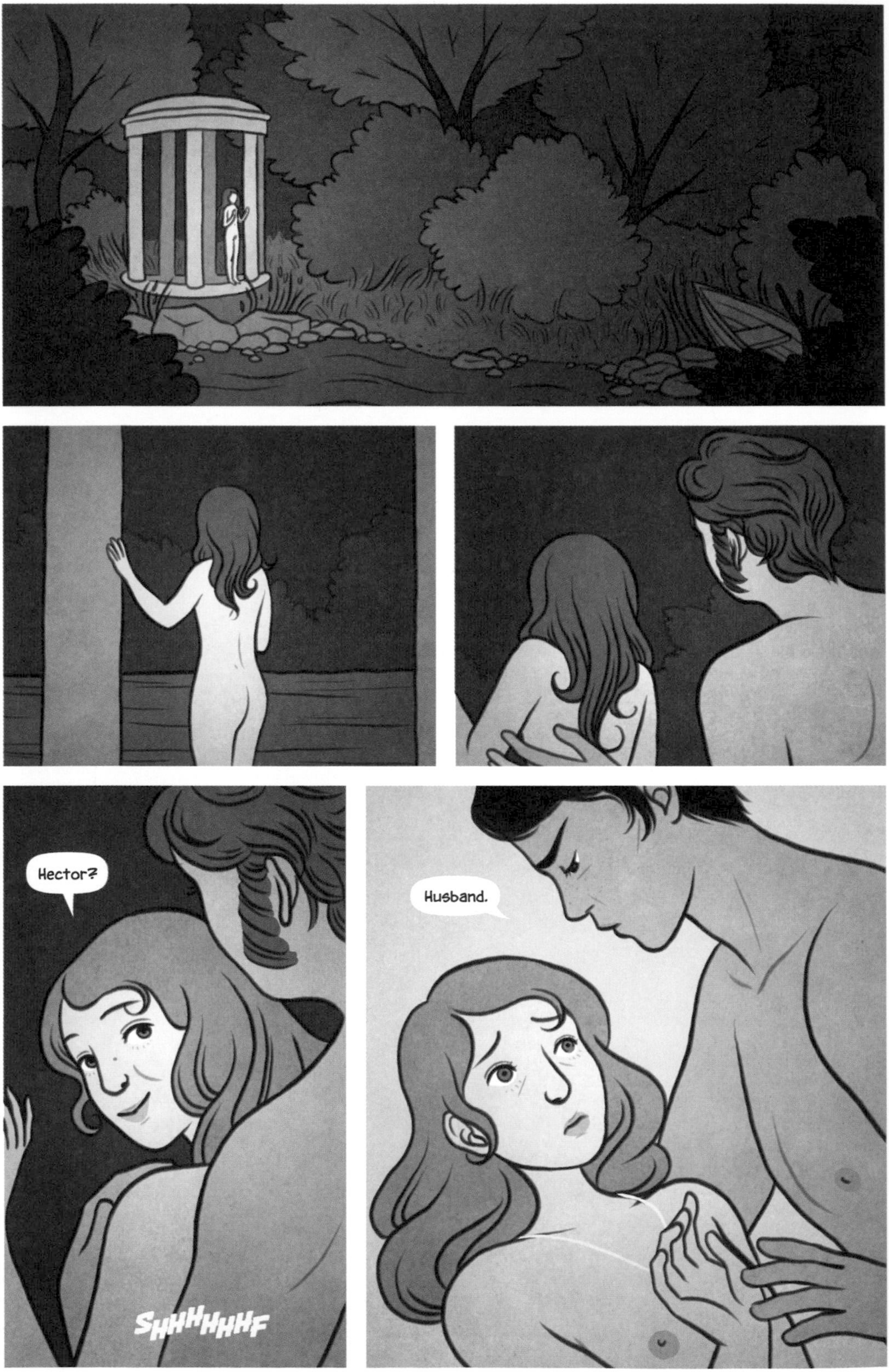
Hector?
SHHHHHHF
Husband.

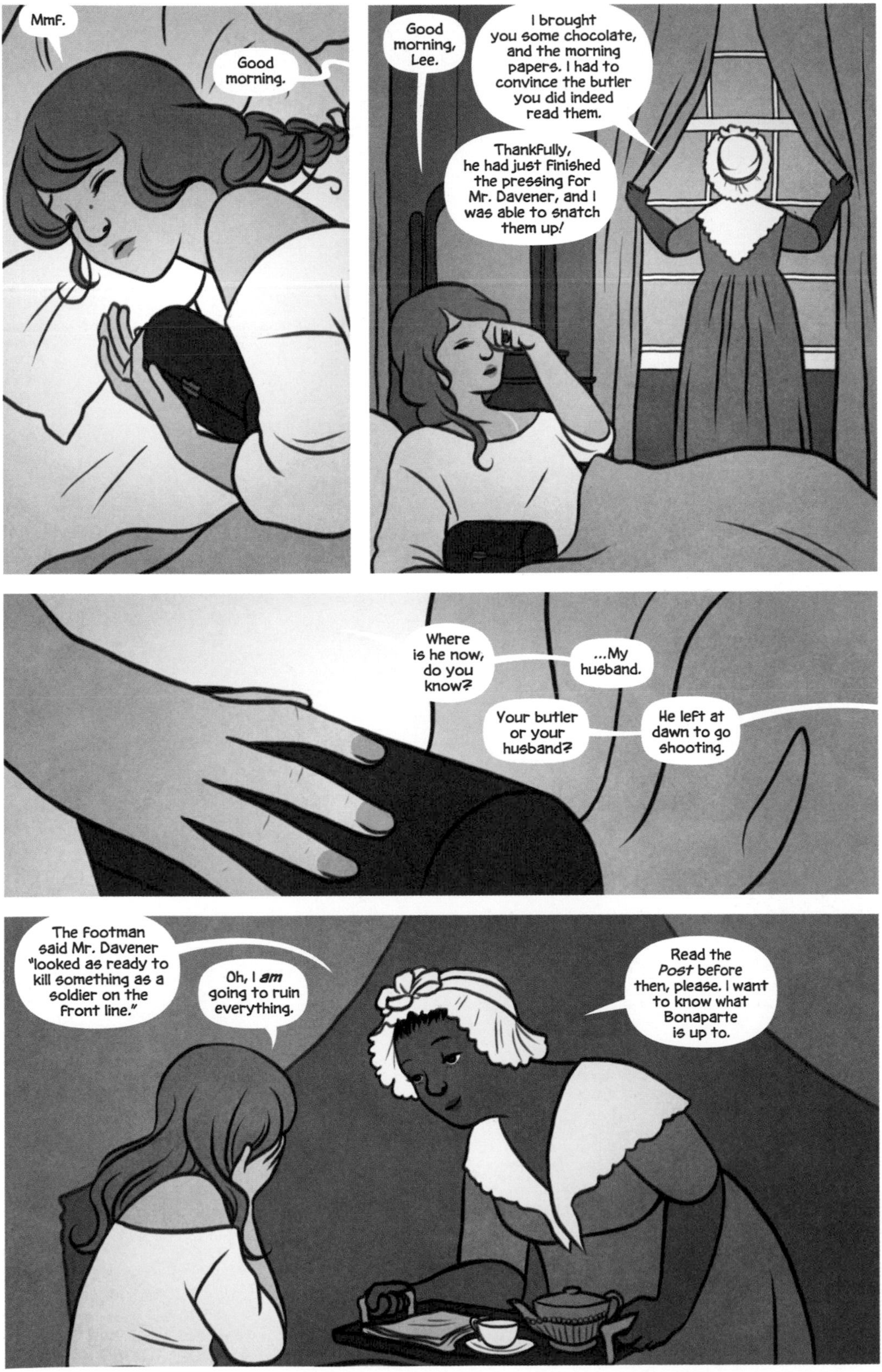
Mmf.
Good morning.
Good morning, Lee.
I brought you some chocolate, and the morning papers. I had to convince the butler you did indeed read them.
Thankfully, he had just finished the pressing for Mr. Davener, and I was able to snatch them up!
Where is he now, do you know?
...My husband.
Your butler or your husband?
He left at dawn to go shooting.
The footman said Mr. Davener "looked as ready to kill something as a soldier on the front line."
Oh, I *am* going to ruin everything.
Read the *Post* before then, please. I want to know what Bonaparte is up to.

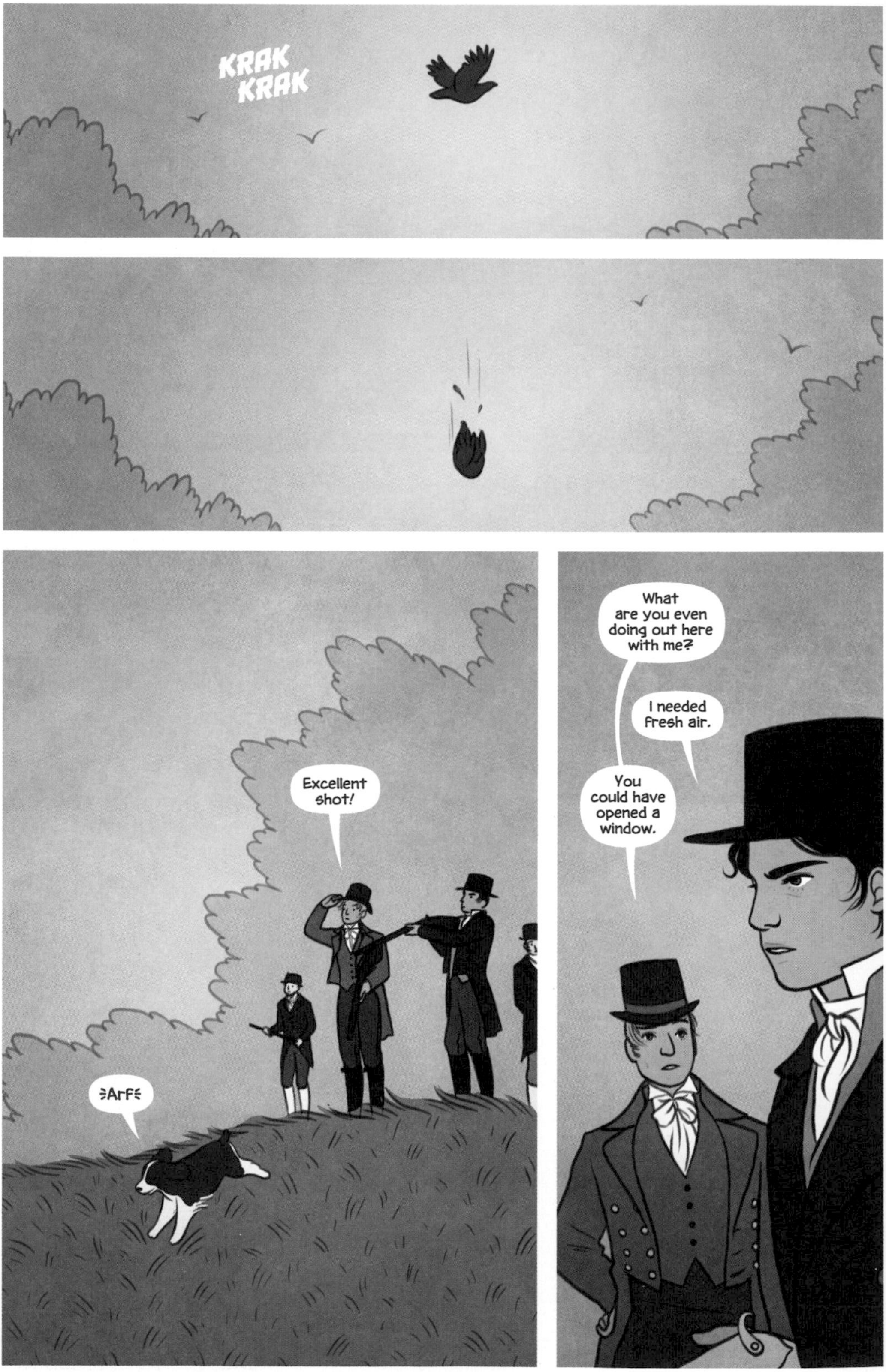
KRAK
KRAK
Excellent shot!
≶Arf≷
What are you even doing out here with me?
I needed fresh air.
You could have opened a window.

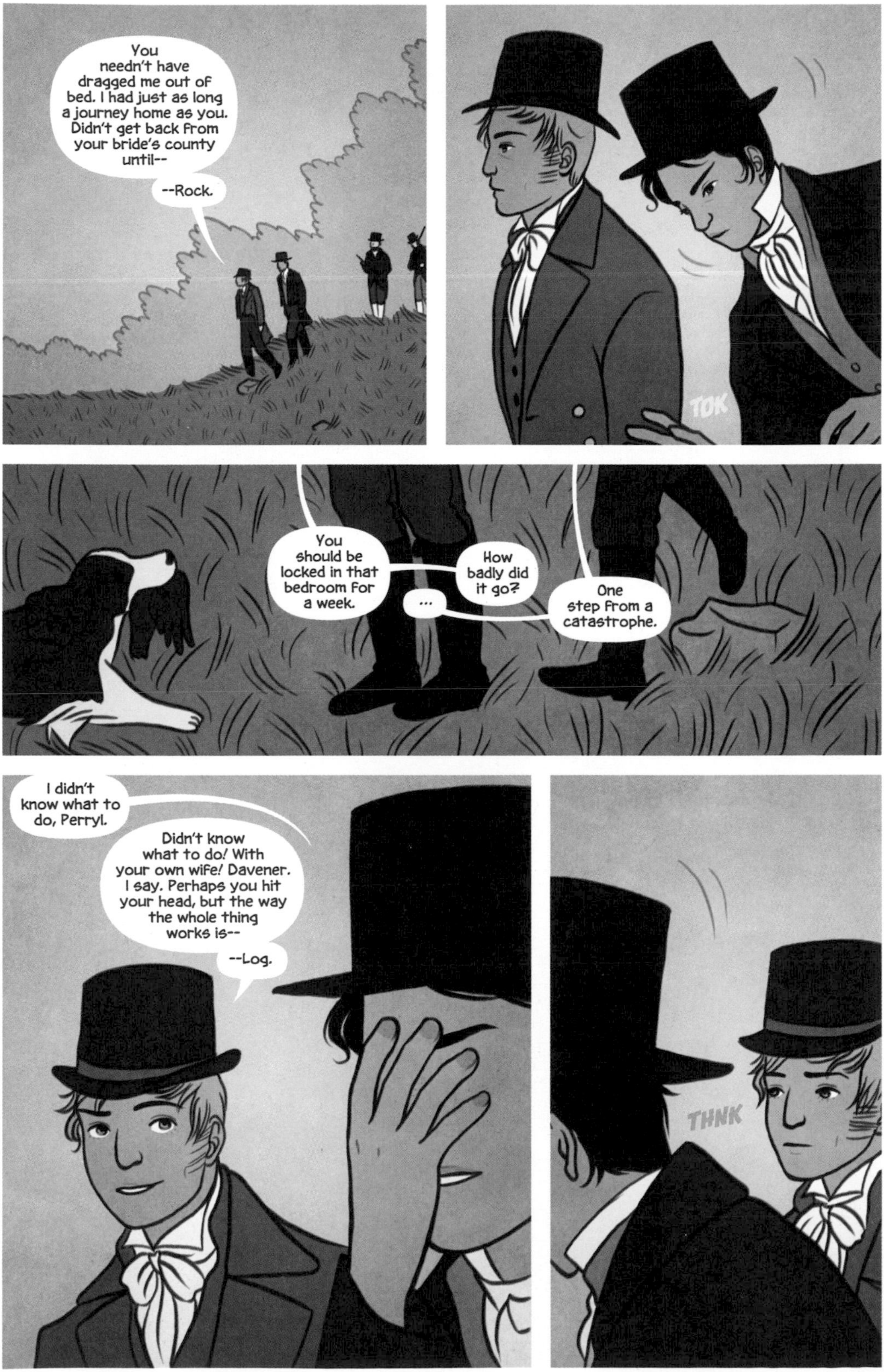
You needn't have dragged me out of bed. I had just as long a journey home as you. Didn't get back from your bride's county until--
--Rock.
TOK
You should be locked in that bedroom for a week.
How badly did it go?
...
One step from a catastrophe.
I didn't know what to do, Perryl.
Didn't know what to do! With your own wife! Davener. I say. Perhaps you hit your head, but the way the whole thing works is--
--Log.
THNK

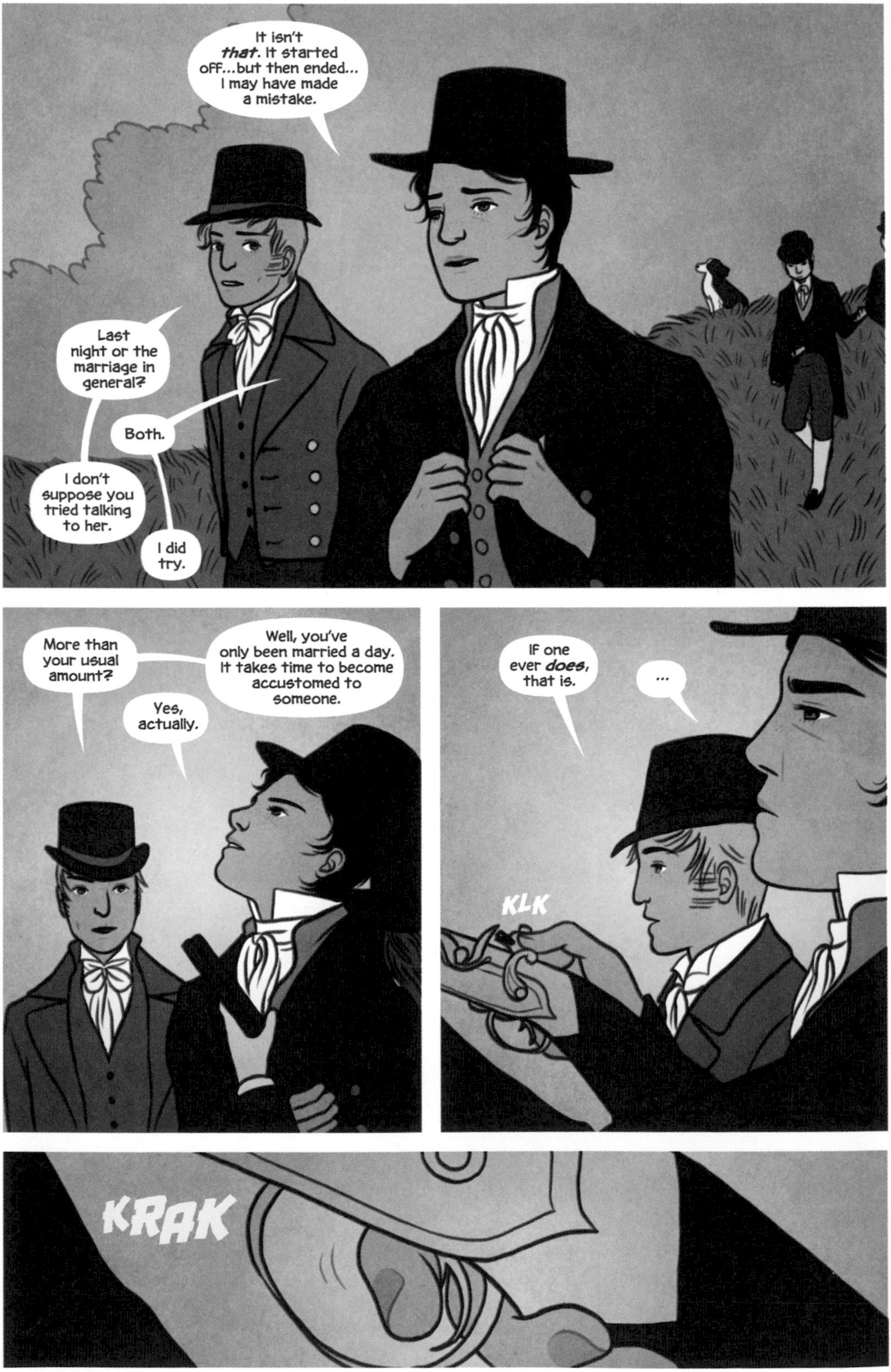
It isn't *that*. It started off...but then ended... I may have made a mistake.
Last night or the marriage in general?
Both.
I don't suppose you tried talking to her.
I did try.
More than your usual amount?
Well, you've only been married a day. It takes time to become accustomed to someone.
Yes, actually.
If one ever *does*, that is.
...
KLK
KRAK

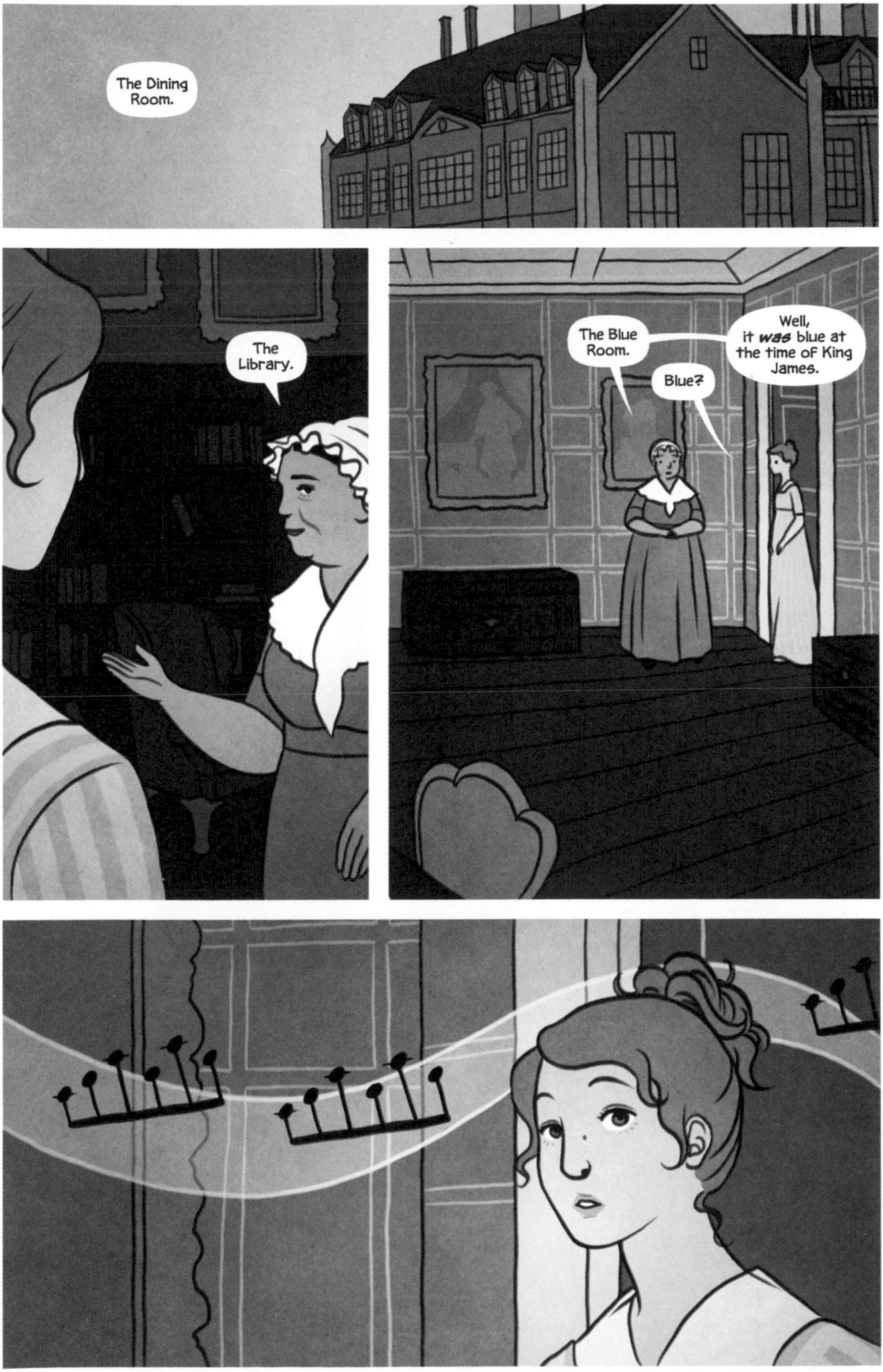
The Dining Room.
The Library.
The Blue Room.
Blue?
Well, it *was* blue at the time of King James.

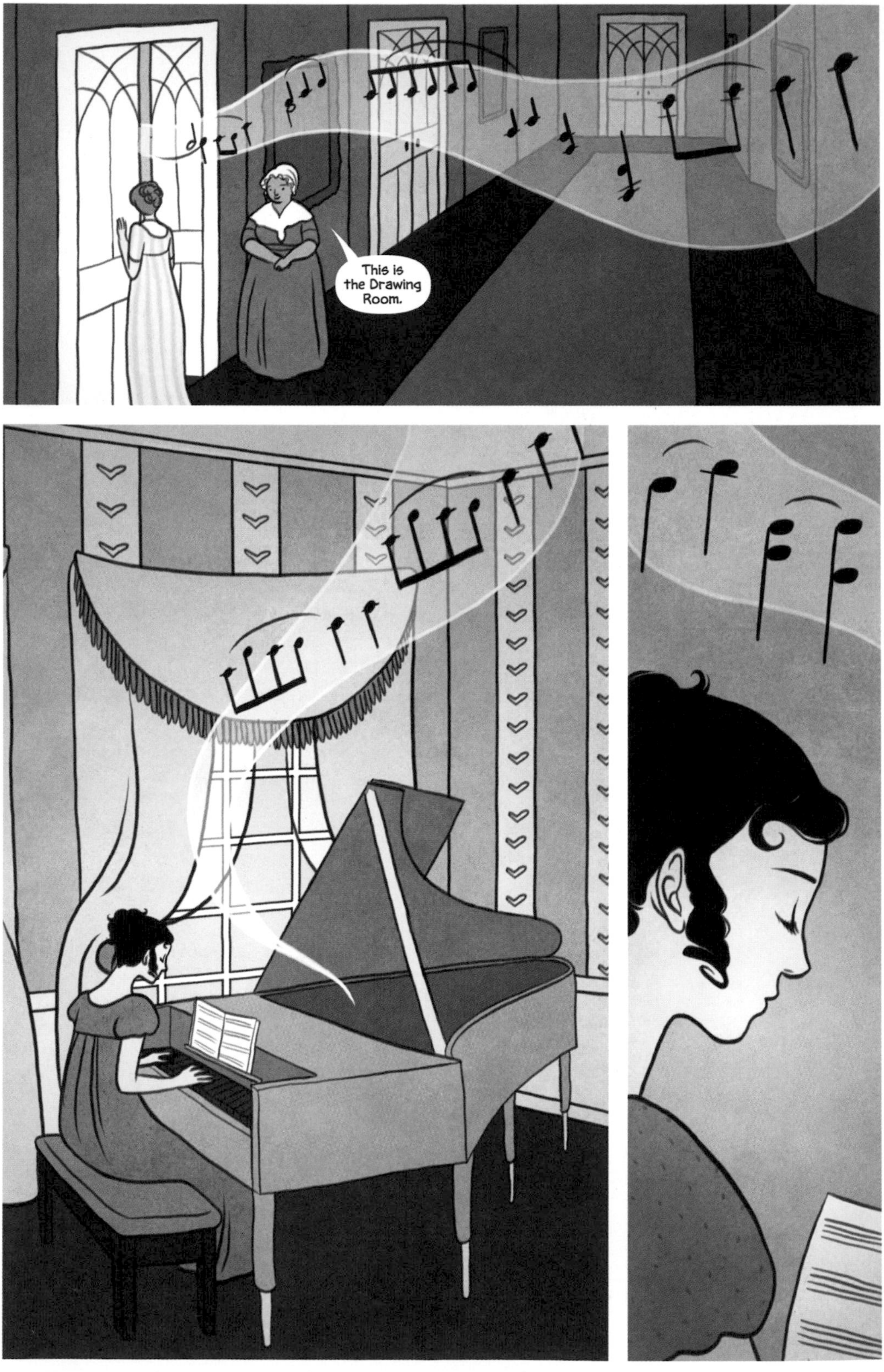
This is the Drawing Room.

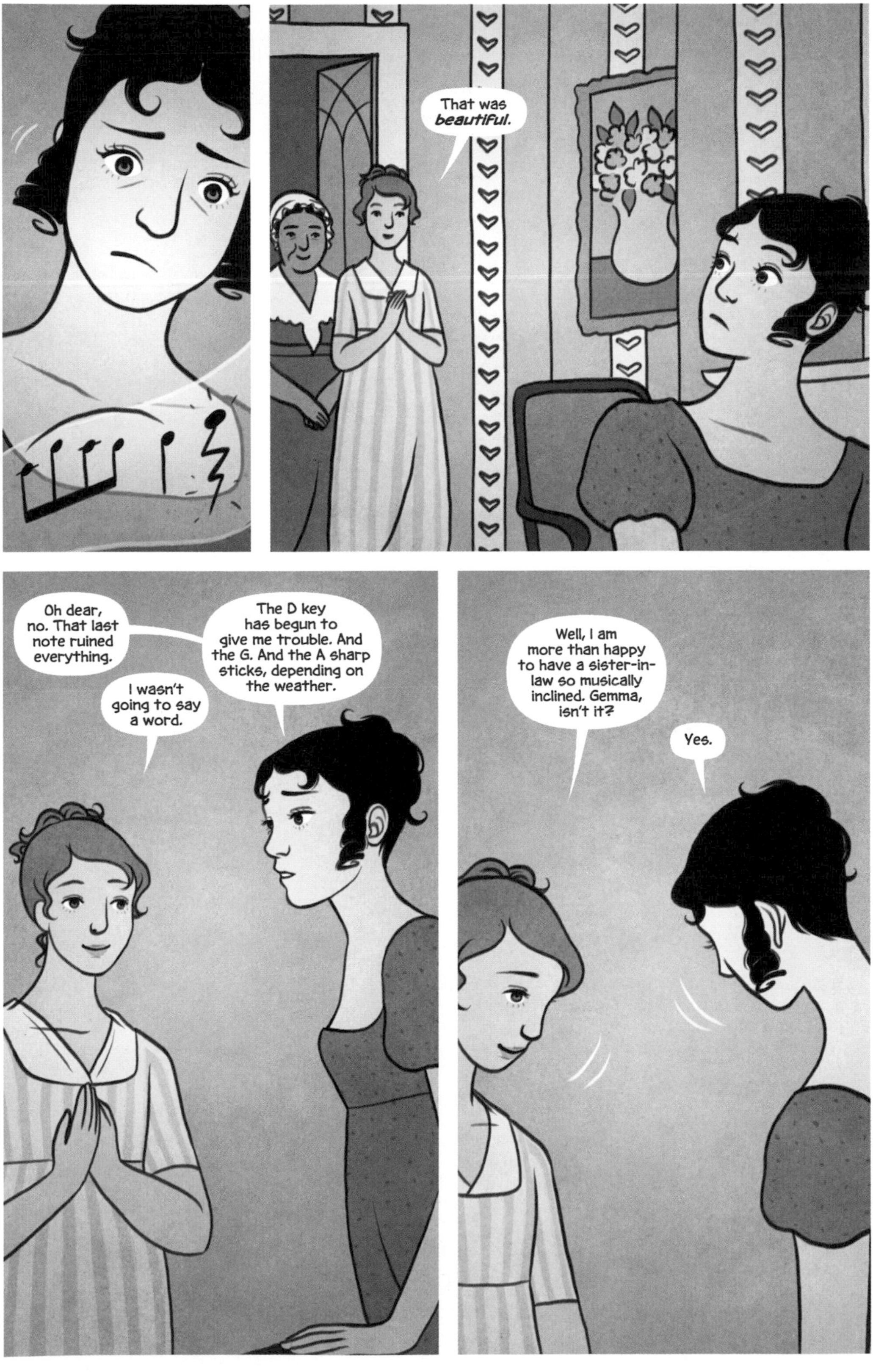

That was *beautiful.*
Oh dear, no. That last note ruined everything.
The D key has begun to give me trouble. And the G. And the A sharp sticks, depending on the weather.
I wasn't going to say a word.
Well, I am more than happy to have a sister-in-law so musically inclined. Gemma, isn't it?
Yes.

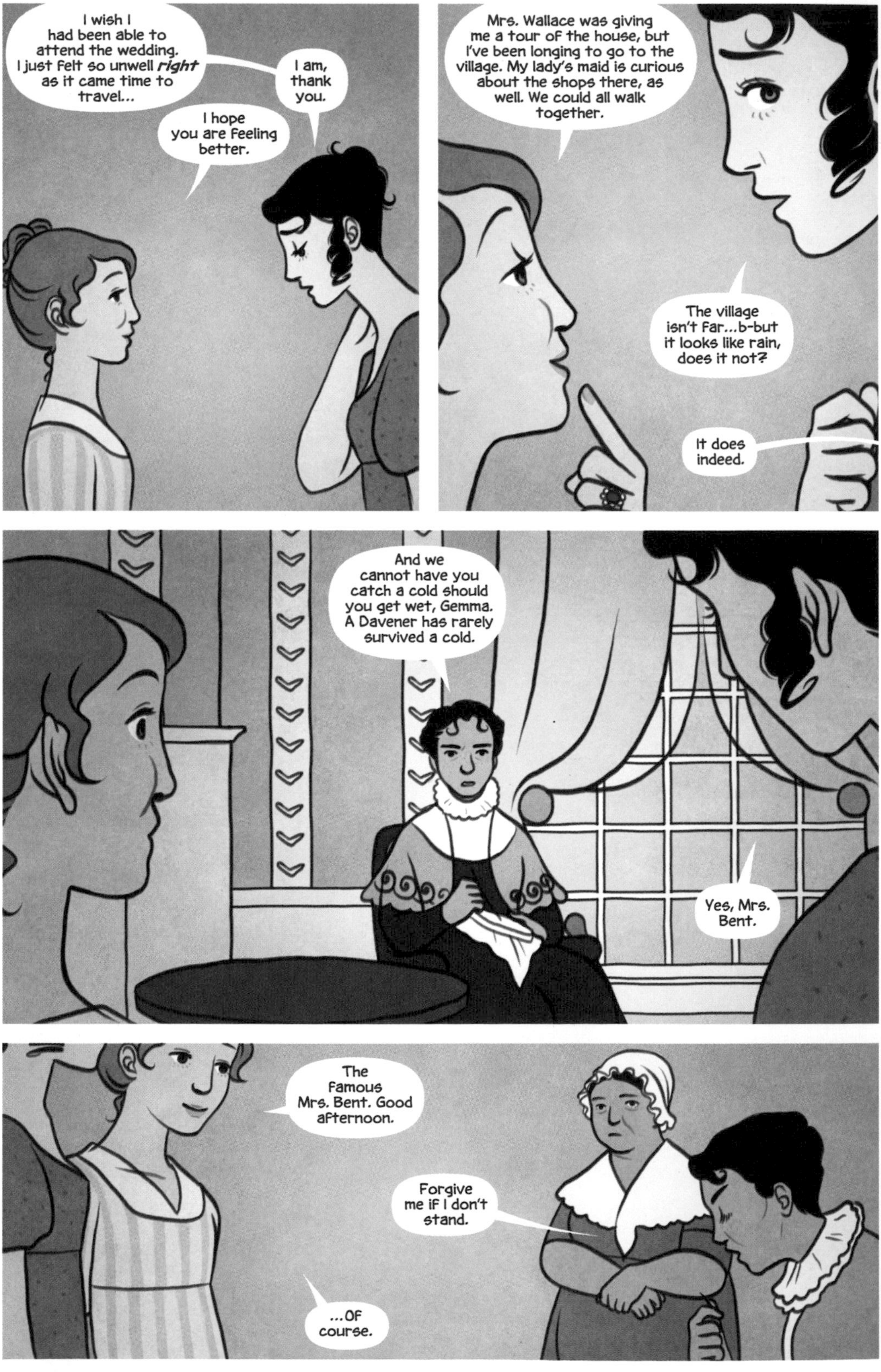
I wish I had been able to attend the wedding. I just felt so unwell *right* as it came time to travel...
I am, thank you.
I hope you are feeling better.
Mrs. Wallace was giving me a tour of the house, but I've been longing to go to the village. My lady's maid is curious about the shops there, as well. We could all walk together.
The village isn't far...b-but it looks like rain, does it not?
It does indeed.
And we cannot have you catch a cold should you get wet, Gemma. A Davener has rarely survived a cold.
Yes, Mrs. Bent.
The famous Mrs. Bent. Good afternoon.
Forgive me if I don't stand.
...Of course.

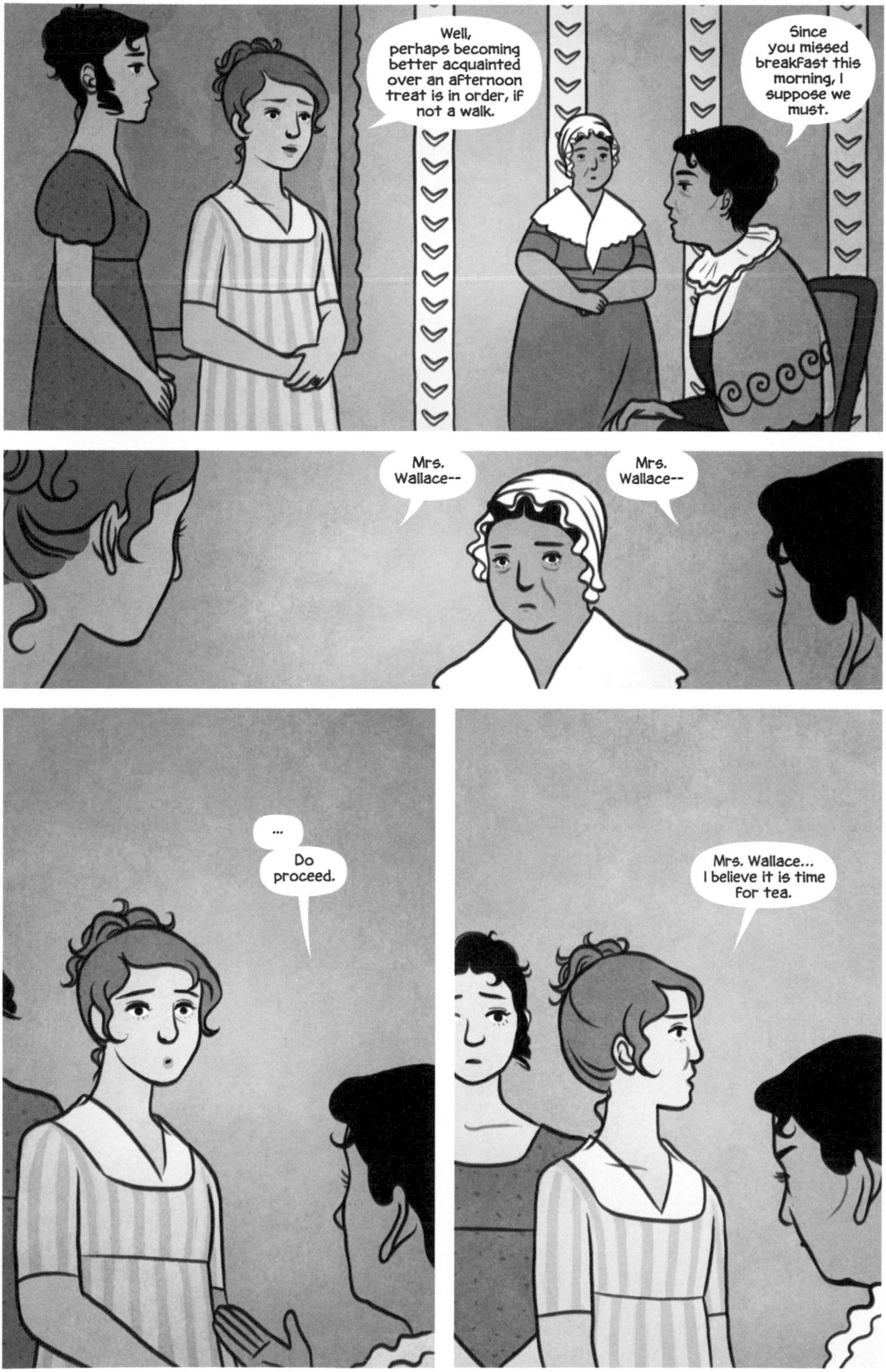
Well, perhaps becoming better acquainted over an afternoon treat is in order, if not a walk.
Since you missed breakfast this morning, I suppose we must.
Mrs. Wallace--
Mrs. Wallace--
...
Do proceed.
Mrs. Wallace... I believe it is time for tea.

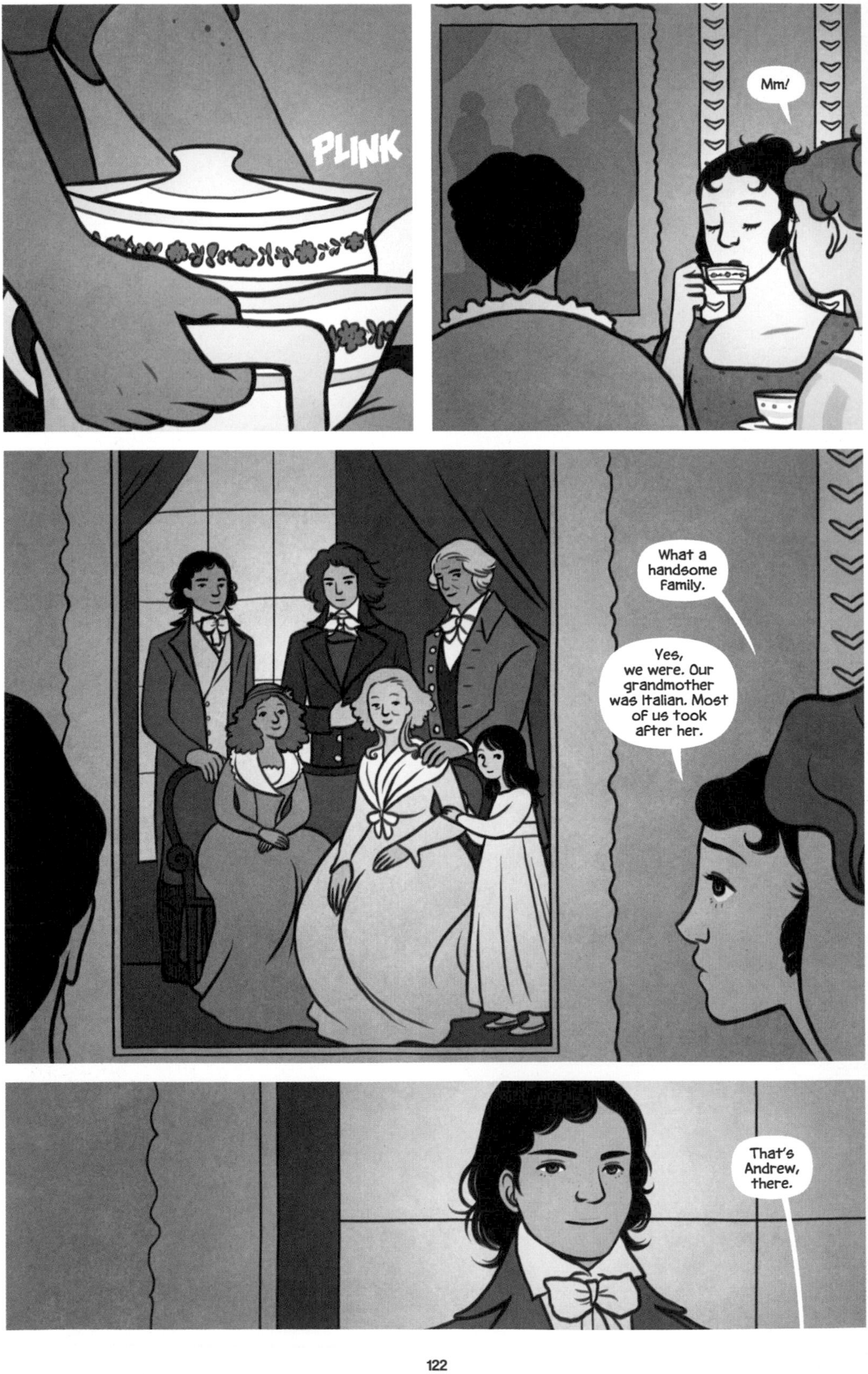
PLINK
Mm!
What a handsome family.
Yes, we were. Our grandmother was Italian. Most of us took after her.
That's Andrew, there.

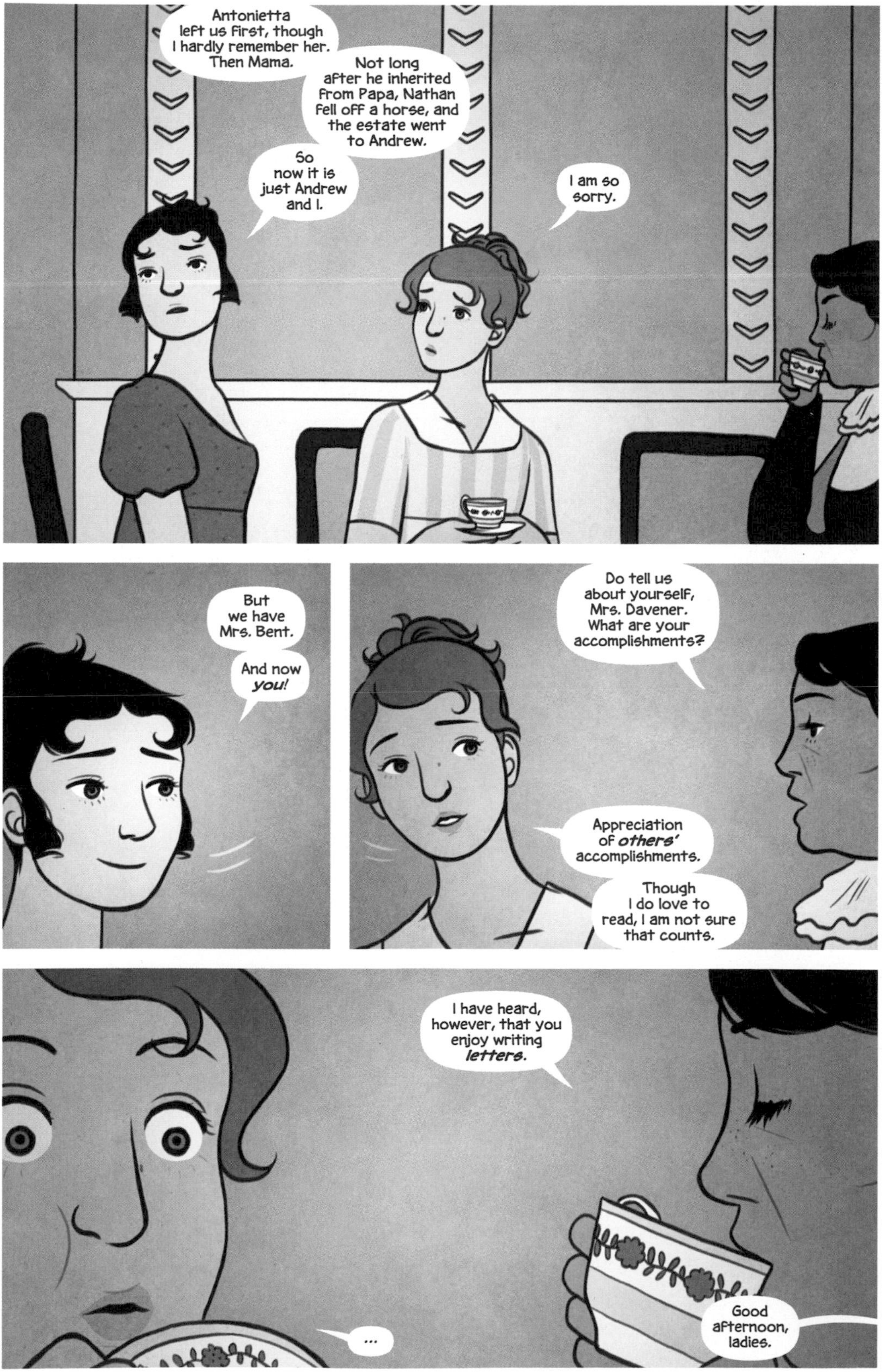
Antonietta left us first, though I hardly remember her. Then Mama.
Not long after he inherited from Papa, Nathan fell off a horse, and the estate went to Andrew.
So now it is just Andrew and I.
I am so sorry.
But we have Mrs. Bent.
And now *you*!
Do tell us about yourself, Mrs. Davener. What are your accomplishments?
Appreciation of *others'* accomplishments.
Though I do love to read, I am not sure that counts.
I have heard, however, that you enjoy writing *letters*.
...
Good afternoon, ladies.

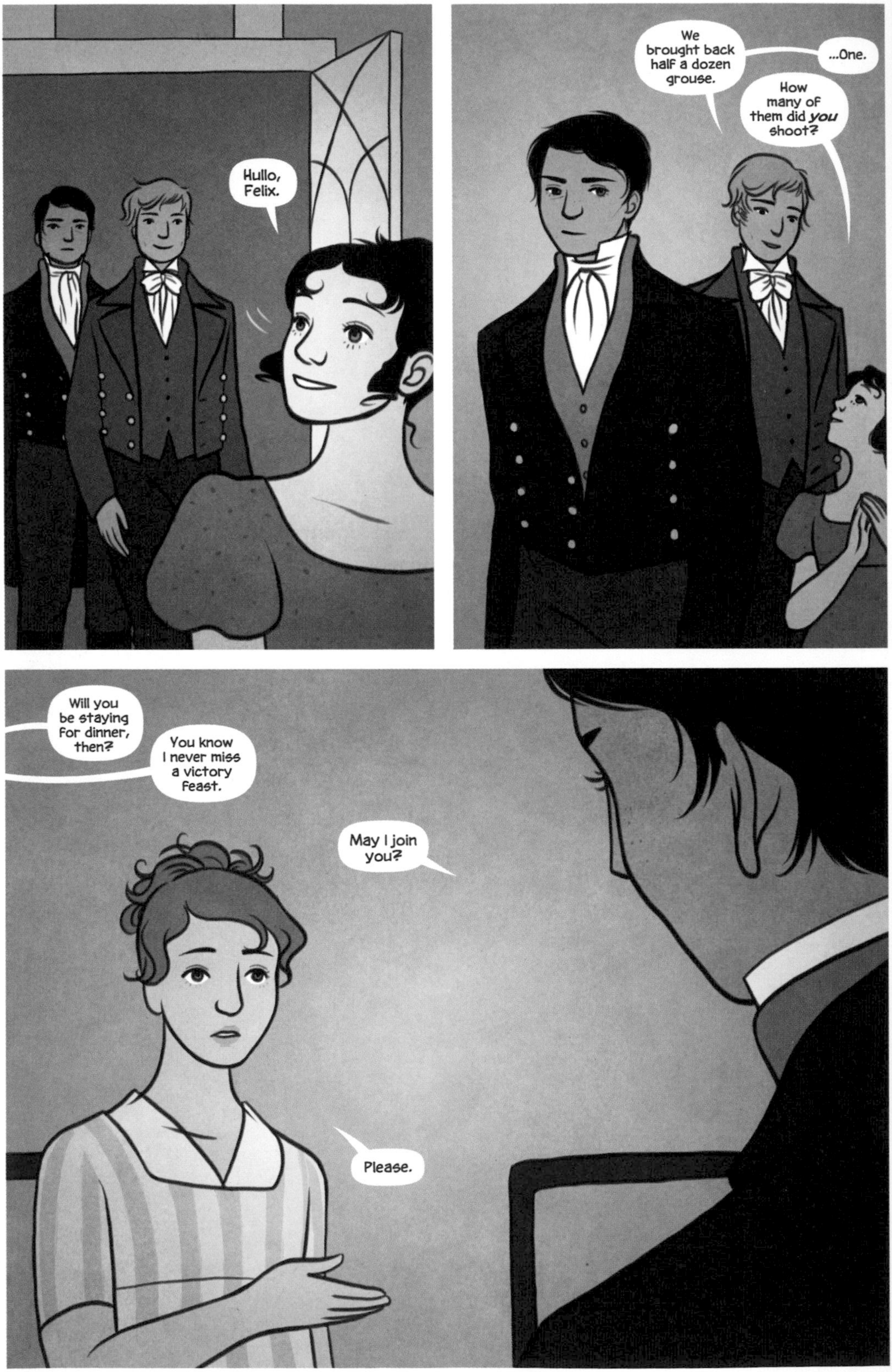

Hullo, Felix.
We brought back half a dozen grouse.
...One.
How many of them did *you* shoot?
Will you be staying for dinner, then?
You know I never miss a victory feast.
May I join you?
Please.

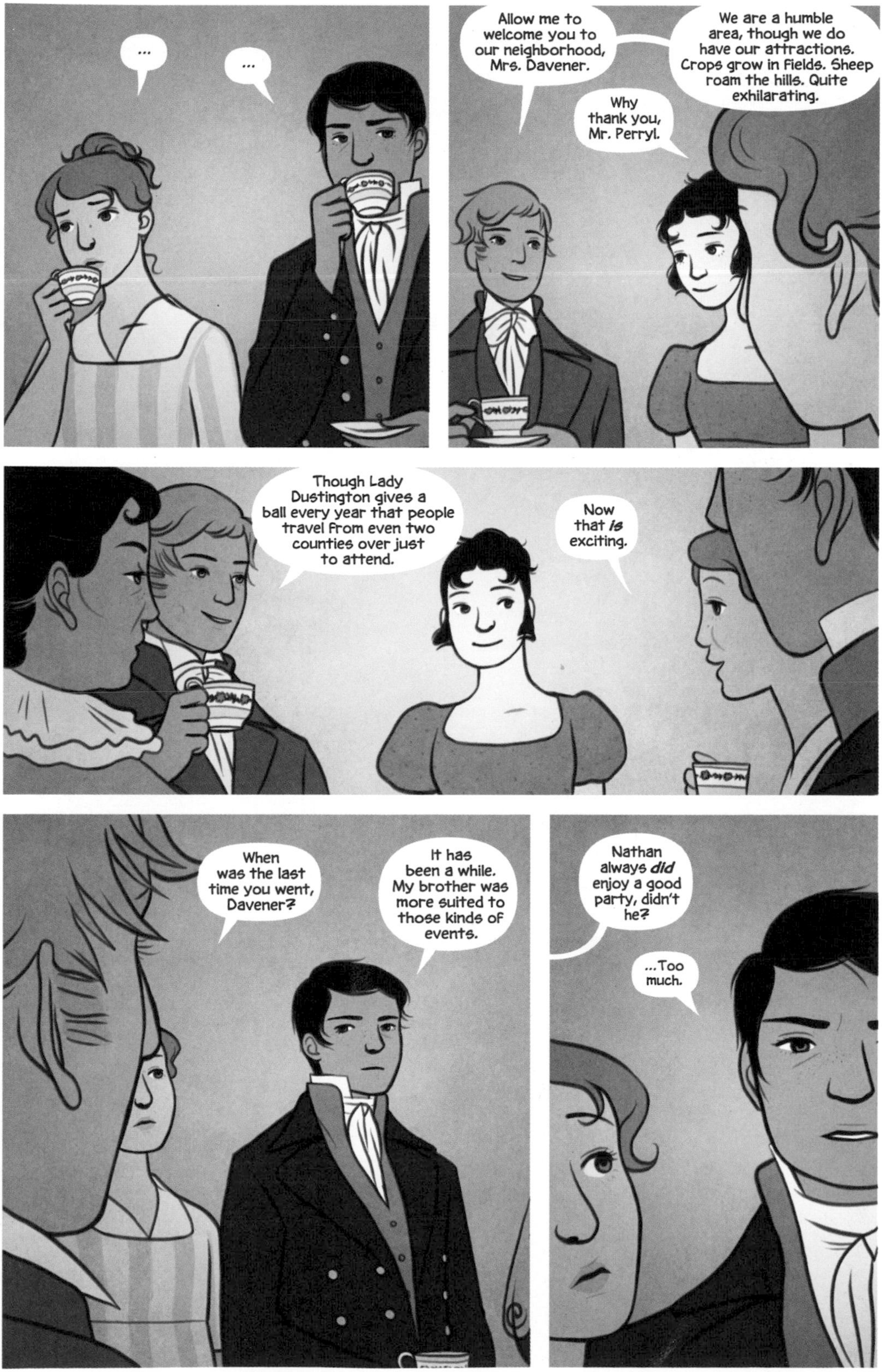
...
...
Allow me to welcome you to our neighborhood, Mrs. Davener.
We are a humble area, though we do have our attractions. Crops grow in fields. Sheep roam the hills. Quite exhilarating.
Why thank you, Mr. Perryl.
Though Lady Dustington gives a ball every year that people travel from even two counties over just to attend.
Now that *is* exciting.
When was the last time you went, Davener?
It has been a while. My brother was more suited to those kinds of events.
Nathan always ***did*** enjoy a good party, didn't he?
...Too much.

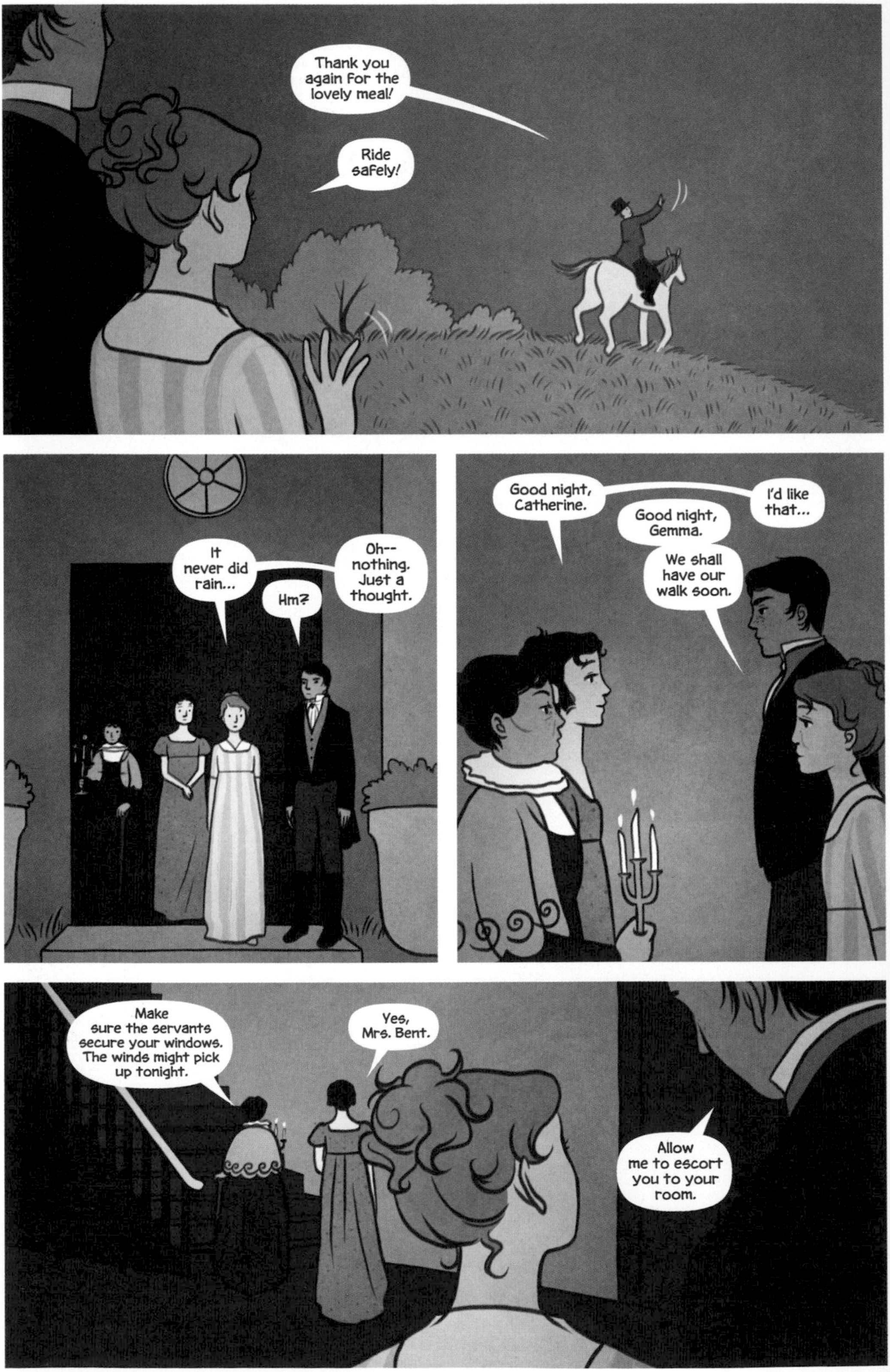

Thank you again for the lovely meal!
Ride safely!
It never did rain...
Hm?
Oh-- nothing. Just a thought.
Good night, Catherine.
Good night, Gemma.
I'd like that...
We shall have our walk soon.
Make sure the servants secure your windows. The winds might pick up tonight.
Yes, Mrs. Bent.
Allow me to escort you to your room.

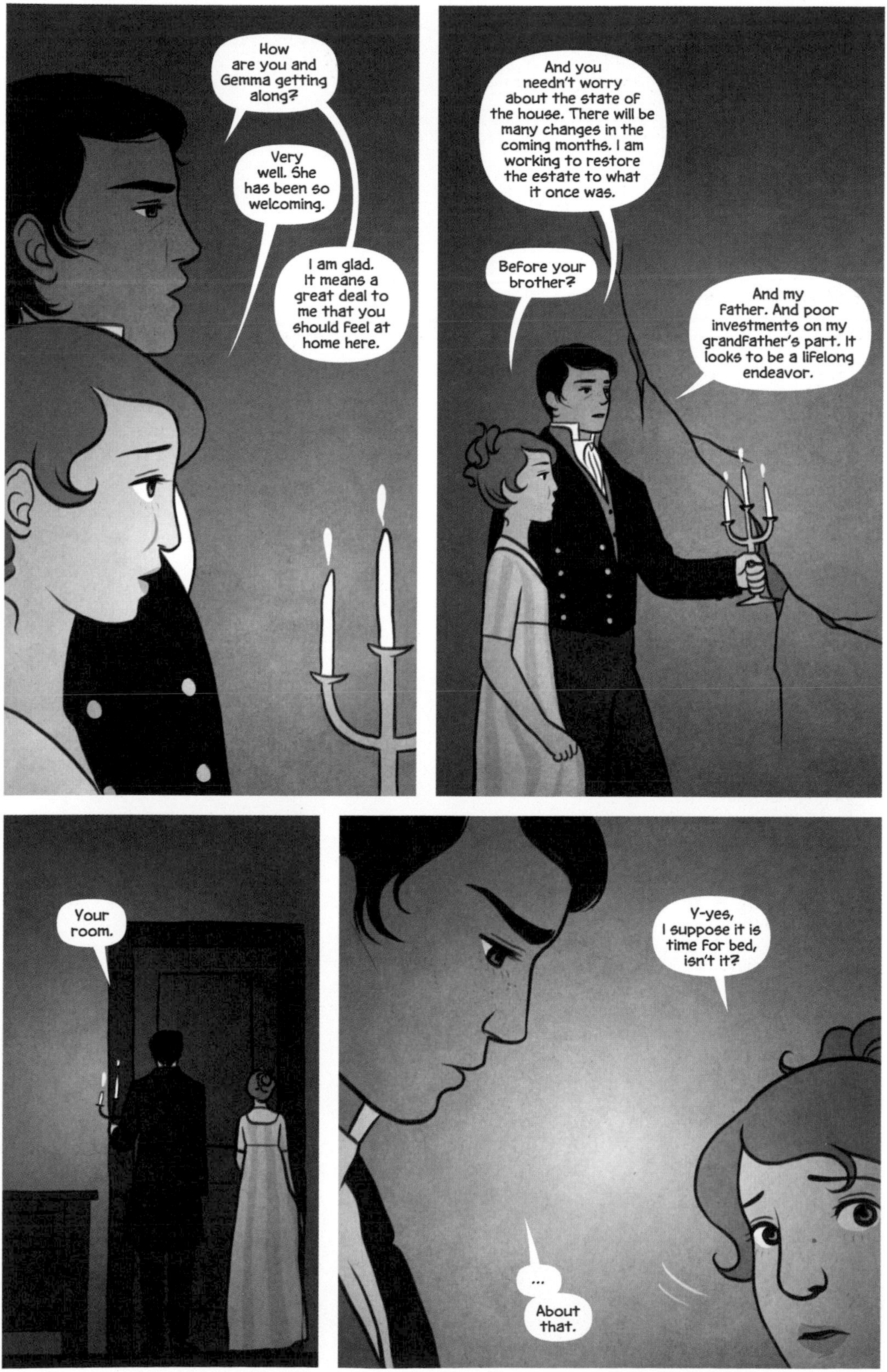
How are you and Gemma getting along?
Very well. She has been so welcoming.
I am glad. It means a great deal to me that you should feel at home here.
And you needn't worry about the state of the house. There will be many changes in the coming months. I am working to restore the estate to what it once was.
Before your brother?
And my father. And poor investments on my grandfather's part. It looks to be a lifelong endeavor.
Your room.
Y-yes, I suppose it is time for bed, isn't it?
...
About that.

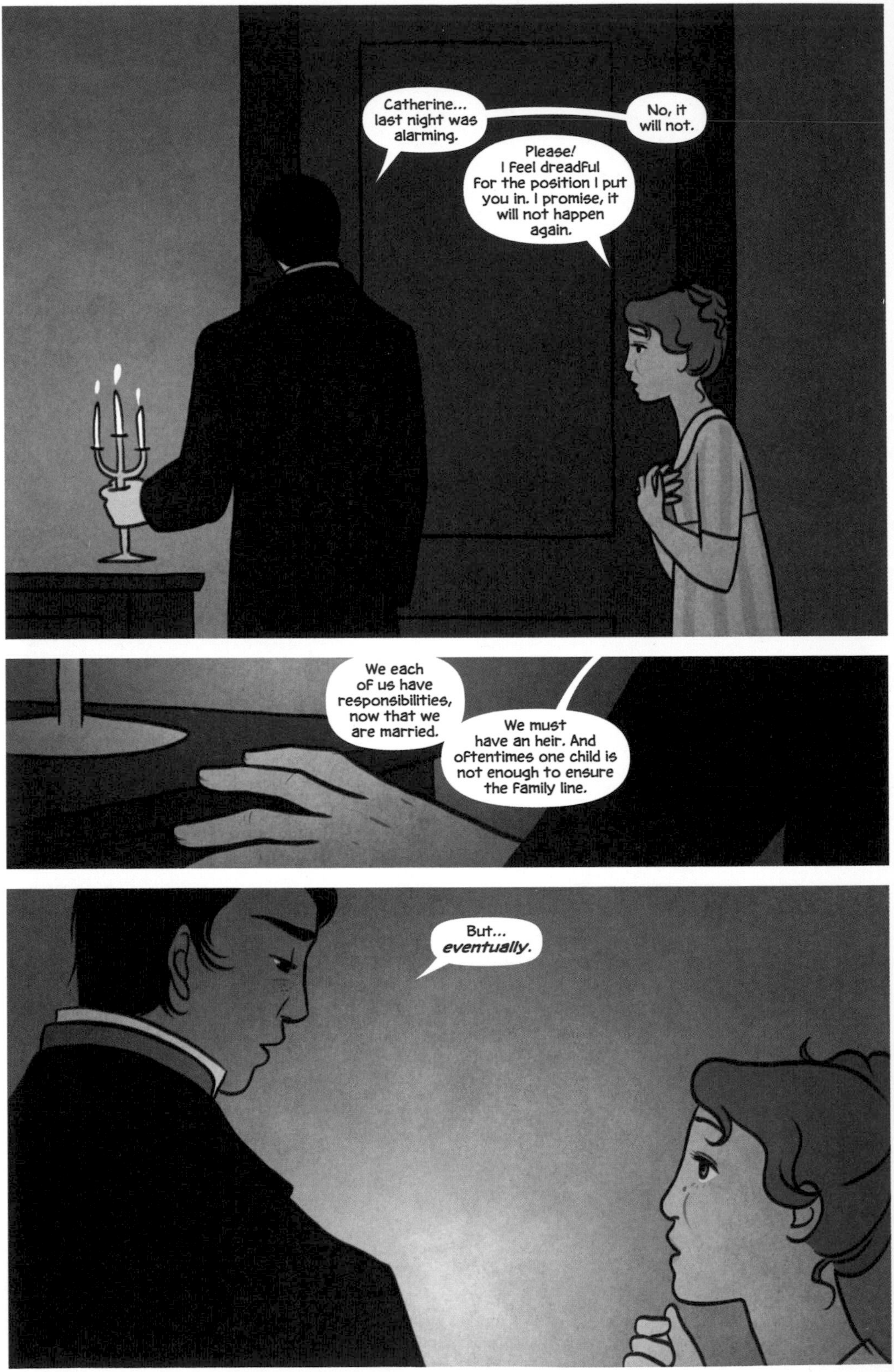
Catherine... last night was alarming.
No, it will not.
Please! I feel dreadful for the position I put you in. I promise, it will not happen again.
We each of us have responsibilities, now that we are married.
We must have an heir. And oftentimes one child is not enough to ensure the family line.
But... *eventually*.

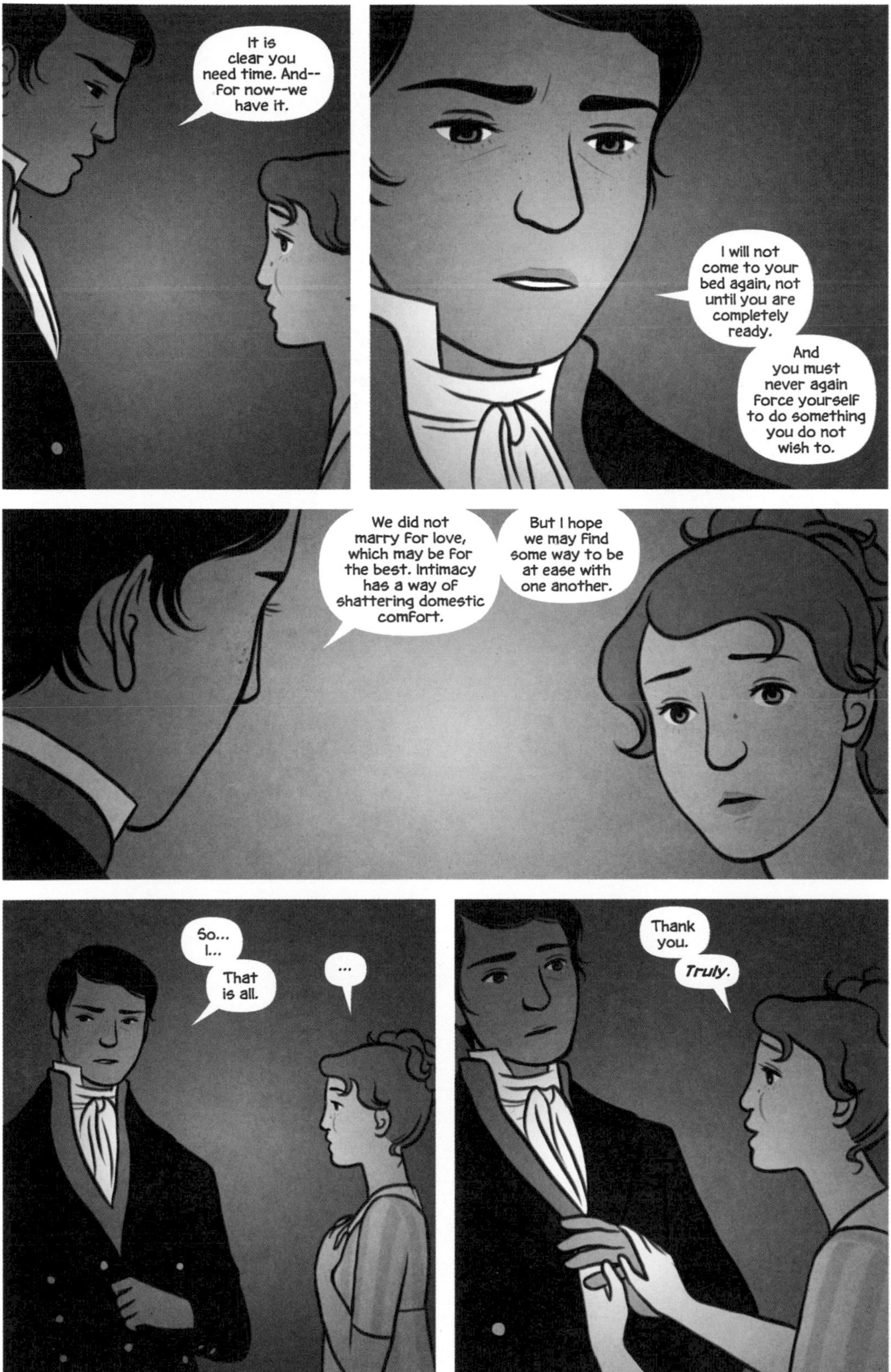
It is clear you need time. And--For now--we have it.
I will not come to your bed again, not until you are completely ready.
And you must never again force yourself to do something you do not wish to.
We did not marry for love, which may be for the best. Intimacy has a way of shattering domestic comfort.
But I hope we may find some way to be at ease with one another.
So... I...
That is all.
...
Thank you.
Truly.

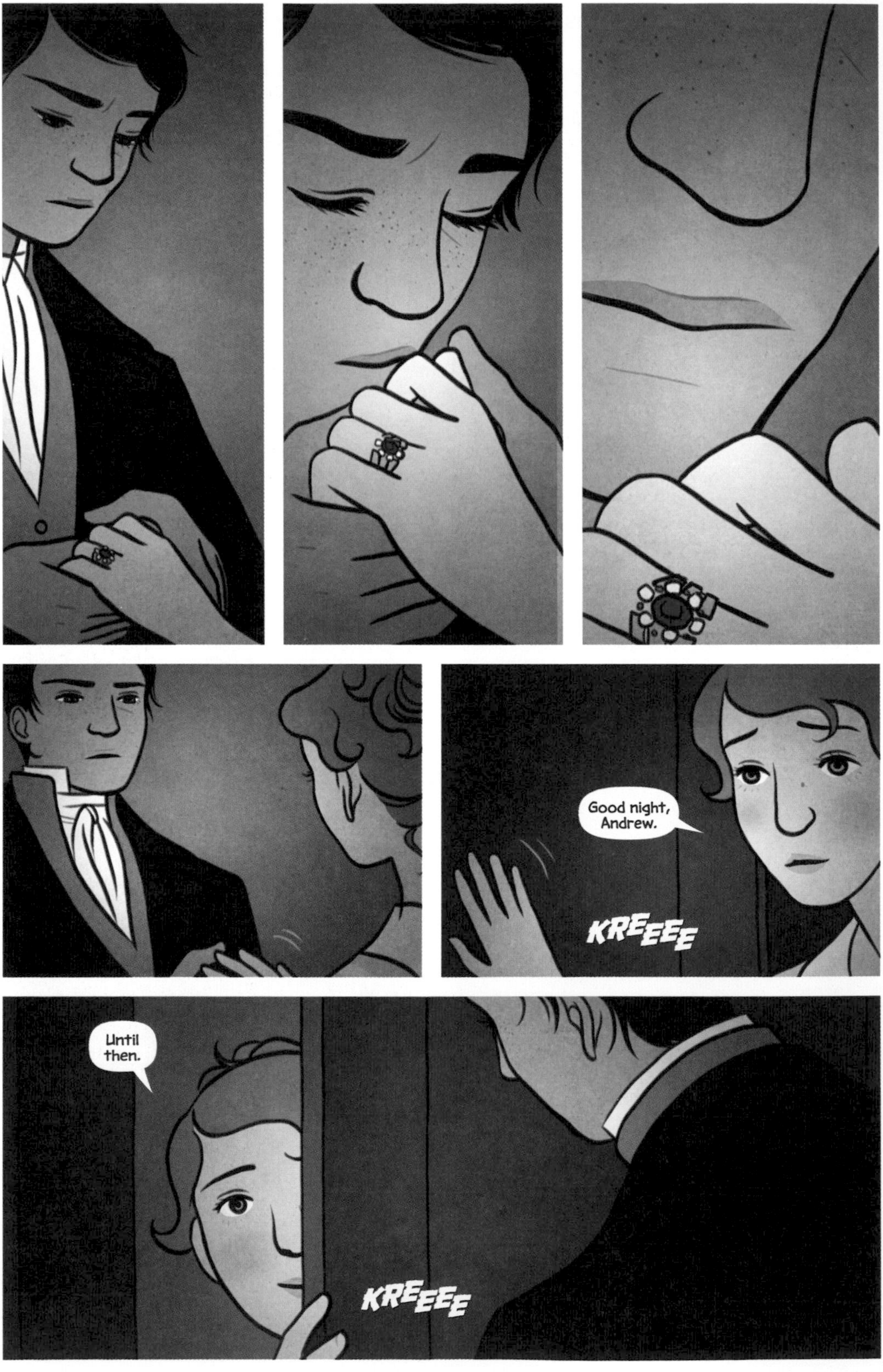
Good night, Andrew.
KREEEE
Until then.
KREEEE

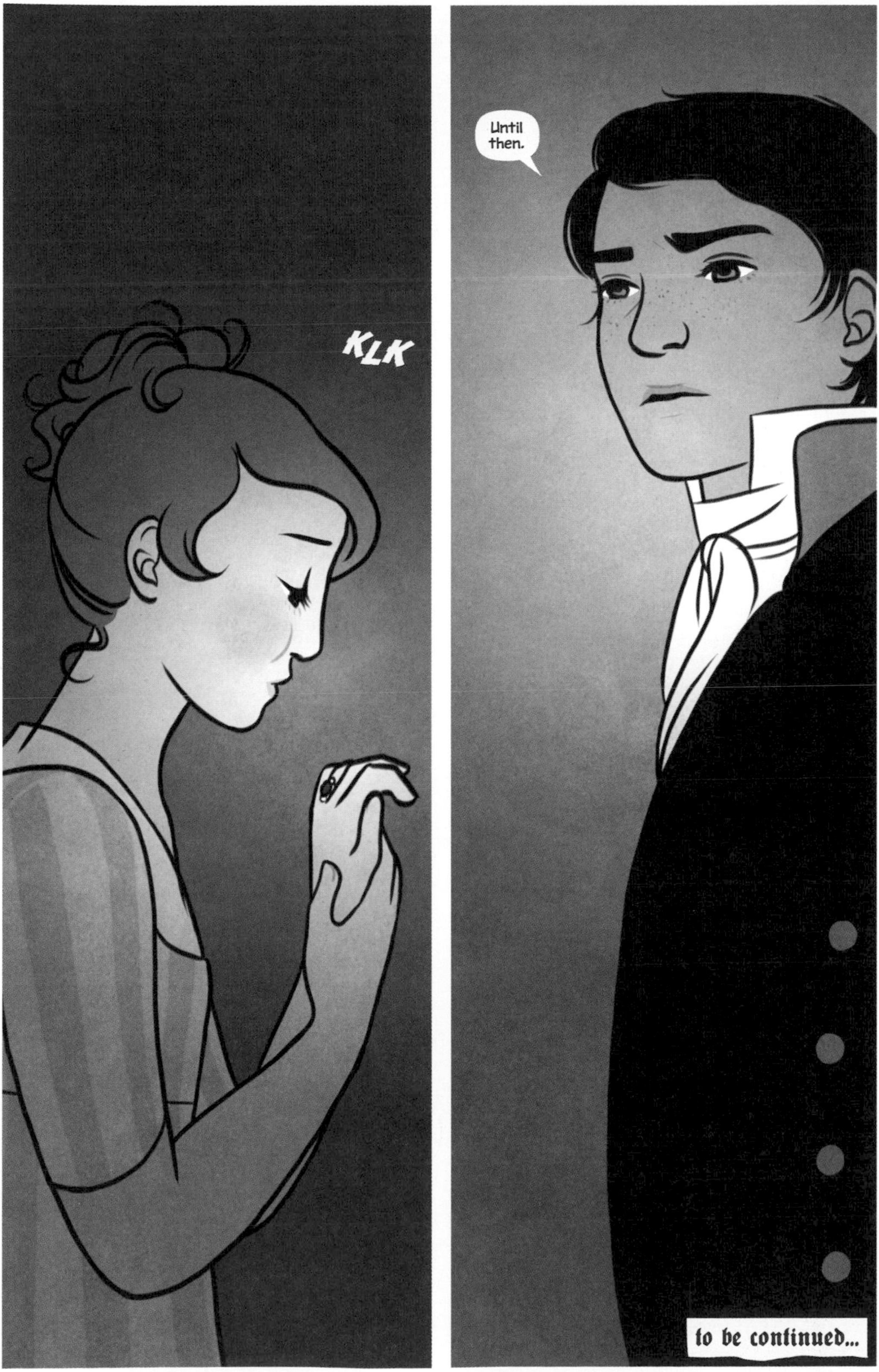
KLK
Until then.
to be continued...

RUINED ROUNDTABLE

The *Ruined* creative team sat down to talk about their work process, favorite time periods, and a little bit of everything.

Sarah Vaughn: Sarah, do you listen to music while you work on pages? If so, what?

Sarah Winifred Searle: I'm all over the place with music, but when I need to set the mood, I fall back on a playlist called "Swoon." It's filled with love songs, from sad to sweet: Mazzy Star's "Fade Into You," Tattle Tale's "Glass Vase Cello Case," Kate Nash's "Nicest Thing," and Richard Thompson's "A Love You Can't Survive." Especially when I'm drawing tense moments, I need some ambiance so I can properly convey those delicious levels of yearning!

SWS: Ryan, it's super cool that you're both a writer and a letterer—how do those very different kinds of work inform each other and your personal creative process?

Ryan Ferrier: Thanks, Sarah! Great question.

I find lettering incredibly informing to my own writing. Having that cognizance going into a script has made me a better writer in terms of pacing and page/panel real estate. Most importantly, it keeps me from over-writing, and reminds me that the art is paramount in storytelling. If I'm lettering a book that I've written, it also allows me to edit on the go; I feel like a better product comes out in the end because you're now working with the art and it becomes more natural and complementary. And who doesn't want another draft to work on while seeing the story come to life? For example, with my series *D4VE,* a huge amount of the humor was added or changed in the final lettering stage. Ideally, I would always letter my own work, though that's not always possible. In the case of lettering other people's books, not only do I get to be part of incredible teams and see other creators' stories come to life, but I get to switch gears a little and enjoy the challenge and the craft. It's also one of the few times I get to listen to music while I work (I can't do that while writing), so it's like having your cake and eating it too. Before comics, I was a graphic designer for close to 12 years, so it's nice to be able to still keep that other passion in my life.

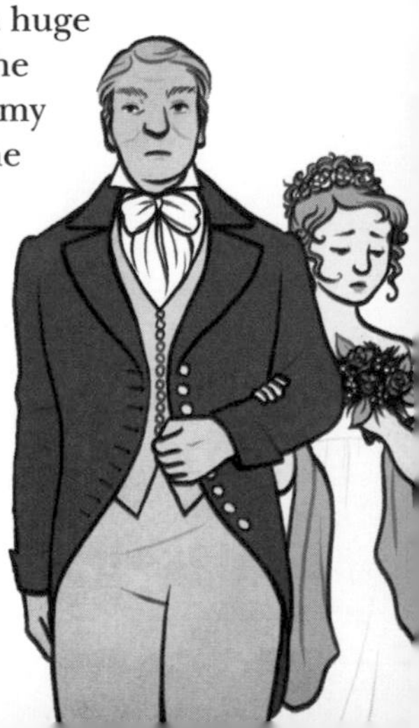

RF: I believe it's Sarah V's turn! Sarah, can you go into your process for *Ruined* a little bit—I'm curious how, if at all, *Ruined* has differed from your other work, in terms of outlining and planning. You and Sarah both are creating a truly remarkable world that is incredibly rich in character, atmosphere, and tone. Given that, and the ways it's being released to audiences, has that changed your process at all? Has the time period in which *Ruined* takes place played a part in that as well?

SV: My process hasn't really changed much for *Ruined.* I'm a very heavy outliner, while also trying to stay as open and flexible to change as possible. I spend a lot of time researching the period, and one piece of info can send me back to rework a chain of events. Consulting with Sarah S. can also result in changing the entire outline! Quite a lot has changed because of our talks, and immensely for the better.

My actual outlining/planning process begins small and expands in a structured way (concept to arcs to issues) until I even have a sentence for the events of each page. Nothing ever happens exactly as I plan it, but it helps to catch problems with flow early on. Things will always change on the fly. Characters will do things that I never expected, and events I think are solid will end up not working anymore, but figuring out how to solve those roadblocks is part of the fun for me.

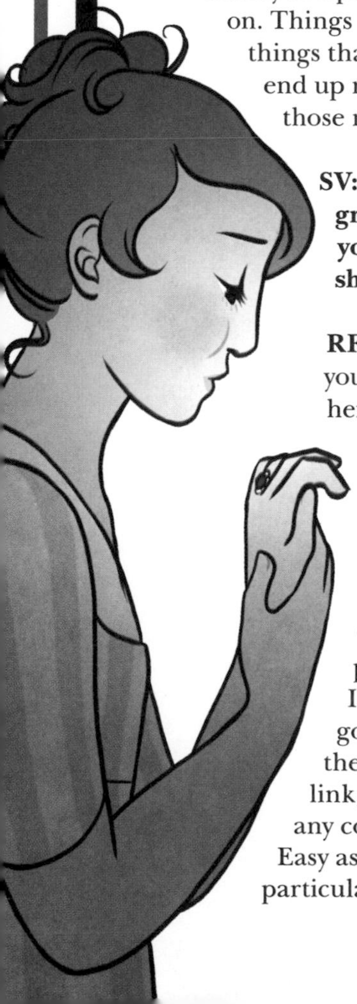

SV: And my question back to Ryan is: You were a graphic designer for 12 years. So much respect to you! What's the most ridiculous client story you can share?

RF: Thanks, Sarah! I really appreciate your insight into your process. It's fascinating to me. Great question, and here's my answer:

I could spend hours telling ridiculous client stories. There are just so, so many. The one that always comes to mind was several years ago—I'm thinking 2009 or 2010. I had designed and built a website for, let's call them, "N." It was a slick looking website, big, bright, and colorful; it was aimed at parents as the product it sold was for pre-teens. So I make this website, and the online demo is ready to go. We're one click away from making N's site live-on-the-internet. My boss and I send N the email with the link, and schedule a call to chat about it and address any concerns, answer questions, receive praise, and so on. Easy as pie, we've done that a hundred times. Not with N in particular, but so far so good.

So we get on the call in my boss's office, me, him, and N—the client—on speaker phone. My boss has the website up on his monitor, and I'm peering on, as does the client, N, on their side of the phone. We roll through five minutes of "this is good, that works, I like that" etc., etc. and then N becomes more abrupt and addresses what clearly had been on their mind since the call started. Sharply, N says, "yes, but you need to remove the 'x' on the site that freezes my internet and makes the site quit!" My boss and I looked at each other, dumbfounded. We asked N to clarify. "The 'x' you put on my website...can you please take it out. It makes the site quit and stop working, and I don't want people to click on it and lose me sales."

My boss and I could not for the lives of us figure it out. My boss becomes panicked, both of us embarrassed at how we could have made an error so grave. While the call continues on speaker phone, we both scour the website, page by page, clicking here and there, trying to figure it out. We pour over the code of the site itself, trying to find this one damn 'x' that makes the site stop working. This damn doomsday button. And nothing. My boss says to N, "uhh, so we can't seem to find the 'x' you're talking about... can you send us a screenshot?" and N replies, "the x! the red x! It's on every single page!" and then it hits us. Like a train to the face. And I watch as my boss' cursor slowly inches up to the top-left of the browser window. Past the green maximize button; past the yellow minimize button; landing on The Red X. Click. The browser closes. N, the client, thought that red x was part of their site. N wanted the website to be a permanent fixture on their user's desktops. So we tell her—my boss and I now wrapping our hands on our faces to stifle the reactions, the tears—that the "red x" is the button to close the "internet window" on the computer.

"Well get rid of it, please. I don't like it," they said.

RF: Sarah S., I believe it's your turn! Sarah, your ability to capture atmosphere and tone so wonderfully in *Ruined*'s time period is unmatched in comics, in my opinion. When seeing your work, I start to think about how that would look contrasted to the darker parts of English history (or the world's). If you were to do a historical-comic, which time period and event would you choose? Doesn't at all have to be "dark," just curious of a specific event that you would tackle, if you ever felt compelled. I can't help but imagine how incredibly your work would look on, say, a Jack the Ripper story, or the Salem Witch Trials.

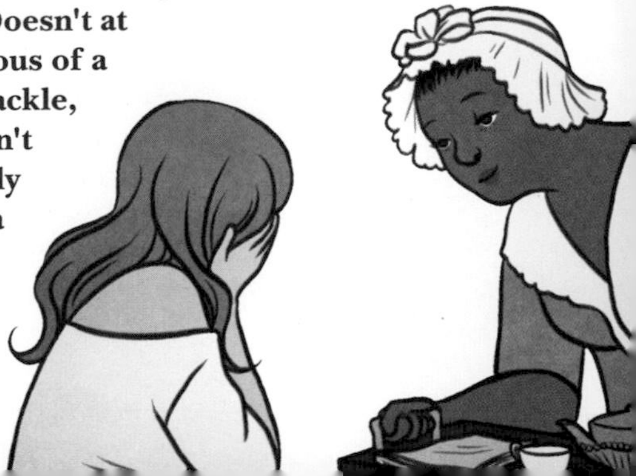

SWS: Oh gosh, thanks so much for the compliments! And no joke, I totally used to live in Salem (I absolutely love historical places like that, surprise surprise).

Right now I'm actually working on another historical comic that I'm both writing and drawing! It's called *Sparks*, and it takes place 100 years after *Ruined*. Two women fall in love while in service as housemaids, and from there they must work toward achieving social and financial independence so they can make a real life together. Back then, it was called a "Boston marriage" when two adult women lived together in a domestic partnership of sorts.

The Edwardian era emerged out of the tight-laced Victorian like a breath of fresh air—women were gaining opportunities to live more on their own terms, the class system and economy began monumental shifts, electricity and other new inventions/ conveniences meant the average person's daily life was changed forever, and British colonialism (particularly the British Raj) hit a turning point. But, at the same time, it still had its limits—feminist efforts were gaining traction, but the foundation of the movement had orientalist, classist, and otherwise problematic roots that made feminism inaccessible to many of the women who needed it the most.

I'm excited to explore this era through the lives of two women from very different backgrounds and how these changes influence their lives, both as a couple and as individuals. I hope I'm able to properly convey such cautiously optimistic complexities through my storytelling so I can do them the justice they deserve!

SWS: Sarah, you've mentioned before that the Georgian era is your favorite, which is the one just before *Ruined* takes place. What is it that intrigues you so much?

SV: It's true, though I should clarify! Visually, my favorite time period is the 1770s. I absolutely love the clothing and the fashion silhouettes. For the wealthy, everything was large and over the top. Women's skirts could be so voluminous an entire adult might hide under them. Men could be just as glamorous as the ladies by powdering and curling their hair, wearing heels and ornate clothing (so much lace!), and putting on makeup. People stuck ships on their heads and glued extra moles or moons or stars to their faces. My eyes just eat it up.

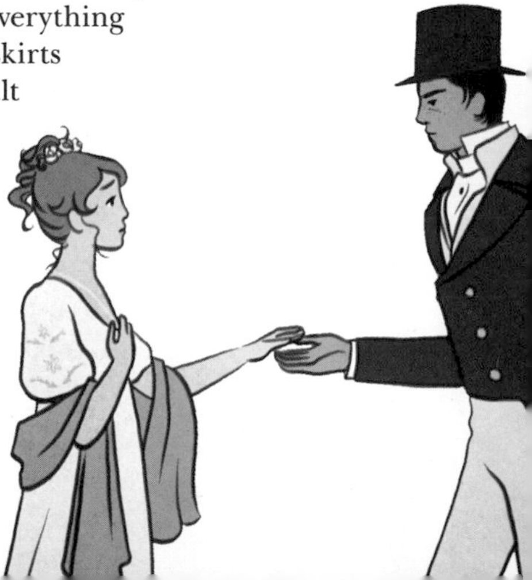

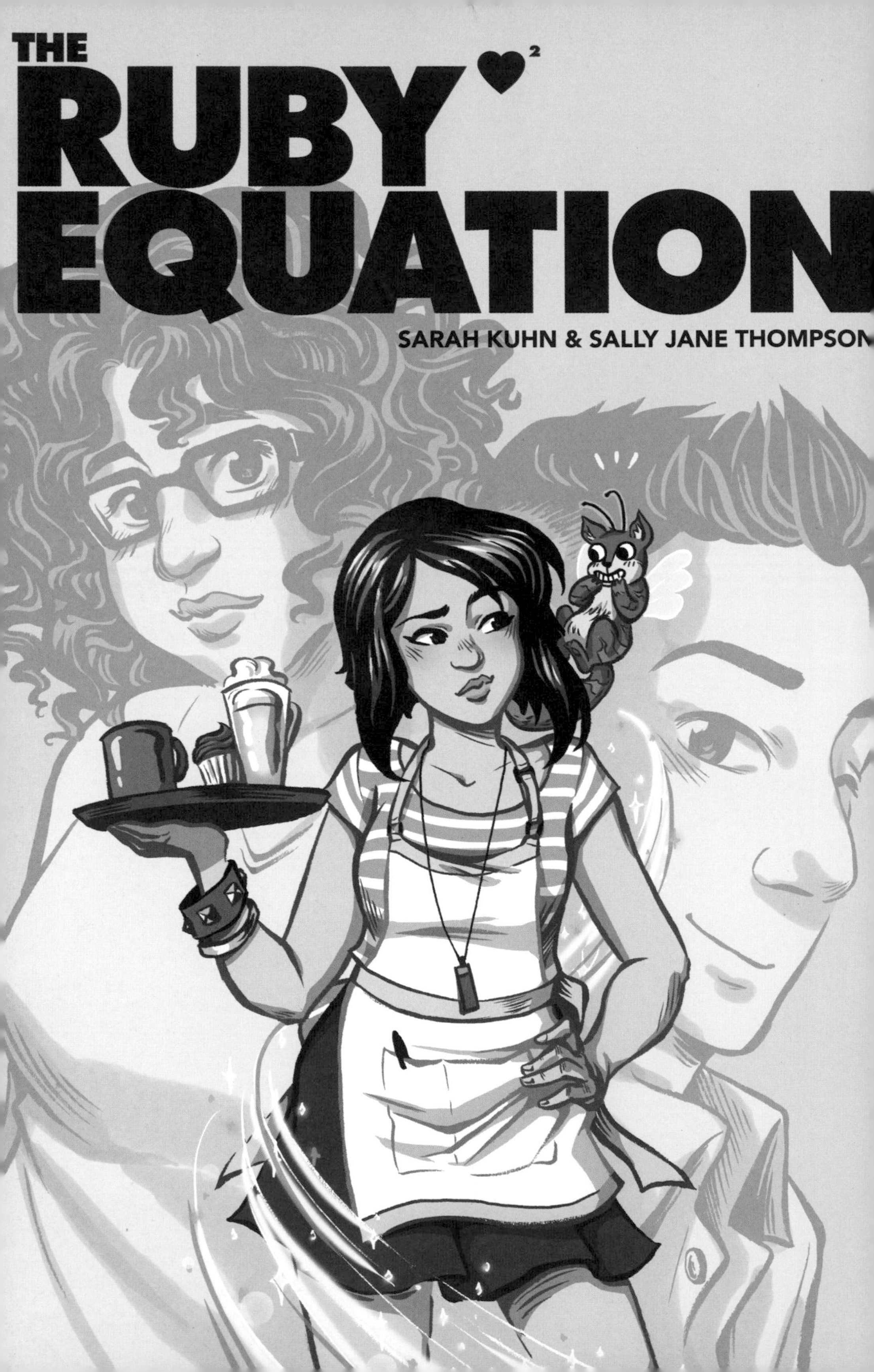
THE
RUBY
EQUATION
SARAH KUHN & SALLY JANE THOMPSON

WRITTEN BY Sarah Kuhn
ILLUSTRATED BY Sally Jane Thompson
COLORED BY Savanna Ganucheau
LETTERED BY Steve Wands
LOGO BY Sonia Harris

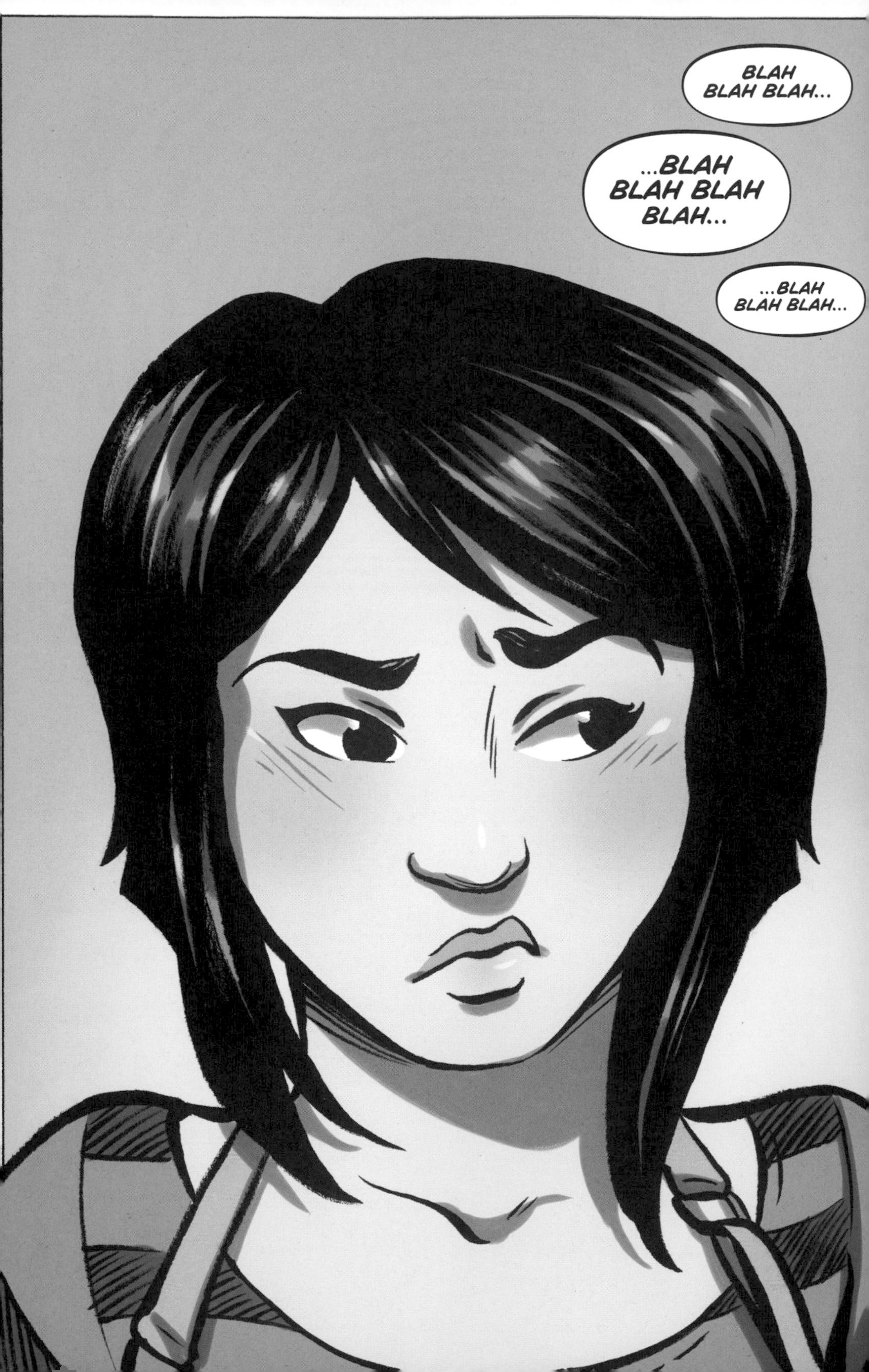
BLAH BLAH BLAH...
...BLAH BLAH BLAH BLAH...
...BLAH BLAH BLAH...

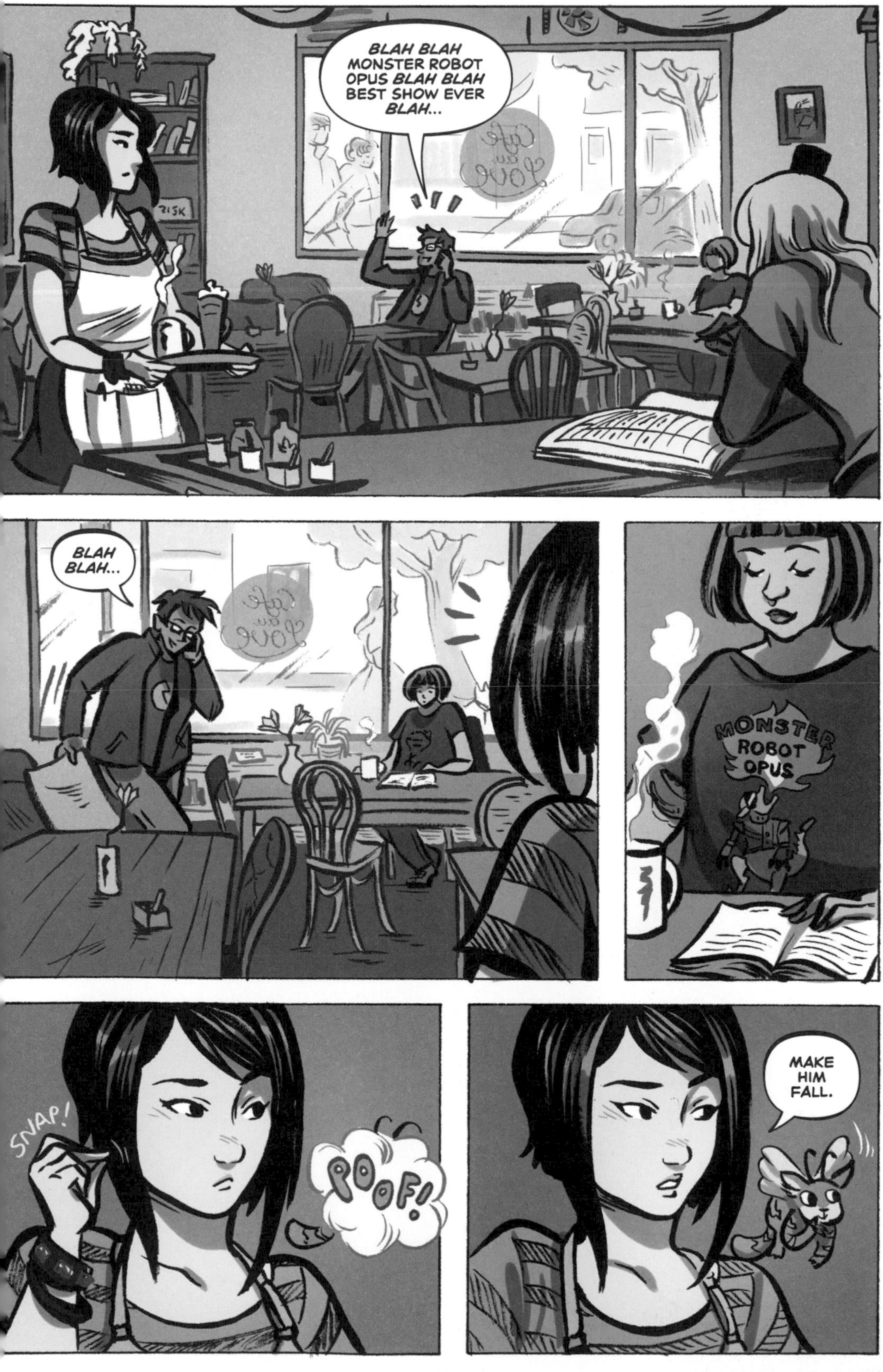
BLAH BLAH MONSTER ROBOT OPUS BLAH BLAH BEST SHOW EVER BLAH...
BLAH BLAH...
MONSTER ROBOT OPUS
SNAP!
POOF!
MAKE HIM FALL.

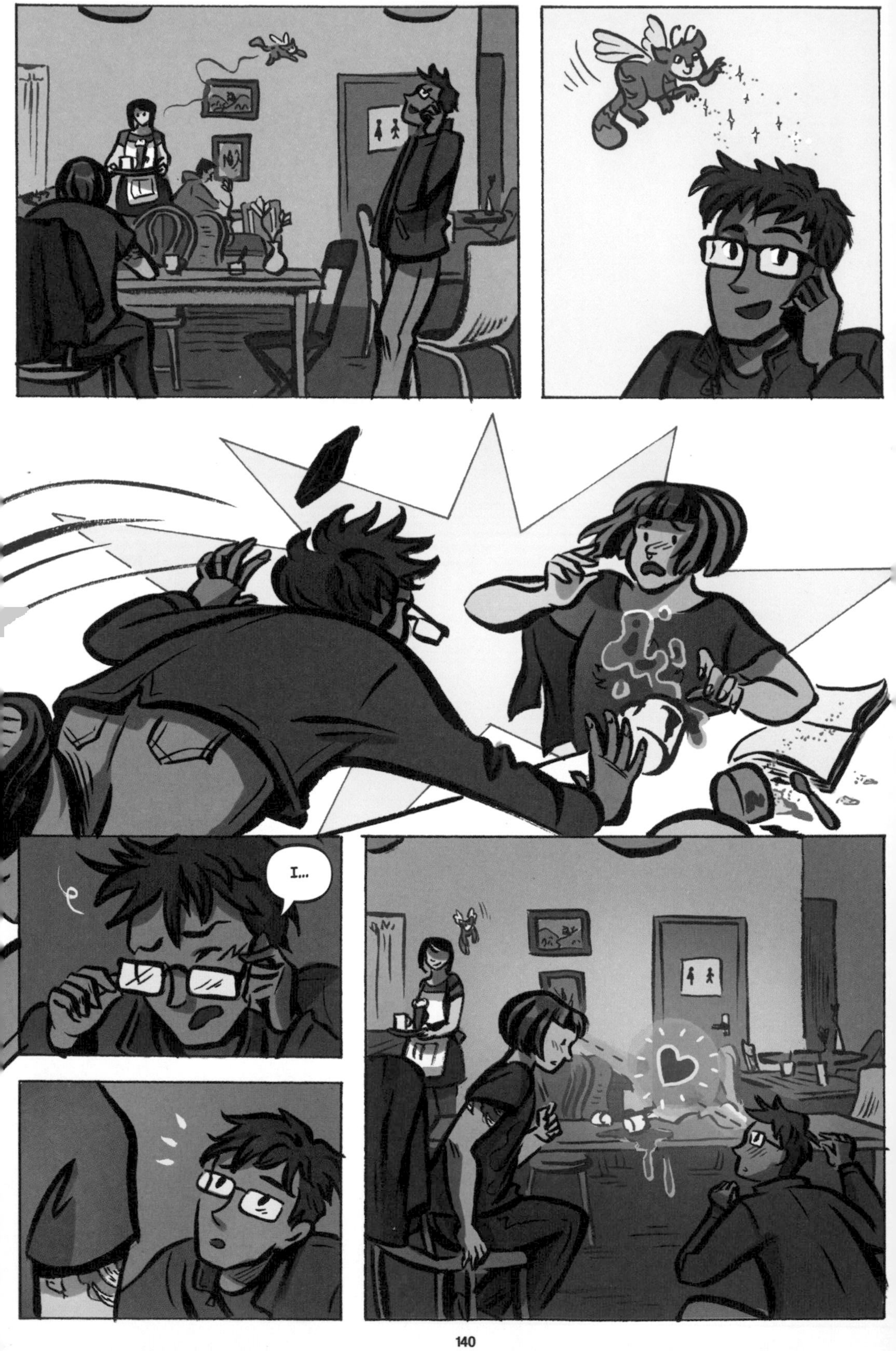

I...

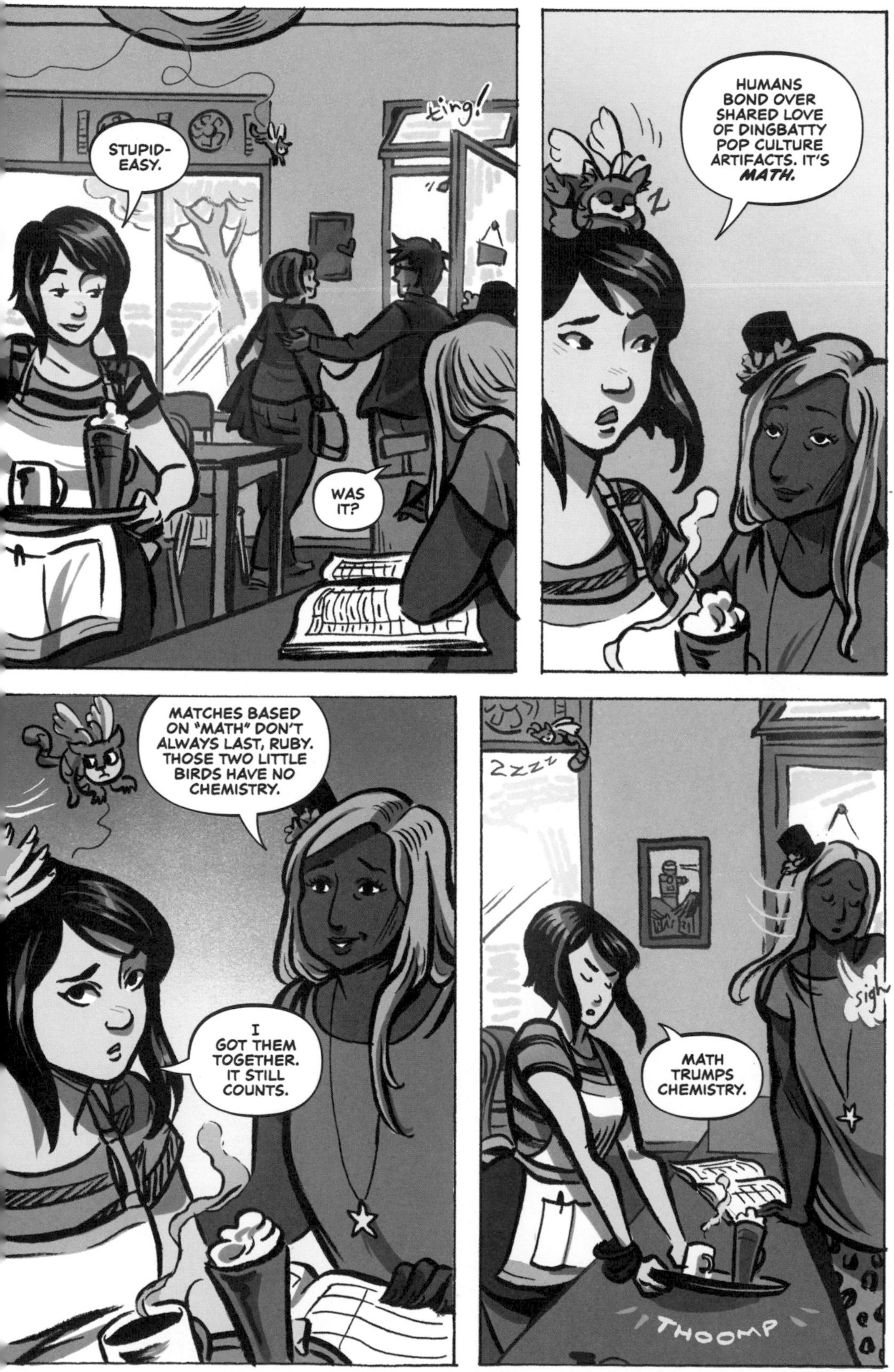
STUPID-EASY.
ting!
WAS IT?
HUMANS BOND OVER SHARED LOVE OF DINGBATTY POP CULTURE ARTIFACTS. IT'S *MATH.*
Z
MATCHES BASED ON "MATH" DON'T ALWAYS LAST, RUBY. THOSE TWO LITTLE BIRDS HAVE NO CHEMISTRY.
I GOT THEM TOGETHER. IT STILL COUNTS.
Zzzz
sigh
MATH TRUMPS CHEMISTRY.
THOOMP

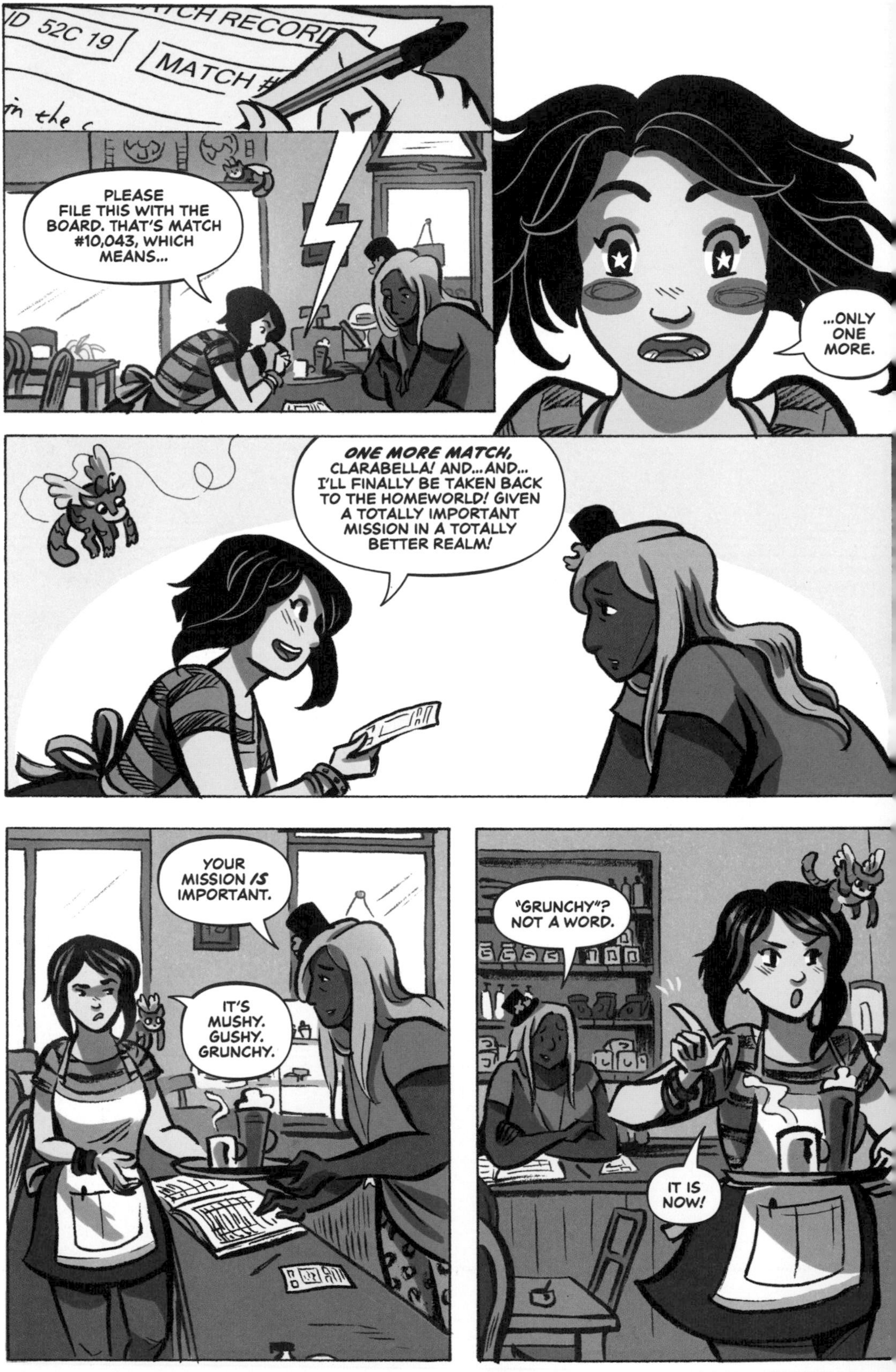
ID 52C 19
MATCH RECORD
MATCH #
PLEASE FILE THIS WITH THE BOARD. THAT'S MATCH #10,043, WHICH MEANS...
...ONLY ONE MORE.
ONE MORE MATCH, CLARABELLA! AND...AND... I'LL FINALLY BE TAKEN BACK TO THE HOMEWORLD! GIVEN A TOTALLY IMPORTANT MISSION IN A TOTALLY BETTER REALM!
YOUR MISSION IS IMPORTANT.
IT'S MUSHY. GUSHY. GRUNCHY.
"GRUNCHY"? NOT A WORD.
IT IS NOW!

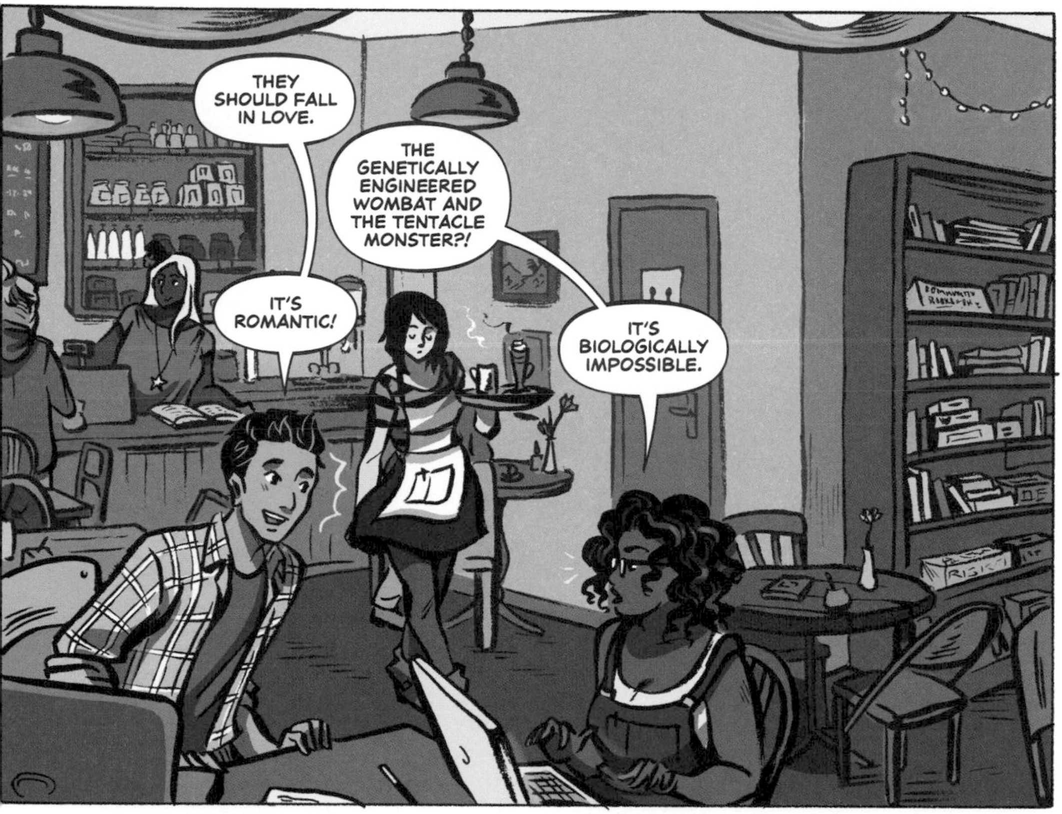
THEY SHOULD FALL IN LOVE.
IT'S ROMANTIC!
THE GENETICALLY ENGINEERED WOMBAT AND THE TENTACLE MONSTER?!
IT'S BIOLOGICALLY IMPOSSIBLE.

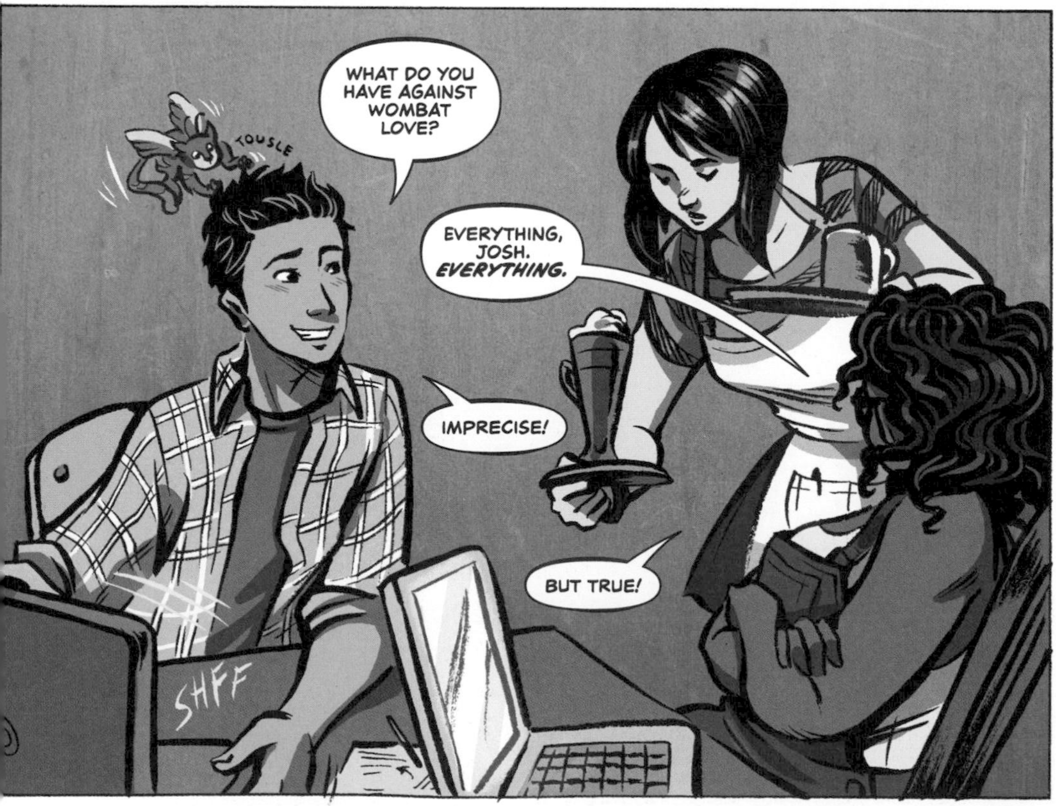
TOUSLE
WHAT DO YOU HAVE AGAINST WOMBAT LOVE?
EVERYTHING, JOSH. ***EVERYTHING.***
IMPRECISE!
BUT TRUE!
SHFF

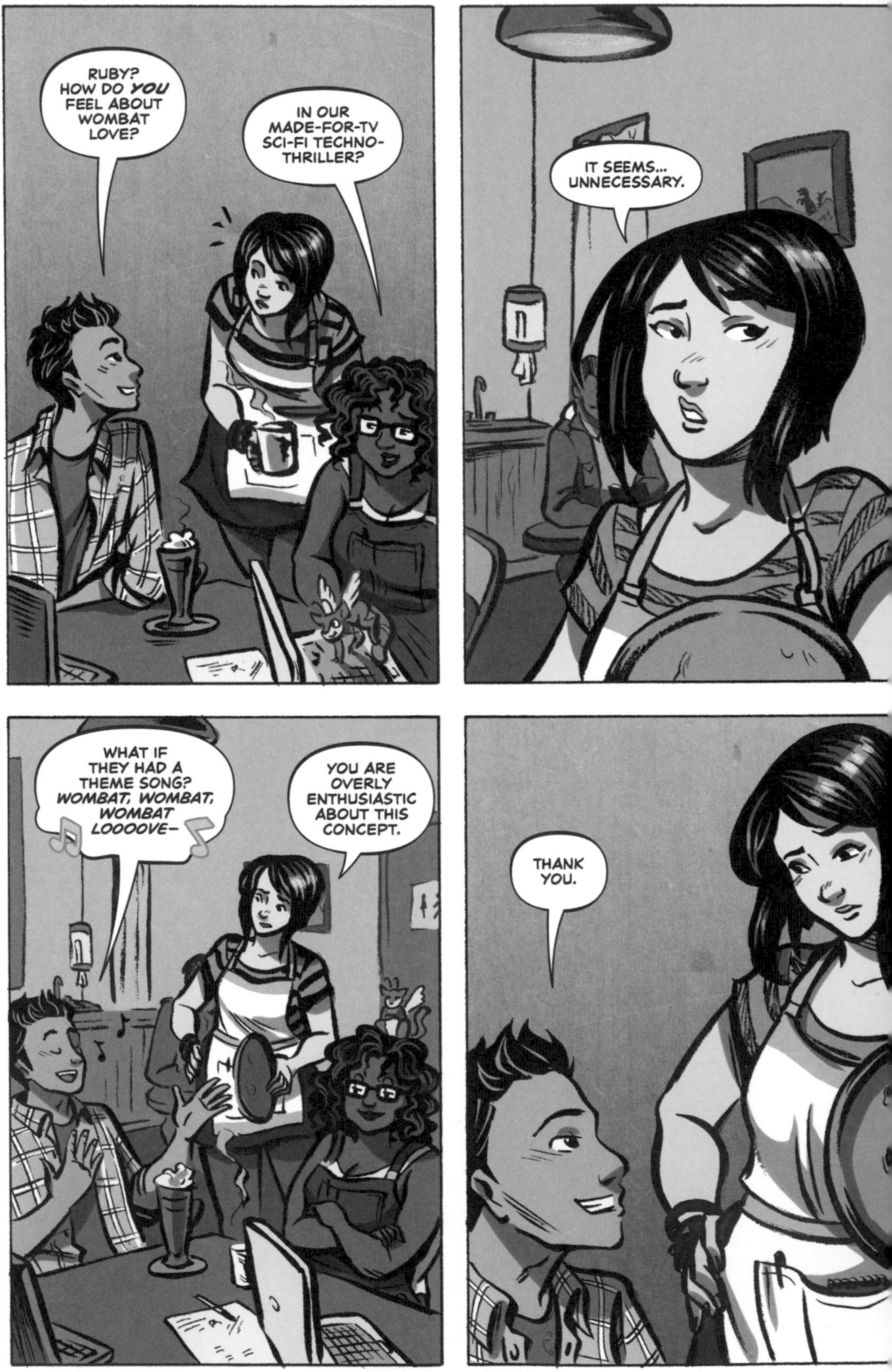
RUBY? HOW DO *YOU* FEEL ABOUT WOMBAT LOVE?
IN OUR MADE-FOR-TV SCI-FI TECHNO-THRILLER?
IT SEEMS... UNNECESSARY.
WHAT IF THEY HAD A THEME SONG? *WOMBAT, WOMBAT, WOMBAT LOOOOVE–*
YOU ARE OVERLY ENTHUSIASTIC ABOUT THIS CONCEPT.
THANK YOU.

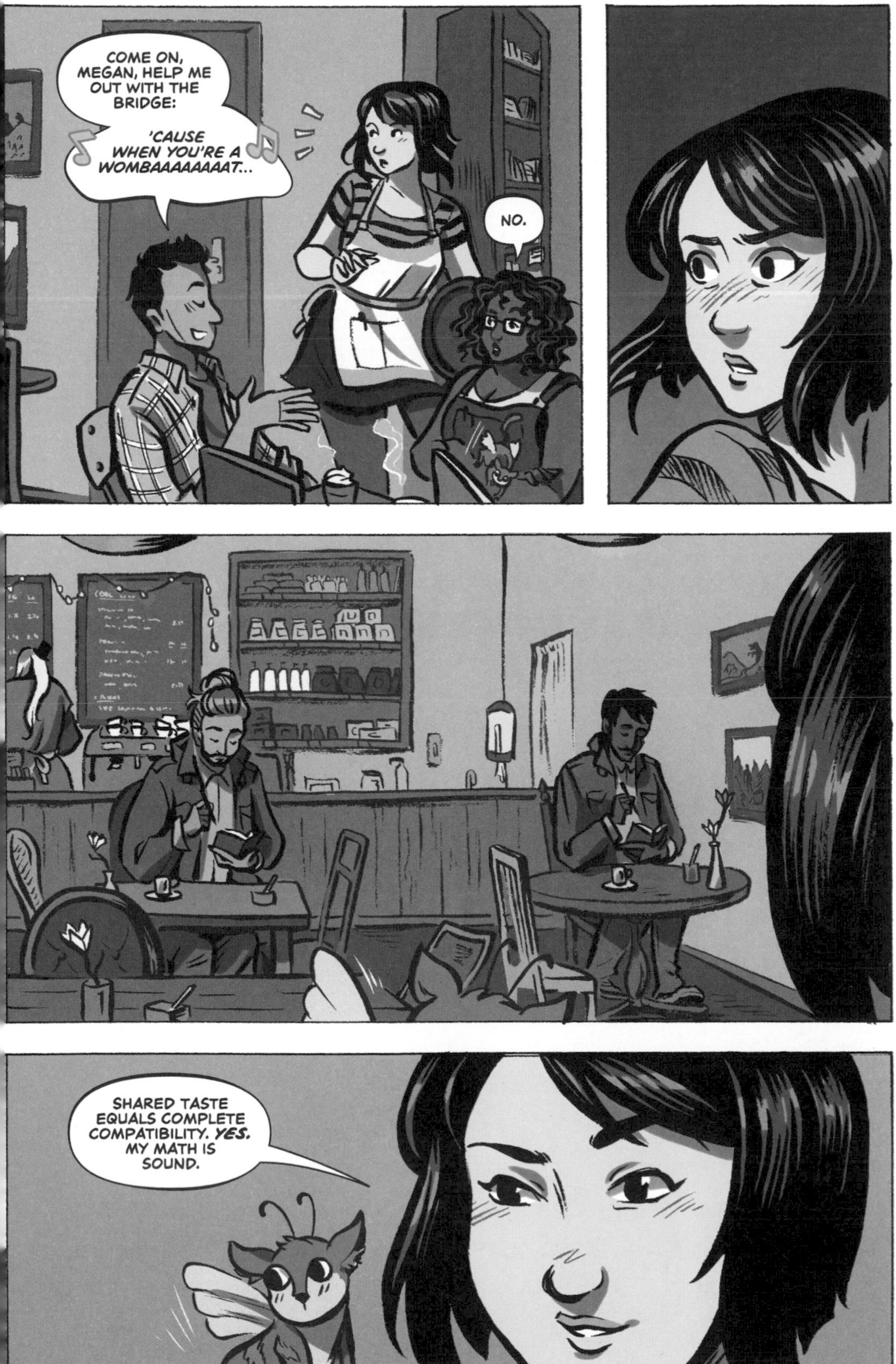
COME ON, MEGAN, HELP ME OUT WITH THE BRIDGE:
'CAUSE WHEN YOU'RE A WOMBAAAAAAAAT...
NO.
SHARED TASTE EQUALS COMPLETE COMPATIBILITY. ***YES.*** MY MATH IS SOUND.

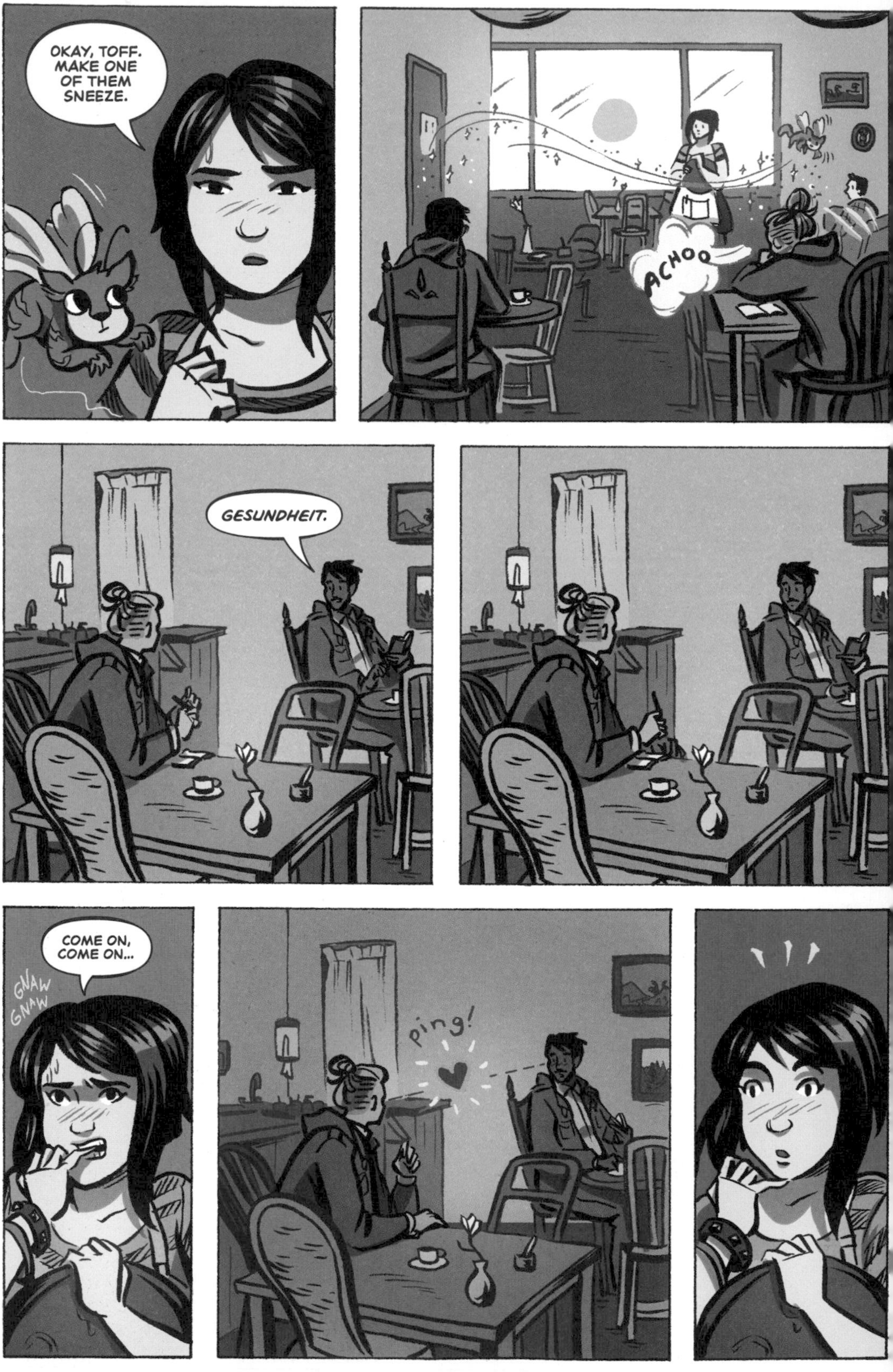
OKAY, TOFF. MAKE ONE OF THEM SNEEZE.
ACHOO
GESUNDHEIT.
COME ON, COME ON...
GNAW GNAW
ping!

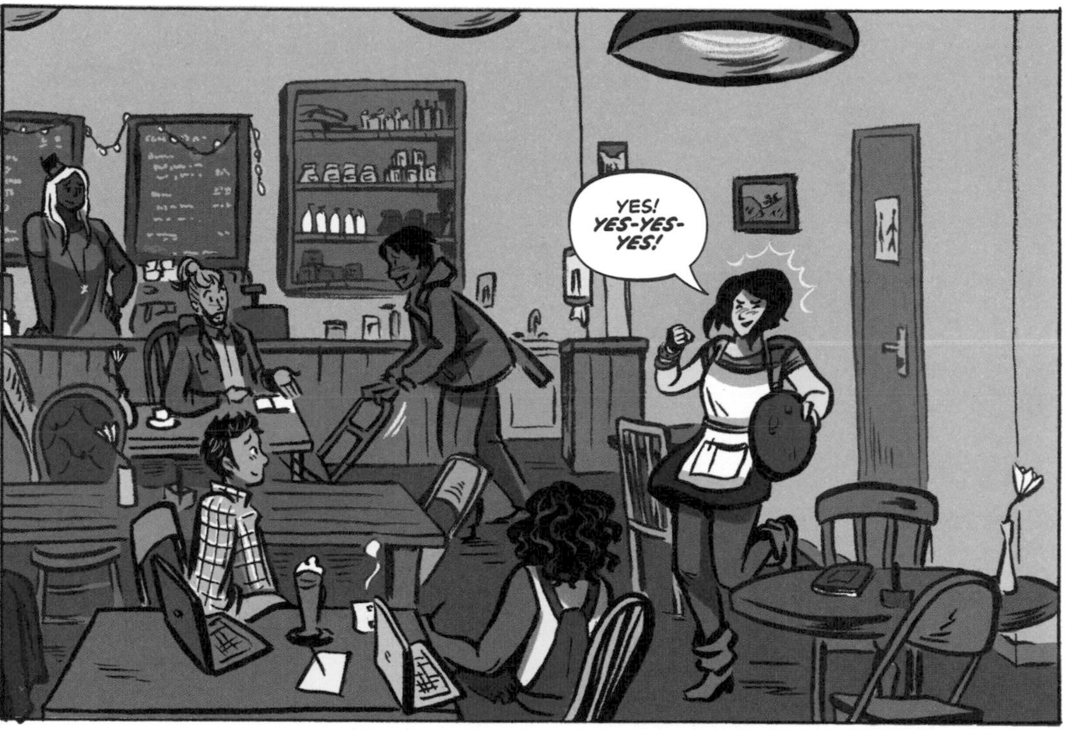
YES! YES-YES-YES!

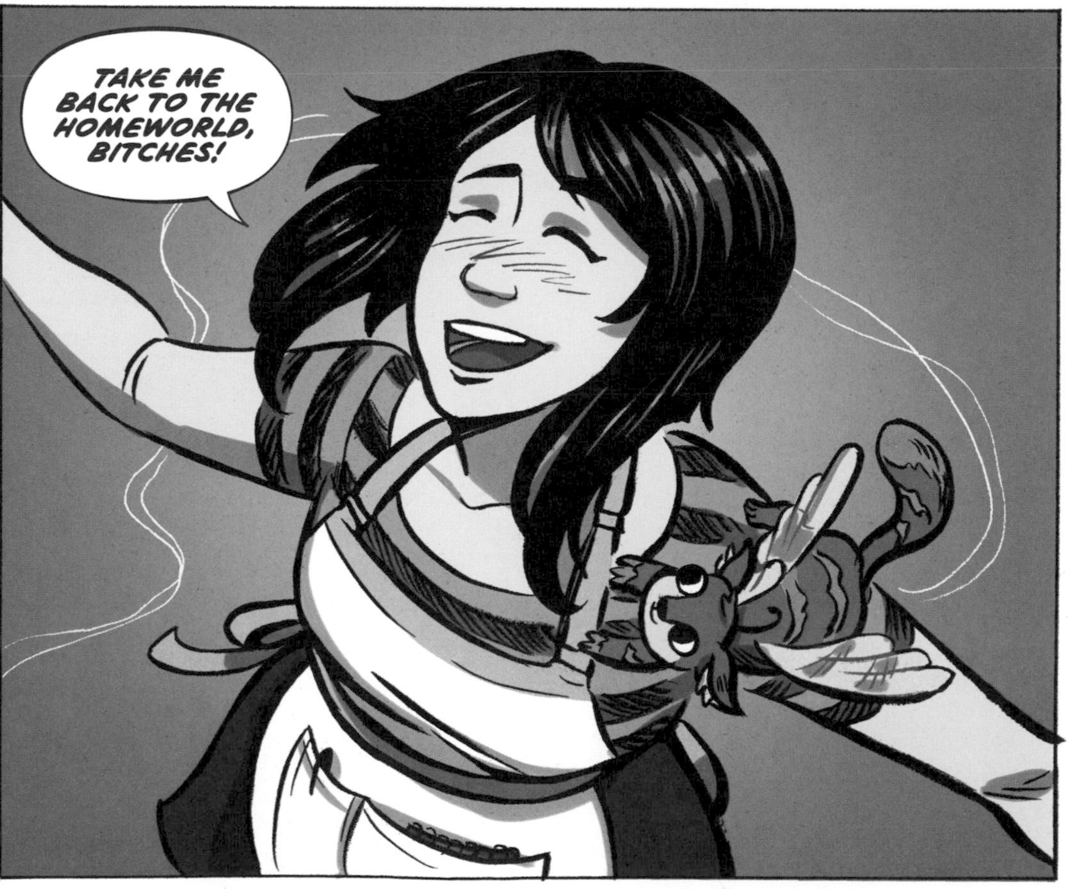
TAKE ME BACK TO THE HOMEWORLD, BITCHES!

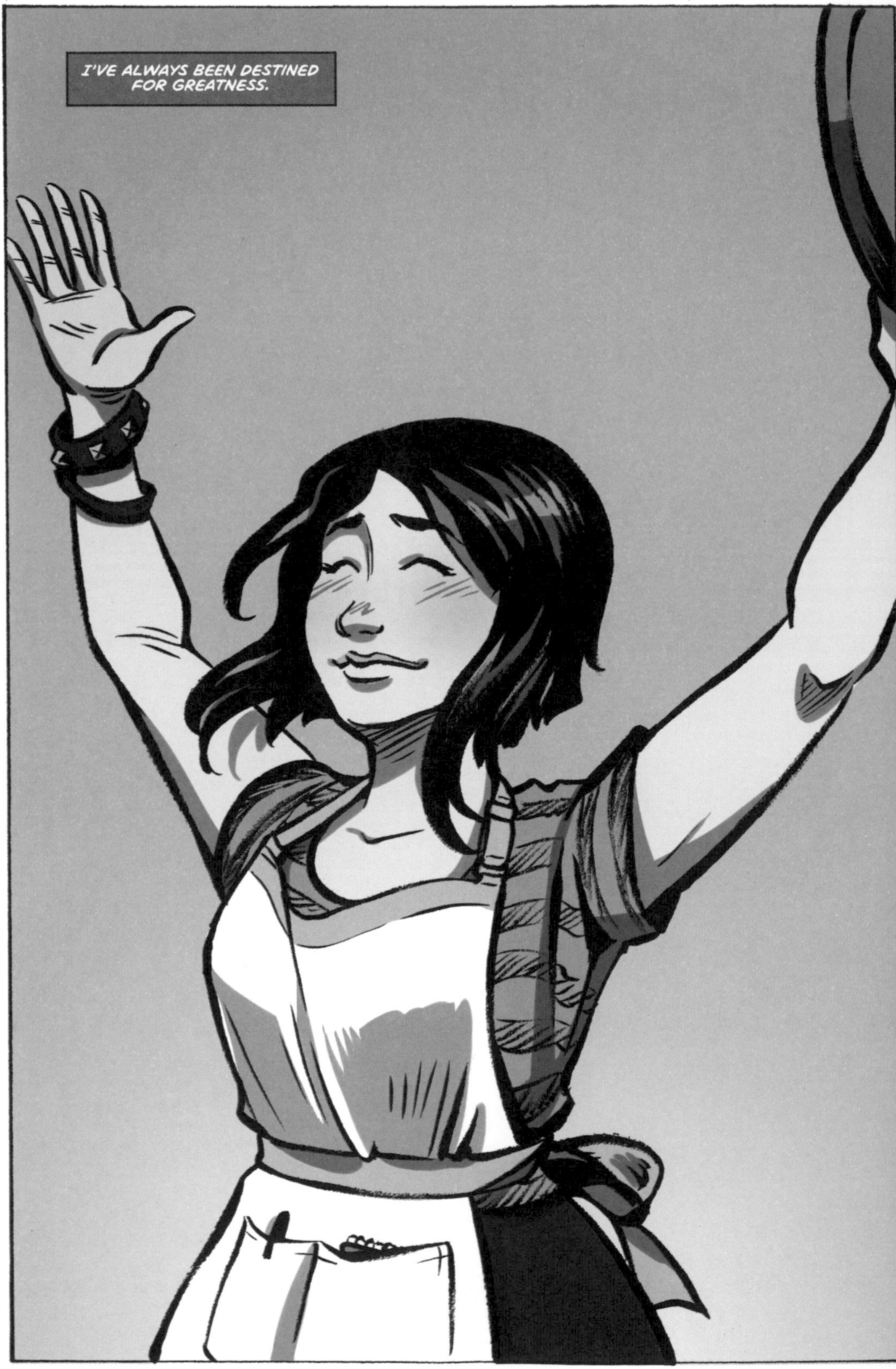
I'VE ALWAYS BEEN DESTINED FOR GREATNESS.

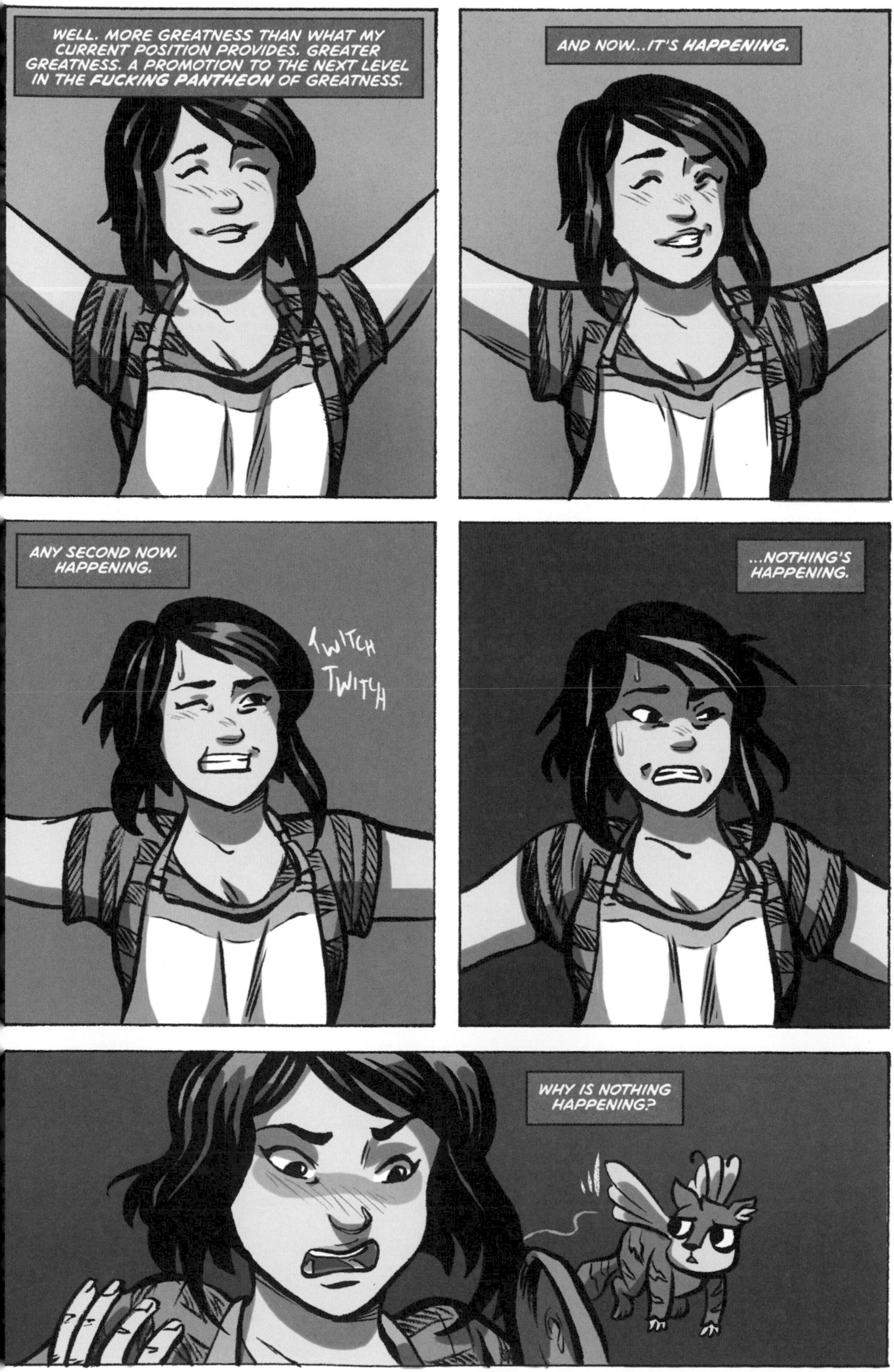
WELL. MORE GREATNESS THAN WHAT MY CURRENT POSITION PROVIDES. GREATER GREATNESS. A PROMOTION TO THE NEXT LEVEL IN THE FUCKING PANTHEON OF GREATNESS.
AND NOW...IT'S HAPPENING.
ANY SECOND NOW. HAPPENING.
TWITCH
TWITCH
...NOTHING'S HAPPENING.
WHY IS NOTHING HAPPENING?

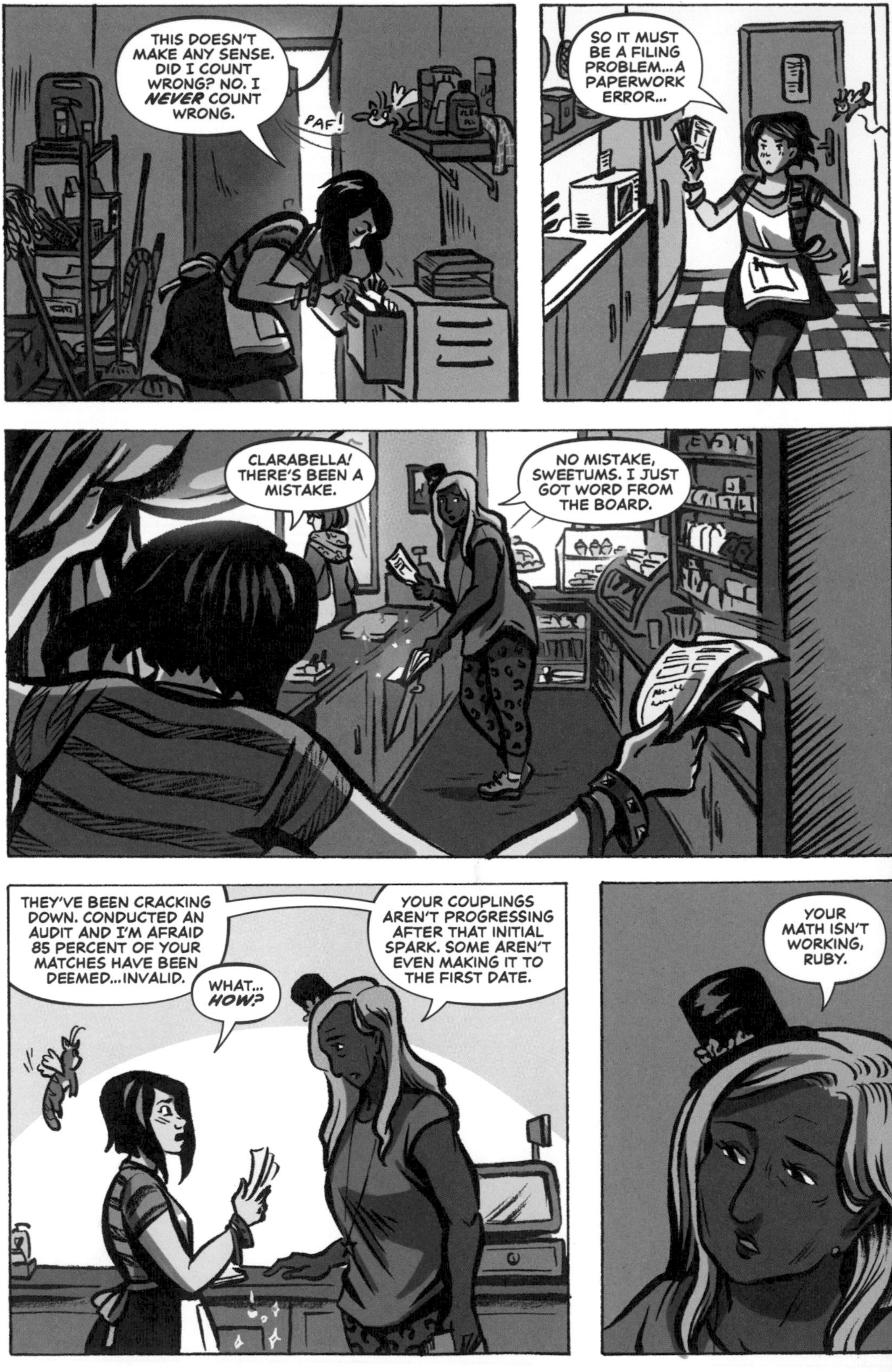
THIS DOESN'T MAKE ANY SENSE. DID I COUNT WRONG? NO. I NEVER COUNT WRONG.
PAF!
SO IT MUST BE A FILING PROBLEM...A PAPERWORK ERROR...
CLARABELLA! THERE'S BEEN A MISTAKE.
NO MISTAKE, SWEETUMS. I JUST GOT WORD FROM THE BOARD.
THEY'VE BEEN CRACKING DOWN. CONDUCTED AN AUDIT AND I'M AFRAID 85 PERCENT OF YOUR MATCHES HAVE BEEN DEEMED...INVALID.
WHAT... HOW?
YOUR COUPLINGS AREN'T PROGRESSING AFTER THAT INITIAL SPARK. SOME AREN'T EVEN MAKING IT TO THE FIRST DATE.
YOUR MATH ISN'T WORKING, RUBY.

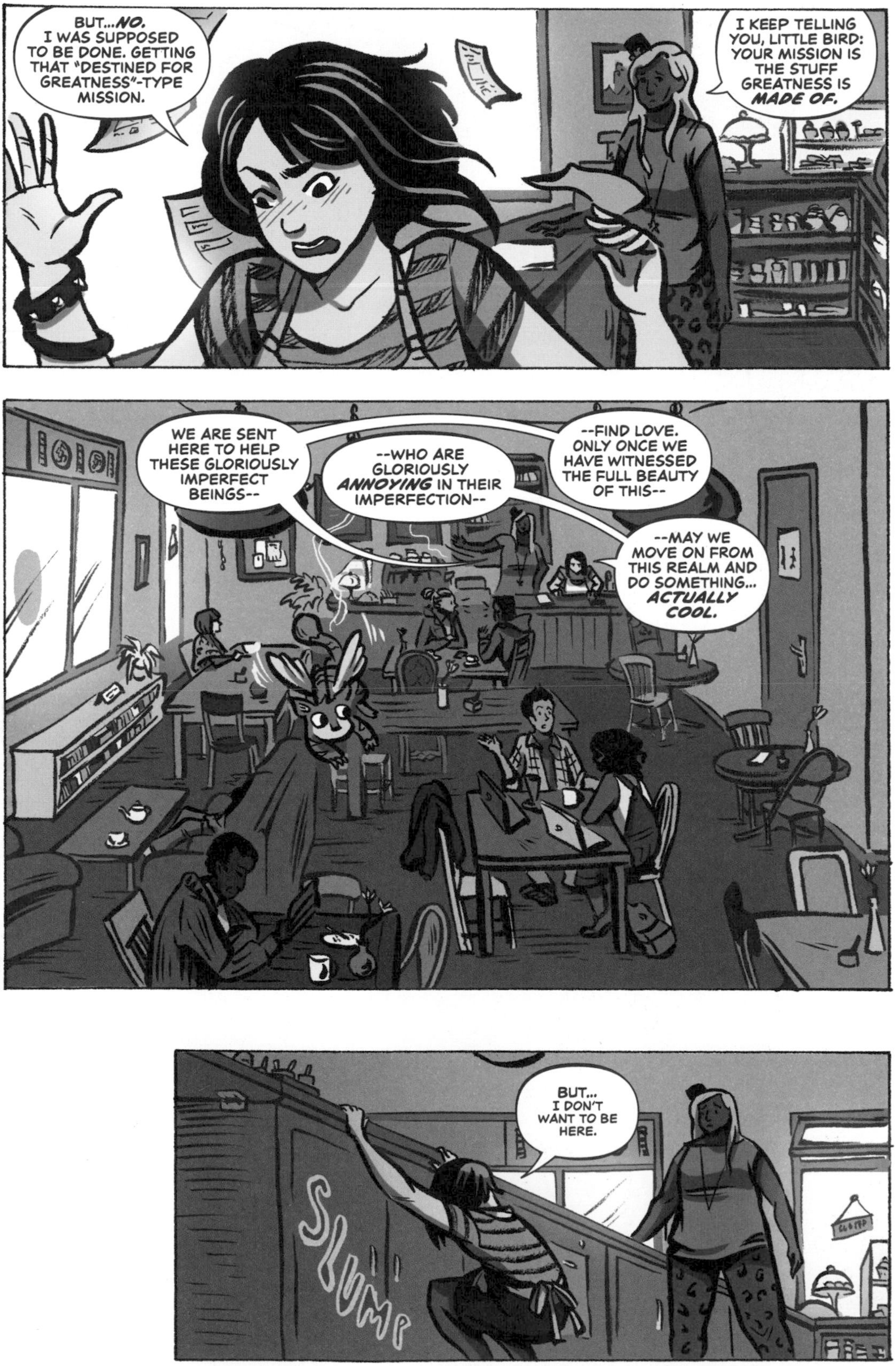
BUT...*NO.* I WAS SUPPOSED TO BE DONE. GETTING THAT "DESTINED FOR GREATNESS"-TYPE MISSION.
I KEEP TELLING YOU, LITTLE BIRD: YOUR MISSION IS THE STUFF GREATNESS IS *MADE OF.*
WE ARE SENT HERE TO HELP THESE GLORIOUSLY IMPERFECT BEINGS--
--WHO ARE GLORIOUSLY *ANNOYING* IN THEIR IMPERFECTION--
--FIND LOVE. ONLY ONCE WE HAVE WITNESSED THE FULL BEAUTY OF THIS--
--MAY WE MOVE ON FROM THIS REALM AND DO SOMETHING... *ACTUALLY COOL.*
BUT... I DON'T WANT TO BE HERE.
SLUMP

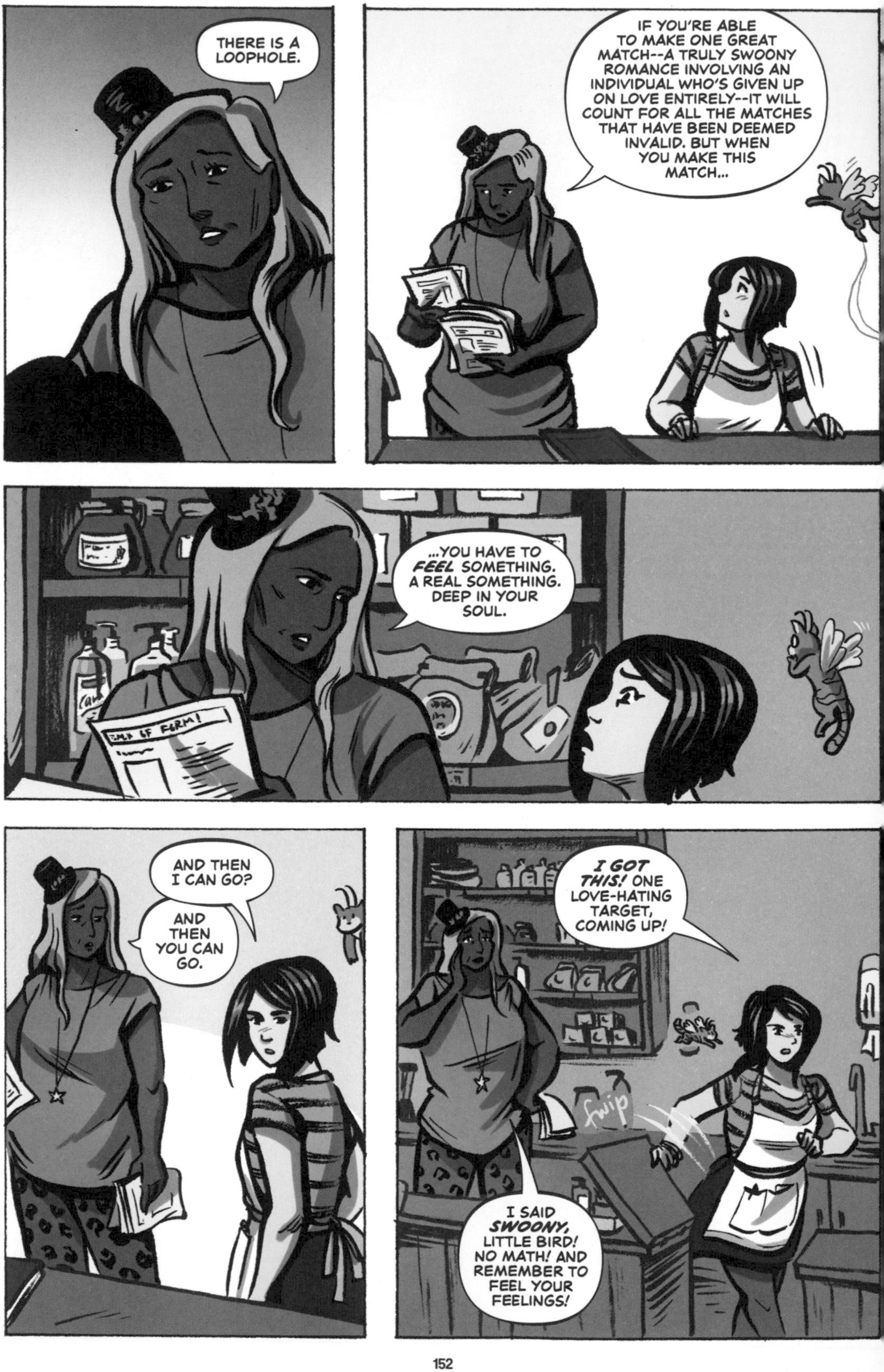
THERE IS A LOOPHOLE.
IF YOU'RE ABLE TO MAKE ONE GREAT MATCH--A TRULY SWOONY ROMANCE INVOLVING AN INDIVIDUAL WHO'S GIVEN UP ON LOVE ENTIRELY--IT WILL COUNT FOR ALL THE MATCHES THAT HAVE BEEN DEEMED INVALID. BUT WHEN YOU MAKE THIS MATCH...
...YOU HAVE TO FEEL SOMETHING. A REAL SOMETHING. DEEP IN YOUR SOUL.
AND THEN I CAN GO?
AND THEN YOU CAN GO.
I GOT THIS! ONE LOVE-HATING TARGET, COMING UP!
fwip
I SAID SWOONY, LITTLE BIRD! NO MATH! AND REMEMBER TO FEEL YOUR FEELINGS!

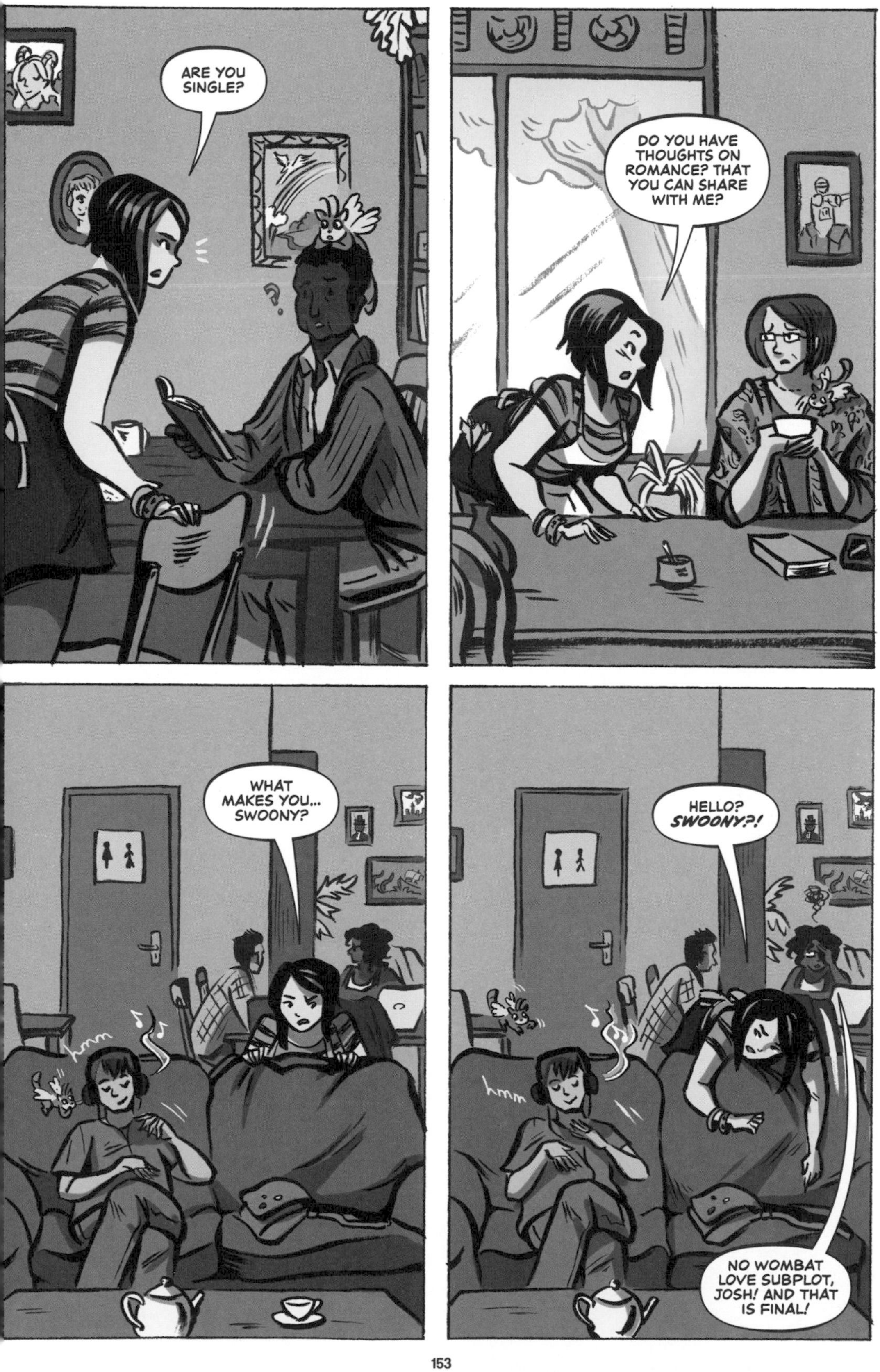
ARE YOU SINGLE?
DO YOU HAVE THOUGHTS ON ROMANCE? THAT YOU CAN SHARE WITH ME?
WHAT MAKES YOU... SWOONY?
hmm
HELLO? *SWOONY?!*
hmm
NO WOMBAT LOVE SUBPLOT, JOSH! AND THAT IS FINAL!

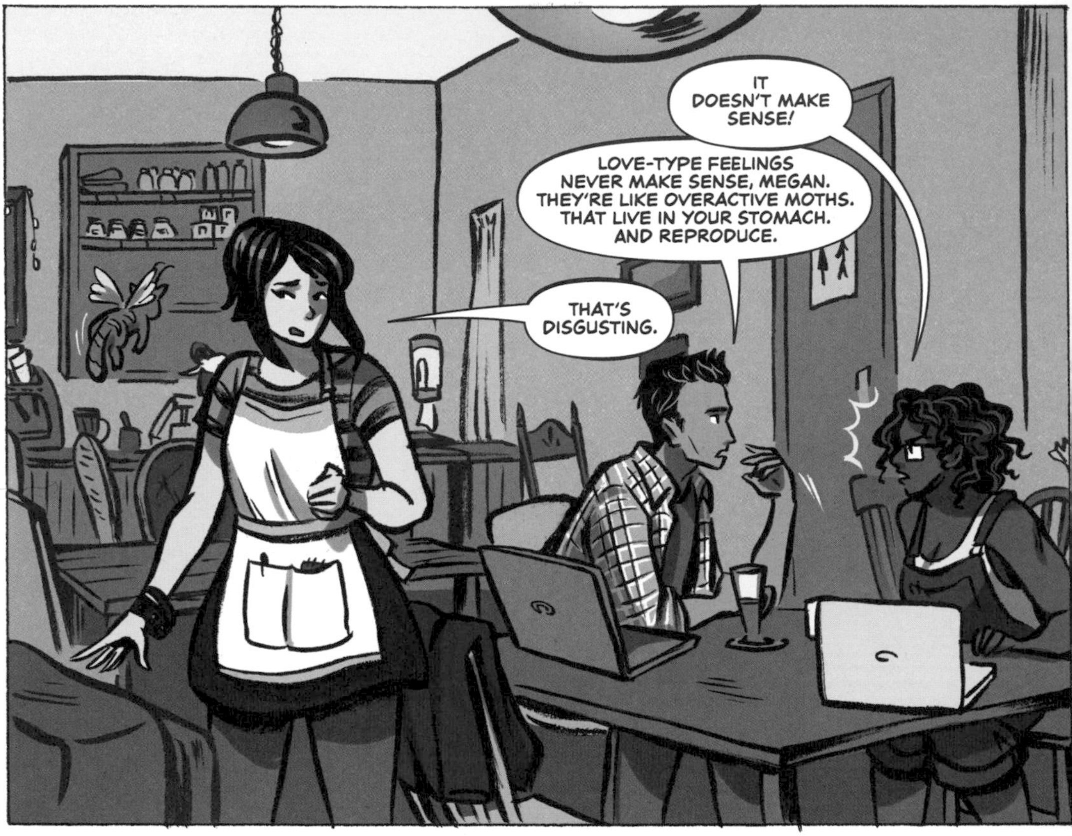
IT DOESN'T MAKE SENSE!
LOVE-TYPE FEELINGS NEVER MAKE SENSE, MEGAN. THEY'RE LIKE OVERACTIVE MOTHS. THAT LIVE IN YOUR STOMACH. AND REPRODUCE.
THAT'S DISGUSTING.

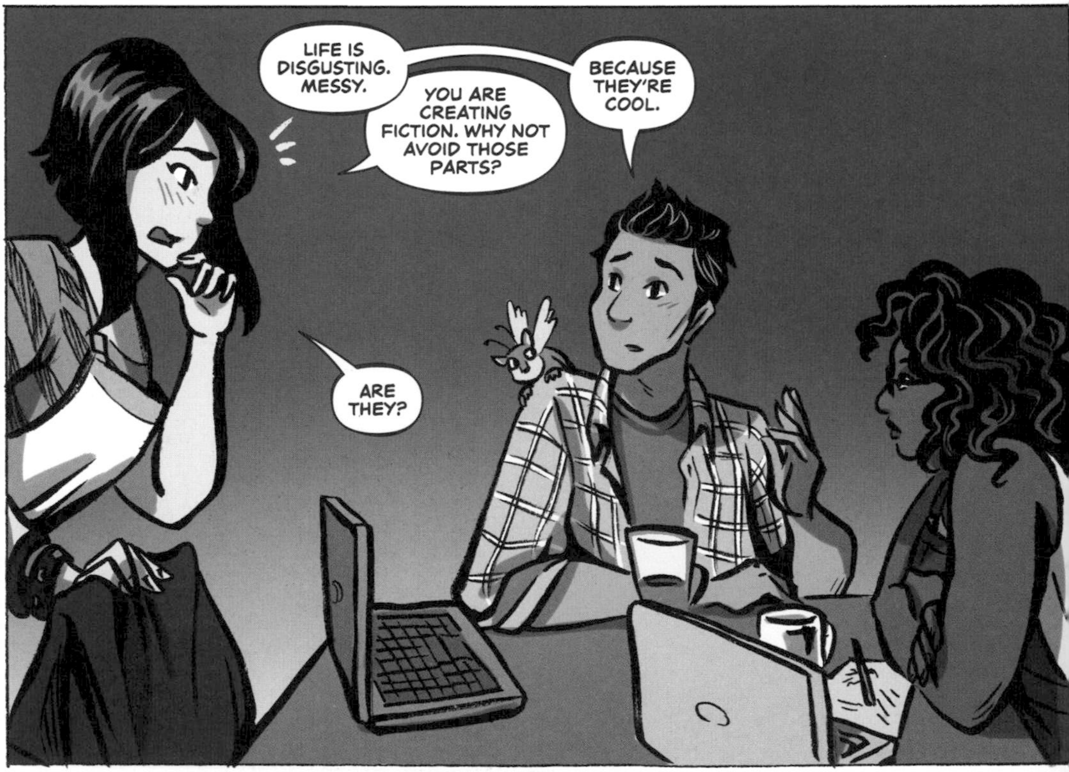
LIFE IS DISGUSTING. MESSY.
YOU ARE CREATING FICTION. WHY NOT AVOID THOSE PARTS?
BECAUSE THEY'RE COOL.
ARE THEY?

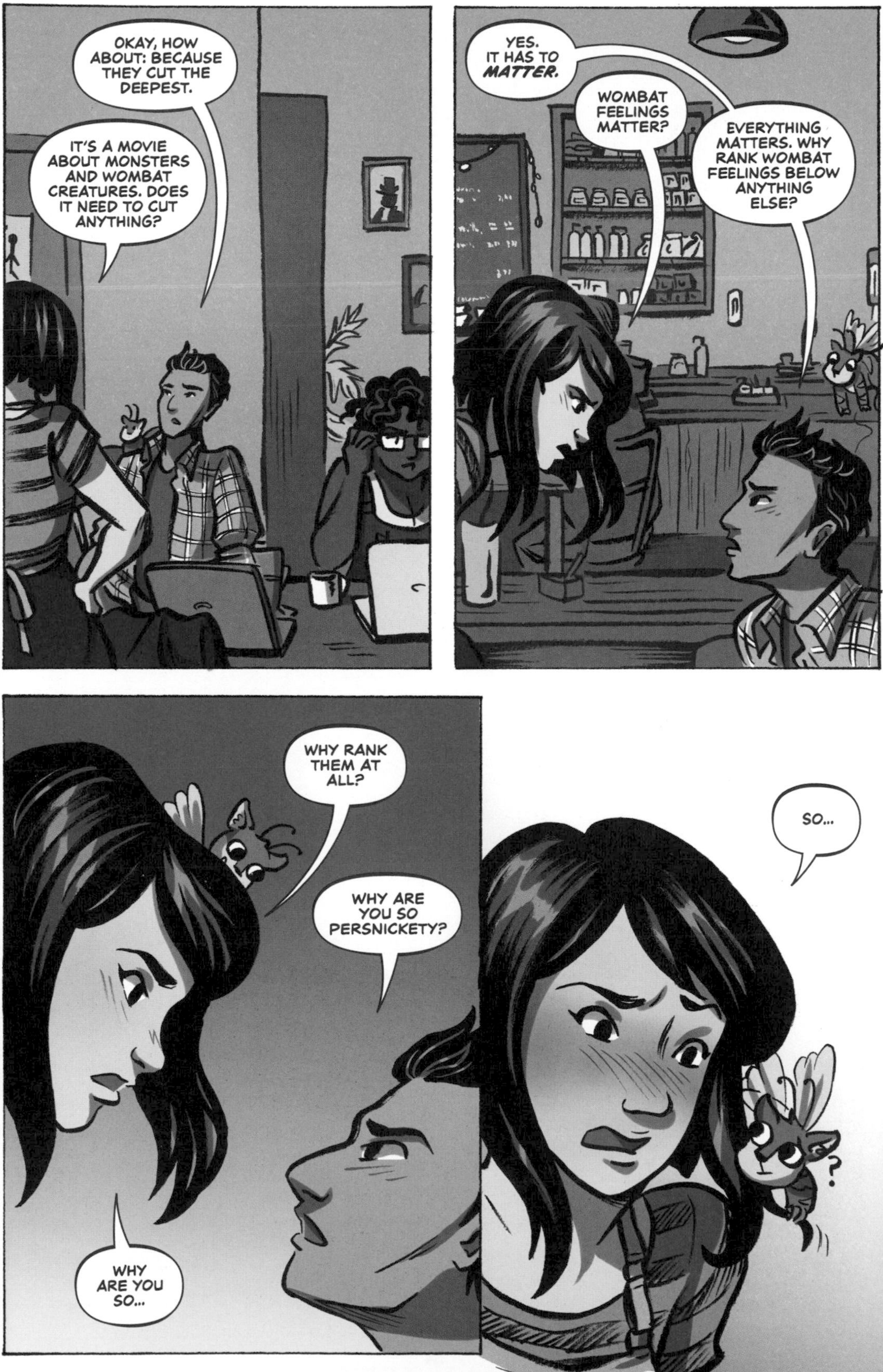
OKAY, HOW ABOUT: BECAUSE THEY CUT THE DEEPEST.
IT'S A MOVIE ABOUT MONSTERS AND WOMBAT CREATURES. DOES IT NEED TO CUT ANYTHING?
YES. IT HAS TO *MATTER.*
WOMBAT FEELINGS MATTER?
EVERYTHING MATTERS. WHY RANK WOMBAT FEELINGS BELOW ANYTHING ELSE?
WHY RANK THEM AT ALL?
WHY ARE YOU SO PERSNICKETY?
WHY ARE YOU SO...
SO...
?

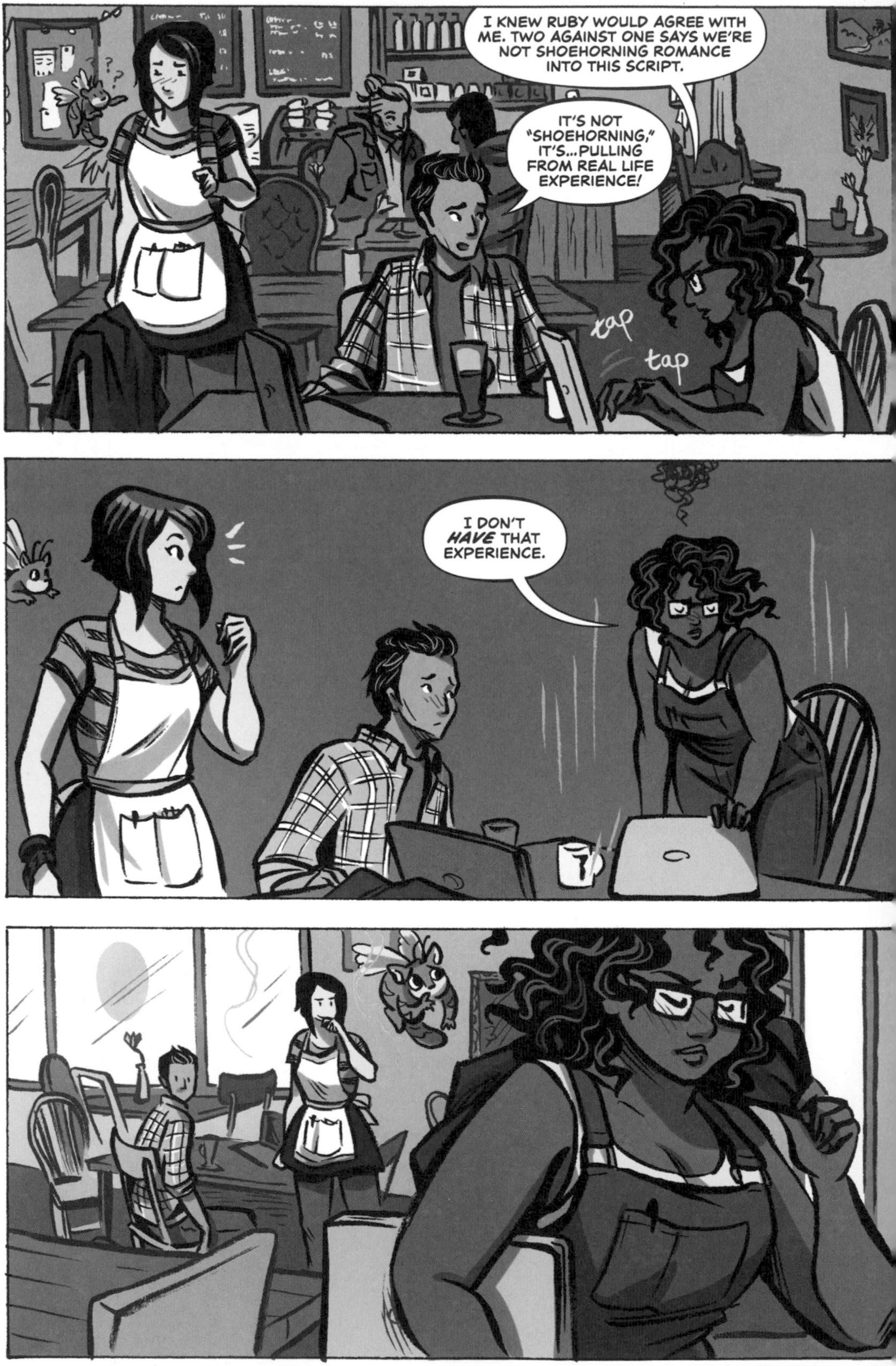
I KNEW RUBY WOULD AGREE WITH ME. TWO AGAINST ONE SAYS WE'RE NOT SHOEHORNING ROMANCE INTO THIS SCRIPT.
IT'S NOT "SHOEHORNING," IT'S...PULLING FROM REAL LIFE EXPERIENCE!
tap
tap
I DON'T *HAVE* THAT EXPERIENCE.

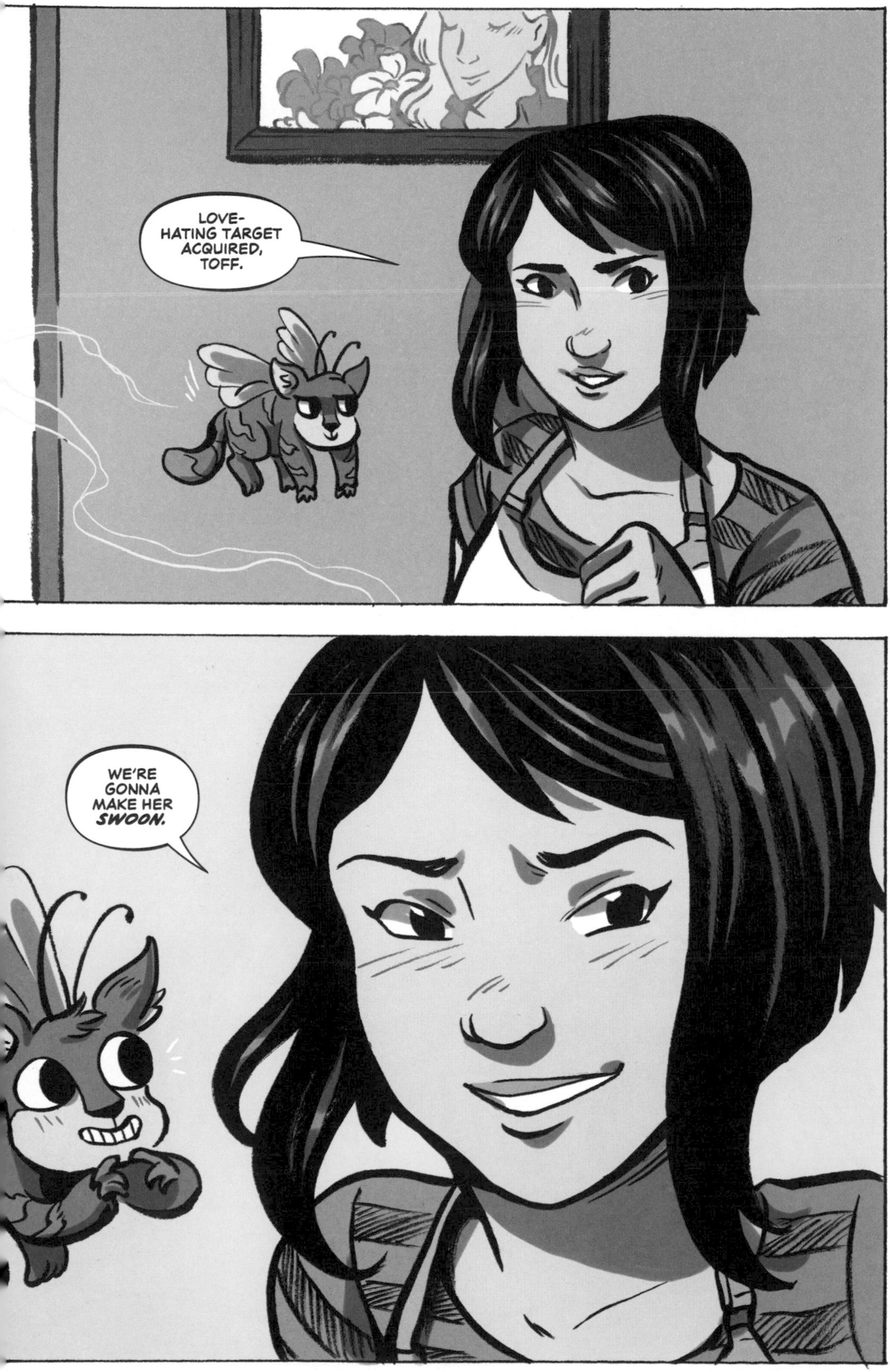
LOVE-HATING TARGET ACQUIRED, TOFF.
WE'RE GONNA MAKE HER *SWOON.*

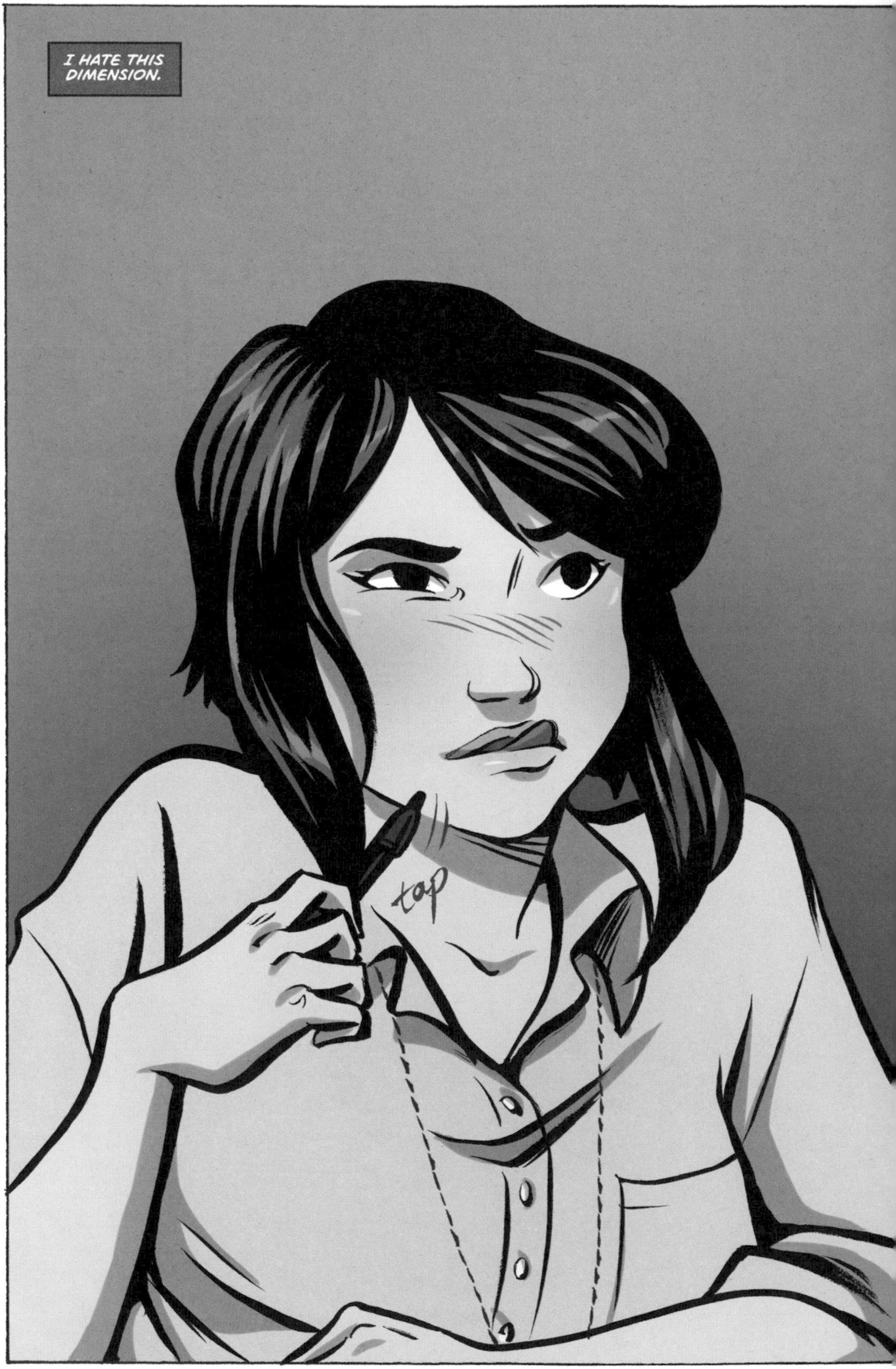
I HATE THIS DIMENSION.
tap

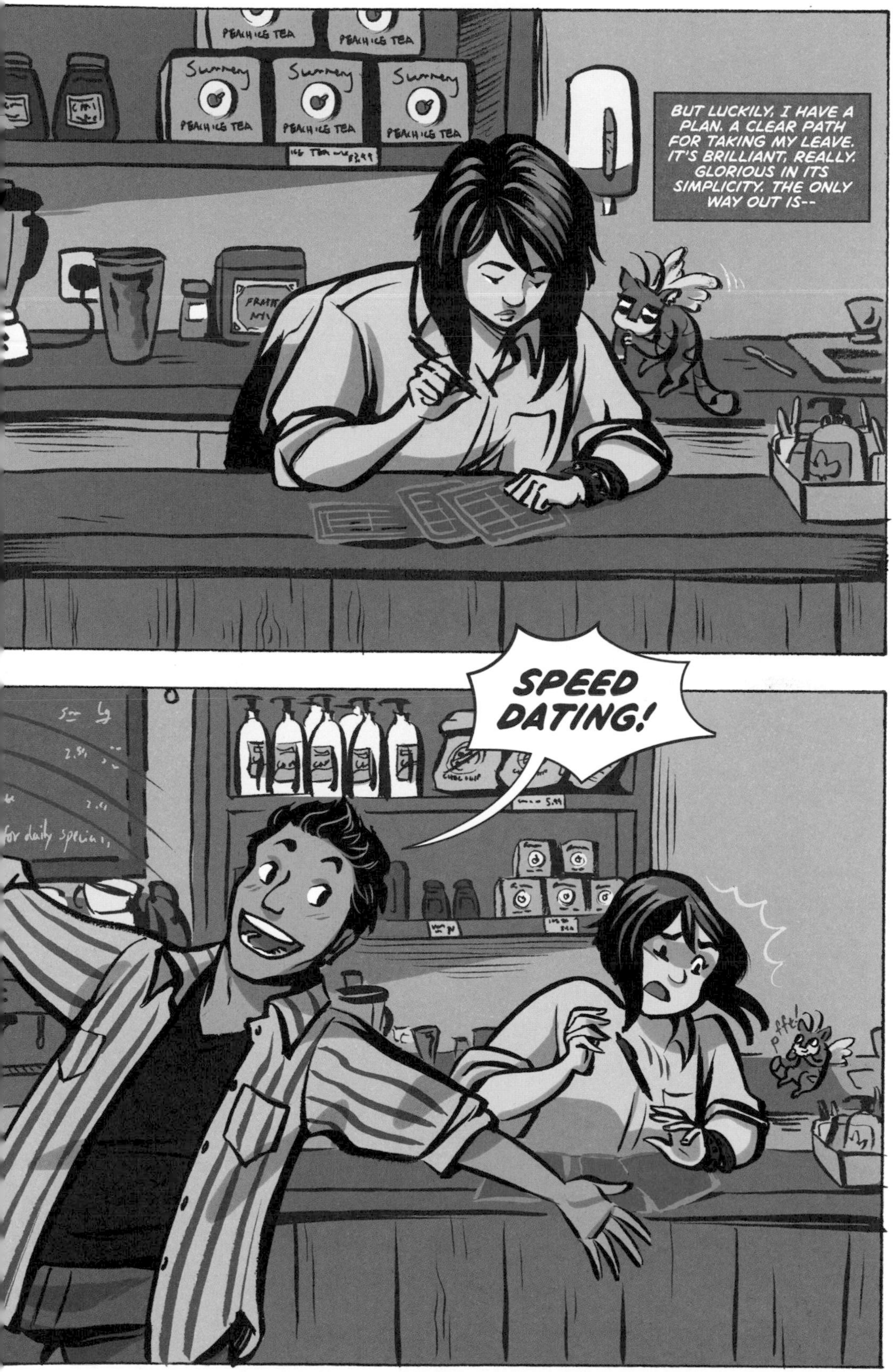
PEACH ICE TEA
Summery
PEACH ICE TEA
BUT LUCKILY, I HAVE A PLAN. A CLEAR PATH FOR TAKING MY LEAVE. IT'S BRILLIANT, REALLY. GLORIOUS IN ITS SIMPLICITY. THE ONLY WAY OUT IS--
SPEED DATING!
pfft!

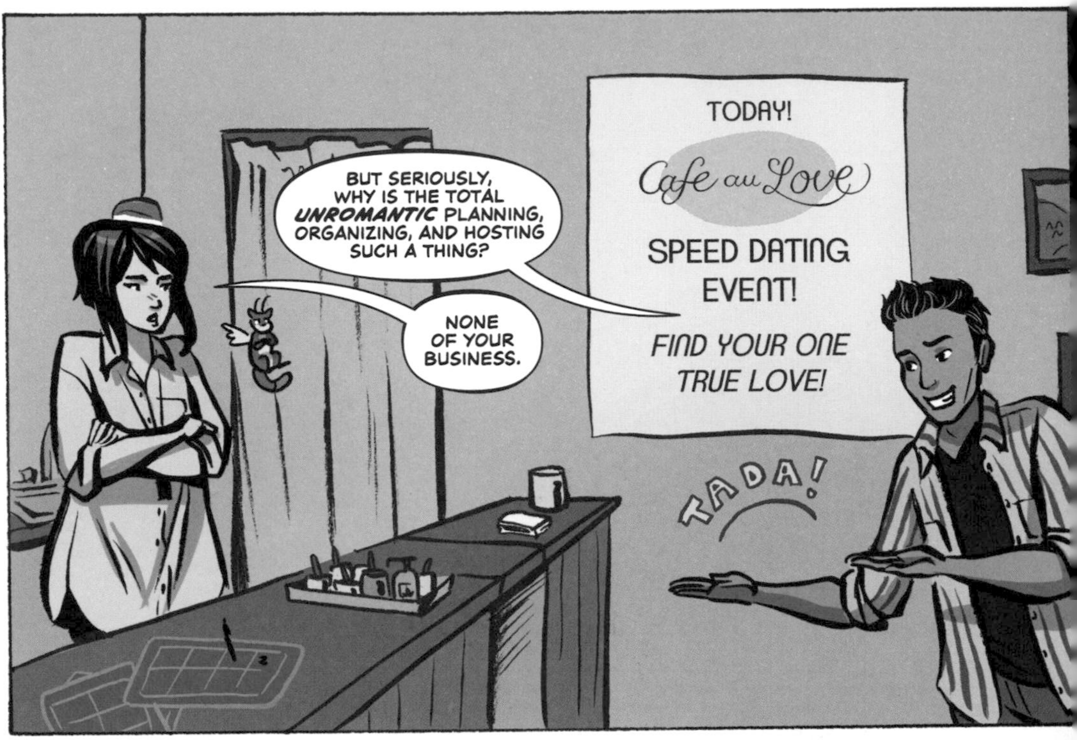
BUT SERIOUSLY, WHY IS THE TOTAL *UNROMANTIC* PLANNING, ORGANIZING, AND HOSTING SUCH A THING?
NONE OF YOUR BUSINESS.
TODAY!
Cafe au Love
SPEED DATING EVENT!
FIND YOUR ONE TRUE LOVE!
TADA!

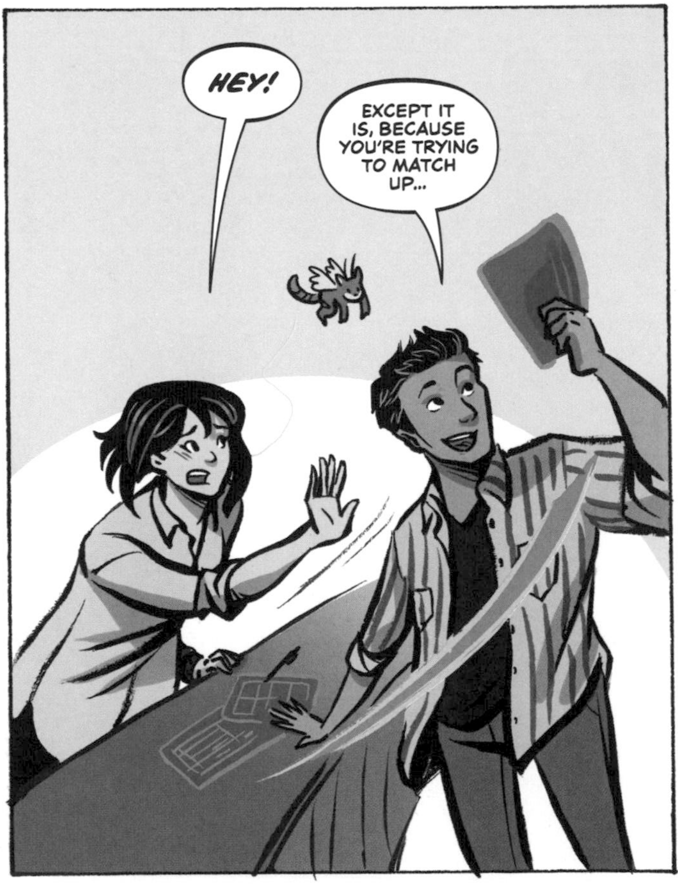
HEY!
EXCEPT IT IS, BECAUSE YOU'RE TRYING TO MATCH UP...

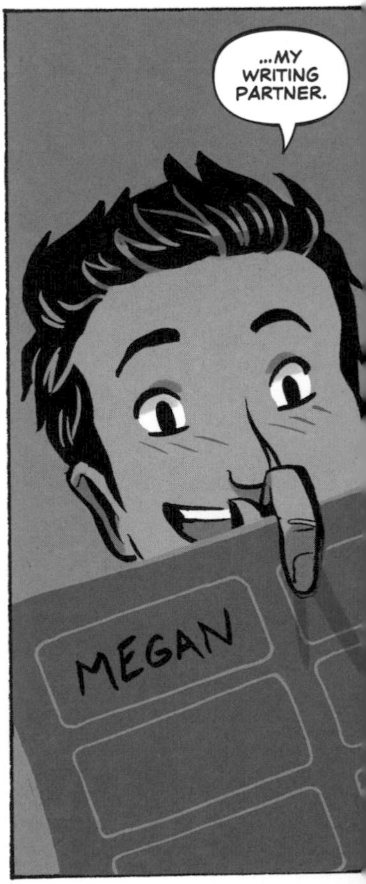
...MY WRITING PARTNER.
MEGAN

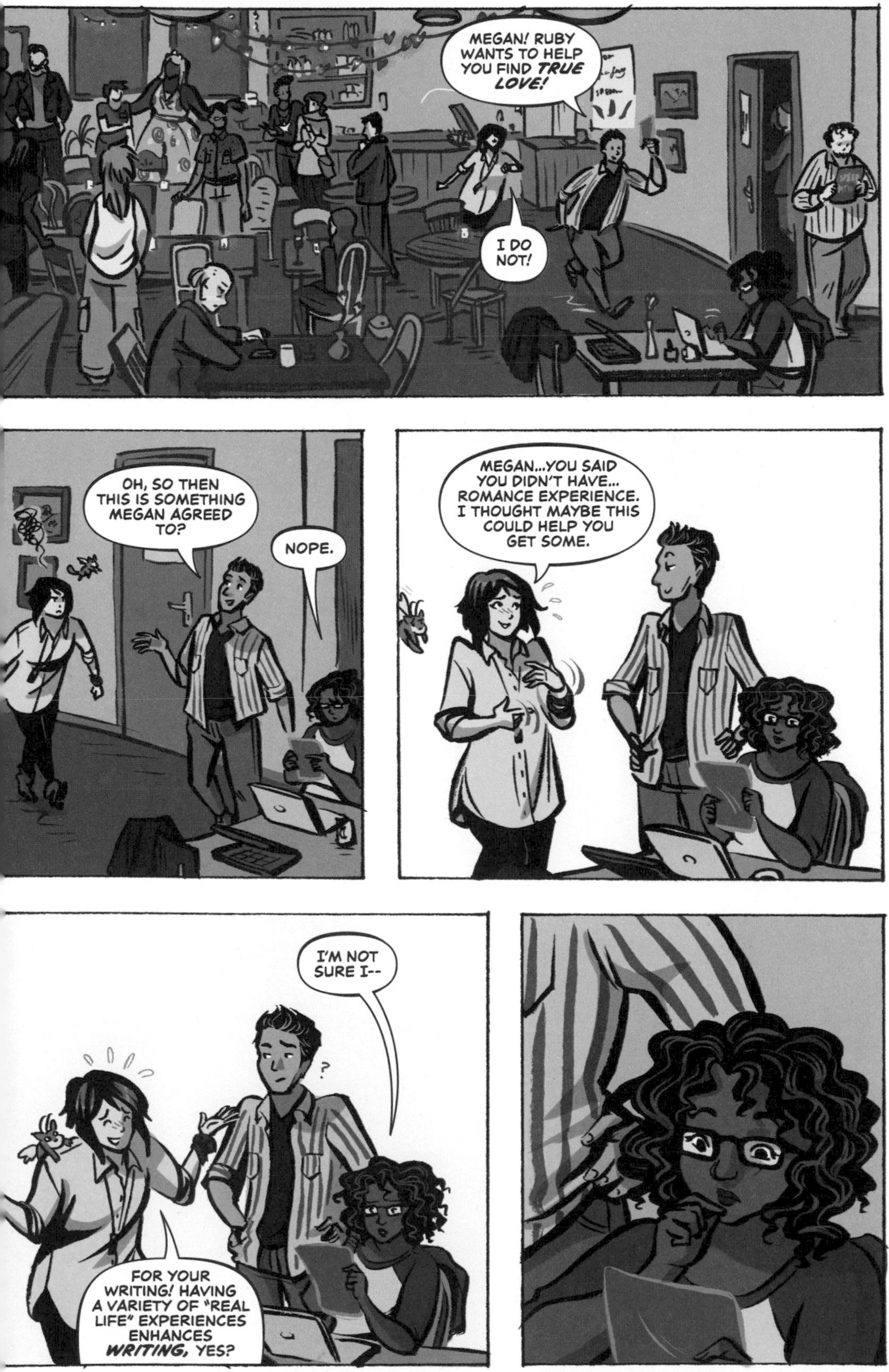
MEGAN! RUBY WANTS TO HELP YOU FIND *TRUE LOVE!*
I DO NOT!
OH, SO THEN THIS IS SOMETHING MEGAN AGREED TO?
NOPE.
MEGAN...YOU SAID YOU DIDN'T HAVE... ROMANCE EXPERIENCE. I THOUGHT MAYBE THIS COULD HELP YOU GET SOME.
I'M NOT SURE I--
FOR YOUR WRITING! HAVING A VARIETY OF "REAL LIFE" EXPERIENCES ENHANCES *WRITING,* YES?

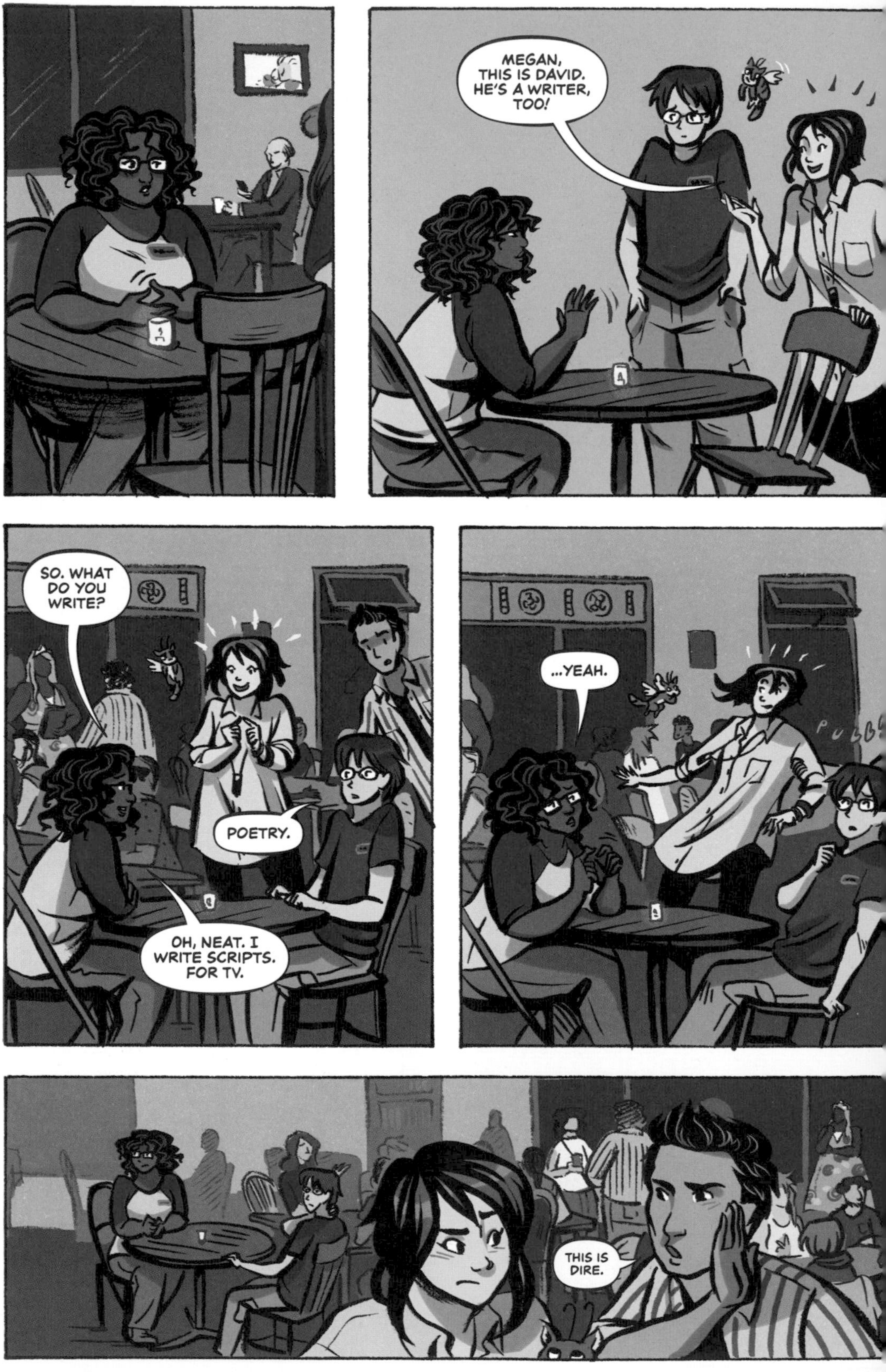
MEGAN, THIS IS DAVID. HE'S A WRITER, TOO!
SO. WHAT DO YOU WRITE?
POETRY.
OH, NEAT. I WRITE SCRIPTS. FOR TV.
...YEAH.
THIS IS DIRE.

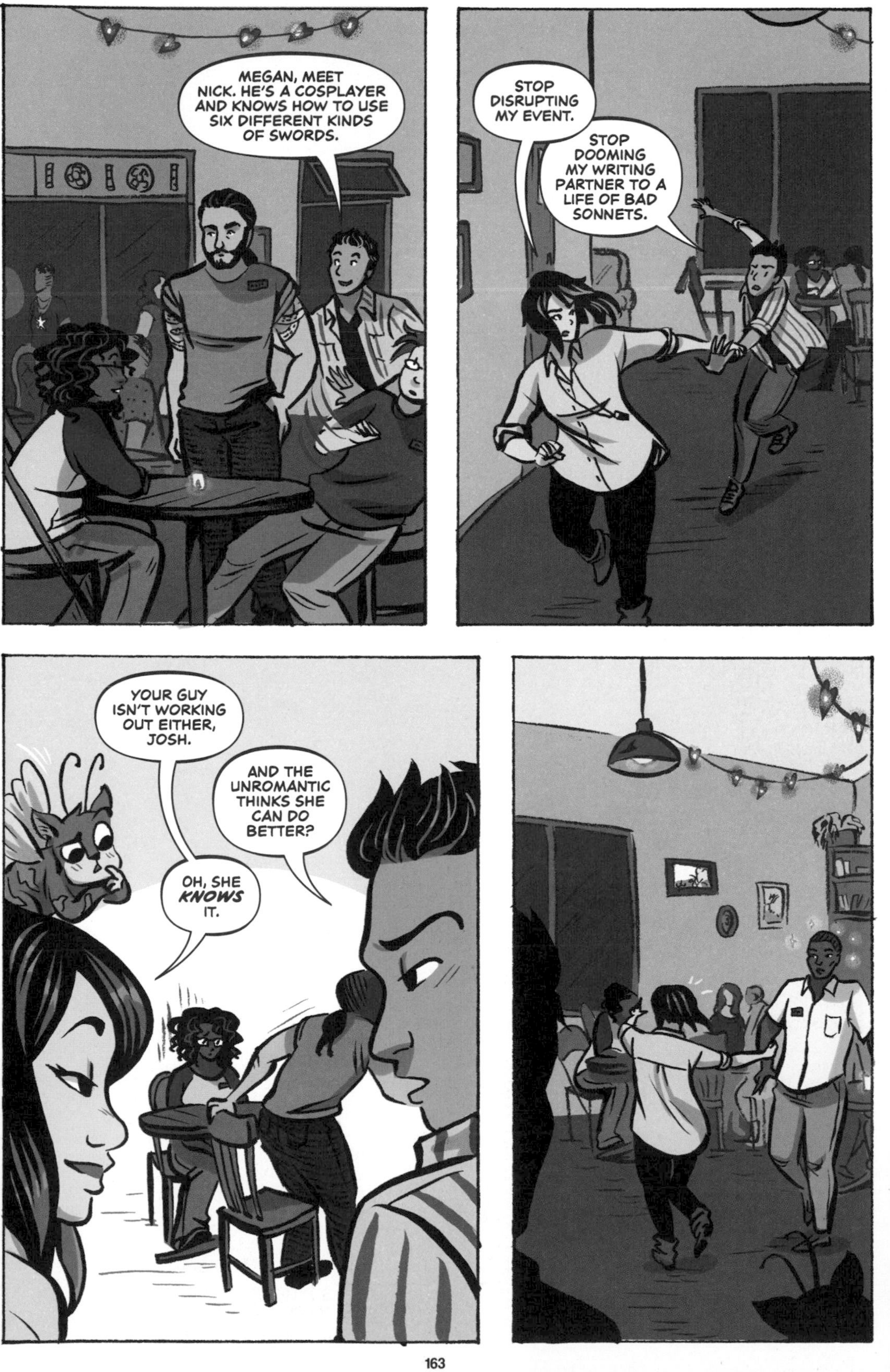
MEGAN, MEET NICK. HE'S A COSPLAYER AND KNOWS HOW TO USE SIX DIFFERENT KINDS OF SWORDS.
STOP DISRUPTING MY EVENT.
STOP DOOMING MY WRITING PARTNER TO A LIFE OF BAD SONNETS.
YOUR GUY ISN'T WORKING OUT EITHER, JOSH.
AND THE UNROMANTIC THINKS SHE CAN DO BETTER?
OH, SHE *KNOWS* IT.

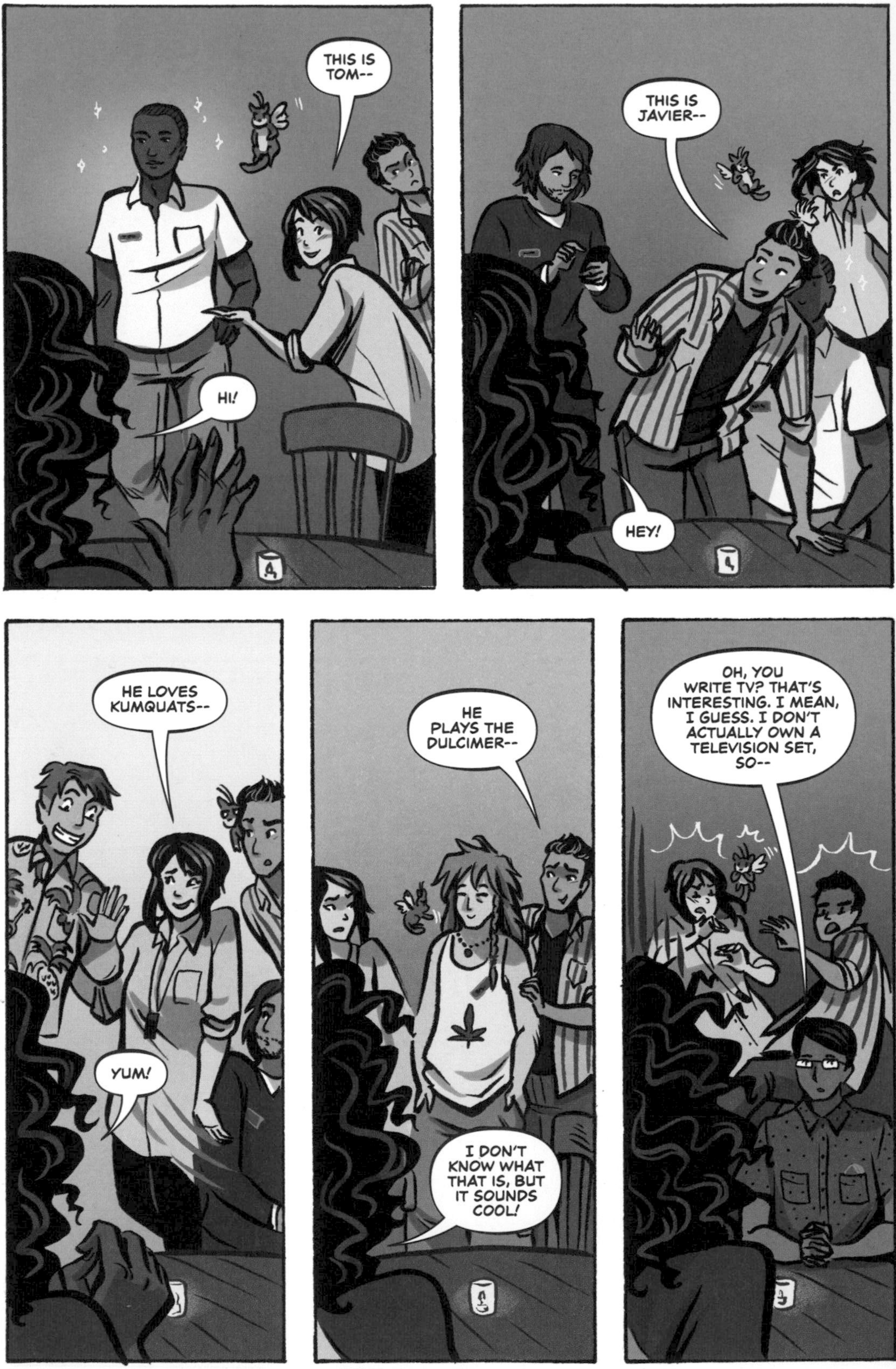
THIS IS TOM--
HI!
THIS IS JAVIER--
HEY!
HE LOVES KUMQUATS--
YUM!
HE PLAYS THE DULCIMER--
I DON'T KNOW WHAT THAT IS, BUT IT SOUNDS COOL!
OH, YOU WRITE TV? THAT'S INTERESTING. I MEAN, I GUESS. I DON'T ACTUALLY OWN A TELEVISION SET, SO--

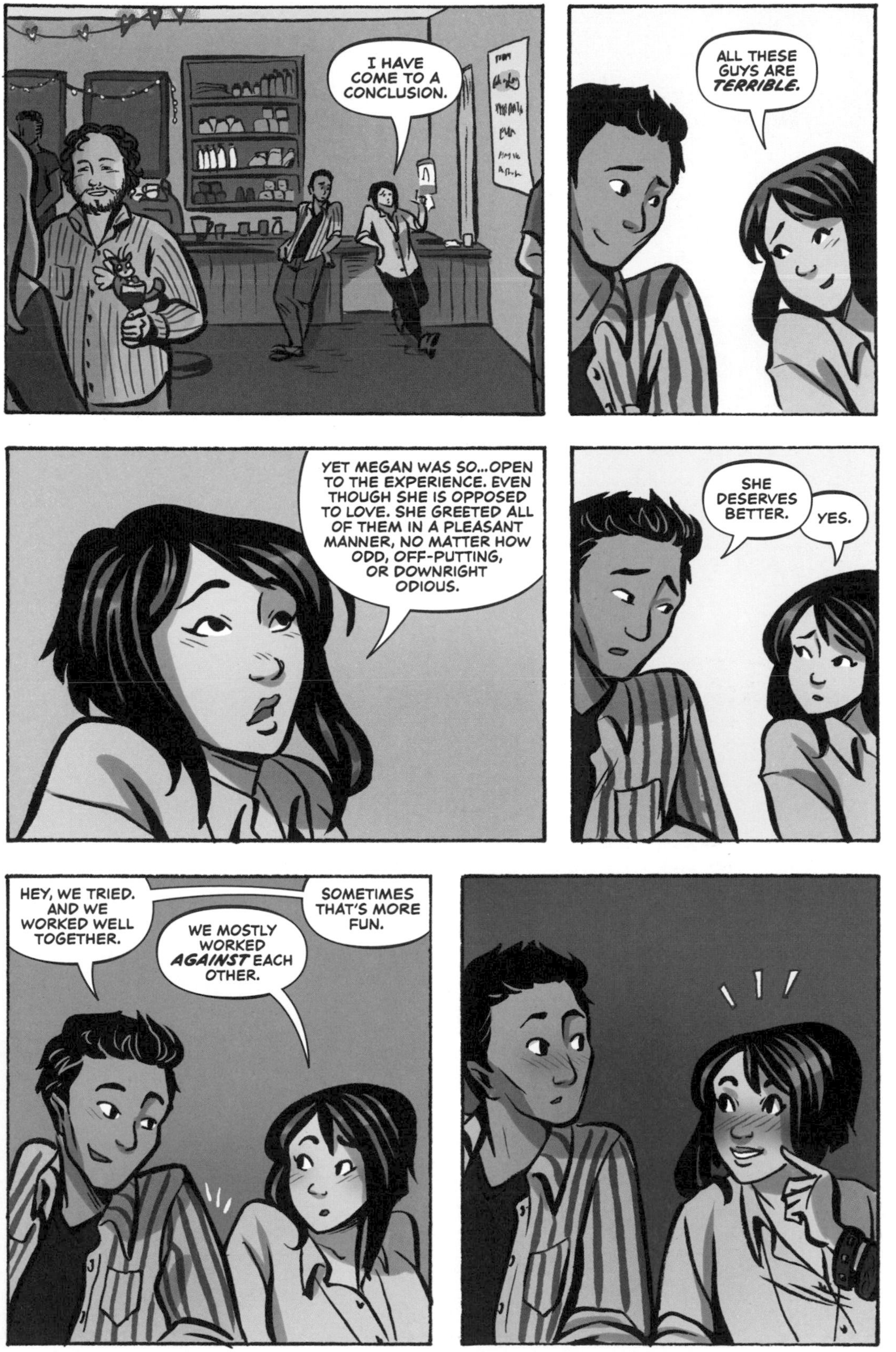
I HAVE COME TO A CONCLUSION.
ALL THESE GUYS ARE *TERRIBLE.*
YET MEGAN WAS SO...OPEN TO THE EXPERIENCE. EVEN THOUGH SHE IS OPPOSED TO LOVE. SHE GREETED ALL OF THEM IN A PLEASANT MANNER, NO MATTER HOW ODD, OFF-PUTTING, OR DOWNRIGHT ODIOUS.
SHE DESERVES BETTER.
YES.
HEY, WE TRIED. AND WE WORKED WELL TOGETHER.
WE MOSTLY WORKED *AGAINST* EACH OTHER.
SOMETIMES THAT'S MORE FUN.

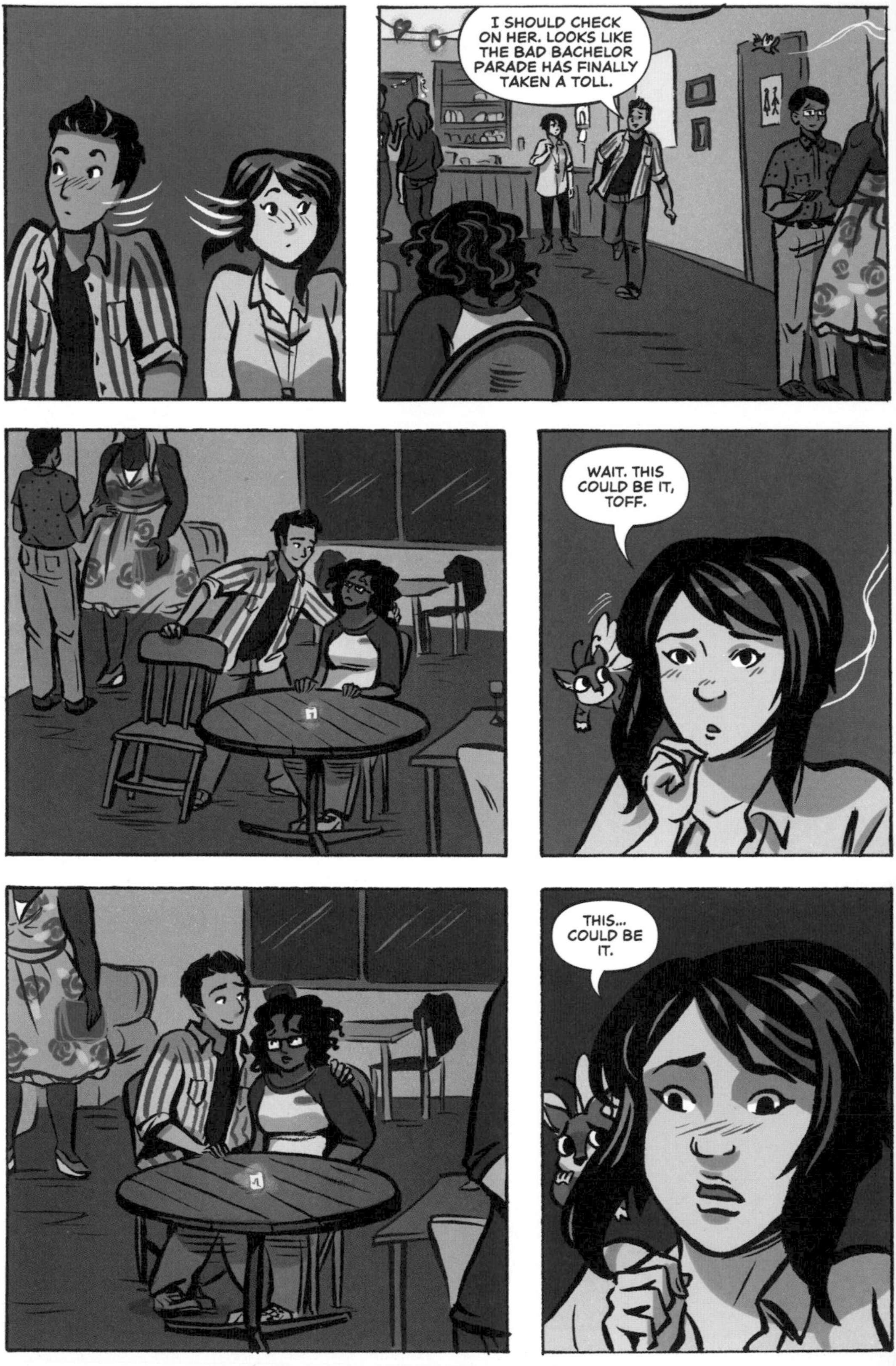
I SHOULD CHECK ON HER. LOOKS LIKE THE BAD BACHELOR PARADE HAS FINALLY TAKEN A TOLL.
WAIT. THIS COULD BE IT, TOFF.
THIS... COULD BE IT.

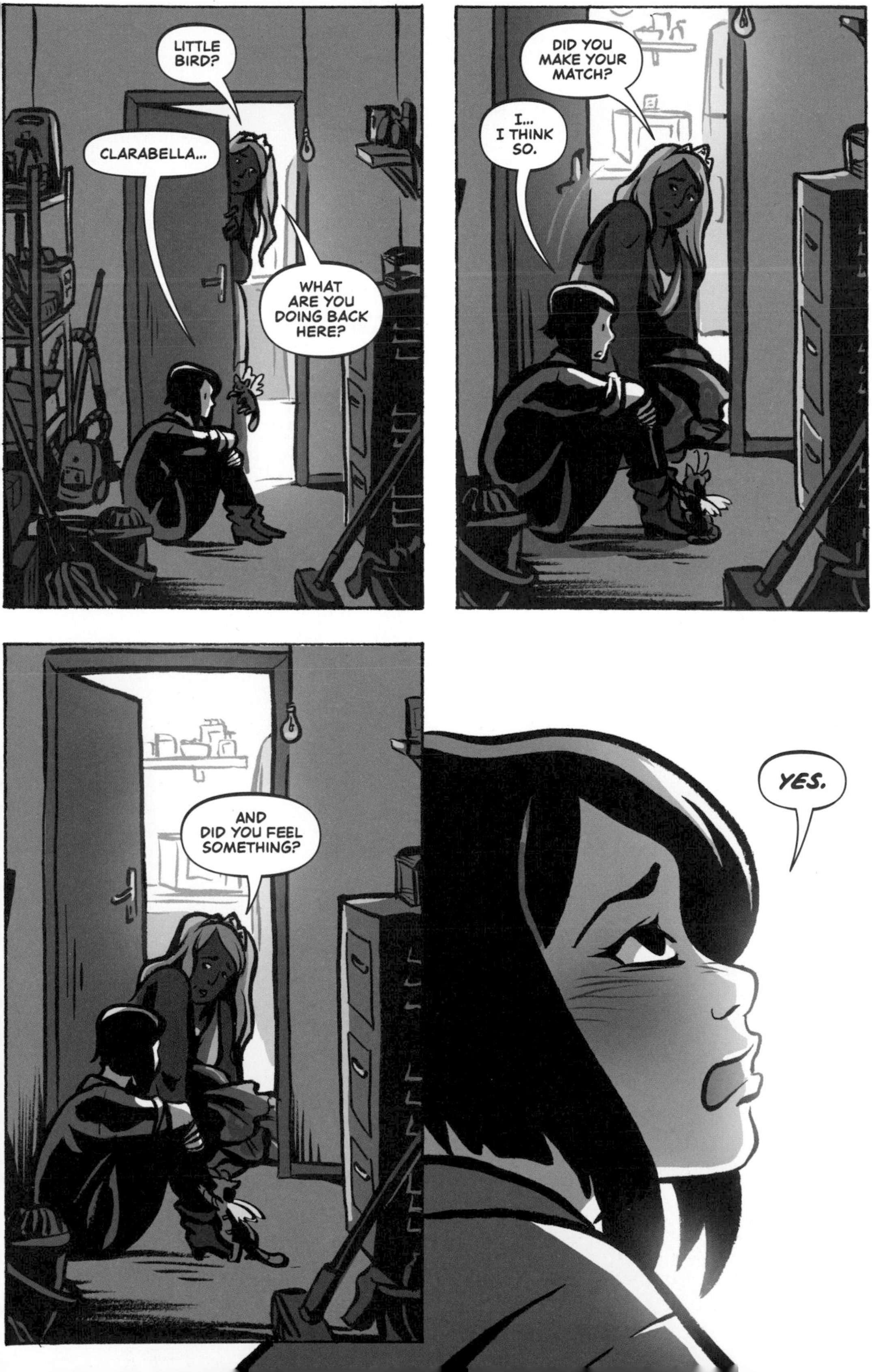
LITTLE BIRD?
CLARABELLA...
WHAT ARE YOU DOING BACK HERE?
DID YOU MAKE YOUR MATCH?
I... I THINK SO.
AND DID YOU FEEL SOMETHING?
YES.

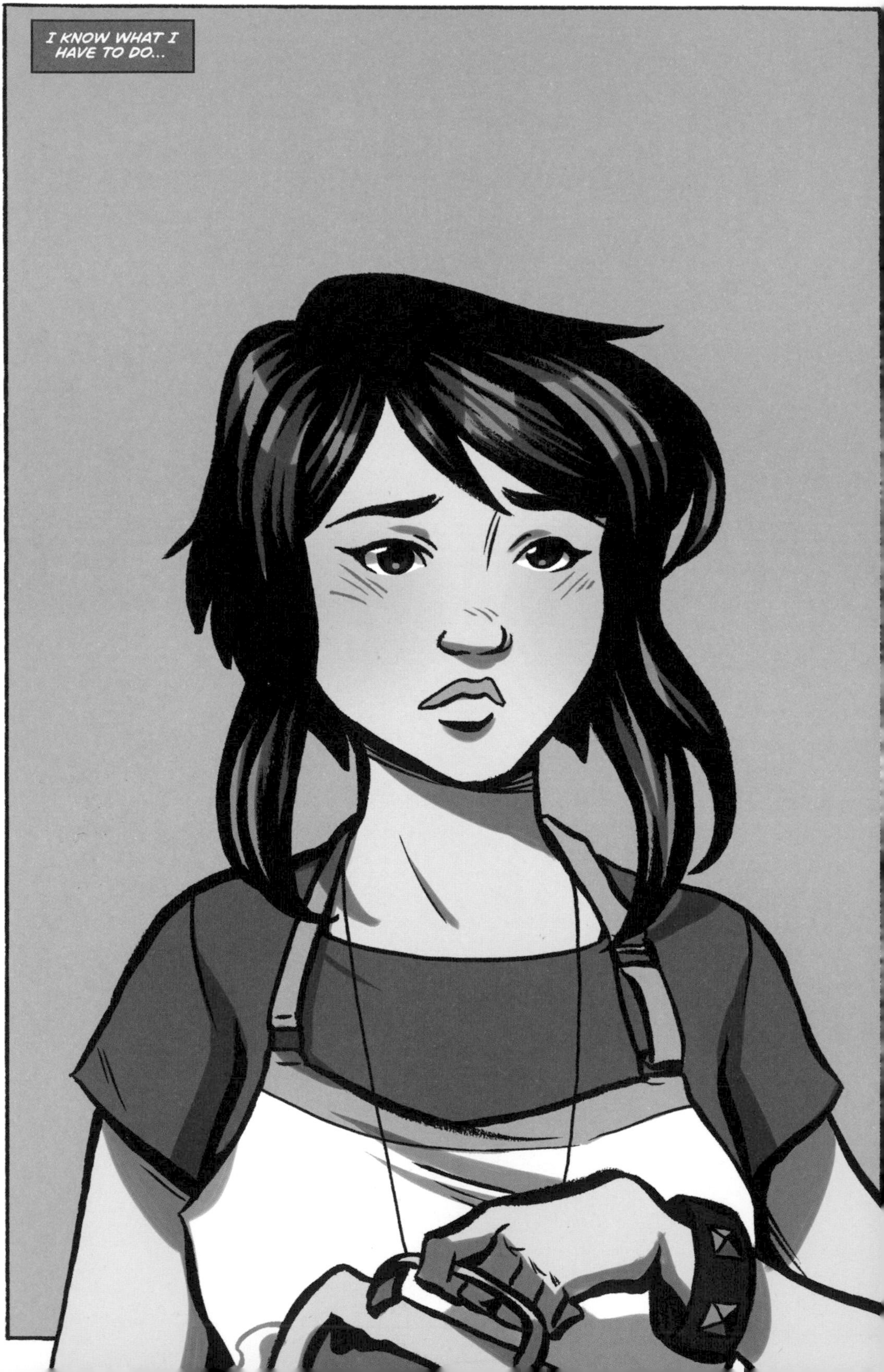
I KNOW WHAT I HAVE TO DO...

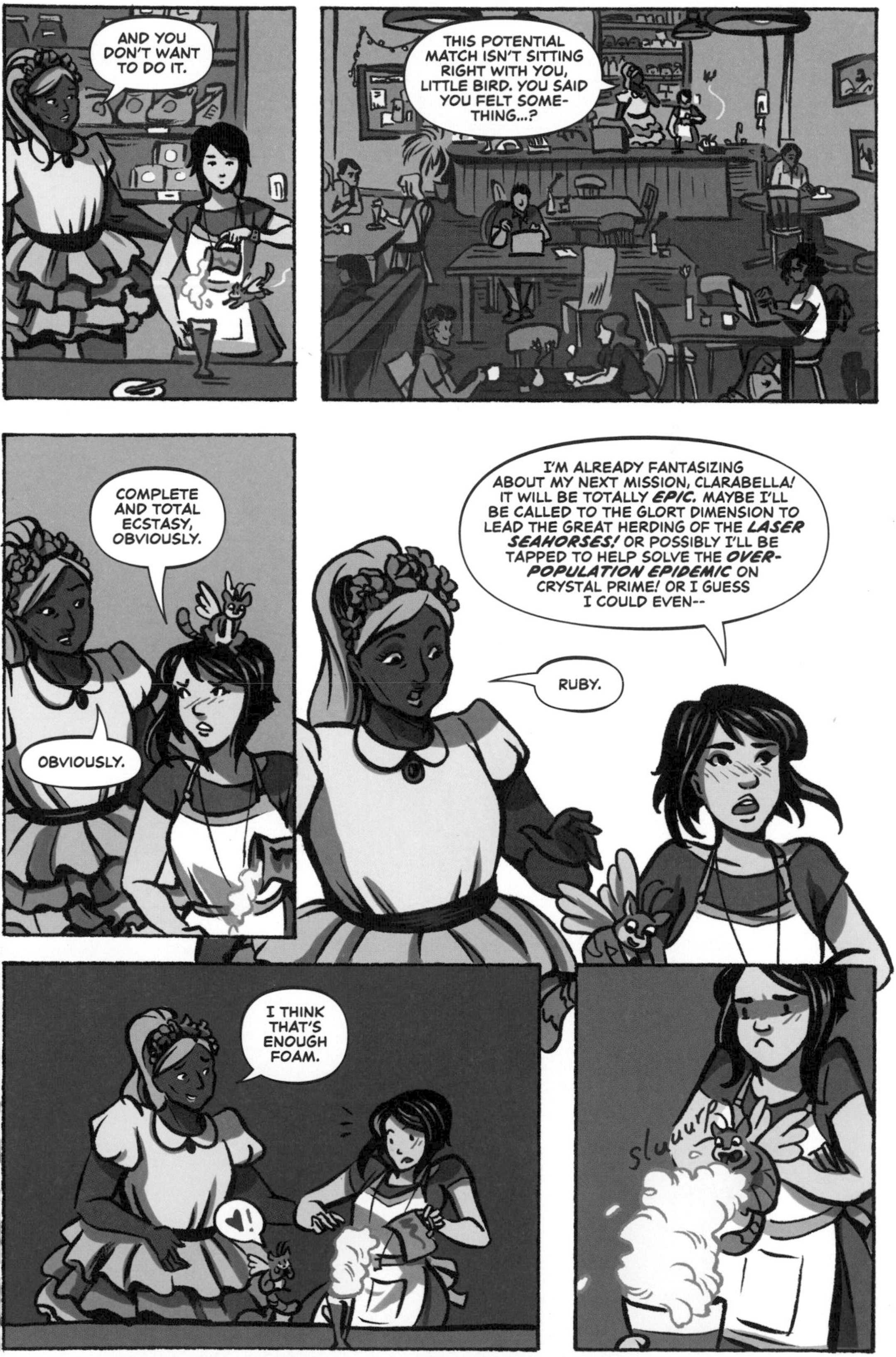
AND YOU DON'T WANT TO DO IT.
THIS POTENTIAL MATCH ISN'T SITTING RIGHT WITH YOU, LITTLE BIRD. YOU SAID YOU FELT SOMETHING...?
COMPLETE AND TOTAL ECSTASY, OBVIOUSLY.
OBVIOUSLY.
I'M ALREADY FANTASIZING ABOUT MY NEXT MISSION, CLARABELLA! IT WILL BE TOTALLY EPIC. MAYBE I'LL BE CALLED TO THE GLORT DIMENSION TO LEAD THE GREAT HERDING OF THE LASER SEAHORSES! OR POSSIBLY I'LL BE TAPPED TO HELP SOLVE THE OVER-POPULATION EPIDEMIC ON CRYSTAL PRIME! OR I GUESS I COULD EVEN--
RUBY.
I THINK THAT'S ENOUGH FOAM.
sluuurp

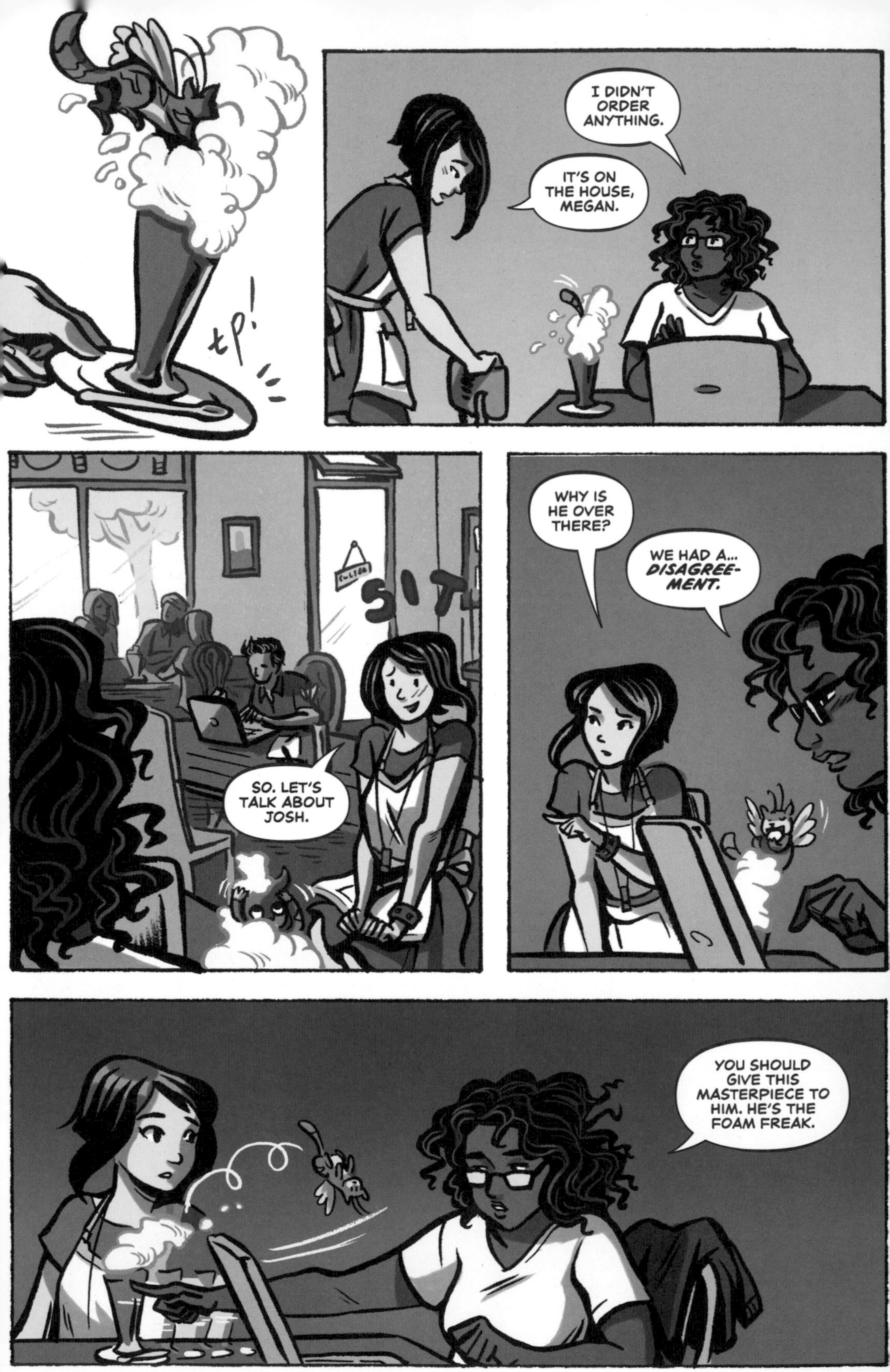
tp!
I DIDN'T ORDER ANYTHING.
IT'S ON THE HOUSE, MEGAN.
SIT
SO. LET'S TALK ABOUT JOSH.
WHY IS HE OVER THERE?
WE HAD A... ***DISAGREEMENT.***
YOU SHOULD GIVE THIS MASTERPIECE TO HIM. HE'S THE FOAM FREAK.

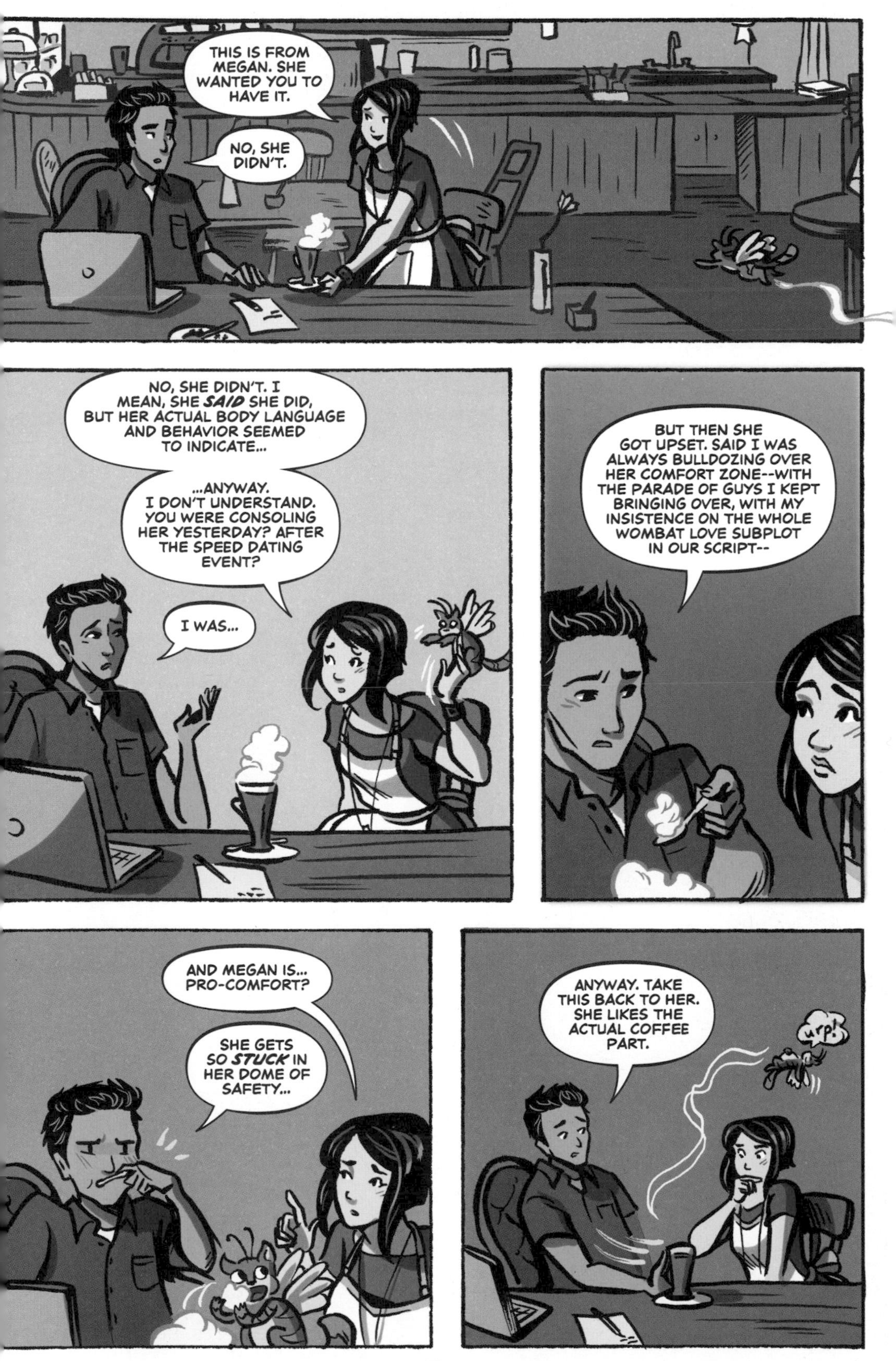
THIS IS FROM MEGAN. SHE WANTED YOU TO HAVE IT.
NO, SHE DIDN'T.
NO, SHE DIDN'T. I MEAN, SHE *SAID* SHE DID, BUT HER ACTUAL BODY LANGUAGE AND BEHAVIOR SEEMED TO INDICATE...
...ANYWAY. I DON'T UNDERSTAND. YOU WERE CONSOLING HER YESTERDAY? AFTER THE SPEED DATING EVENT?
I WAS...
BUT THEN SHE GOT UPSET. SAID I WAS ALWAYS BULLDOZING OVER HER COMFORT ZONE--WITH THE PARADE OF GUYS I KEPT BRINGING OVER, WITH MY INSISTENCE ON THE WHOLE WOMBAT LOVE SUBPLOT IN OUR SCRIPT--
AND MEGAN IS... PRO-COMFORT?
SHE GETS SO *STUCK* IN HER DOME OF SAFETY...
ANYWAY. TAKE THIS BACK TO HER. SHE LIKES THE ACTUAL COFFEE PART.
urp!

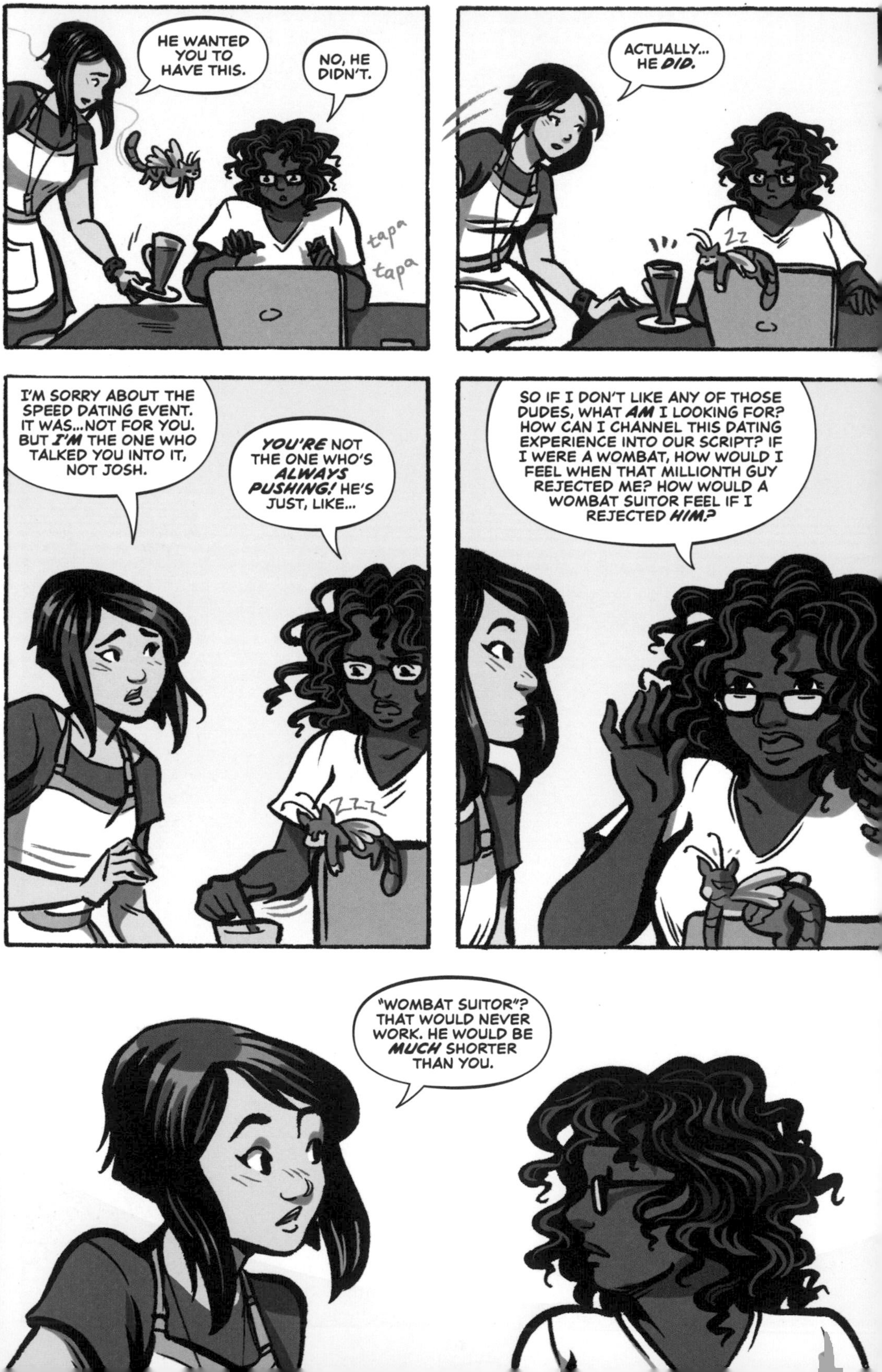
HE WANTED YOU TO HAVE THIS.
NO, HE DIDN'T.
tapa tapa
ACTUALLY... HE *DID.*
Zz
I'M SORRY ABOUT THE SPEED DATING EVENT. IT WAS...NOT FOR YOU. BUT *I'M* THE ONE WHO TALKED YOU INTO IT, NOT JOSH.
YOU'RE NOT THE ONE WHO'S *ALWAYS PUSHING!* HE'S JUST, LIKE...
ZZZ
SO IF I DON'T LIKE ANY OF THOSE DUDES, WHAT *AM* I LOOKING FOR? HOW CAN I CHANNEL THIS DATING EXPERIENCE INTO OUR SCRIPT? IF I WERE A WOMBAT, HOW WOULD I FEEL WHEN THAT MILLIONTH GUY REJECTED ME? HOW WOULD A WOMBAT SUITOR FEEL IF I REJECTED *HIM?*
"WOMBAT SUITOR"? THAT WOULD NEVER WORK. HE WOULD BE *MUCH* SHORTER THAN YOU.

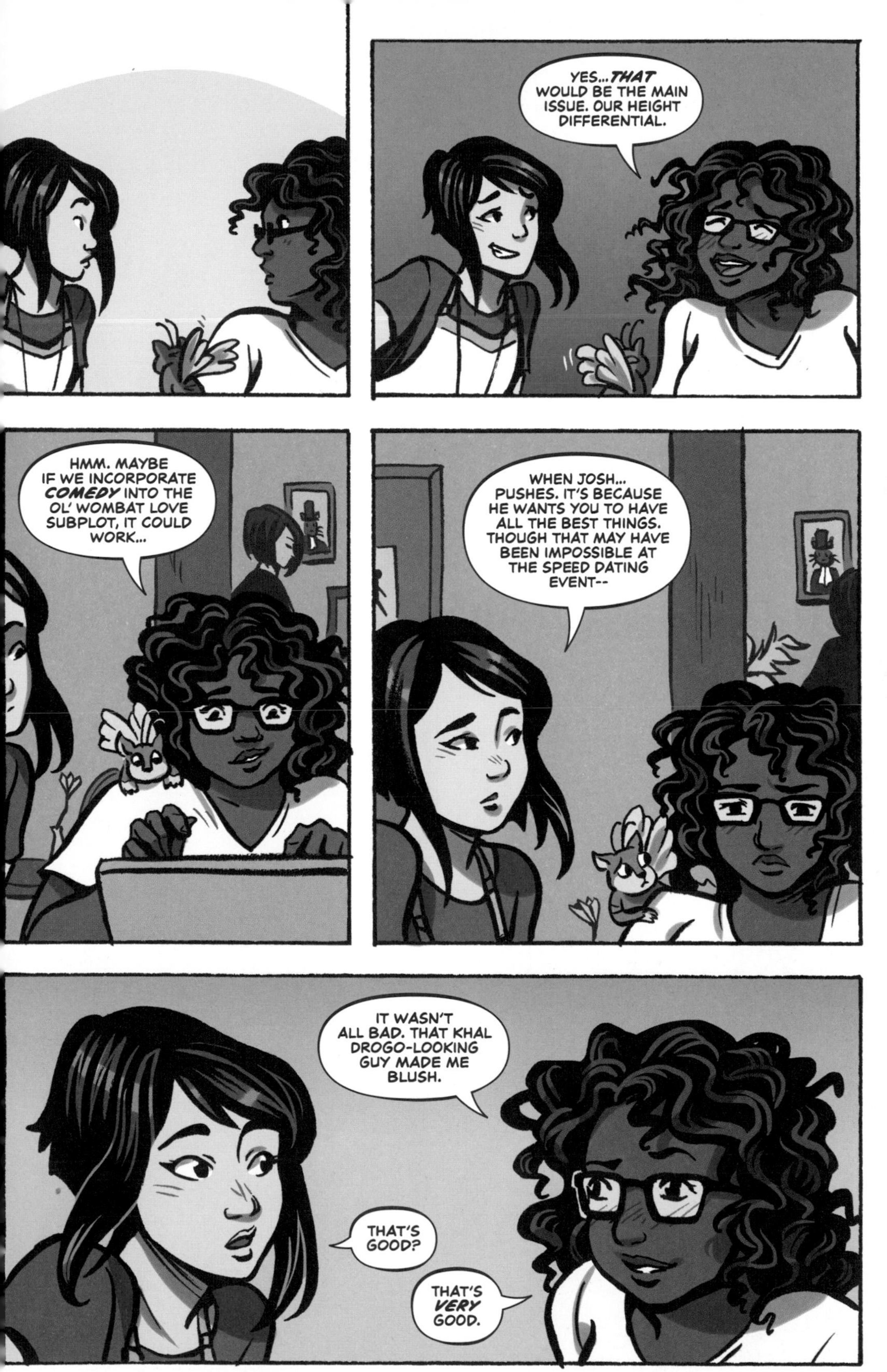
YES...THAT WOULD BE THE MAIN ISSUE. OUR HEIGHT DIFFERENTIAL.
HMM. MAYBE IF WE INCORPORATE COMEDY INTO THE OL' WOMBAT LOVE SUBPLOT, IT COULD WORK...
WHEN JOSH... PUSHES. IT'S BECAUSE HE WANTS YOU TO HAVE ALL THE BEST THINGS. THOUGH THAT MAY HAVE BEEN IMPOSSIBLE AT THE SPEED DATING EVENT--
IT WASN'T ALL BAD. THAT KHAL DROGO-LOOKING GUY MADE ME BLUSH.
THAT'S GOOD?
THAT'S VERY GOOD.

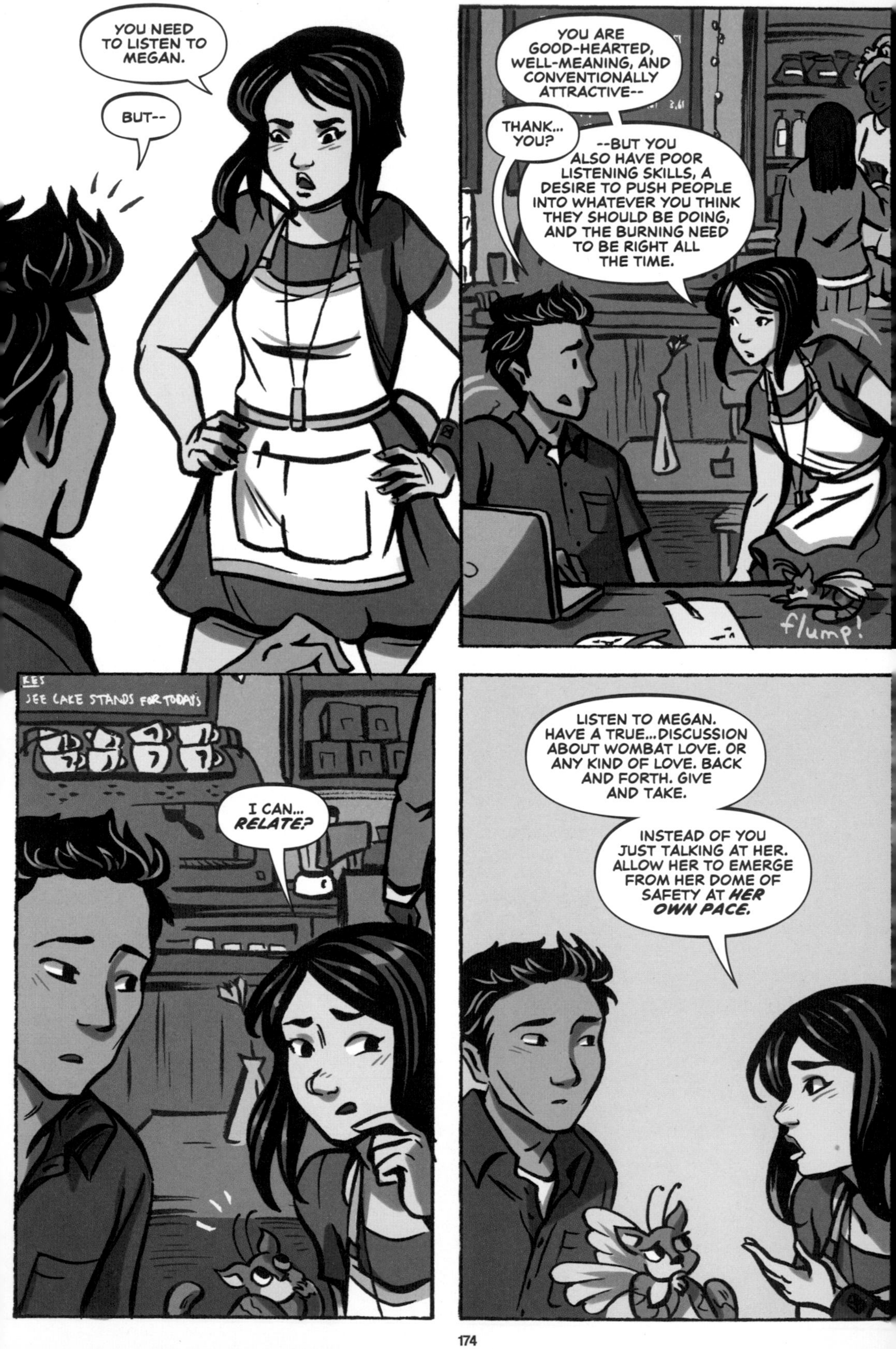

YOU NEED TO LISTEN TO MEGAN.
BUT--
YOU ARE GOOD-HEARTED, WELL-MEANING, AND CONVENTIONALLY ATTRACTIVE--
THANK... YOU?
--BUT YOU ALSO HAVE POOR LISTENING SKILLS, A DESIRE TO PUSH PEOPLE INTO WHATEVER YOU THINK THEY SHOULD BE DOING, AND THE BURNING NEED TO BE RIGHT ALL THE TIME.
flump!
SEE CAKE STANDS FOR TODAY'S
I CAN... *RELATE?*
LISTEN TO MEGAN. HAVE A TRUE...DISCUSSION ABOUT WOMBAT LOVE. OR ANY KIND OF LOVE. BACK AND FORTH. GIVE AND TAKE.
INSTEAD OF YOU JUST TALKING AT HER. ALLOW HER TO EMERGE FROM HER DOME OF SAFETY AT *HER OWN PACE.*

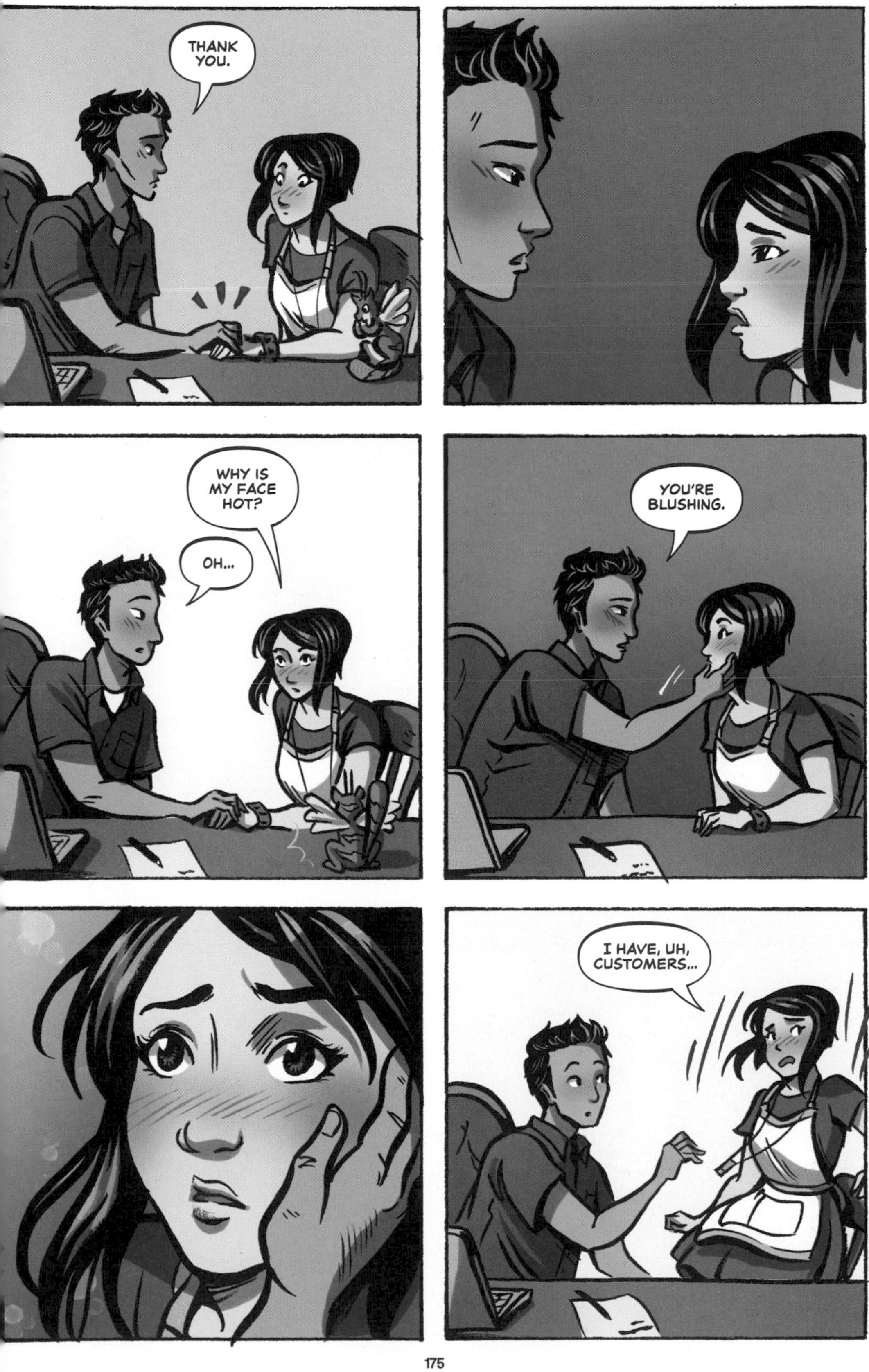
THANK YOU.
WHY IS MY FACE HOT?
OH...
YOU'RE BLUSHING.
I HAVE, UH, CUSTOMERS...

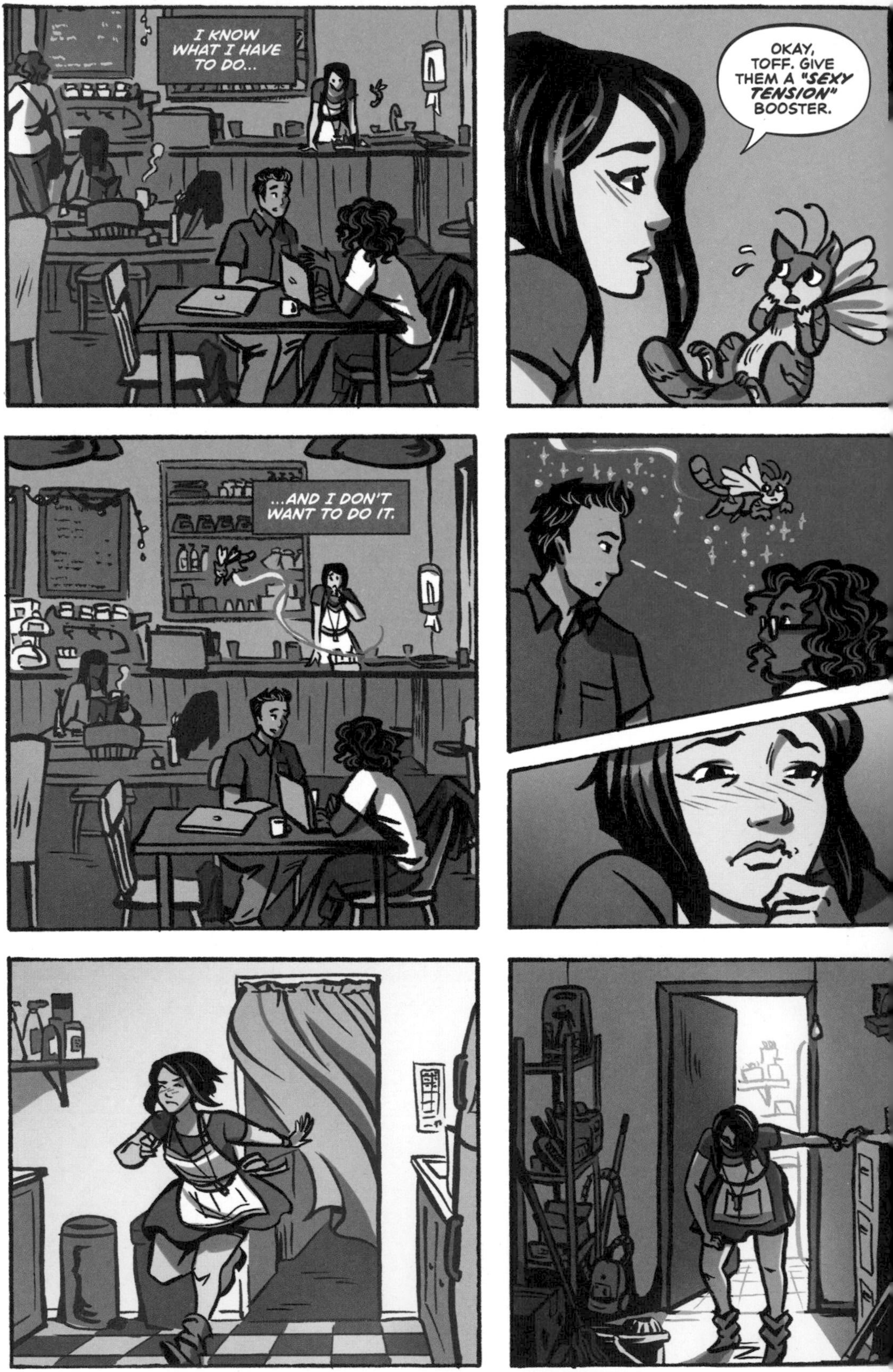
I KNOW WHAT I HAVE TO DO...
OKAY, TOFF. GIVE THEM A "SEXY TENSION" BOOSTER.
...AND I DON'T WANT TO DO IT.

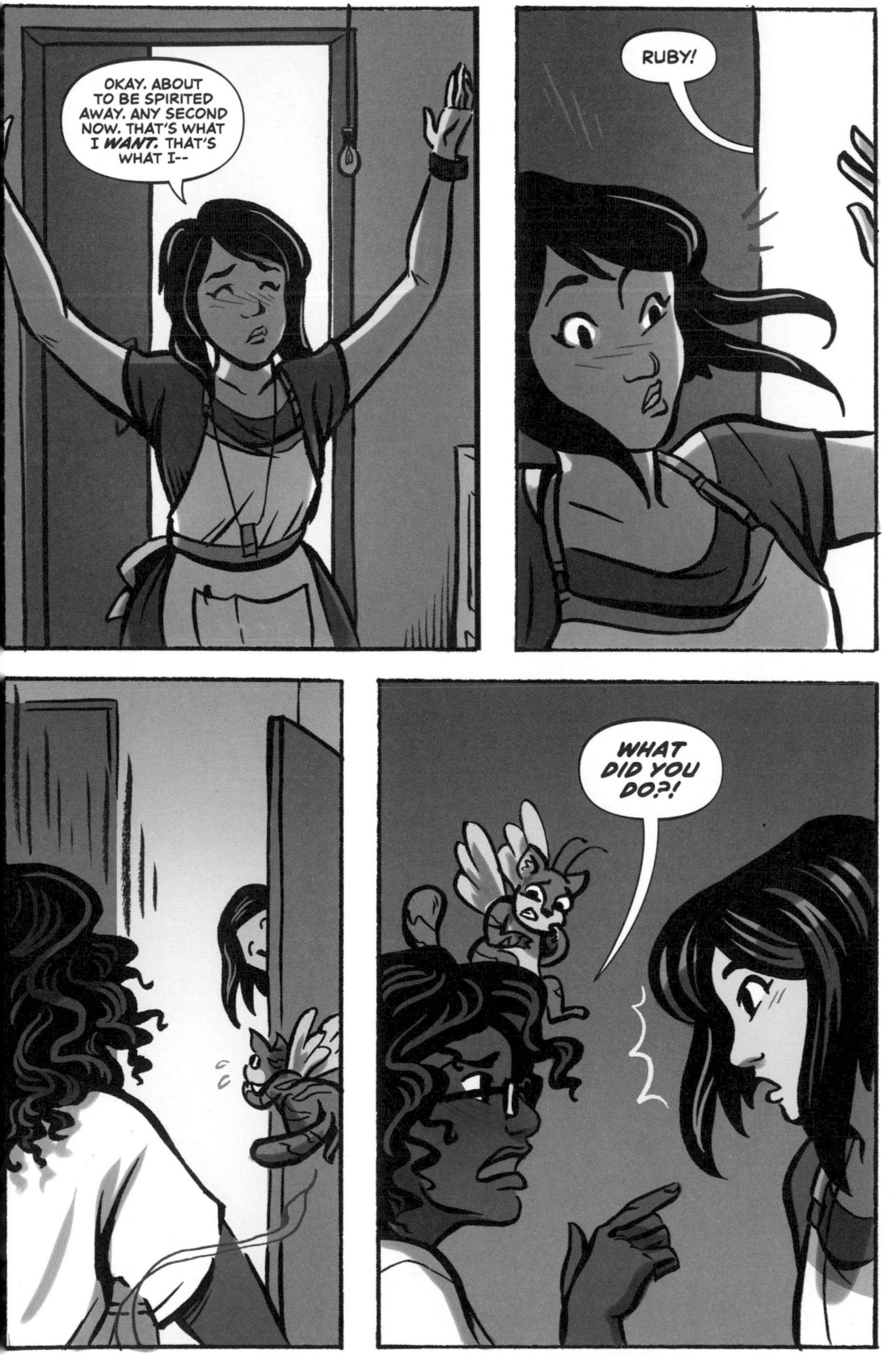
OKAY. ABOUT TO BE SPIRITED AWAY. ANY SECOND NOW. THAT'S WHAT I *WANT.* THAT'S WHAT I--
RUBY!
WHAT DID YOU DO?!

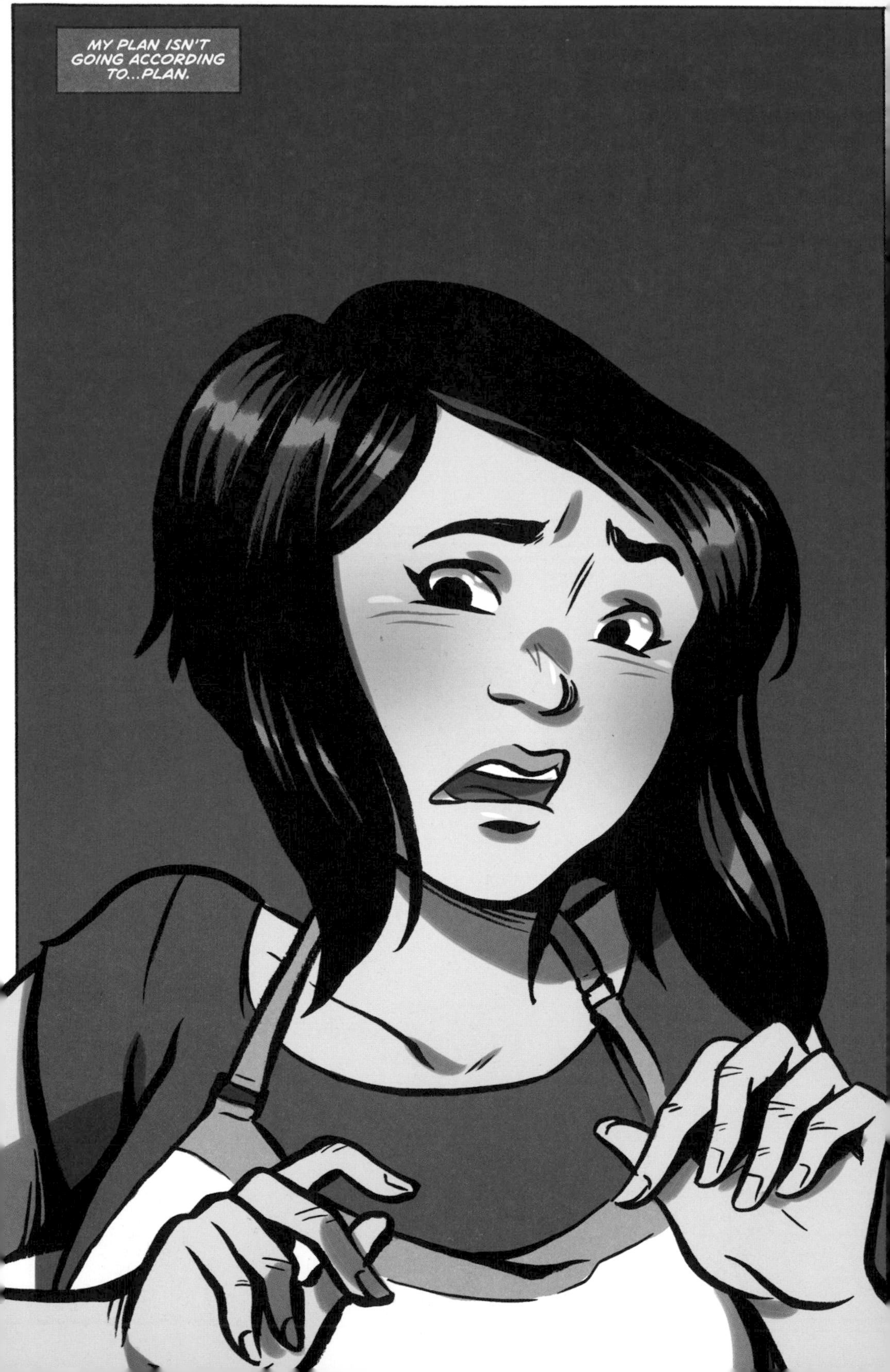
MY PLAN ISN'T GOING ACCORDING TO...PLAN.

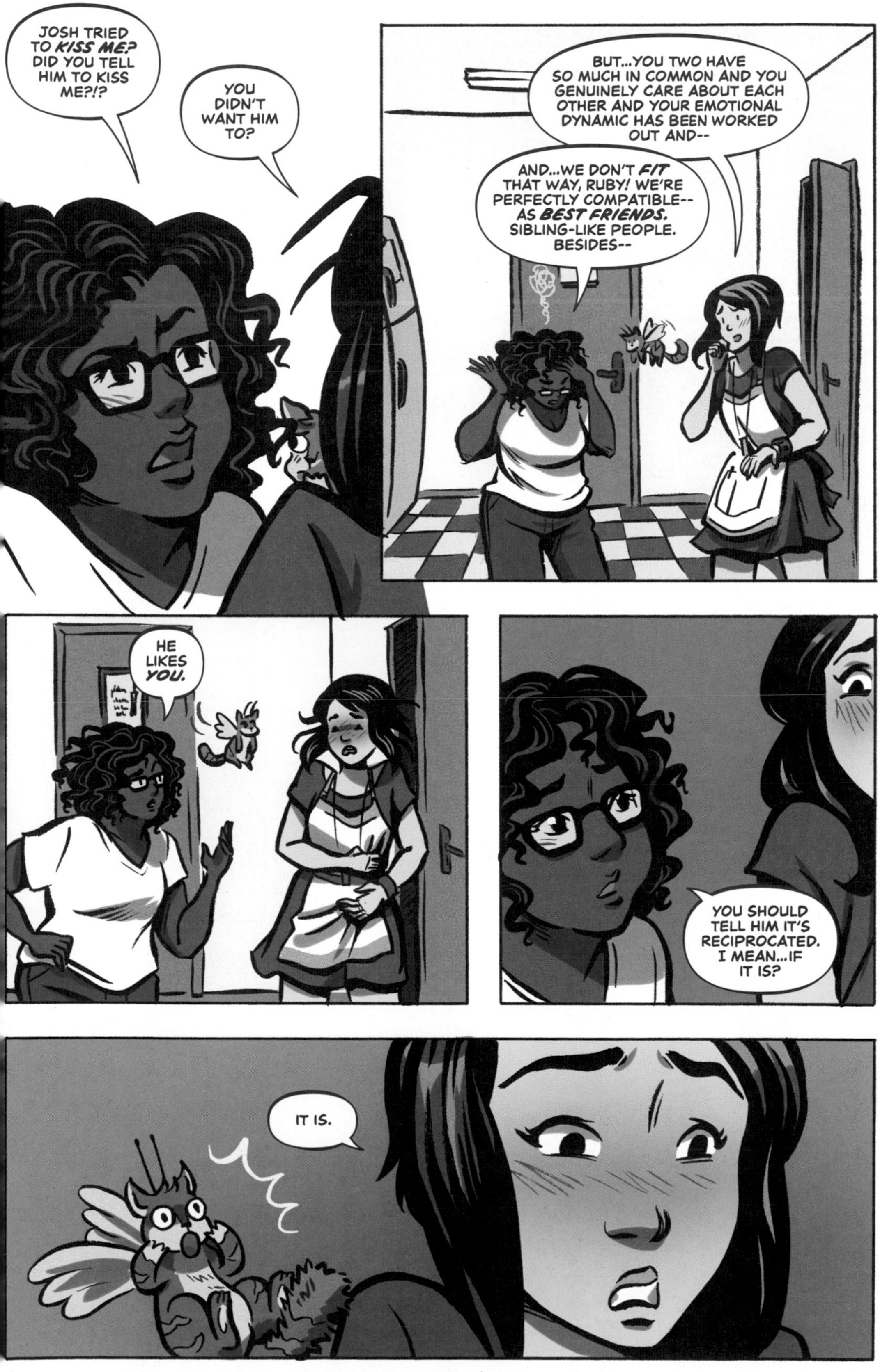
JOSH TRIED TO KISS ME? DID YOU TELL HIM TO KISS ME?!?
YOU DIDN'T WANT HIM TO?
BUT...YOU TWO HAVE SO MUCH IN COMMON AND YOU GENUINELY CARE ABOUT EACH OTHER AND YOUR EMOTIONAL DYNAMIC HAS BEEN WORKED OUT AND--
AND...WE DON'T FIT THAT WAY, RUBY! WE'RE PERFECTLY COMPATIBLE-- AS BEST FRIENDS. SIBLING-LIKE PEOPLE. BESIDES--
HE LIKES YOU.
YOU SHOULD TELL HIM IT'S RECIPROCATED. I MEAN...IF IT IS?
IT IS.

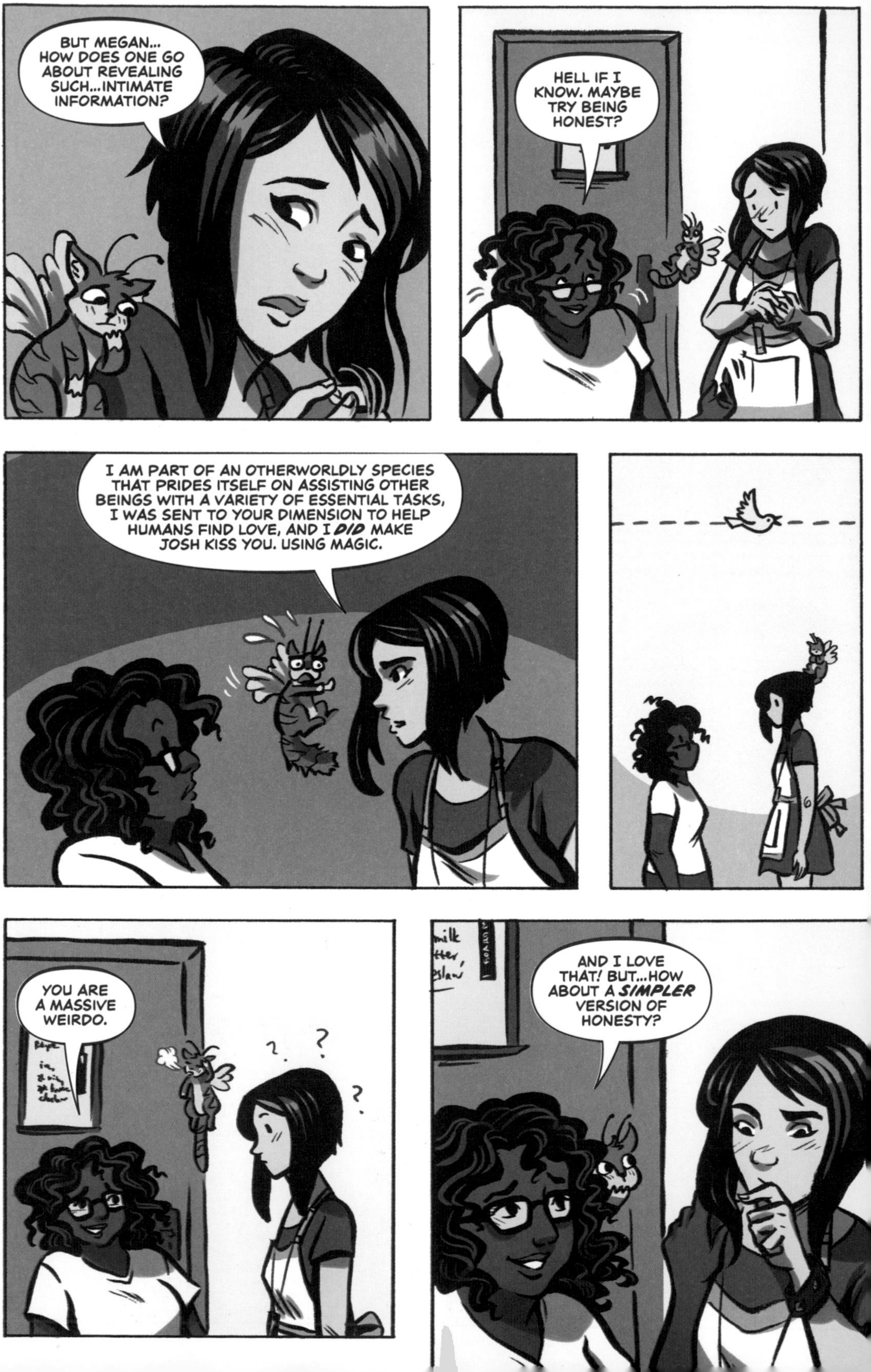
BUT MEGAN... HOW DOES ONE GO ABOUT REVEALING SUCH...INTIMATE INFORMATION?
HELL IF I KNOW. MAYBE TRY BEING HONEST?
I AM PART OF AN OTHERWORLDLY SPECIES THAT PRIDES ITSELF ON ASSISTING OTHER BEINGS WITH A VARIETY OF ESSENTIAL TASKS, I WAS SENT TO YOUR DIMENSION TO HELP HUMANS FIND LOVE, AND I *DID* MAKE JOSH KISS YOU. USING MAGIC.
YOU ARE A MASSIVE WEIRDO.
? ? ?
AND I LOVE THAT! BUT...HOW ABOUT A *SIMPLER* VERSION OF HONESTY?

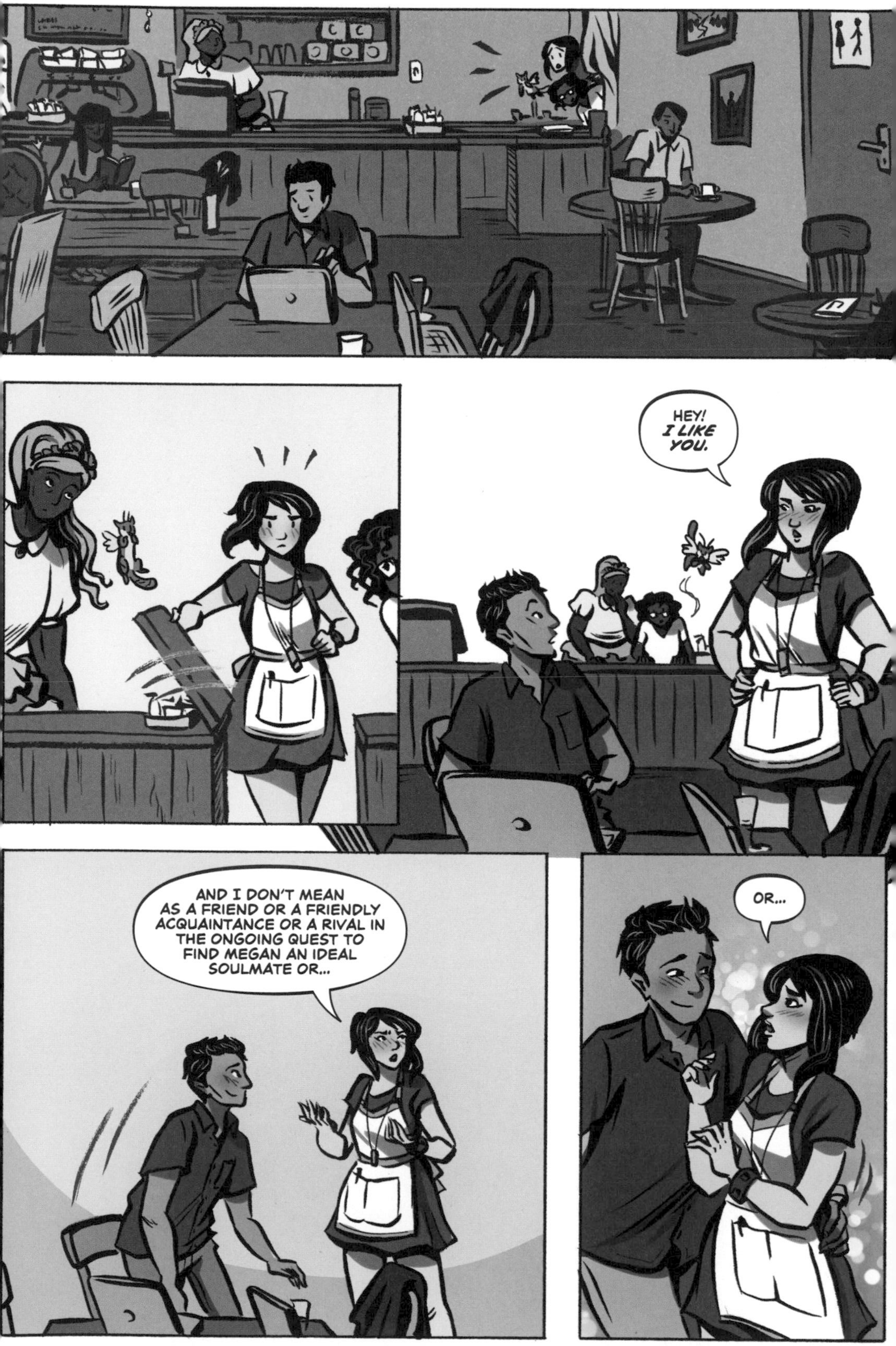
HEY! I LIKE YOU.
AND I DON'T MEAN AS A FRIEND OR A FRIENDLY ACQUAINTANCE OR A RIVAL IN THE ONGOING QUEST TO FIND MEGAN AN IDEAL SOULMATE OR...
OR...

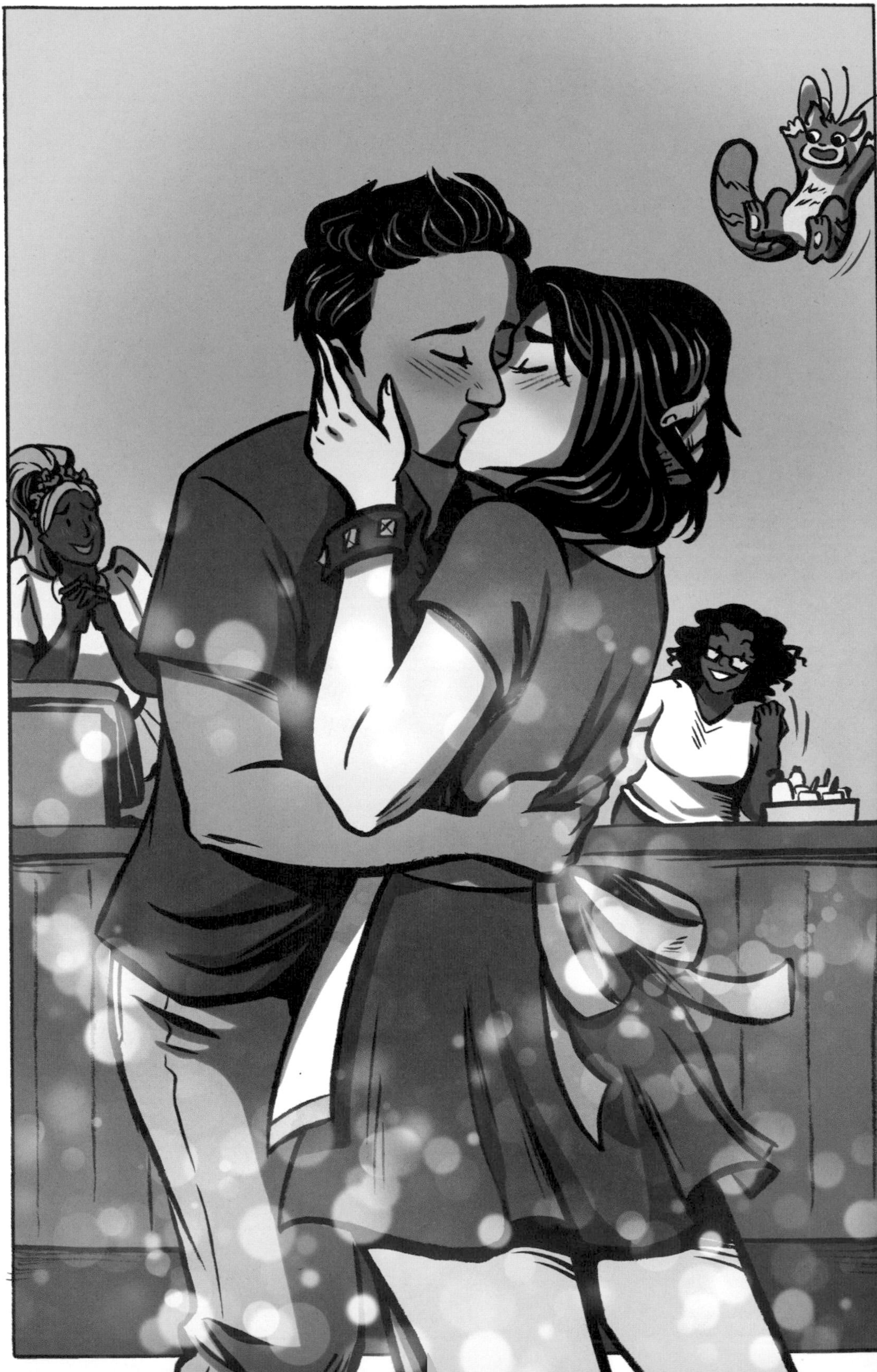

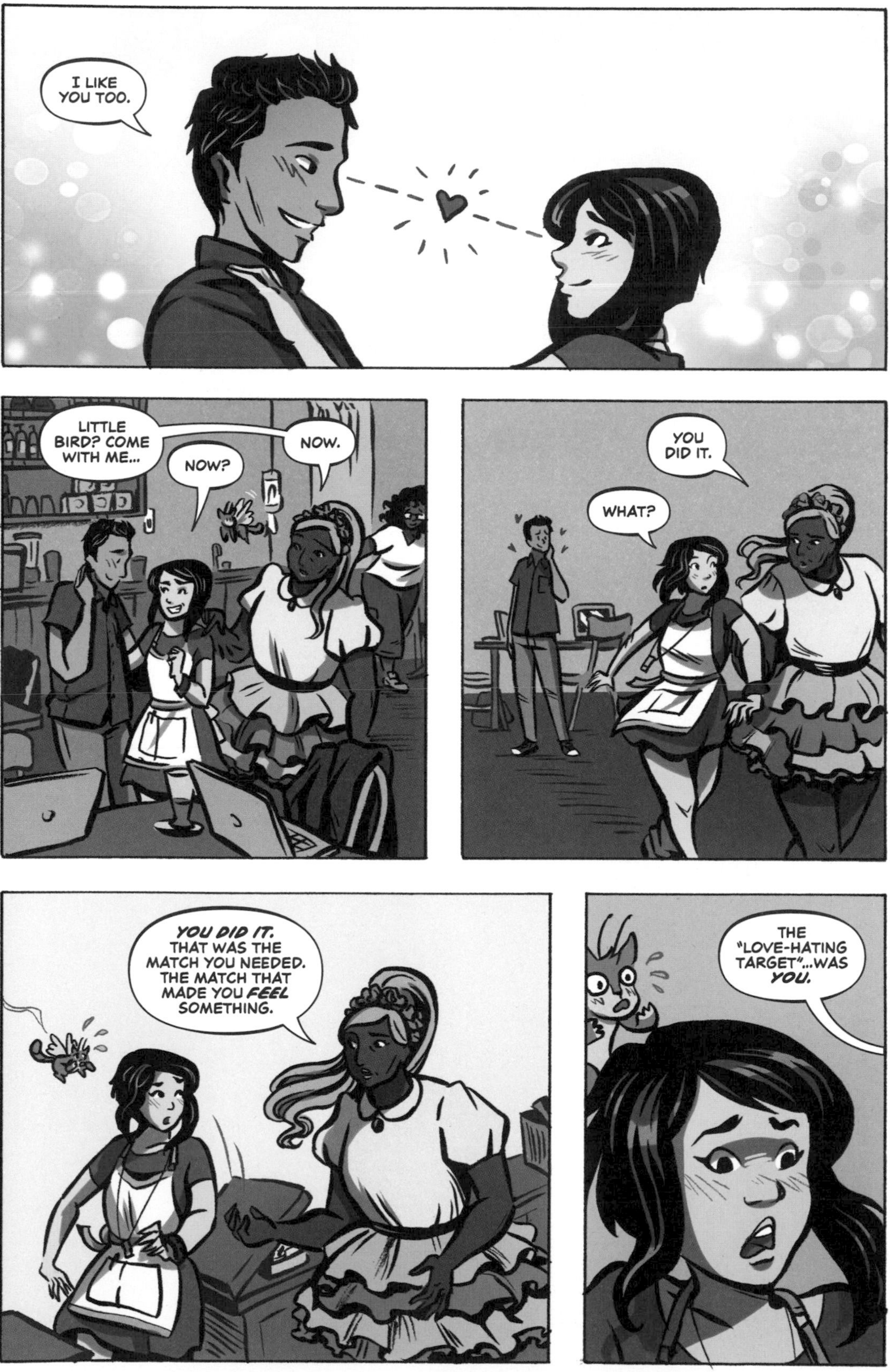
I LIKE YOU TOO.
LITTLE BIRD? COME WITH ME...
NOW?
NOW.
YOU DID IT.
WHAT?
YOU DID IT. THAT WAS THE MATCH YOU NEEDED. THE MATCH THAT MADE YOU FEEL SOMETHING.
THE "LOVE-HATING TARGET"...WAS YOU.

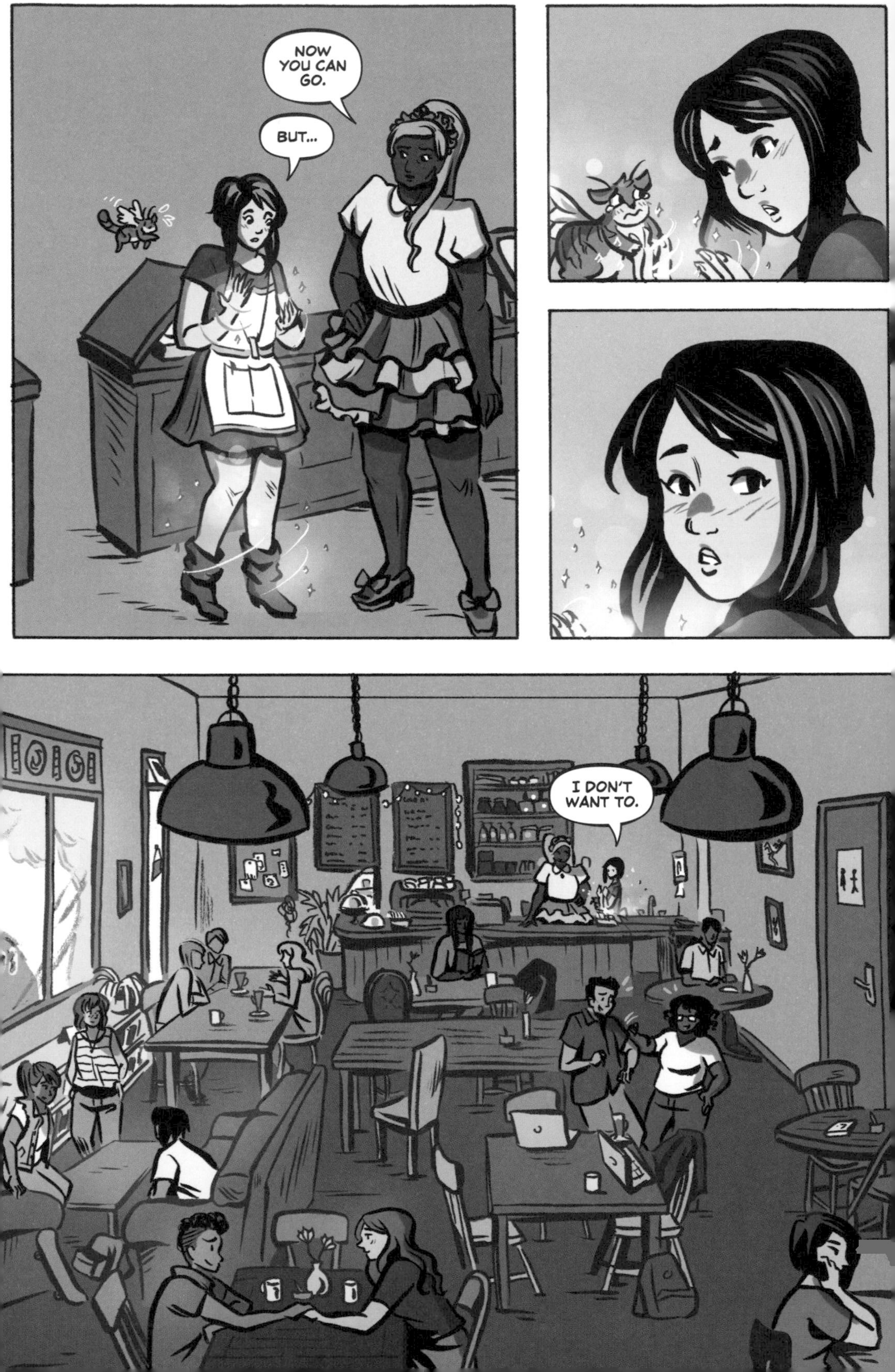
NOW YOU CAN GO.
BUT...
I DON'T WANT TO.

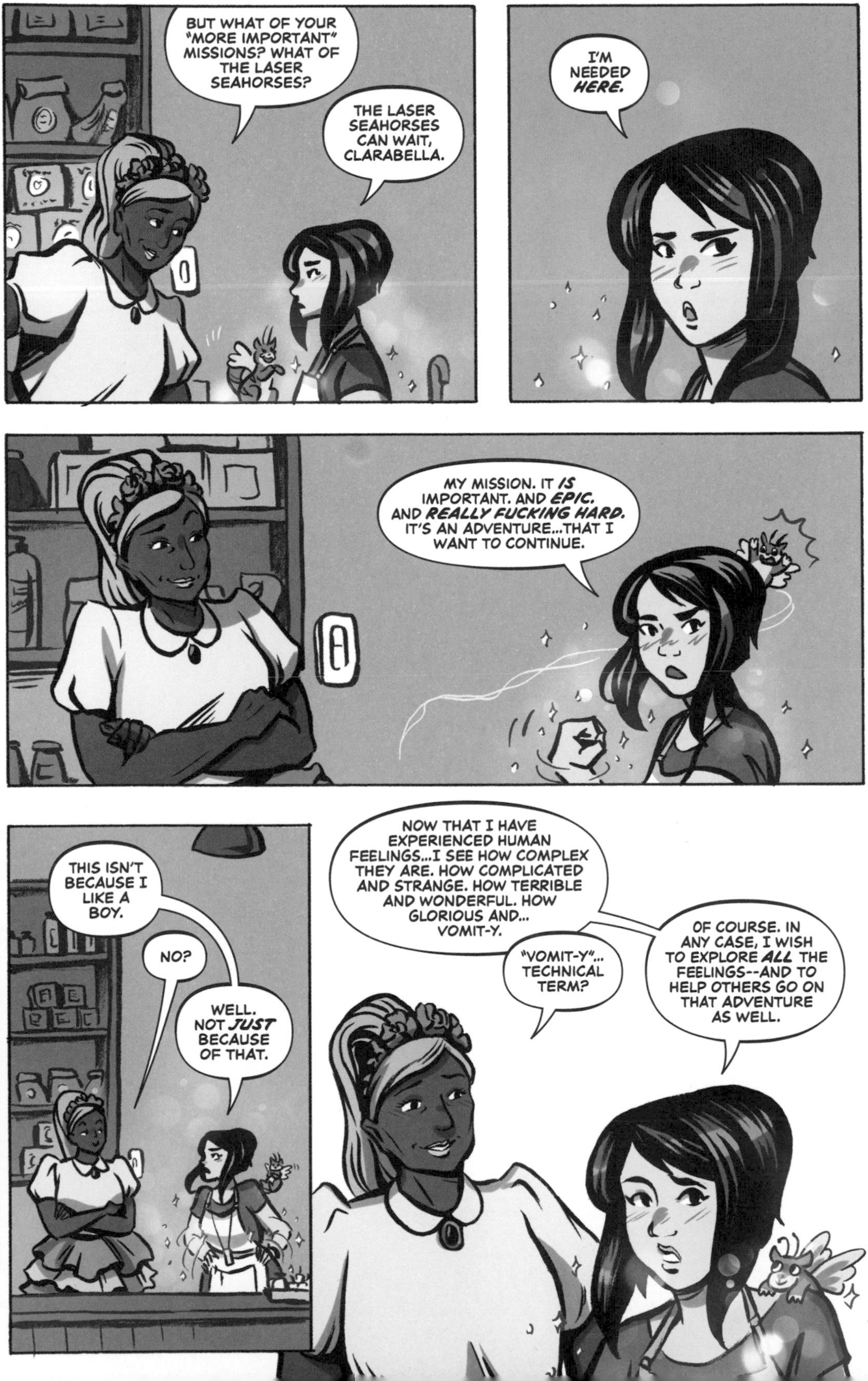
BUT WHAT OF YOUR "MORE IMPORTANT" MISSIONS? WHAT OF THE LASER SEAHORSES?
THE LASER SEAHORSES CAN WAIT, CLARABELLA.
I'M NEEDED *HERE.*
MY MISSION. IT *IS* IMPORTANT. AND *EPIC.* AND *REALLY FUCKING HARD.* IT'S AN ADVENTURE...THAT I WANT TO CONTINUE.
THIS ISN'T BECAUSE I LIKE A BOY.
NO?
WELL. NOT *JUST* BECAUSE OF THAT.
NOW THAT I HAVE EXPERIENCED HUMAN FEELINGS...I SEE HOW COMPLEX THEY ARE. HOW COMPLICATED AND STRANGE. HOW TERRIBLE AND WONDERFUL. HOW GLORIOUS AND... VOMIT-Y.
"VOMIT-Y"... TECHNICAL TERM?
OF COURSE. IN ANY CASE, I WISH TO EXPLORE *ALL* THE FEELINGS--AND TO HELP OTHERS GO ON THAT ADVENTURE AS WELL.

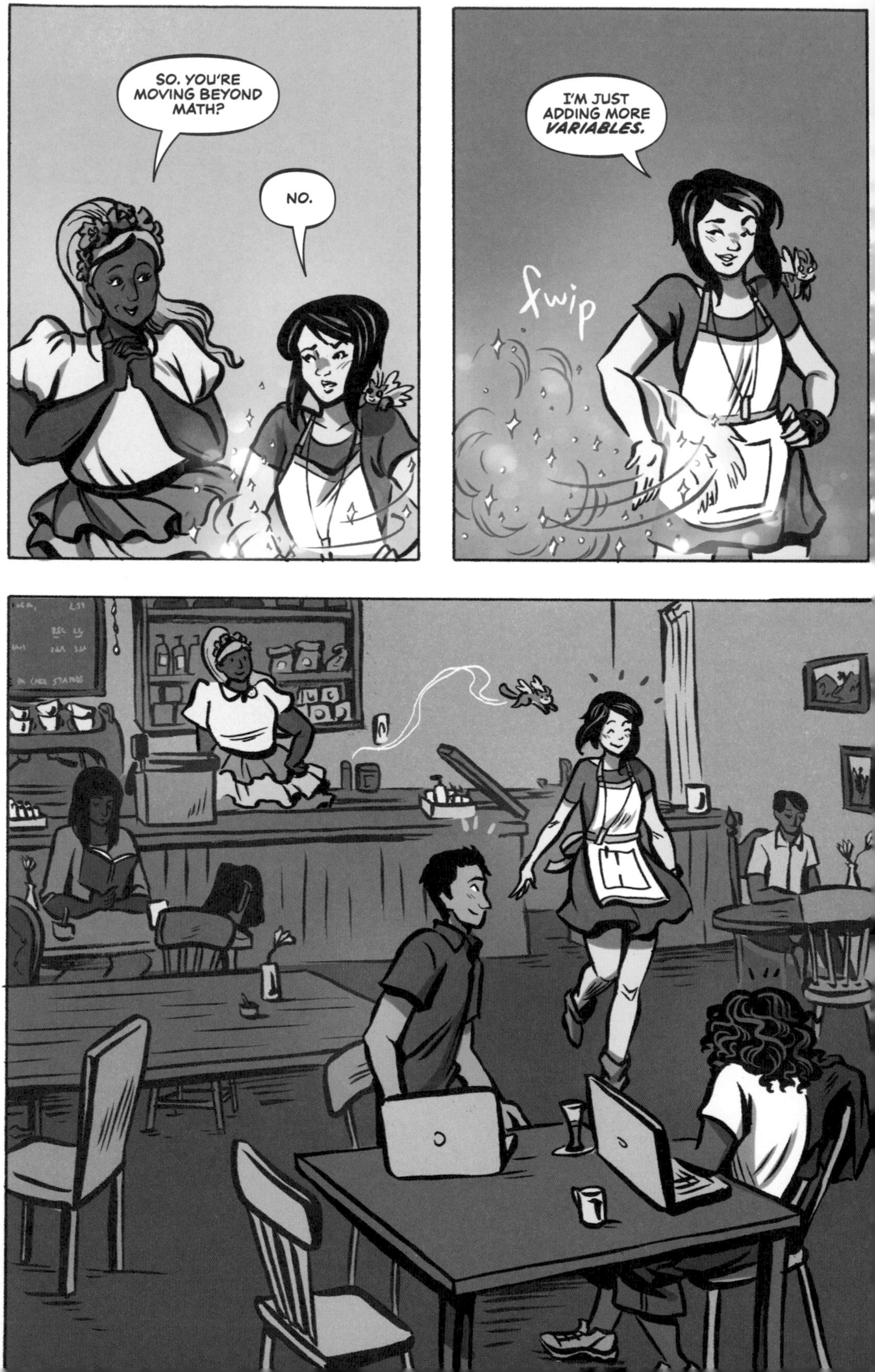
SO. YOU'RE MOVING BEYOND MATH?
NO.
I'M JUST ADDING MORE *VARIABLES.*
fwip

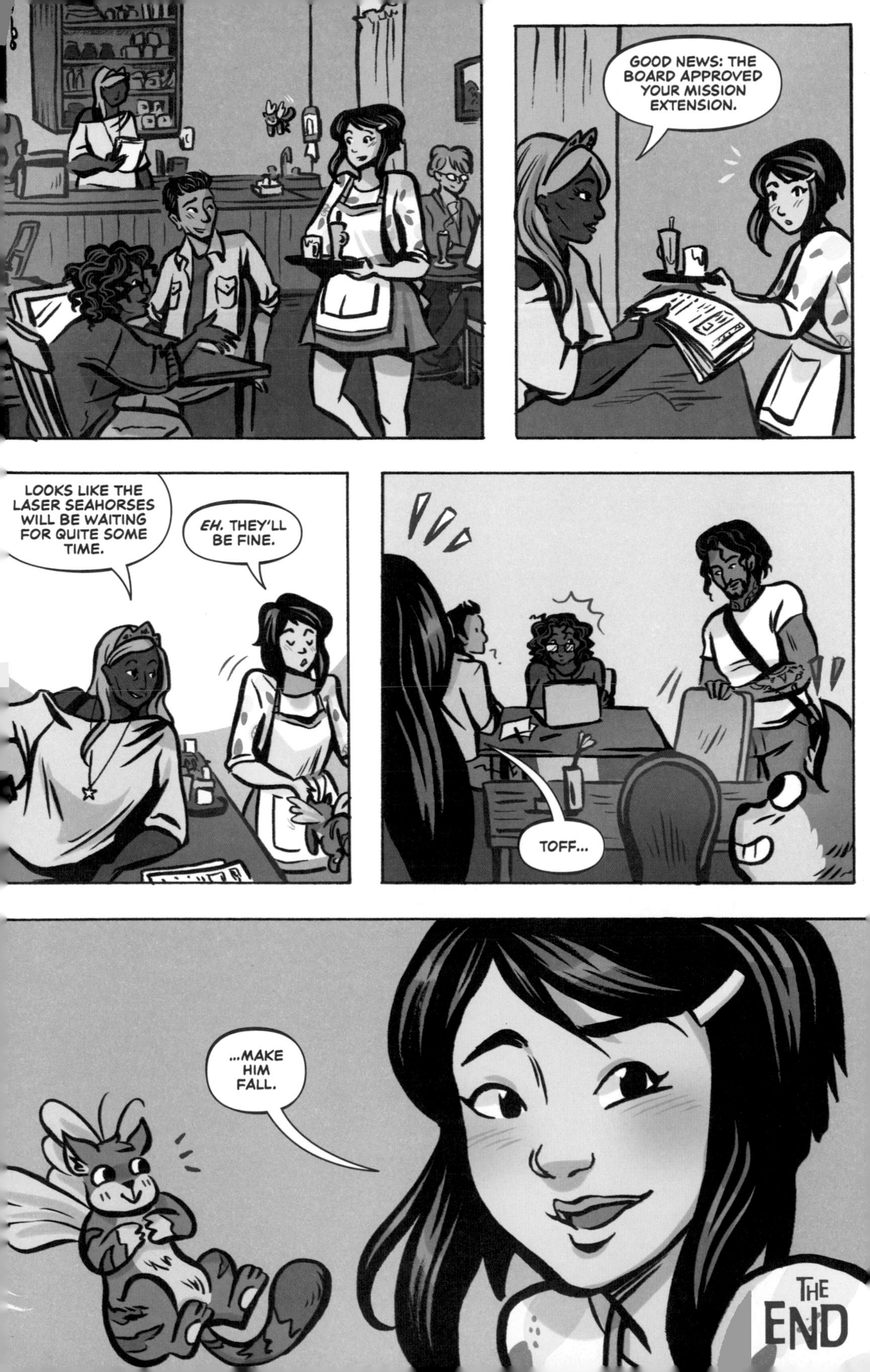
GOOD NEWS: THE BOARD APPROVED YOUR MISSION EXTENSION.
LOOKS LIKE THE LASER SEAHORSES WILL BE WAITING FOR QUITE SOME TIME.
EH. THEY'LL BE FINE.
TOFF...
...MAKE HIM FALL.
THE END

THE RUBY EQUATION ROUNDTABLE

To say farewell to *The Ruby Equation*, the entire creative team sat down for a roundtable chat about how they all work and what they each brought to the table in the process.

Sarah Kuhn: Sally, how do you approach those initial sketches of a new character? I loved how you instantly captured the attitudes and expressiveness of Ruby and Co. (Not to mention their outfits, which I consider to be one of those important parts of any character.)

Sally Jane Thompson: I totally agree on how important clothes are to communicating personality! The more I know about what sort of person the character is at the start, the better, as that needs to come out through their design. Beyond that, I usually try and leave myself room in my very first sketches to experiment, and try and think of times when other characters or people have given me the feeling I'm after—the sort of expressions and gestures that remind me of that character. I also think through their day, their lifestyle, so that I can come up with clothes that express their personality but also fit their lives and world. The secondary characters are affected by the first as I always want to make sure I have a variety of features, hairstyles, and body types, so once the main characters are there I can try and make sure there's not too much repetition. The *Ruby* characters were all set fairly fast as your descriptions already had a lot of thought put into the style of the characters as an extension of their personalities. So the character with the widest variety of initial designs was definitely Toff!

SJT: Savanna, once the first pages of story get sent to you, how do you start figuring out what the right look and palette is for that story?

Savanna Ganucheau: Well, if the creators have a look in mind, I'll go from that. But If I have nothing to work from, I usually start by looking through my giant folder of palettes. Also, I like to look at photographs or even classical paintings for color ideas. For *Ruby*, I really wanted something that looked vibrant, but also calming. There are so many colors going on in the cafe, and I didn't want the palette to be overwhelming. So, the colors I ended up with are the result of those thoughts. Initially it's a lot of trial and error... mixing and matching seeing what looks best. Peaches, cool browns, teals, and light yellow make up the majority of *Ruby*'s palette.

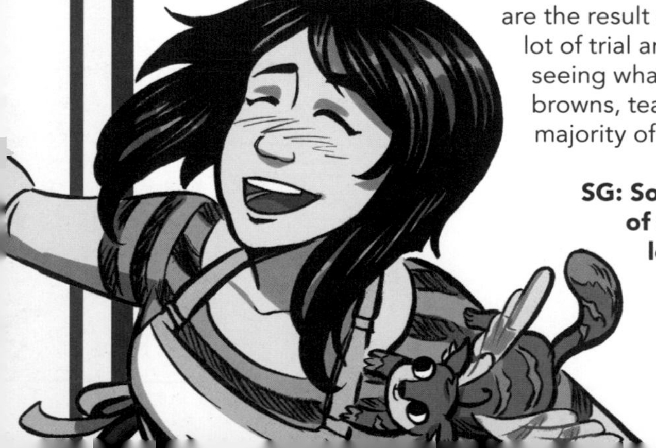

SG: So, Steve: What's the best piece of advice you've received as a letterer?

Steve Wands: Best piece of advice? Don't stop believing.

But in reality, probably to not let yourself get jaded or dragged down by negative aspects of the comics beast we love. I can't credit a sole individual with that advice, but if you're around enough positive people it becomes a mindset. So I try to keep it positive and remember why the hell I got into this. This especially applies to lettering, because it can quickly become a grind. Often a letterer's job is to make up for lost time.

SW: Now for Sarah—what's your ideal place to write? Is there a particular time or place in which your muse strikes?

SK: I write a lot in coffee shops, which is actually what inspired *Ruby*'s setting—I'm part of a writing group called the Shamers that has a regular set of cafe-type spots we frequent, wherein we sit together and shame each other into writing. That sense of camaraderie and community keeps me productive and inspired and ensures that I don't devolve into a weeping bag of feelings lying on the floor and eating her own hair. And of course coffee shops also make for a lot of great people-watching, which gave me plenty of ideas for *Ruby*'s cast. Josh and Megan are like their own little version of the Shamers, really, right down to all the weird conversations about wombat plot points. As far as preferred times of day, I've gotten to the point where I can write just about any time, anywhere (even if I like the coffee shops best), but I tend to have my most productive moments post-lunch. I do best after I've been fed.

SK: So, Steve! What's the biggest challenge of lettering/balloon placement when a panel or page has a lot of dialogue—and how do you deal with it? I know our last issue of *Ruby* had some long-ass speeches.

SW: I love me some coffee. Usually when there is a whole lot of words, I usually ask myself, do writers get paid by the word?! But then I start slapping in on the page and roughing out placement. Sometimes I will have to go in and break up sections of text to fit the art, using more balloons, or cutting around the art, so characters' heads might pop over a balloon. When desperate I'll resort to breaking over the panel borders, and if there's so much text that it could literally fill the whole panel (which I've seen before) then I'll reach out the editor(s) and writer and ask them to get real about it. Which never happened in *Ruby*, there was always just the right amount of text!

SW: Sally... I've heard from someone (possibly you) that you draw on the computer and then print out the drawing and then ink it. Do you not scratch the screen? How is this possible?

SJT: Ha! My set-up's fairly simple... I much prefer drawing on paper, but digital's good for speed, so I compromise. The roughs are done digitally (using, at the moment, my very old Wacom Graphire tablet that I've had since I was a teenager. I keep thinking one day I'll upgrade to a Cintiq or similar, but that day has not yet come!). This lets me resize and adjust things at an early stage, as well as test out text on busy pages to make sure I leave enough room.

Once roughs are approved, I print them out in cyan on drawing paper, and ink with brush and ink, and various brushpens, since inking is the part I really like to keep doing traditionally. I love the feel of a brush on paper. Once scanned, I can get rid of the printed cyan lines in Photoshop, and do any last touch-ups or fixes before they're ready for colour!

SJT: Sarah, as someone who works in both comics and prose, what goes into deciding what shape/format a project will be, and how does working across those two formats relate (or separate!) for you?

SK: I usually come up with ideas that I think (perhaps mistakenly!) could work well in a variety of media—but then I'll tailor them depending on how something is pitched or sold. Or sometimes that decision might hinge on an element of the story I really want to explore. I thought my novel, *Heroine Complex*, could also make a good comic book or TV show, but there was something about getting into the really long internal monologue of an extremely neurotic superheroine that I wanted to explore in prose. When Janelle asked me to pitch for *Fresh Romance*, I tried to think of ideas that would have a fun visual element—I always thought of *Ruby*'s world looking bright and bubbly, sort of like the visual equivalent of candy. And all of you guys totally brought that to life: expanded upon the candyness and enhanced it with your own amazing ideas and unique flair! As far as how working across formats relates: I think I'm always trying to convey—as clearly and specifically as possible—the picture that's happening in my head. In prose, I'm trying to describe it so the reader feels like they're totally living in the story, seeing what I'm seeing. In comics, I try to describe it for the artist(s), who will likely take it to the next level and paint a much better picture than the one going on in my brain. With Ruby, I knew her facial expressions would be key to the story, so I tried to describe those in the scripts in as much detail as possible, to really link them to whatever specific crazy emotion she was having. And once again, y'all brought it and

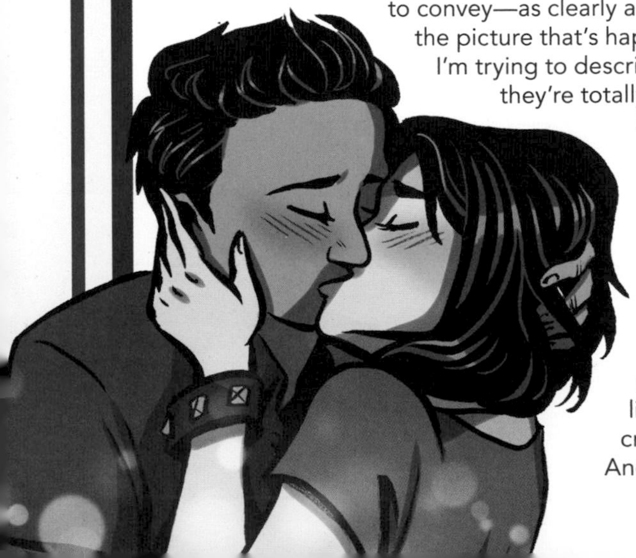

made it even more awesome than I imagined.

SK: Savanna, how do you come up with all those great little touches that enhance your coloring work—all the sparkles in this issue, for example, or the different colored backgrounds that really bring out the emotions of the characters?

SG: Well, the sparkles in the last issue are just Bokeh textures that I've layered over (I used the "screen" layer setting). As for the colors in the backgrounds, I really enjoy color theory and how humans react to colors. So, I usually have the script open while I'm coloring. I like to make sure the colorful backgrounds give off the same emotional cues that the dialogue does. There are so many different little coloring techniques that you can use, and I think coloring is all about trying new things. *Ruby* was nice because Sally's art really lent itself to me experimenting with colors, layer settings, and textures. I really had an amazing time working on *Ruby*, and I just wanted to say thank you all so much. GO S-TEAM!

SK: That's two rounds! Janelle, do you want us to ask each other any further Q's or is there anything you would like to ask us?

SW: I say we turn the heat lamps on to Janelle and ask her the tough questions...

Janelle Asselin: I'll add this question for all of you instead: what was your favorite part of working on *The Ruby Equation*?

SW: I'd have to say being part of something new and fresh. Yes, that's my favorite. It takes a lot of balls (or courage if you prefer) to put something new into the world, and I was stoked to be part of that.

SJT: In a general sense, designing and drawing something with such an unabashedly fun, pop-y vibe has been like a breath of fresh air! In a specific sense, any page where I got to draw Toff Expressions™ was pretty much my favorite.

SK: From a writing standpoint, my favorite part is always figuring out how to make people kiss. From a process standpoint, I really loved the talks the team had about all that little minutiae stuff that is actually quite important: what colors people like to wear, what kinds of coffee drinks Josh and Megan prefer, if Toff's various proposed color schemes made him look like a Popple (which is totally a good thing), what Ruby's inner monologue text would look like, and how many sparkles we needed on the big kiss page. (The answer to that last one was, of course, all of them. All of the sparkles!)

SG: *Ruby Equation* was a blast to work on. It's such an adorable comic, I really loved coloring it. My favorite part is that it allowed me to use bright colors and sparkles! If I could work on comics with sparkles all the time... I would. I think for me *Ruby* was really refreshing; it's youthful, bright, and fun. I hope to work on more comics just like it.

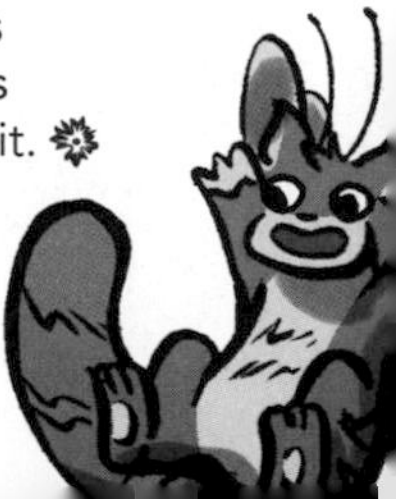

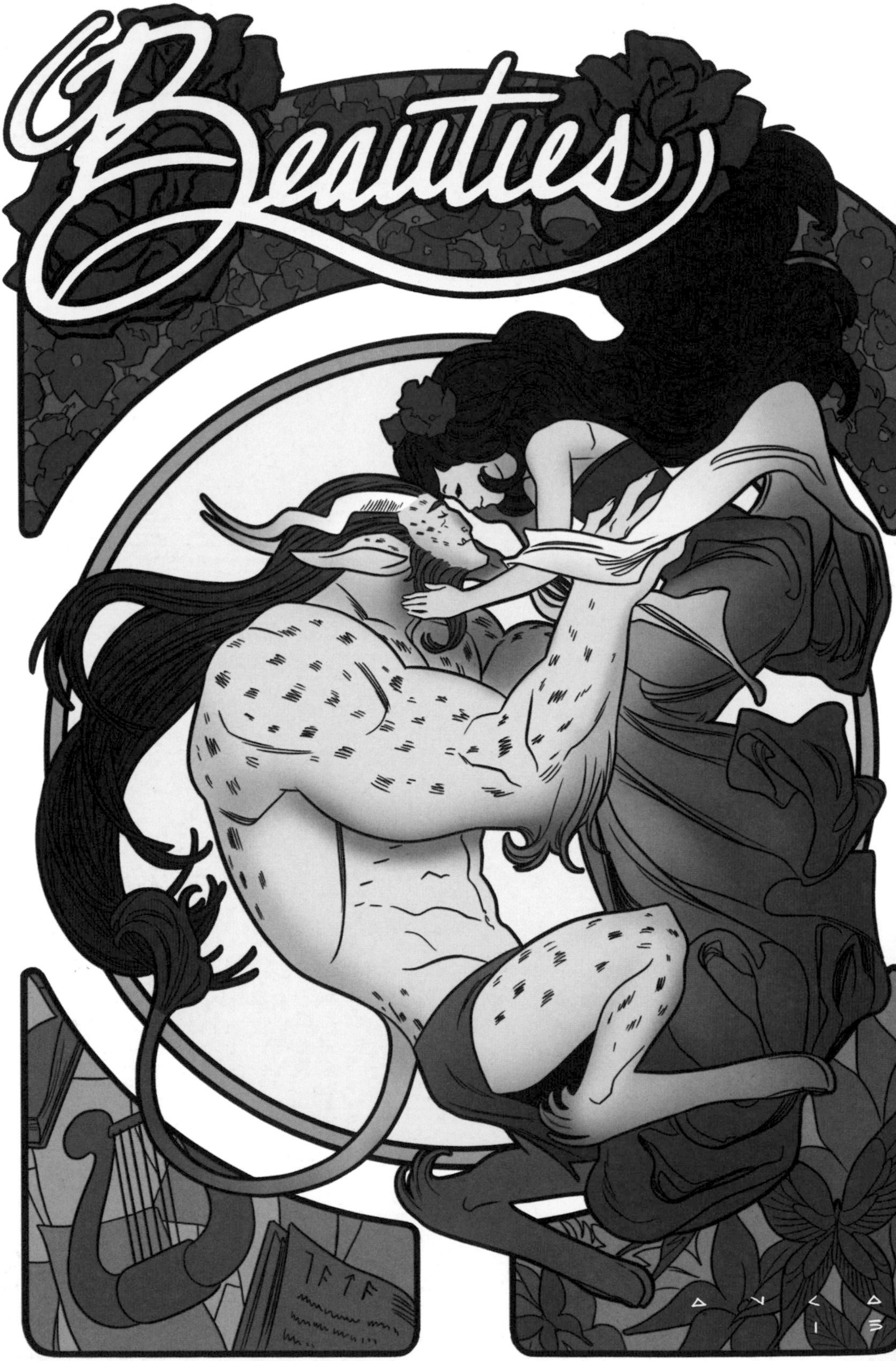
Beauties

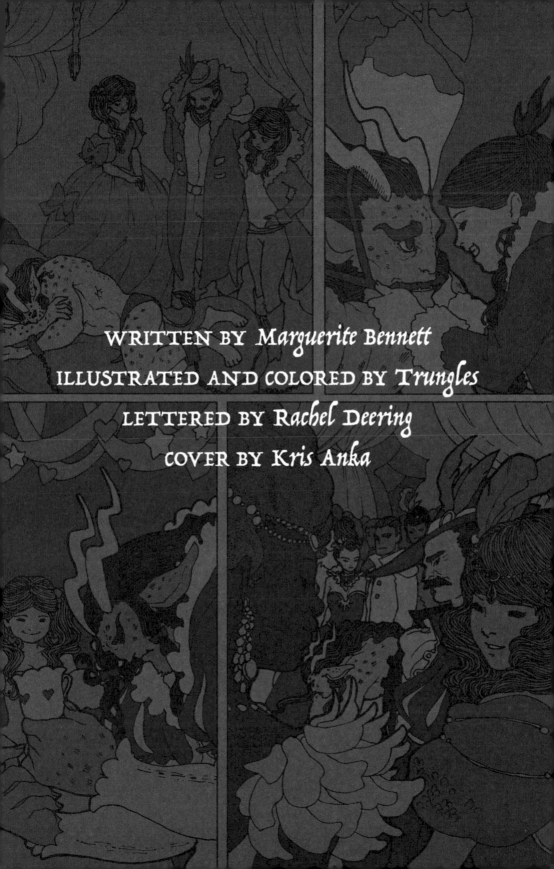

WRITTEN BY *Marguerite Bennett*
ILLUSTRATED AND COLORED BY *Trungles*
LETTERED BY *Rachel Deering*
COVER BY *Kris Anka*

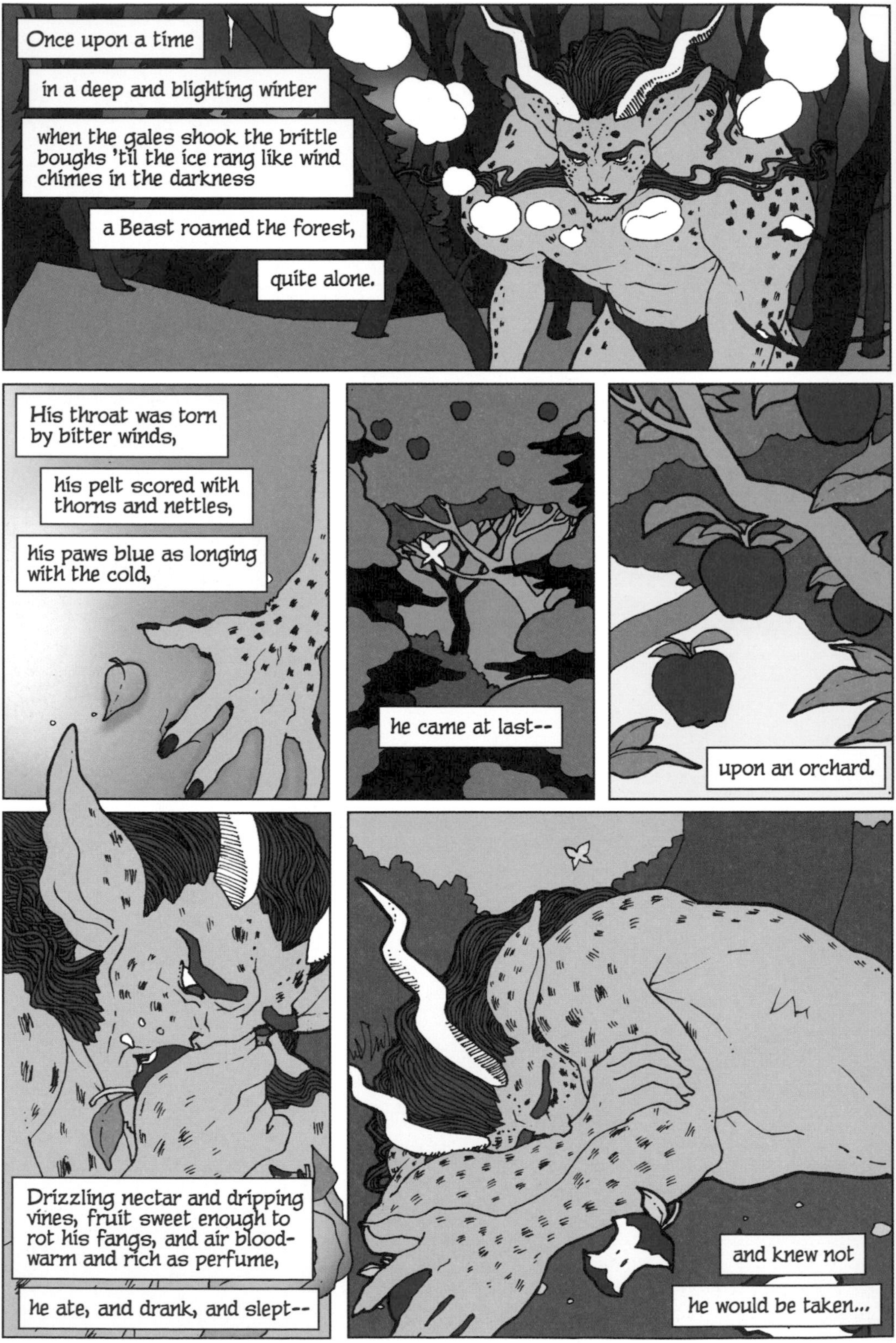
Once upon a time
in a deep and blighting winter
when the gales shook the brittle boughs 'til the ice rang like wind chimes in the darkness
a Beast roamed the forest,
quite alone.
His throat was torn by bitter winds,
his pelt scored with thorns and nettles,
his paws blue as longing with the cold,
he came at last--
upon an orchard.
Drizzling nectar and dripping vines, fruit sweet enough to rot his fangs, and air blood-warm and rich as perfume,
he ate, and drank, and slept--
and knew not
he would be taken...

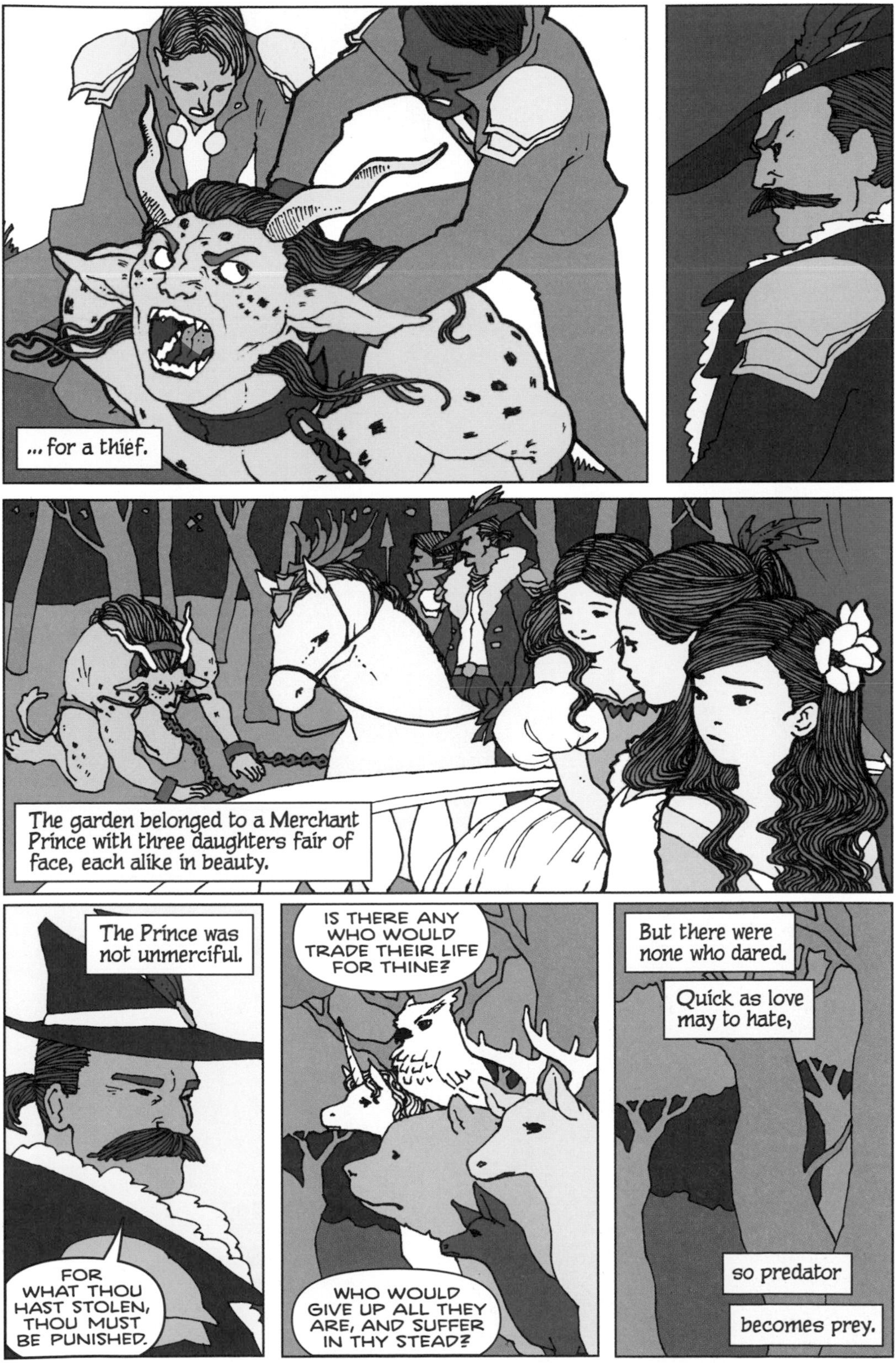
... for a thief.
The garden belonged to a Merchant Prince with three daughters fair of face, each alike in beauty.
The Prince was not unmerciful.
FOR WHAT THOU HAST STOLEN, THOU MUST BE PUNISHED.
IS THERE ANY WHO WOULD TRADE THEIR LIFE FOR THINE?
WHO WOULD GIVE UP ALL THEY ARE, AND SUFFER IN THY STEAD?
But there were none who dared.
Quick as love may to hate,
so predator
becomes prey.

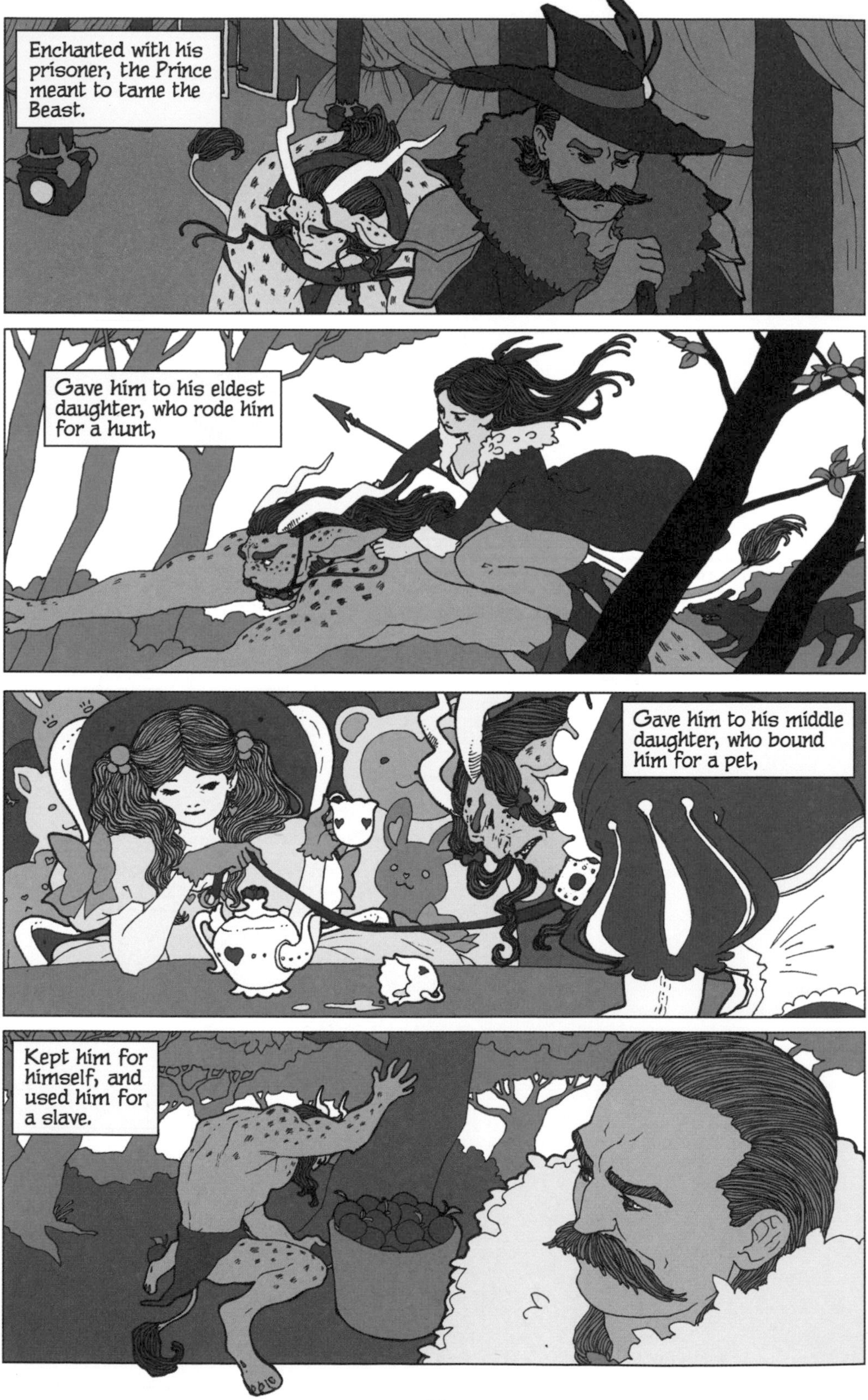
Enchanted with his prisoner, the Prince meant to tame the Beast.
Gave him to his eldest daughter, who rode him for a hunt,
Gave him to his middle daughter, who bound him for a pet,
Kept him for himself, and used him for a slave.

But the youngest daughter,

no sweeter, no shyer, no fairer than her sisters,

stole through the wood and the parlor and the orchard

and took his paw, trembling, and asked him,

WHAT IS THY NAME?

KRÁSNÁ.

KRÁSNÁ.

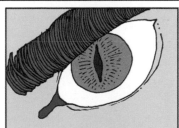

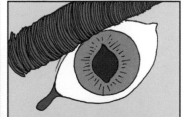

197

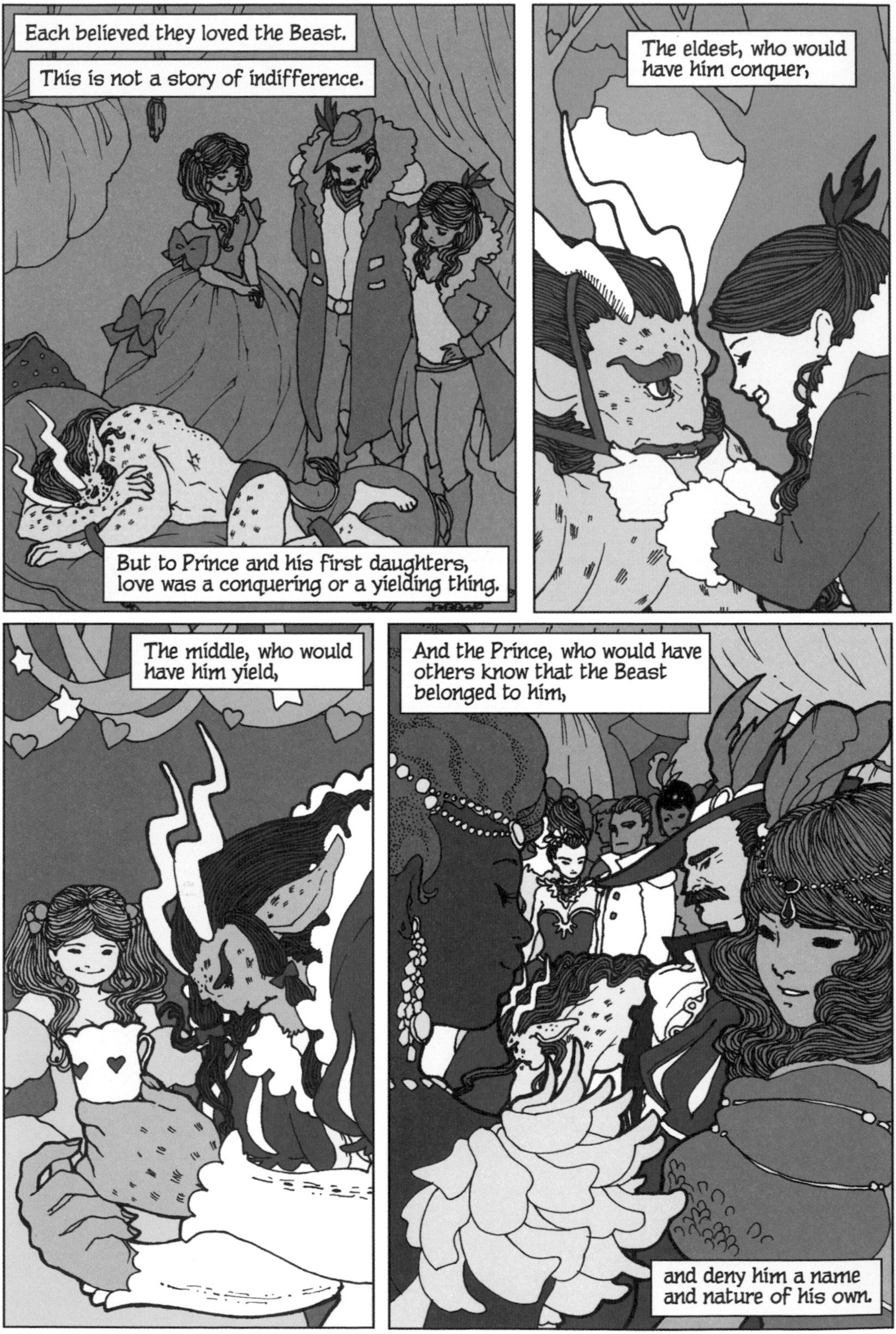
Each believed they loved the Beast.
This is not a story of indifference.
But to Prince and his first daughters, love was a conquering or a yielding thing.
The eldest, who would have him conquer,
The middle, who would have him yield,
And the Prince, who would have others know that the Beast belonged to him,
and deny him a name and nature of his own.

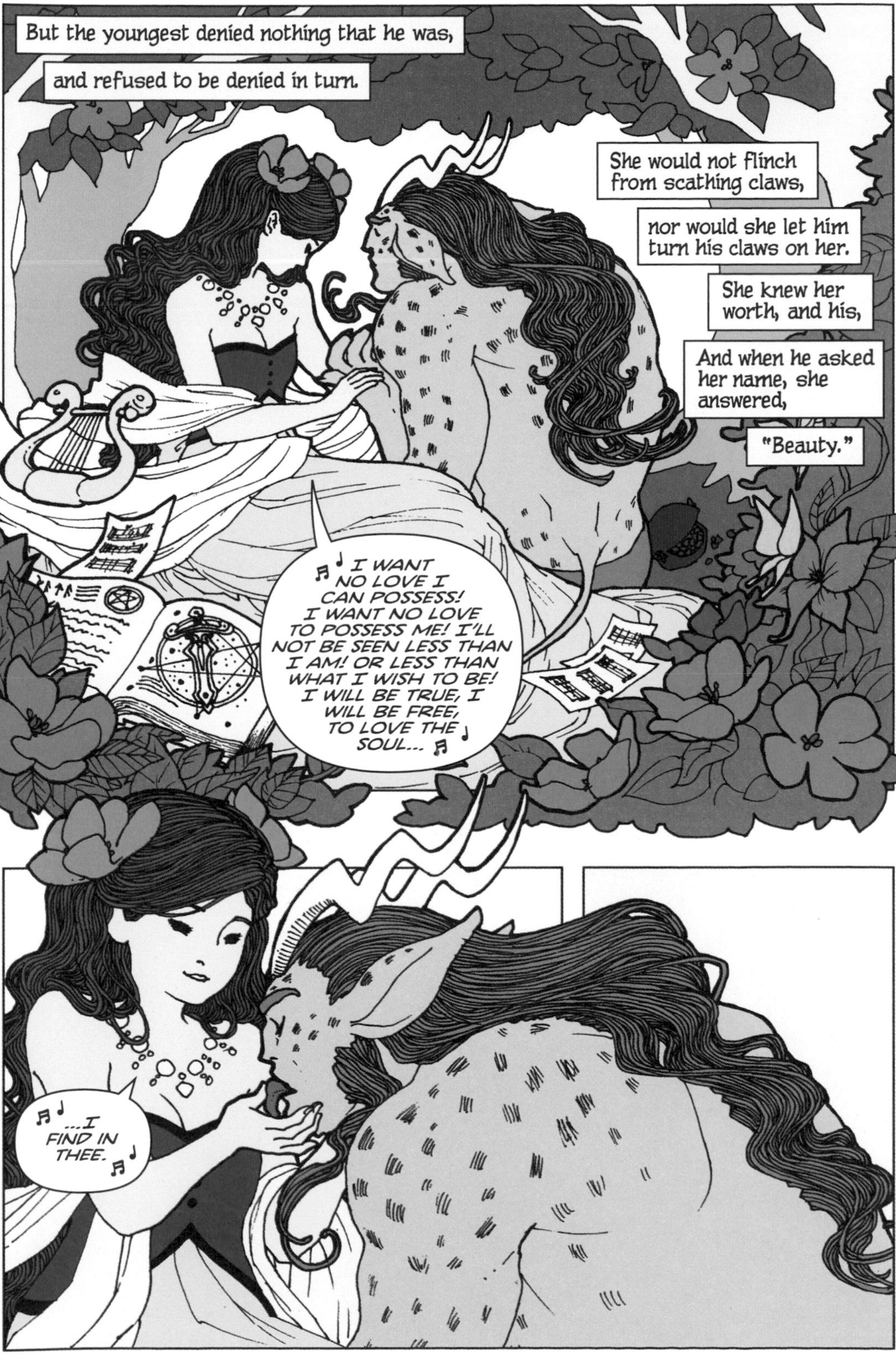

But the youngest denied nothing that he was,
and refused to be denied in turn.
She would not flinch from scathing claws,
nor would she let him turn his claws on her.
She knew her worth, and his,
And when he asked her name, she answered,
"Beauty."
I WANT NO LOVE I CAN POSSESS! I WANT NO LOVE TO POSSESS ME! I'LL NOT BE SEEN LESS THAN I AM! OR LESS THAN WHAT I WISH TO BE! I WILL BE TRUE, I WILL BE FREE, TO LOVE THE SOUL...
...I FIND IN THEE.

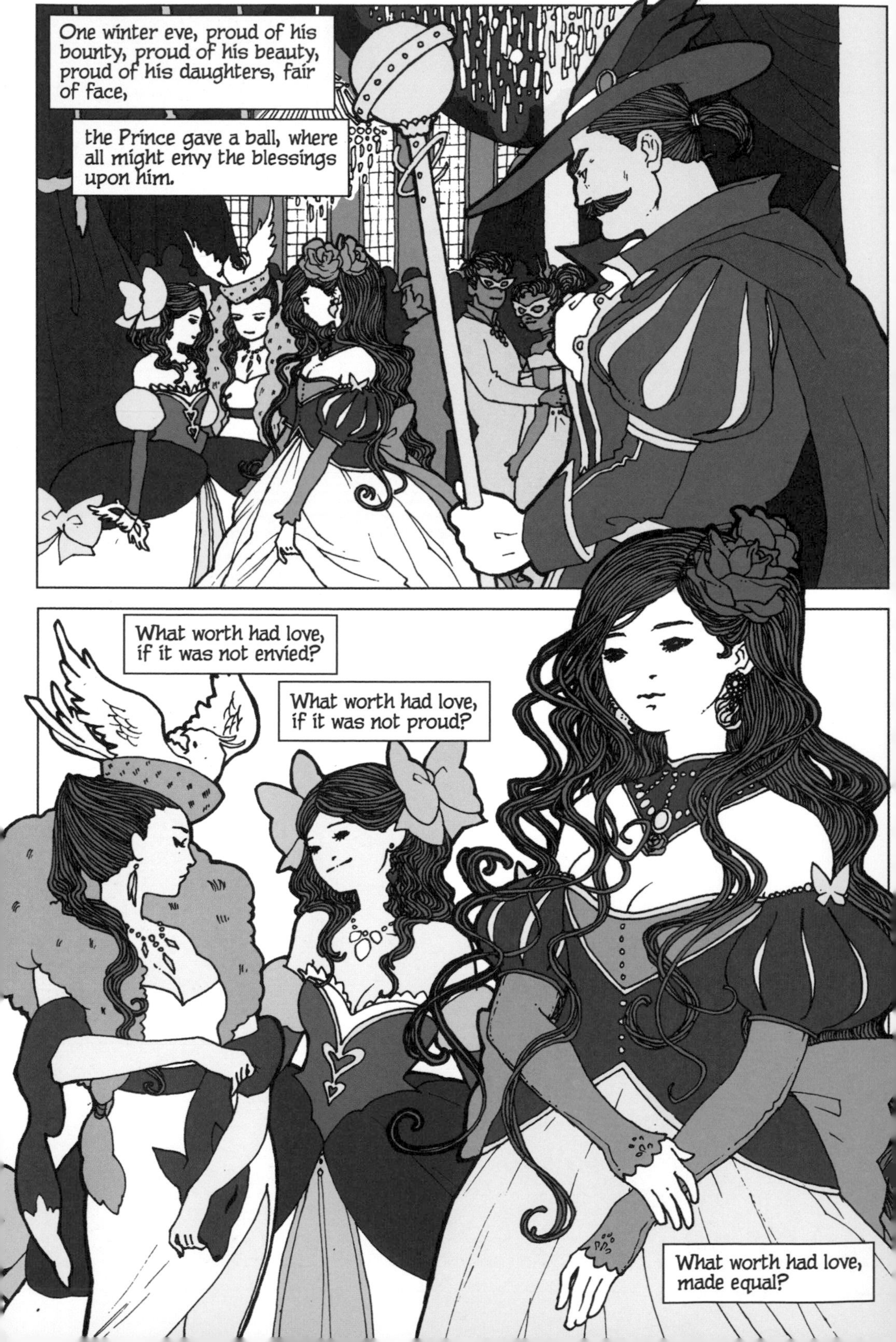
One winter eve, proud of his bounty, proud of his beauty, proud of his daughters, fair of face,
the Prince gave a ball, where all might envy the blessings upon him.
What worth had love, if it was not envied?
What worth had love, if it was not proud?
What worth had love, made equal?

The Prince ushered forth the Beast--an indulgence, an amusement.

The Beast was to show how tame love had made him.

He was to show how wild love had kept him.

He was a possession, inhuman,

a toy for those to whom lovers are playthings.

NO...

NO MORE.

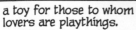

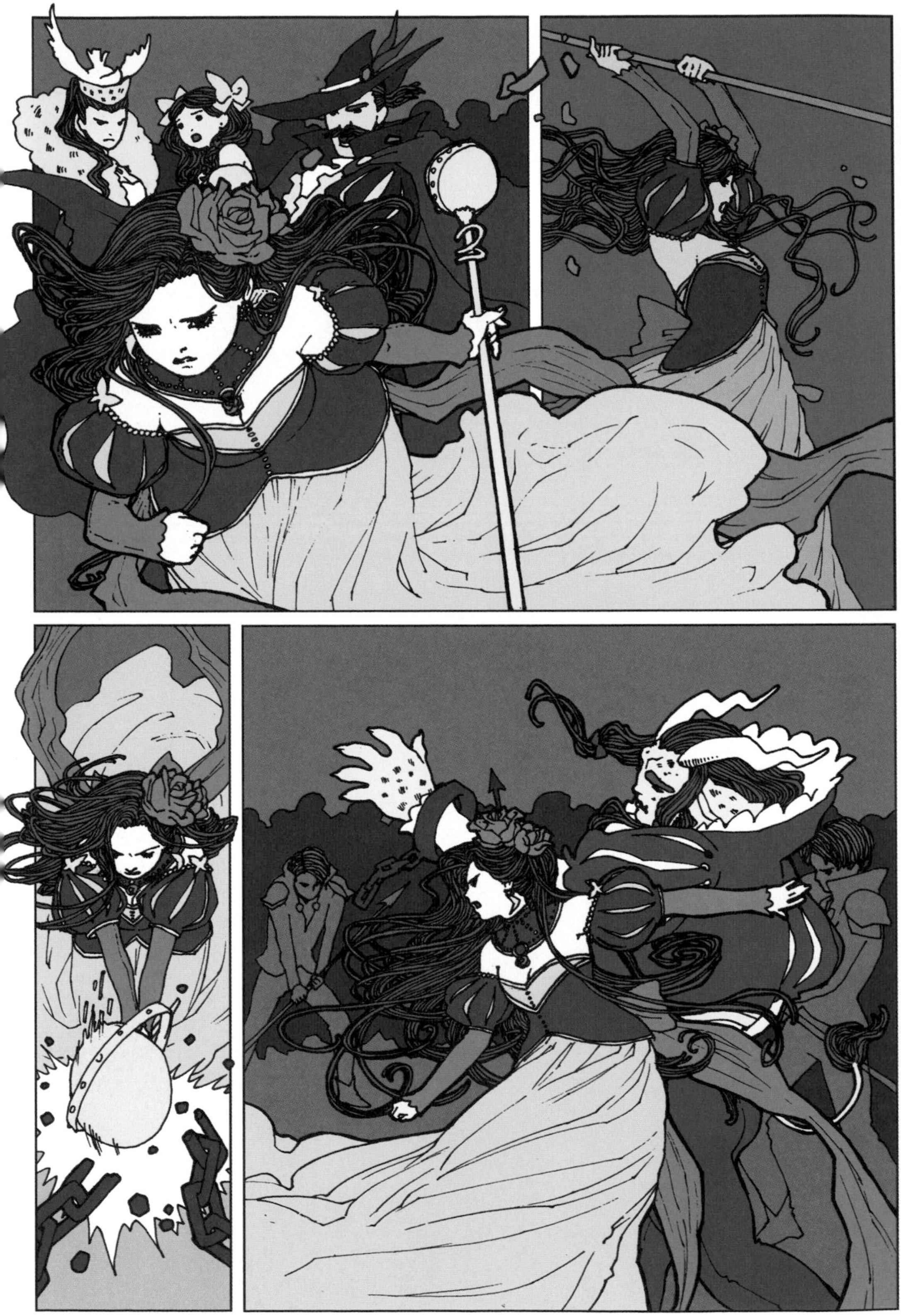

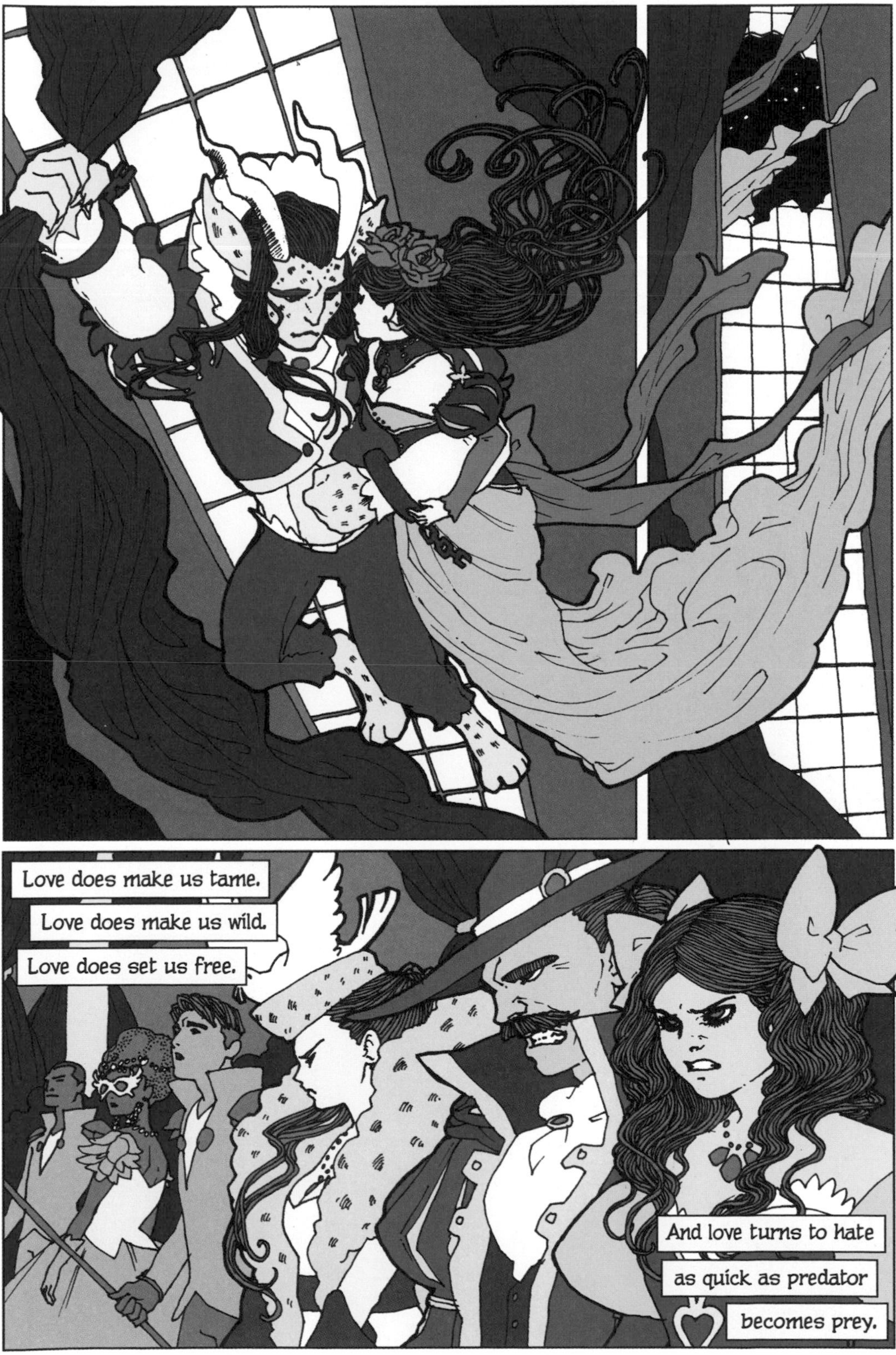
Love does make us tame.
Love does make us wild.
Love does set us free.
And love turns to hate
as quick as predator
becomes prey.

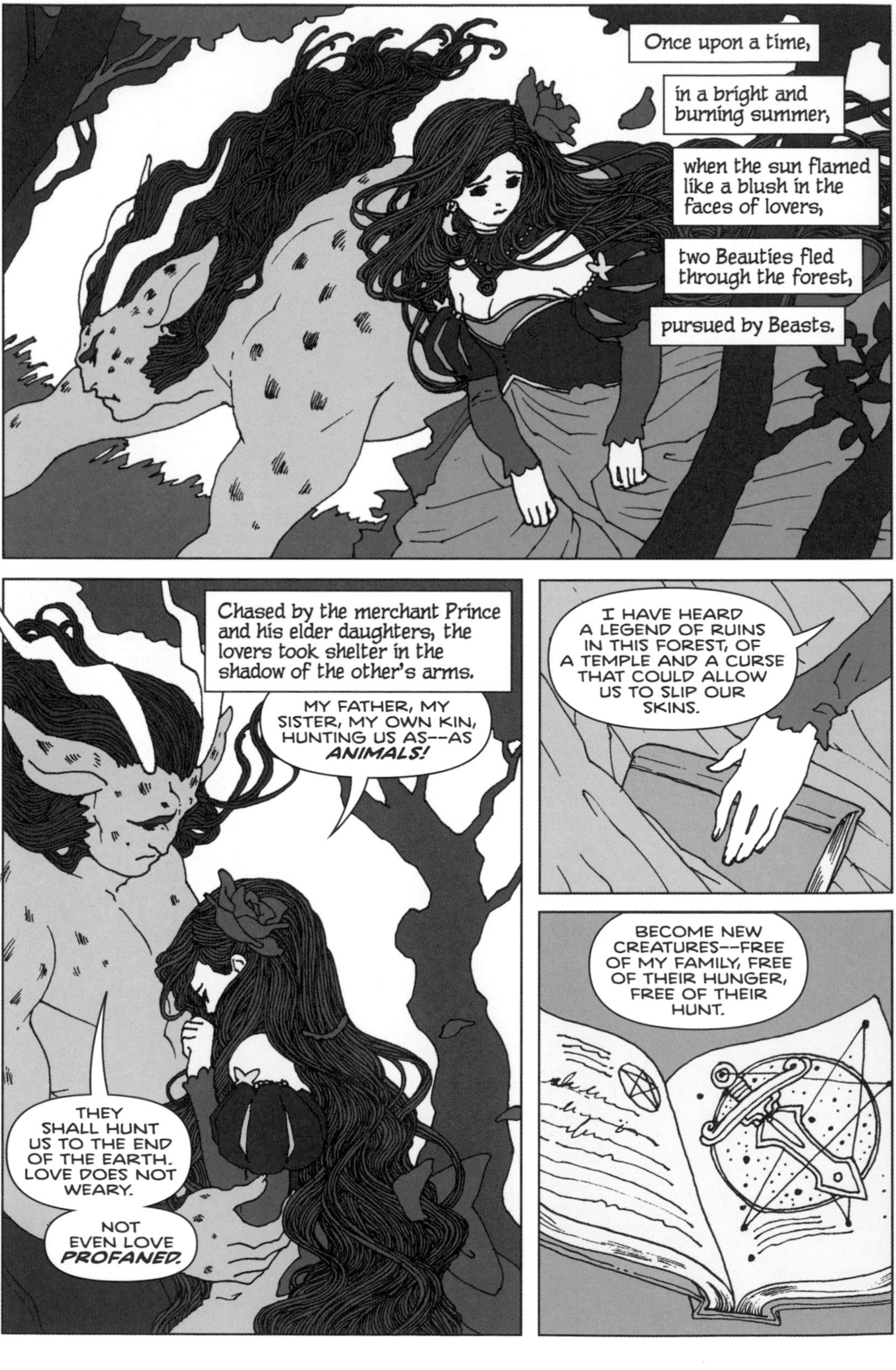
Once upon a time,
in a bright and burning summer,
when the sun flamed like a blush in the faces of lovers,
two Beauties fled through the forest,
pursued by Beasts.
Chased by the merchant Prince and his elder daughters, the lovers took shelter in the shadow of the other's arms.
MY FATHER, MY SISTER, MY OWN KIN, HUNTING US AS--AS *ANIMALS!*
THEY SHALL HUNT US TO THE END OF THE EARTH. LOVE DOES NOT WEARY.
NOT EVEN LOVE *PROFANED.*
I HAVE HEARD A LEGEND OF RUINS IN THIS FOREST, OF A TEMPLE AND A CURSE THAT COULD ALLOW US TO SLIP OUR SKINS.
BECOME NEW CREATURES--FREE OF MY FAMILY, FREE OF THEIR HUNGER, FREE OF THEIR HUNT.

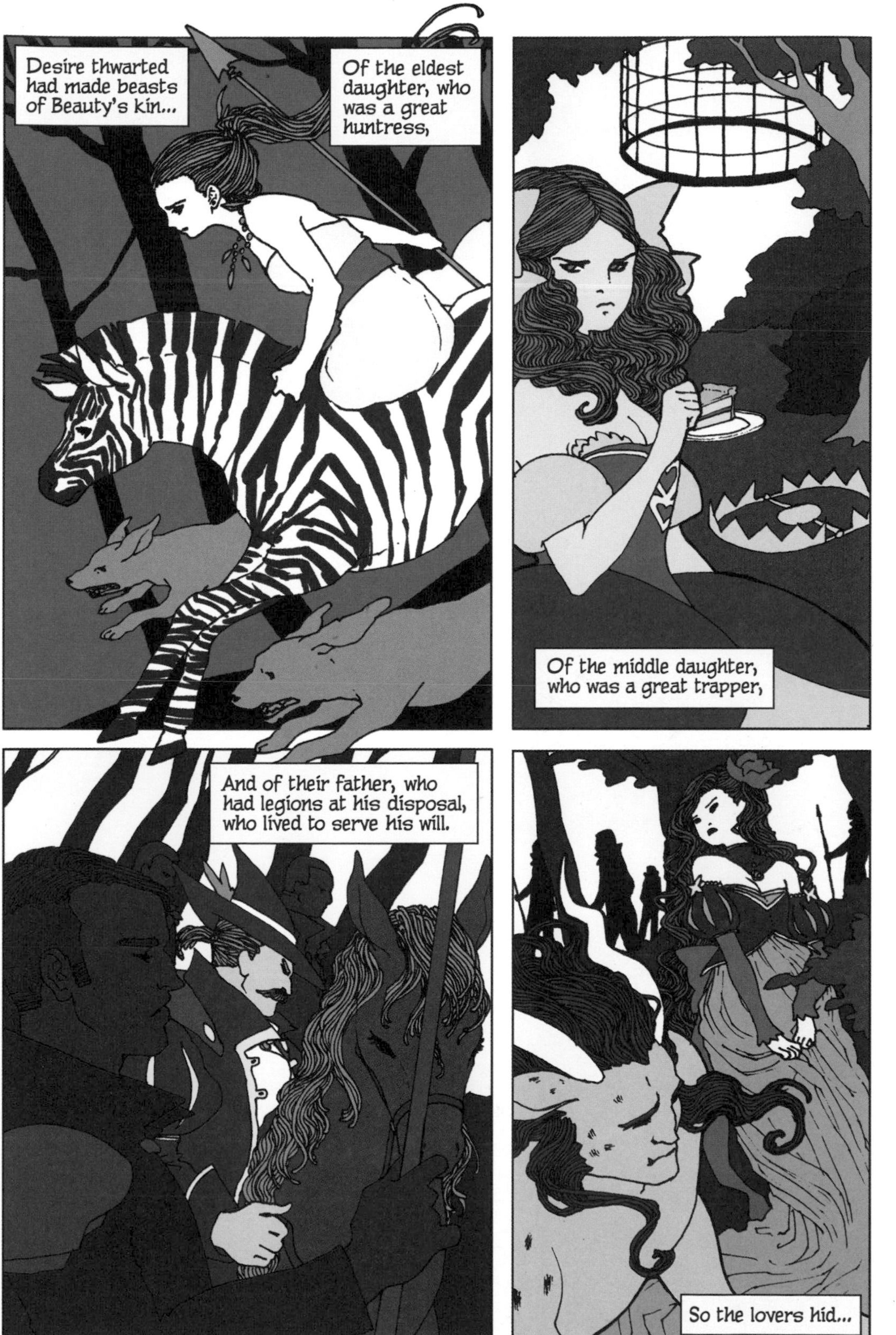
Desire thwarted had made beasts of Beauty's kin...
Of the eldest daughter, who was a great huntress,
Of the middle daughter, who was a great trapper,
And of their father, who had legions at his disposal, who lived to serve his will.
So the lovers hid...

...and came upon a dark and holy place.

ON, HUNTERS! ON, HOUNDS!

A Temple...

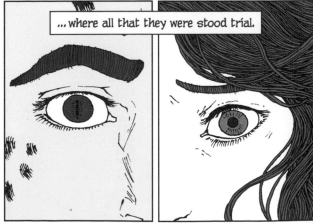

...where all that they were stood trial.

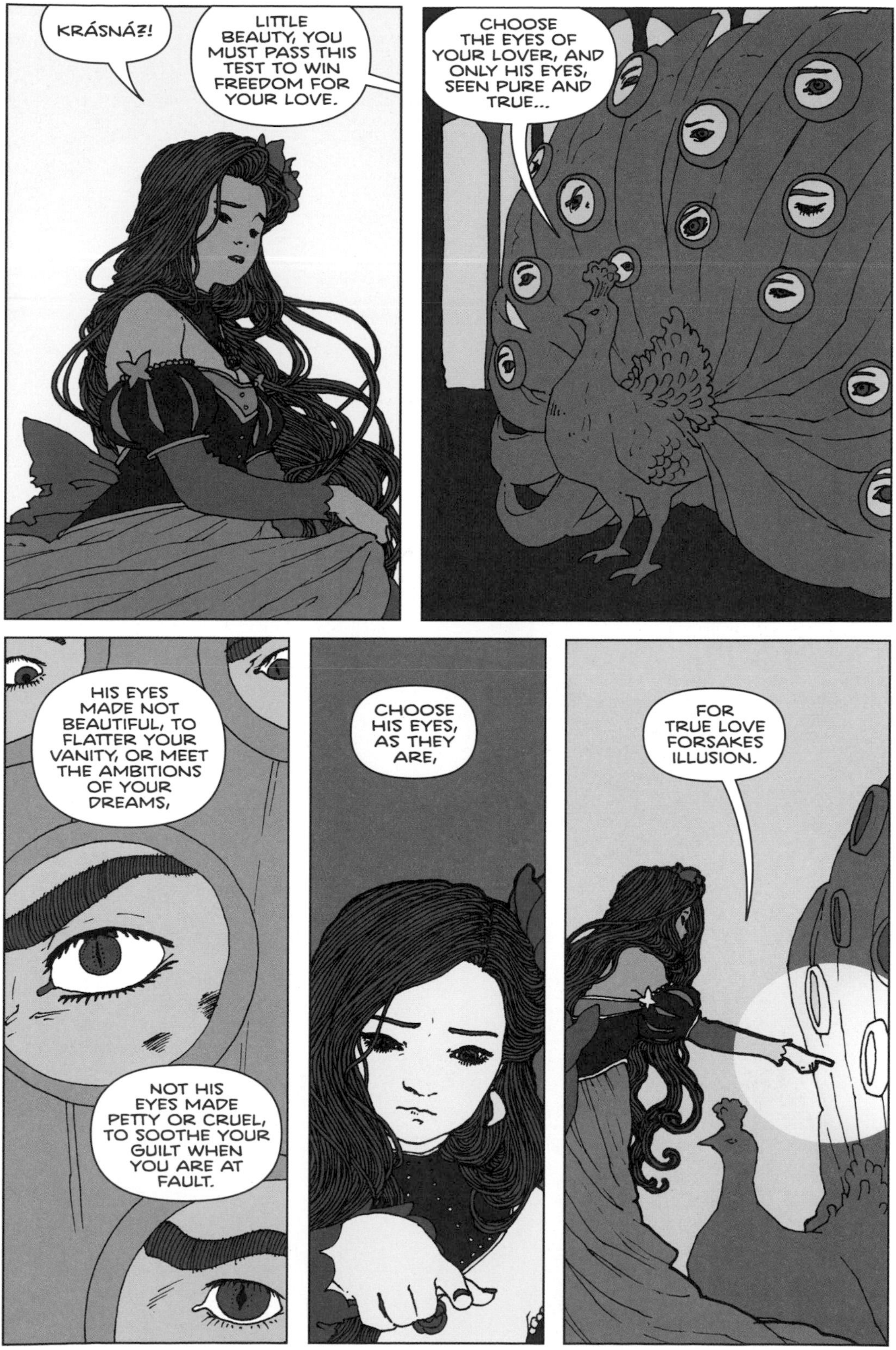

KRÁSNÁŽ!
LITTLE BEAUTY, YOU MUST PASS THIS TEST TO WIN FREEDOM FOR YOUR LOVE.
CHOOSE THE EYES OF YOUR LOVER, AND ONLY HIS EYES, SEEN PURE AND TRUE...
HIS EYES MADE NOT BEAUTIFUL, TO FLATTER YOUR VANITY, OR MEET THE AMBITIONS OF YOUR DREAMS,
NOT HIS EYES MADE PETTY OR CRUEL, TO SOOTHE YOUR GUILT WHEN YOU ARE AT FAULT.
CHOOSE HIS EYES, AS THEY ARE,
FOR TRUE LOVE FORSAKES ILLUSION.

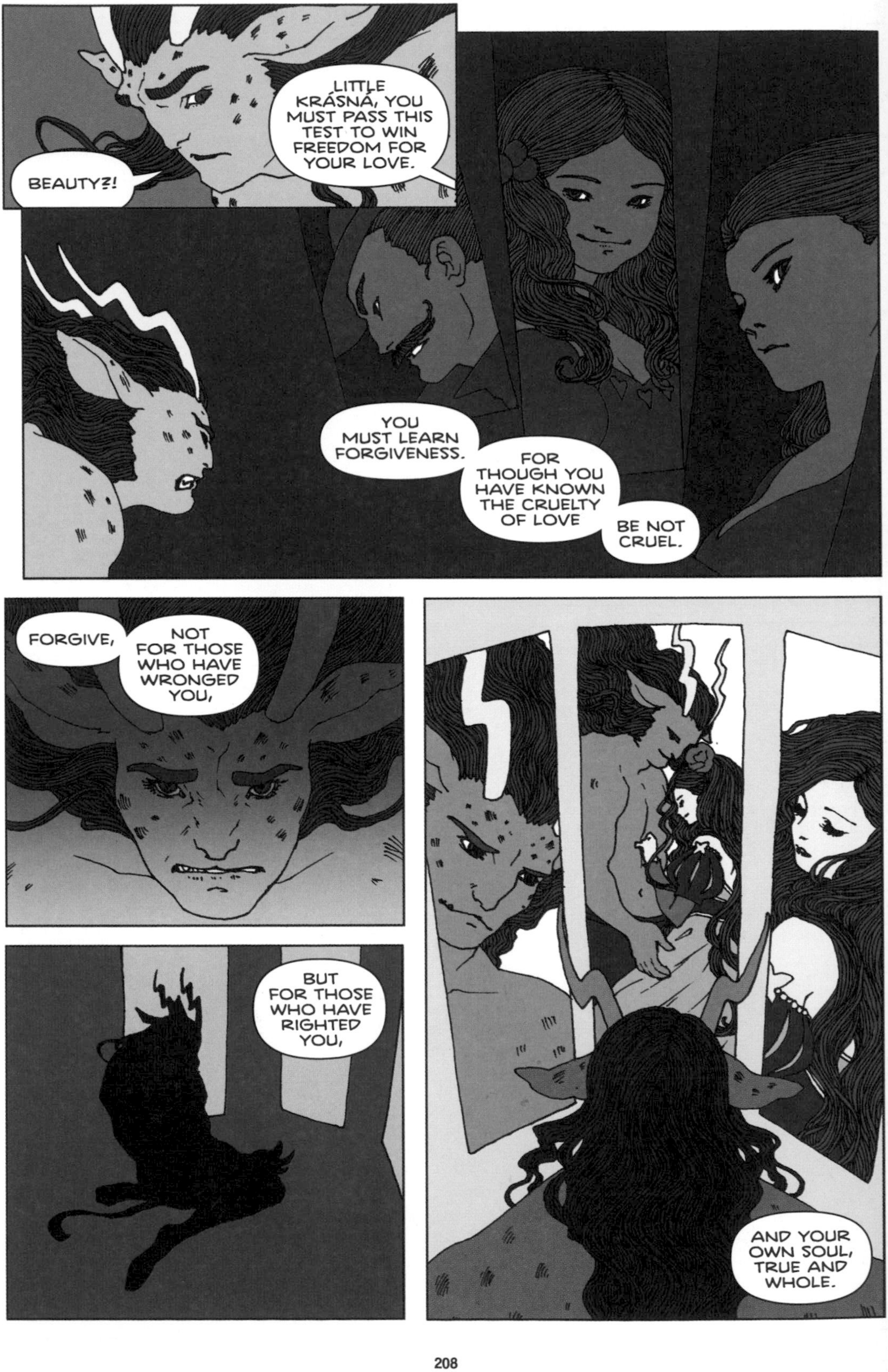
LITTLE KRÁSNÁ, YOU MUST PASS THIS TEST TO WIN FREEDOM FOR YOUR LOVE.
BEAUTY?!
YOU MUST LEARN FORGIVENESS.
FOR THOUGH YOU HAVE KNOWN THE CRUELTY OF LOVE
BE NOT CRUEL.
FORGIVE,
NOT FOR THOSE WHO HAVE WRONGED YOU,
BUT FOR THOSE WHO HAVE RIGHTED YOU,
AND YOUR OWN SOUL, TRUE AND WHOLE.

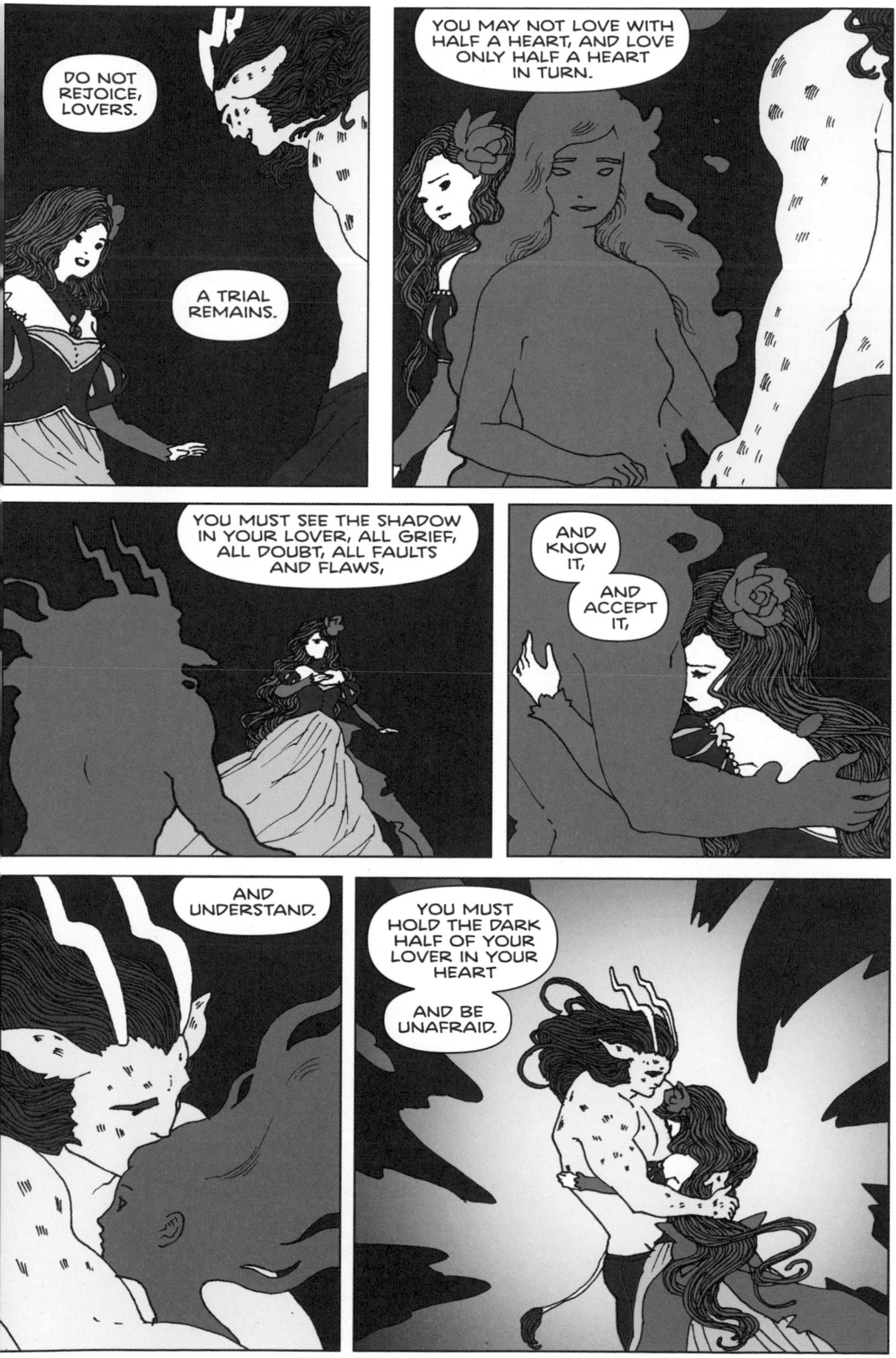
DO NOT REJOICE, LOVERS.
A TRIAL REMAINS.
YOU MAY NOT LOVE WITH HALF A HEART, AND LOVE ONLY HALF A HEART IN TURN.
YOU MUST SEE THE SHADOW IN YOUR LOVER, ALL GRIEF, ALL DOUBT, ALL FAULTS AND FLAWS,
AND KNOW IT,
AND ACCEPT IT,
AND UNDERSTAND.
YOU MUST HOLD THE DARK HALF OF YOUR LOVER IN YOUR HEART
AND BE UNAFRAID.

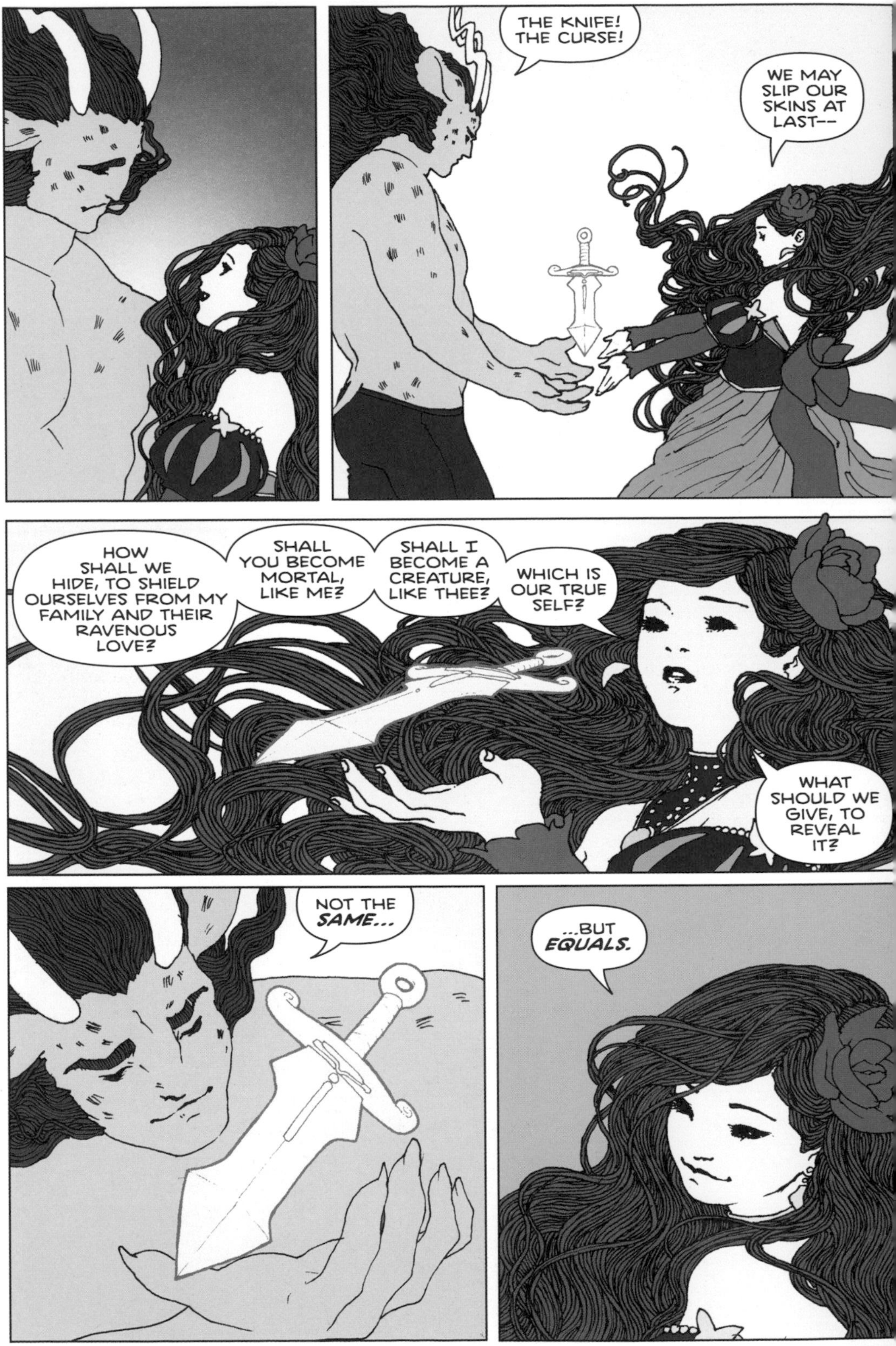
THE KNIFE! THE CURSE!
WE MAY SLIP OUR SKINS AT LAST--
HOW SHALL WE HIDE, TO SHIELD OURSELVES FROM MY FAMILY AND THEIR RAVENOUS LOVE?
SHALL YOU BECOME MORTAL, LIKE ME?
SHALL I BECOME A CREATURE, LIKE THEE?
WHICH IS OUR TRUE SELF?
WHAT SHOULD WE GIVE, TO REVEAL IT?
NOT THE SAME...
...BUT EQUALS.

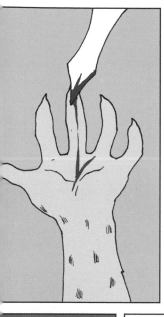
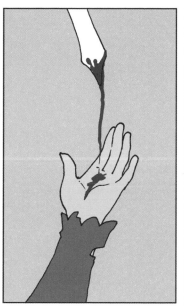
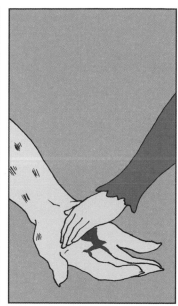

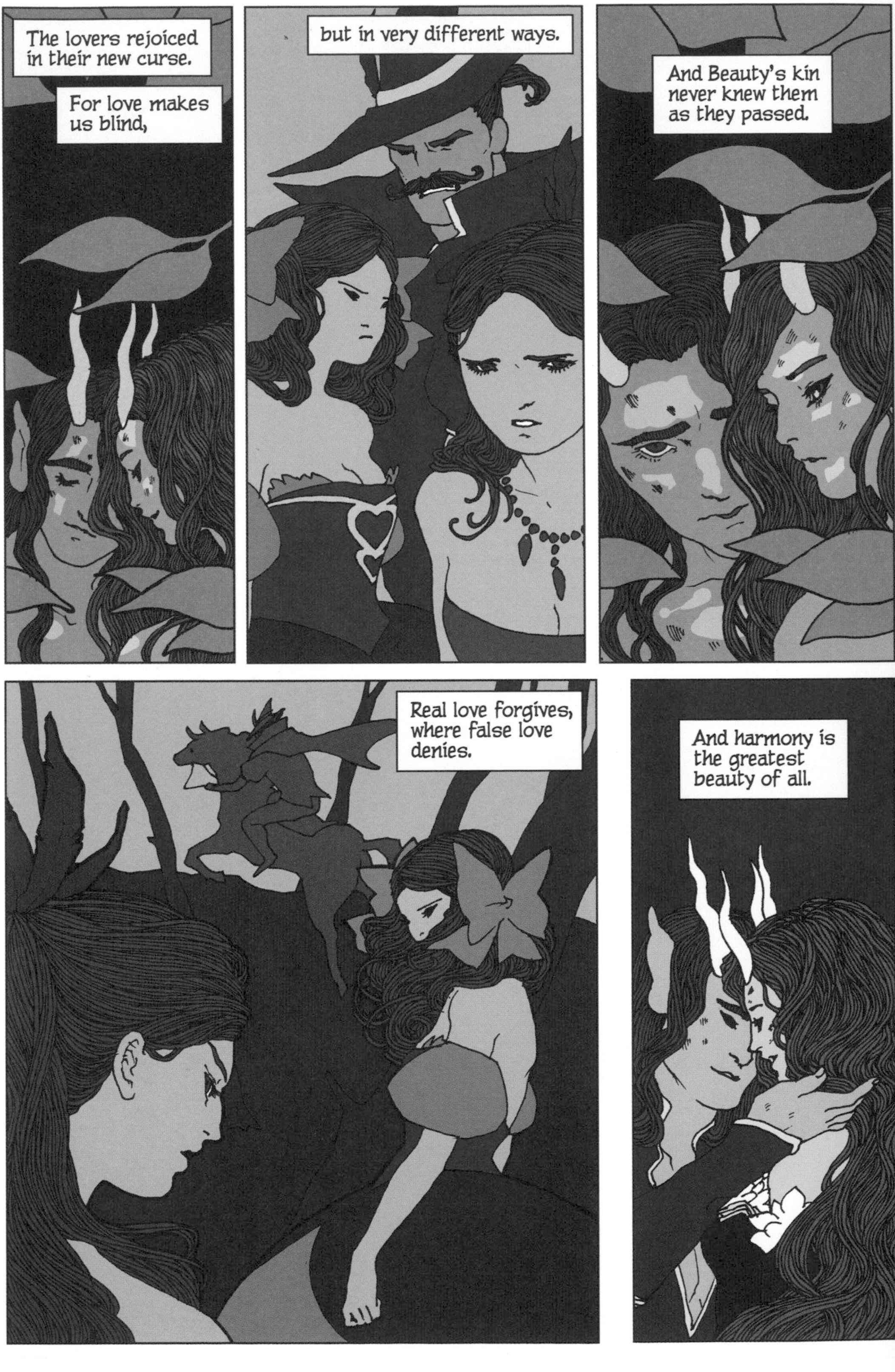
The lovers rejoiced in their new curse.
For love makes us blind,
but in very different ways.
And Beauty's kin never knew them as they passed.
Real love forgives, where false love denies.
And harmony is the greatest beauty of all.

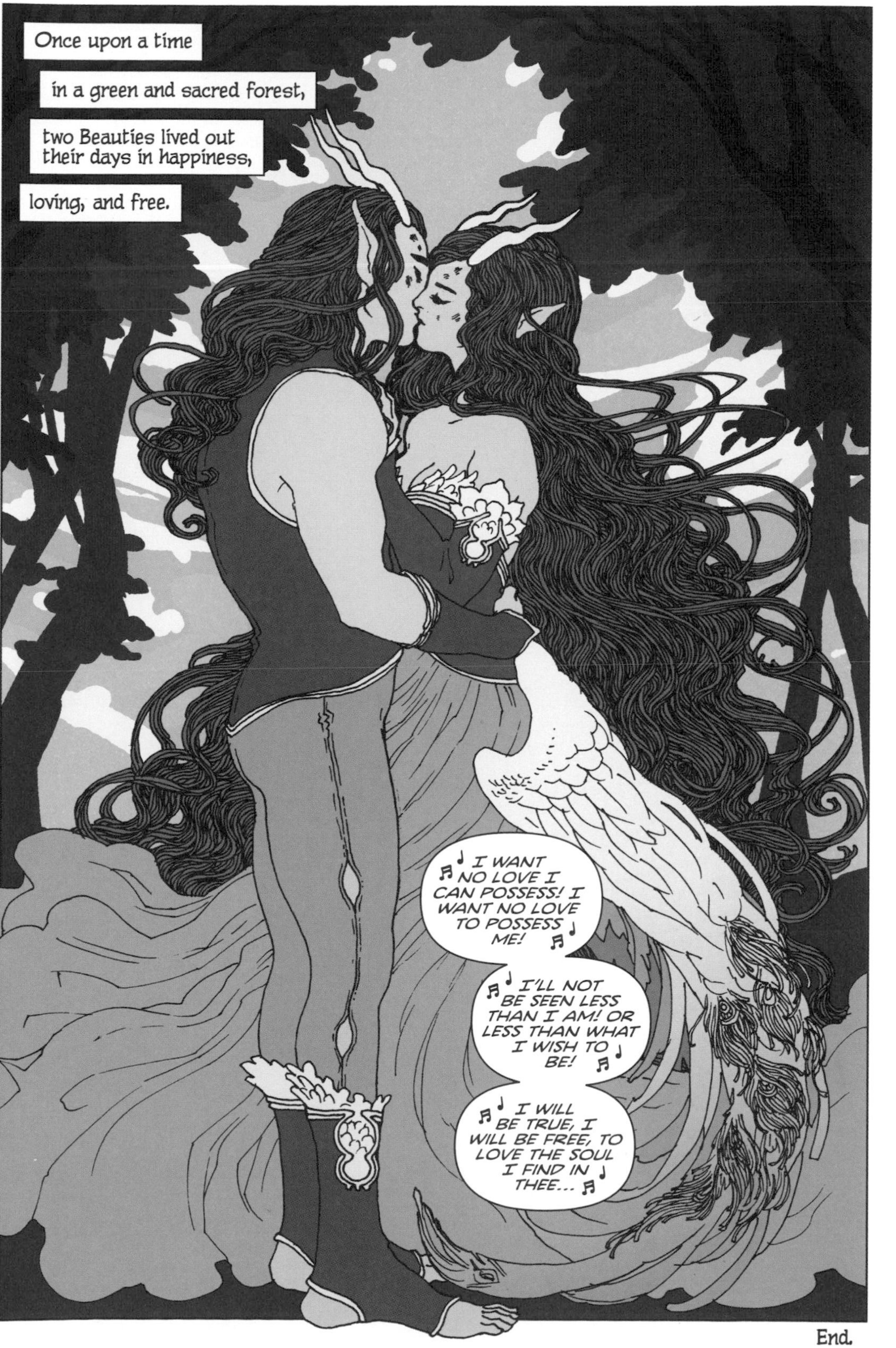
Once upon a time
in a green and sacred forest,
two Beauties lived out their days in happiness,
loving, and free.
I WANT NO LOVE I CAN POSSESS! I WANT NO LOVE TO POSSESS ME!
I'LL NOT BE SEEN LESS THAN I AM! OR LESS THAN WHAT I WISH TO BE!
I WILL BE TRUE, I WILL BE FREE, TO LOVE THE SOUL I FIND IN THEE...

End.

BEAUTIES ROUNDTABLE

The *Beauties* creative team had a nice long chat about their inspiration, work process, and mutual admiration society.

Marguerite Bennett: Trung! Would you like to start with your design process and how we avoided "the furry question"? ;)

Trungles: Oh my goodness, that's a fun one!

Without digging into our correspondences, I remember being very deliberate in the design for Krásná and working around some special criteria. First, he would primarily be animal in nature with human-like characteristics. Second, he would not follow the archetypical format of boar, bear, and bull to which most folks are accustomed. And last, he would be elegant and lithe. I wanted to remove him from that western visual canon and include animals toward which I gravitate. I settled on the horns of a gazelle and the pattern and build of a jaguar to imply a bit more precision and grace in his physicality.

Krásná ended up reminding me of a kirin, a mythical animal I was familiar with growing up, which I loved. It's also noteworthy that we had a conversation about how to make Krásná attractive without treading full-gait into furry territory, which was an interesting challenge. I tried to sort of let Krásná have moments where there are echoes of humanity without letting go of the overall animal. Ultimately, it was the writing and the thematic explorations that overcame the Furry Question.

T: I've got a couple questions!

Marguerite, we've touched on our mutual love of fairy tales before, but what in particular about *Beauty and the Beast* or its themes inclined to you to a little exploration and remixing of your own? There's so many versions and so many different themes depending on the story's context. How did you go about crafting the themes of love in the story?

MB: Cheers! The themes in *Beauty and the Beast* in general are some of those dearest and most intriguing to me—power, beauty,

personhood, and sacrifice. I've always enjoyed the elements in play in the classic story—masculine power in strength, feminine strength in sacrifice, imprisonment, wealth, etc, and how the two lovers challenge and tame one another. I wanted to see them arrive at a happy ending as equals. Even where we begin, it is not a case of our Beauty being put into our Beast's power—but nor is it a case of our Beast being placed in our Beauty's power. They are both trapped within different confines, but are permitted to discover each other as equals.

I also, frankly, wanted to introduce sensuality into play. Because we have (bizarrely) taken folk stories and decided that their magical elements mean that they are not serious literature, and that literature that is not serious is meant for children, we often remake fairy stories and folktales with a muting and banking of strong emotional and physical elements of love. We brush abusive relationships, insincere love, and even power dynamics present in S&M relationships. One day I hope to unpack it all for a reader, haha.

T: Rachel, your lettering is really wonderful! How do you balance the aesthetic, compositional, and practical considerations of lettering from page to page? I don't know a lot about the lettering process and am not well attuned to all the work that goes into, but I loved how everything turned out.

Rachel Deering: First of all, thank you so much for the kind words! I'm glad you were happy with how the letters worked with your art. As for how I approach designing a page, I typically let the artwork dictate the flow of the letters. Great artists will naturally provide a flow for letters. If a designer has a sharp enough eye to spot the flow, it makes their job a lot easier and they look a lot better. That was certainly the case with *Beauties*!

RD: Marguerite, you use music throughout the comic to help express the desires of your characters. How important is music to you as a writer, and what types of music do you enjoy most?

MB: Thank you, Rachel! Music is (frustratingly) very important to me as a writer, and I have been drawn to precisely the medium that has the most trouble conveying it, haha. I include songs in nearly all my comics (and in some cases, cursing myself all the while, go back and add songs with unnecessarily

complicated rhyme schemes to stories because they are true to character and period, despite all the extra work entailed). In the case of *Beauties*, I wanted the story to read as sort of a poem or lyric ballad, with rhythm and poetic word choices to create a lovely, lilting cadence when read aloud—the closest I can get to expressing music in comics. Thanks for asking! :)

In terms of my own music, I love everything from Rammstein to Disney, but if you can get me some moody singers with wild, weird lyrics, or else perpetually whisper-singing through lost love, I am a happy camper. ;)

MB: Rachel, I'm frankly a sucker for different fonts. What goes into creating or selecting the style that will be immersive for a reader? We've gotten more compliments on the lettering for *Beauties* than any story I've ever worked on. :)

RD: It pleases me to know that people are enjoying my work! Thanks to y'all for having me. As for font choice, I always try to find a letter set that echoes both the weight and character of the line work. If the art is made up of delicate, organic lines, I'll choose a light, rounder font. If the pages are full of thick, sharp lines, I'll go with something angular and heavy. It's all about blending in for me. I'd rather people assume the artist lettered the book than to stand out and draw attention to myself.

RD: Trung, many of the panels in this story have a very stained glass aesthetic, putting me in mind of a bolder sort of Mucha-esque composition. Who or what influenced your style most?

T: Good question! I have a sort of funny combination of influences. While I was in school, I spent a lot of time looking at turn-of-the-century children's book illustrators. My work finds a lot of its themes

and compositions from Edmund Dulac, Arthur Rackham, Rose O'Neill, and Harry Clarke. Harry Clarke did a fair amount of stained glass work, too, so I definitely have a fair bit of that Jugendstil aesthetic in me. I also grew up reading a lot of *Tintin* and some *Little Nemo*. I'm really attracted to that clear-line style. The flat colors and stained glass aesthetic complement that line style really nicely, so I try to keep it simple.

I think above all, my biggest influence in general is, oddly, Chihiro Iwasaki, a Japanese illustrator whose work looks pretty different from mine. I read *The Crane Maiden* when I was a kid, and the way she illustrated the images stuck with me. I like the textures, the shapes, and the sweetly economical details in the figures. They're beautiful. Thanks for the question!

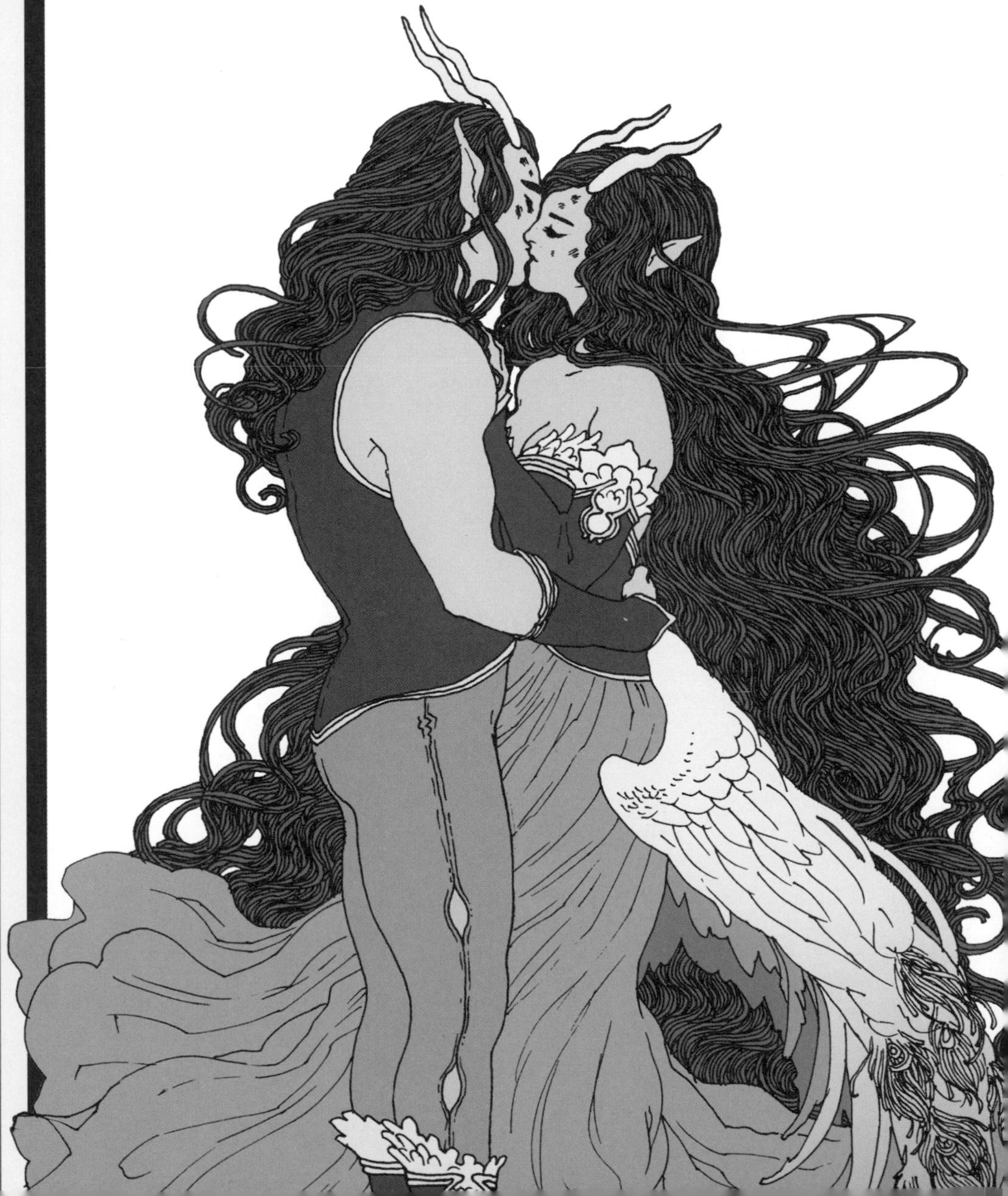

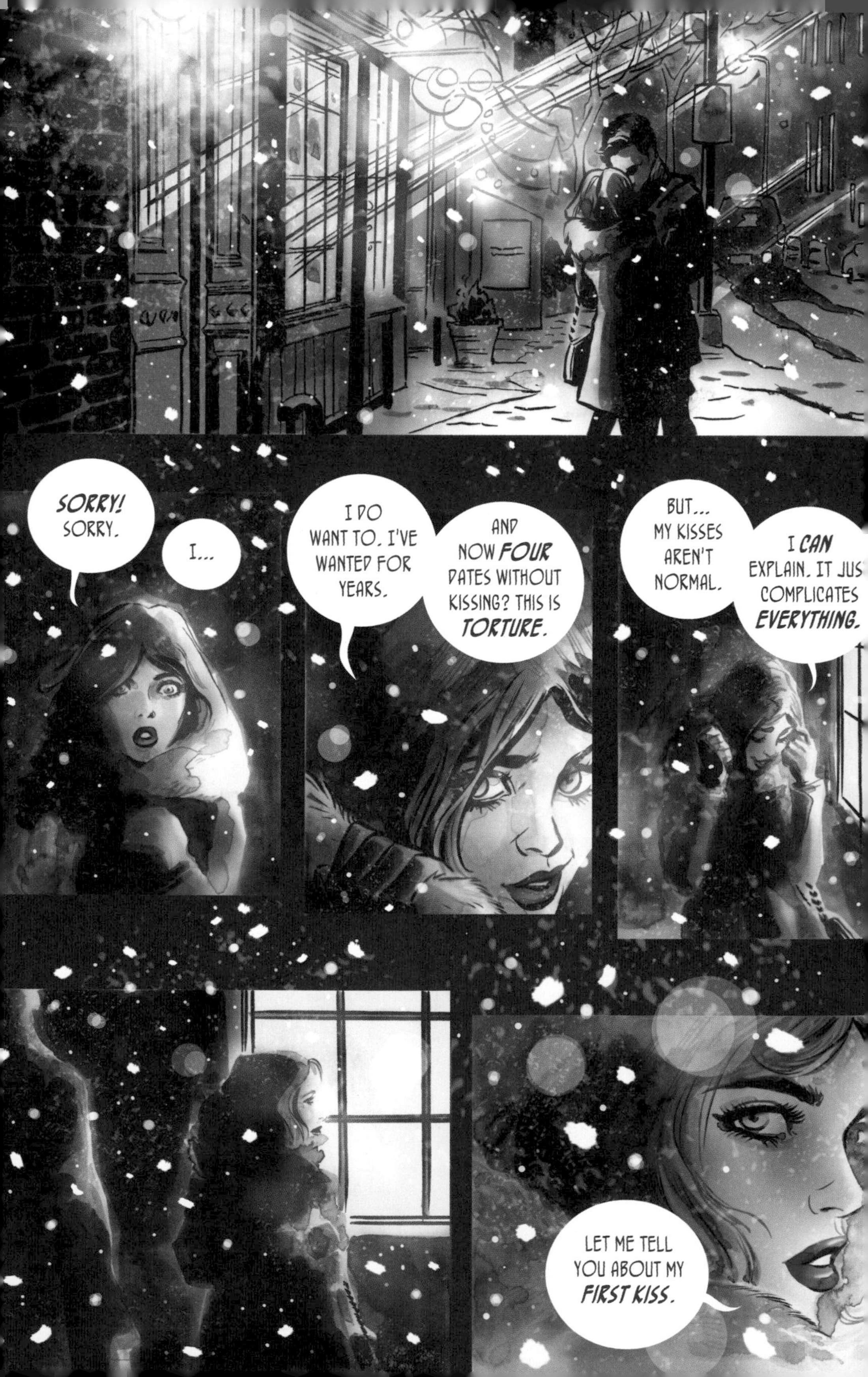

SORRY! SORRY.
I...
I DO WANT TO. I'VE WANTED FOR YEARS.
AND NOW FOUR DATES WITHOUT KISSING? THIS IS TORTURE.
BUT... MY KISSES AREN'T NORMAL.
I CAN EXPLAIN. IT JUS COMPLICATES EVERYTHING.
LET ME TELL YOU ABOUT MY FIRST KISS.

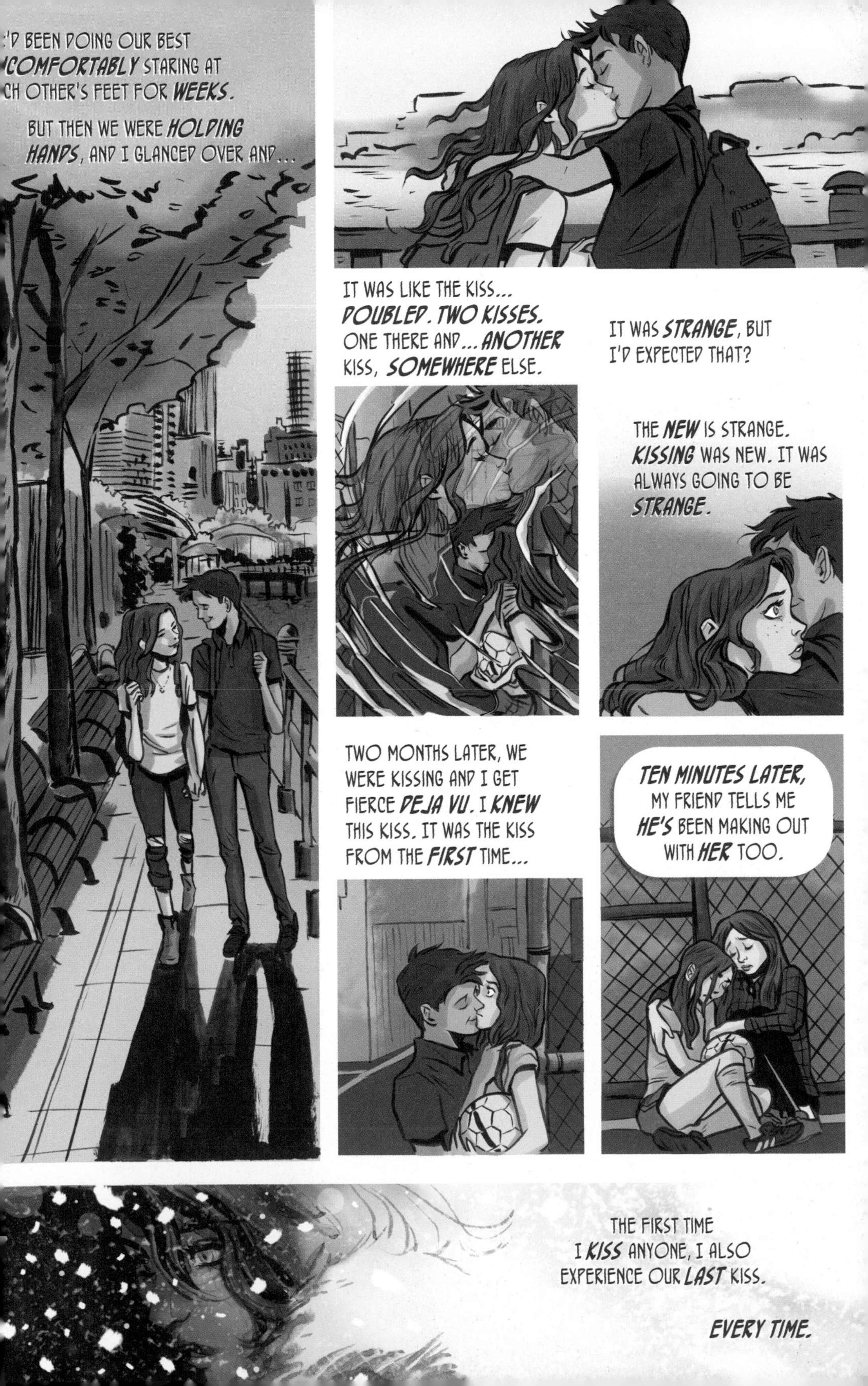

'D BEEN DOING OUR BEST COMFORTABLY STARING AT CH OTHER'S FEET FOR WEEKS.
BUT THEN WE WERE HOLDING HANDS, AND I GLANCED OVER AND...
IT WAS LIKE THE KISS... DOUBLED. TWO KISSES. ONE THERE AND... ANOTHER KISS, SOMEWHERE ELSE.
IT WAS STRANGE, BUT I'D EXPECTED THAT?
THE NEW IS STRANGE. KISSING WAS NEW. IT WAS ALWAYS GOING TO BE STRANGE.
TWO MONTHS LATER, WE WERE KISSING AND I GET FIERCE DEJA VU. I KNEW THIS KISS. IT WAS THE KISS FROM THE FIRST TIME...
TEN MINUTES LATER, MY FRIEND TELLS ME HE'S BEEN MAKING OUT WITH HER TOO.
THE FIRST TIME I KISS ANYONE, I ALSO EXPERIENCE OUR LAST KISS.
EVERY TIME.

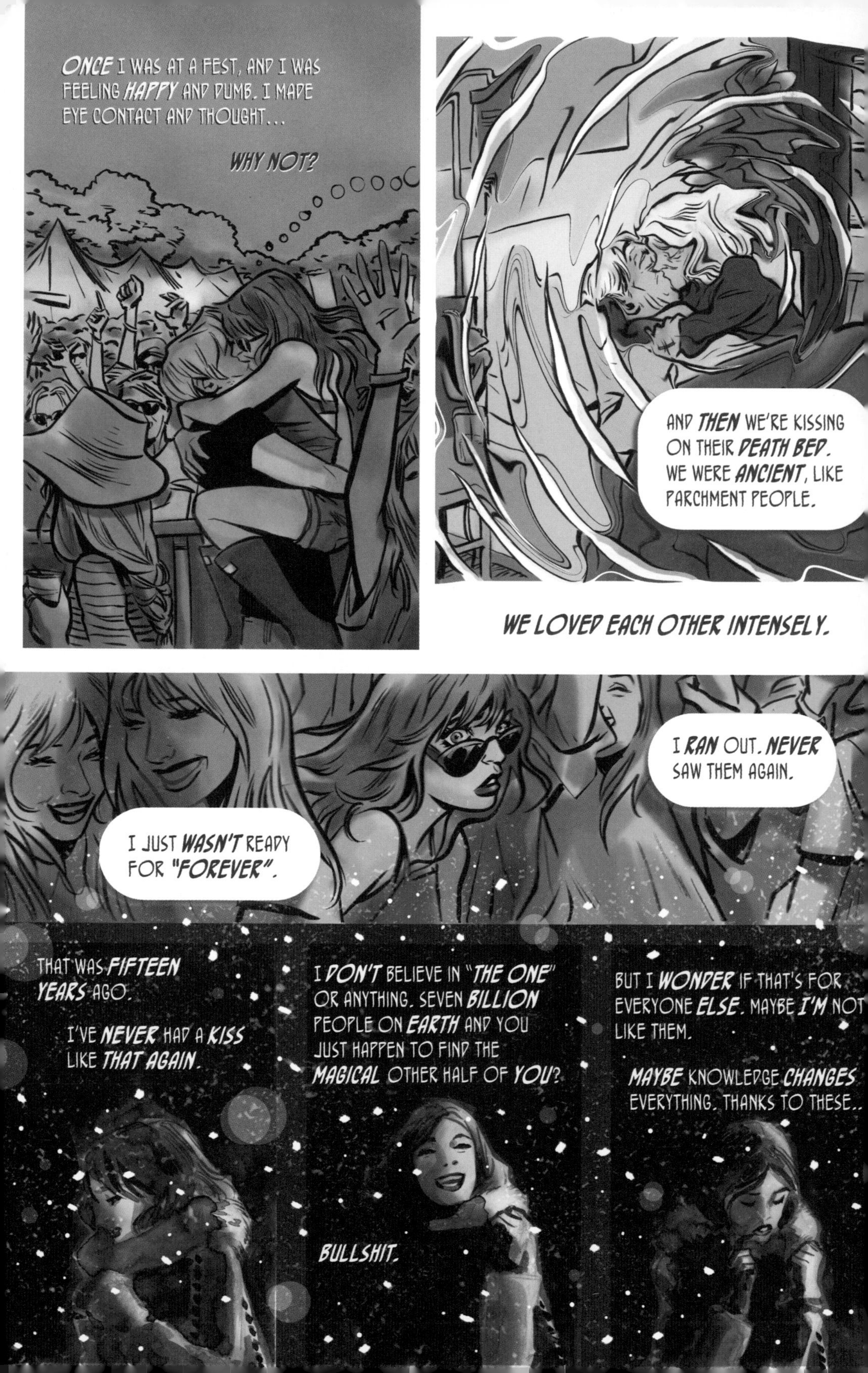
ONCE I WAS AT A FEST, AND I WAS FEELING HAPPY AND DUMB. I MADE EYE CONTACT AND THOUGHT...
WHY NOT?
AND THEN WE'RE KISSING ON THEIR DEATH BED. WE WERE ANCIENT, LIKE PARCHMENT PEOPLE.
WE LOVED EACH OTHER INTENSELY.
I RAN OUT. NEVER SAW THEM AGAIN.
I JUST WASN'T READY FOR "FOREVER".
THAT WAS FIFTEEN YEARS AGO.
I'VE NEVER HAD A KISS LIKE THAT AGAIN.
I DON'T BELIEVE IN "THE ONE" OR ANYTHING. SEVEN BILLION PEOPLE ON EARTH AND YOU JUST HAPPEN TO FIND THE MAGICAL OTHER HALF OF YOU?
BULLSHIT.
BUT I WONDER IF THAT'S FOR EVERYONE ELSE. MAYBE I'M NOT LIKE THEM.
MAYBE KNOWLEDGE CHANGES EVERYTHING. THANKS TO THESE..

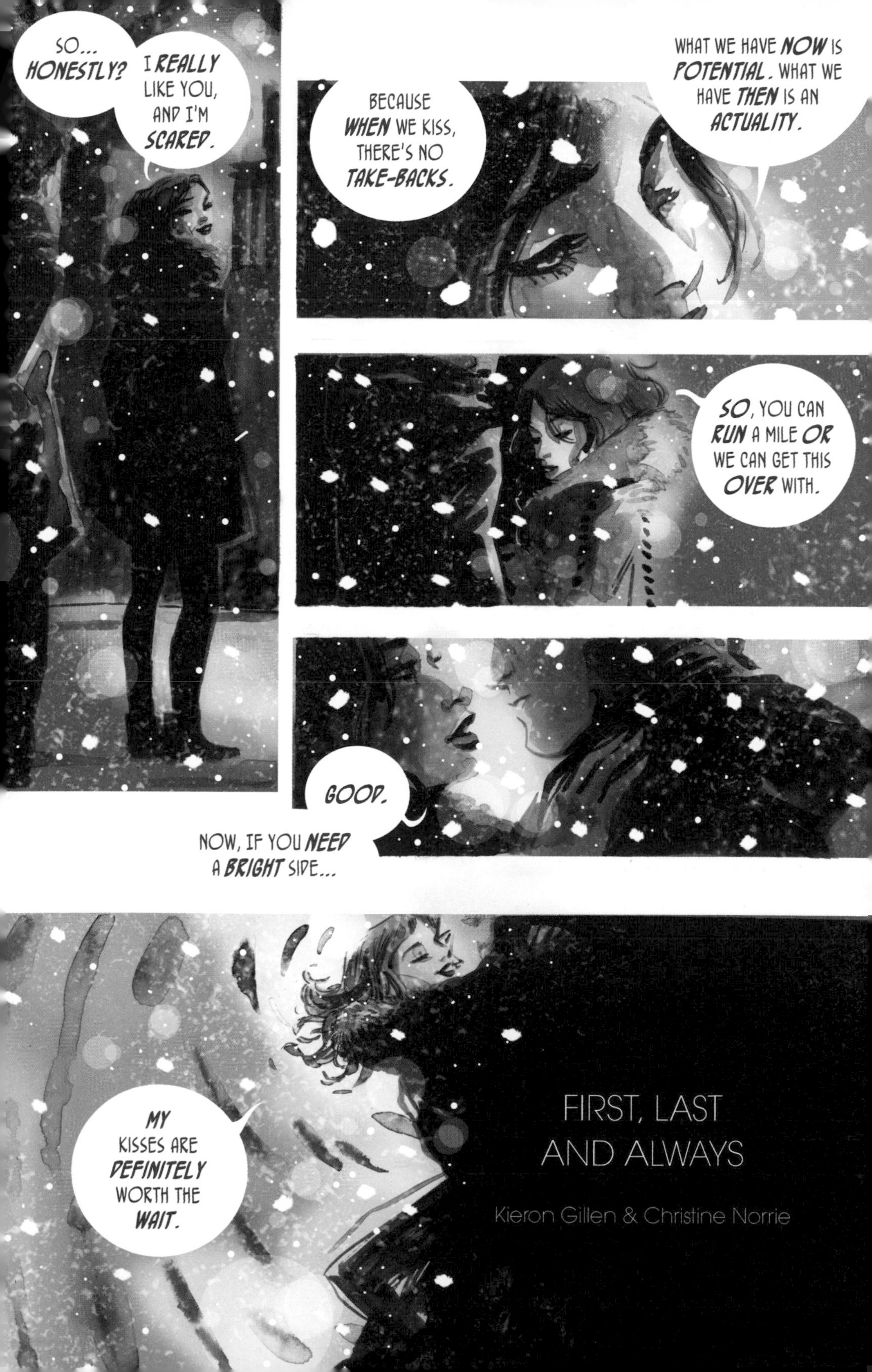
SO... HONESTLY?
I REALLY LIKE YOU, AND I'M SCARED.
BECAUSE WHEN WE KISS, THERE'S NO TAKE-BACKS.
WHAT WE HAVE NOW IS POTENTIAL. WHAT WE HAVE THEN IS AN ACTUALITY.
SO, YOU CAN RUN A MILE OR WE CAN GET THIS OVER WITH.
GOOD.
NOW, IF YOU NEED A BRIGHT SIDE...
MY KISSES ARE DEFINITELY WORTH THE WAIT.
FIRST, LAST AND ALWAYS
Kieron Gillen & Christine Norrie

A look at upcoming *Fresh Romance* comics!

LOVE AND SPROCKETS by Taneka Stotts and Genue Revuelta

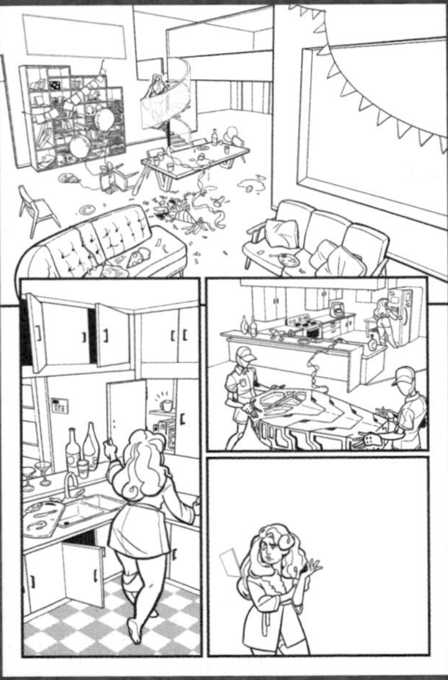

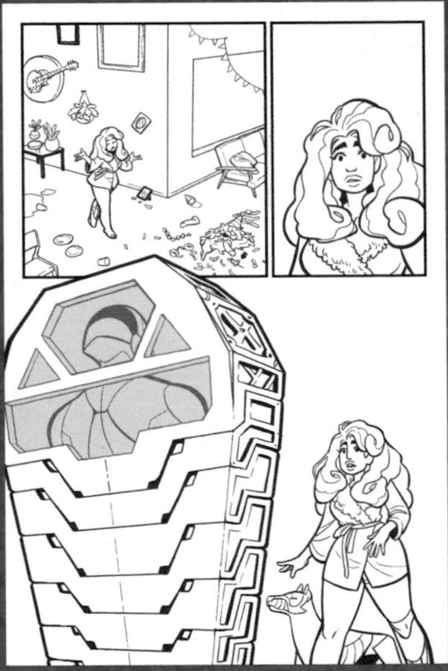

PURPLE LOVE BALLOON by Marcy Cook and Maya Kern

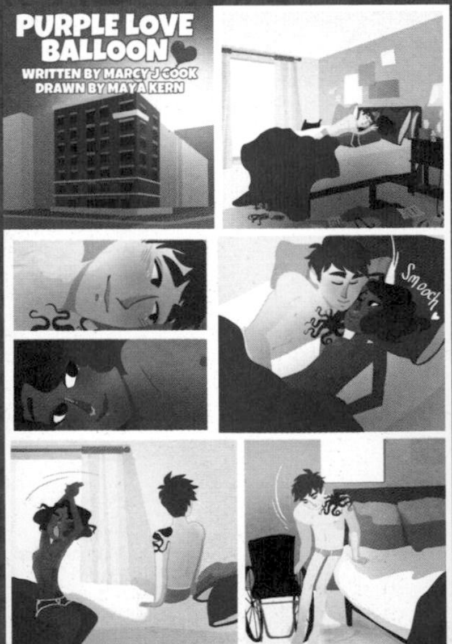
PURPLE LOVE BALLOON
WRITTEN BY MARCY J COOK
DRAWN BY MAYA KERN
Smooch

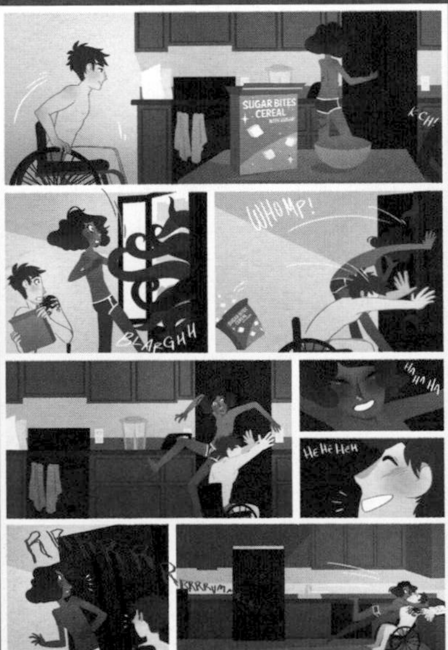
SUGAR BITES CEREAL
K-CH!
BLARGHH
WHOMP!
HA HA HA
HEHEHEH